Fredrick J. Long is Assistant Professor of
New Testament at Bethel College,
Mishawaka, Indiana.

ANCIENT RHETORIC AND PAUL'S APOLOGY

Second Corinthians is Paul's apology to the Corinthians for failing to visit them, using rhetorical persuasion in his letters, and appearing unapproved for the collection. The scholarly consensus maintains that 2 Corinthians is a conglomeration of letters due to its literary and logistical inconsistencies. Consequently, most interpretations of 2 Corinthians treat only parts of it. However, a new consensus is emerging. Fredrick Long situates the text within classical literary and rhetorical conventions and argues for its unity from numerous parallels with ancient apology in the tradition of Andocides, Socrates, Isocrates, and Demosthenes. He provides a comprehensive survey and rigorous genre analysis of ancient forensic discourse in support of his claims, and shows how the unified message of Paul's letter can be recovered. His study will be of relevance to classicists and New Testament scholars alike.

FREDRICK J. LONG is Assistant Professor of New Testament at Bethel College, Mishawaka, Indiana.

SOCIETY FOR NEW TESTAMENT STUDIES

MONOGRAPH SERIES

General Editor: Richard Bauckham

131

ANCIENT RHETORIC AND PAUL'S APOLOGY

SOCIETY FOR NEW TESTAMENT STUDIES

MONOGRAPH SERIES

Titles in the series

Ancient Rhetoric and Paul's Apology

The Compositional Unity of 2 Corinthians

FREDRICK J. LONG

PUBLISHED BY THE PRESS SYNDICATE OF THE UNIVERSITY OF CAMBRIDGE
The Pitt Building, Trumpington Street, Cambridge, United Kingdom

CAMBRIDGE UNIVERSITY PRESS
The Edinburgh Building, Cambridge, CB2 2RU, UK
40 West 20th Street, New York, NY 10011–4211, USA
477 Williamstown Road, Port Melbourne, VIC 3207, Australia
Ruiz de Alarcón 13, 28014 Madrid, Spain
Dock House, The Waterfront, Cape Town 8001, South Africa

http://www.cambridge.org

First published 2004

Printed in the United Kingdom at the University Press, Cambridge

Typeface Times 10/12 pt.   *System* LʌTEX 2$_\varepsilon$ [TB]

A catalogue record for this book is available from the British Library

Library of Congress Cataloguing in Publication data
Long, Fredrick J., 1966–
Ancient rhetoric and Paul's apology: the compositional unity of 2 Corinthians / by
Fredrick J. Long.
    p.   cm. – (Society for New Testament Studies monograph series; 131)
Includes bibliographical references and indexes.
ISBN 0 521 84233 6
1. Bible. N.T. Corinthians, 2nd, 10–13 – Criticism, interpretation, etc.   2. Rhetoric in the
Bible.   3. Rhetoric, Ancient.   I. Title.   II. Monograph series (Society for New
Testament Studies); 131.
BS2675.6.R54L66   2004
227′.3066–dc22   2004045711

ISBN 0 521 84233 6 hardback

For my wife, Shannon,
and
our five lovely little rascals, Hannah, Nathan, Gabby,
Sam, and David

CONTENTS

FIGURES

TABLES

PREFACE

It is entirely appropriate to give thanks where many thanks are due. First, I devote this work and give thanks to my Savior God, Jesus Christ, the incarnated Lord, who sustained me throughout this entire project and who inspired the apostle Paul in the first place to such a high degree of commitment and eloquence. To my lovely and courageous wife, Shannon, to whom I also devote this work, many thanks are given, beyond what words can express. I am indebted, too, to my parents, Dr. James I. and Lois E. Long, for their encouragement over the years, particularly as I finished this project.

I also want to acknowledge my wise dissertation advisor, Dr. Carol Stockhausen, who helped me get hooked on Paul's rhetoric, and the other members of my dissertation committee, Dr. Julian Hills, who impressed on me the importance of literary form and excellence in scholarship, although I am still aspiring, Father Bill Kurz, who particularly encouraged my submission to SNTSMS, and Drs. Brad Hinze and Michel Barnes, who encouraged me in my project.

Vernon Robbins, Duane Watson, David Amador-Hester, and Troy Martin also have provided encouragement and inspiration, as have the members of the Rhetoric of Religious Antiquity group working on socio-rhetorical criticism. In particular, my thesis was shaped in conversation with Ben Witherington III, who was so generous as to read through my opening chapter and offer many helpful suggestions while I was starting my dissertation. Also, I want to mention my mentor and friend David Bauer, who has provided support and inspiration as an inductive exegete from my formative years at Asbury Theological Seminary.

My colleagues at Bethel College have continued to spur me on, often checking eagerly on my progress. Thanks to all. The interlibrary loan personnel at Bethel will be happy that I am done, particularly Mr. Mark Root. For the hundreds of requests that he so faithfully accepted and fulfilled, I give my thanks.

Most recently, many thanks are due to Professor Kim Peterson, and our Bethel student April Stier, who helped me reduce my 161,000-word dissertation into an updated and lean 100,000-word monograph. April went the extra mile to assist me in this task. Also, I want to thank Daniel Loeser for helping me with the difficult task of indexing, which increases the value of this monograph. I think that both Daniel and April have bright futures ahead of them.

ABBREVIATIONS

AB	Anchor Bible
ACNT	Augsburg Commentary on the New Testament
ACS	American Classical Studies
AGRL	Aspects of Greek and Roman Life
AJP	*American Journal of Philology*
AnBib	Analecta Biblica
ASH	Ancient Society and History
AusBR	*Australian Biblical Review*
AUSS	*Andrews University Seminary Studies*
BDB	Brown–Driver–Briggs, *A Hebrew and English Lexicon of the Old Testament*
BETL	Bibliotheca Ephemeridum Theologicarum Lovaniensium
BFT	Biblical Foundations in Theology
BHTh	Beiträge zur historischen Theologie
Bijdr	*Bijdragen: Tidjschrift voor Philosophia en Theologie*
BJS	Brown Judaic Studies
BSGRT	Bibliotheca Scriptorum Graecorum et Romanorum Teubneriana
CBET	Contributions to Biblical Exegesis and Theology
CB NTS	Coniectanea Biblica. New Testament Series
CBQ	*Catholic Biblical Quarterly*
CCS	Cambridge Classical Studies
CGLC	Cambridge Greek and Latin Classics
CJ	*Classical Journal*
CP	*Classical Philology*
CQ	*Classical Quarterly*
CommQ	*Communications Quarterly*
CSSJ	*Central States Speech Journal*
ESEC	Emory Studies in Early Christianity
ExpTim	*Expository Times*
FF	Foundations and Facets

GBS	Guides to Biblical Scholarship
GRBS	*Greek, Roman, and Byzantine Studies*
HAW	Handbuch der Altertumswissenschaft
HNTC	Harper's New Testament Commentaries
HSCP	*Harvard Studies in Classical Philology*
HTR	*Harvard Theological Review*
HUNT	Hermeneutische Untersuchungen zur Theologie
ICC	International Critical Commentary
JBL	*Journal of Biblical Literature*
JCE	*Journal of Christian Education*
JHUSHPS	Johns Hopkins University Studies in Historical and Political Science
JLT	*Journal of Literature and Theology*
JRH	*Journal of Religious History*
JSNT	*Journal for the Study of the New Testament*
JSNTSup	Journal for the Study of the New Testament Supplement Series
JTS	*Journal of Theological Studies*
KEK	Kritisch-exegetischer Kommentar über das Neue Testament (Meyer-Kommentar)
LCL	Loeb Classical Library
LEC	Library of Early Christianity
LSCP	London Studies in Classical Philology
LSJ	Liddell and Scott, *A Greek–English Lexicon*, rev. by H. Jones
LXX	Septuagint
MBCB	*Mnemosyne: Bibliotheca Classica Batava*
MBCBSup	Mnemosyne Bibliotheca Classica Batava Supplement
MBPS	Mellen Biblical Press Series
NASB	New American Standard Bible
NCBC	New Century Bible Commentary
Neot	*Neotestamentica*
NICNT	The New International Commentary on the New Testament
NovT	*Novum Testamentum*
NovTSup	Novum Testamentum Supplements
NTS	*New Testament Studies*
OCG	Oratory of Classical Greece
PhilRhet	*Philosophy and Rhetoric*
PRSt	*Perspectives in Religious Studies*

PW	Pauly–Wissowa, *Real-Enzyklopädie der classische Altertumswissenschaft*
QJS	*Quarterly Journal of Speech*
QJSE	*Quarterly Journal of Speech Education*
RSQ	*Rhetoric Society Quarterly*
SBLDS	Society of Biblical Literature Dissertation Series
SBLRBS	Society of Biblical Literature Resources for Biblical Study
SBLSBS	Society of Biblical Literature Sources for Biblical Study
SCJ	*The Southern Communication Journal*
SEÅ	*Svensk exegetisk årsbok*
SemeiaSt	Semeia Studies
SJG	Schriftenreihe der Juristischen Gesellschaft
SNTSMS	Society for New Testament Studies Monograph Series
SPhiloMS	Studia Philonica Monograph Series
SSCJ	*Southern Speech Communication Journal*
TAPA	*Transactions of the American Philological Association*
TynBul	*Tyndale Bulletin*
WBC	Word Biblical Commentary
WGRW	Writings from the Greco-Roman World
WPRC	*Working Papers in Rhetoric and Communication*
WUNT	Wissenschaftliche Untersuchungen zum Neuen Testament
ZNW	*Zeitschrift für die neutestamentliche Wissenschaft und die Kunde der älteren Kirche*

1

AN APOLOGY FOR THE UNITY OF 2 CORINTHIANS

Introduction and overview

Ever since Johann S. Semler's commentary on 2 Corinthians in 1776, scholars have debated its compositional unity. After Semler, a *flood* of partition theories followed (see the surveys of Hyldahl, 1973, Betz, 1985, and Bieringer, 1994b).

Interpreters typically assume that 2 Corinthians is a composite letter of two or more letters or letter fragments. The number of individual letters and their respective order (also in relation to 1 Corinthians) vary greatly. Scholars have held to as few as two distinct letters: chaps. 1–9 and chaps. 10–13 (e.g., Bruce, 1971). Others have argued that 2 Corinthians contains five distinct letters or fragments: 1.1–2.13 with 7.5–16; 2.14–7.4 (excluding 6.14–7.1); chap. 8; chap. 9; chaps. 10–13 (e.g., Betz, 1985; cf. Bornkamm, 1965) or more (e.g., Schmithals, 1973). Furthermore, 2 Corinthians 6.14–7.1 is considered non-Pauline material. It is standard in current scholarship to ask where to find these smaller letters and how best to understand them according to epistolary and rhetorical conventions.

Considerable confusion results when interpreting 2 Corinthians and reconstructing Paul's theology. Presently, interpreters are left to determine the meaning of parts of 2 Corinthians on the basis of hypothetically reconstructed letters placed in a reconstructed chronological sequence in order to understand the reconstructed situation and Paul's theological response(s). Moreover, if 2 Corinthians is not understood as a unity, an ambiguity arises concerning how the church can adequately appropriate this composite letter in its final form (see Kurz, 1996, who attempts to overcome this dilemma through a canonical–critical approach).

So, the questions of this study are: Was 2 Corinthians as we have it today written and received as a complete letter? If so, how was it crafted so as to achieve its desired ends? My thesis is that Paul composed 2 Corinthians as a rhetorically unified apology drawing on the well-known Greco-Roman forensic tradition. This rhetorical unity is seen on at least two levels. First, the letter evidences substantial parallels in Greco-Roman forensic oratory in terms of speech arrangement (*exordium, narratio, divisio, partitio, probatio, refutatio*, self-adulation, and *peroratio*), forensic *topoi* associated with the qualitative *stasis* (e.g., intentions, authority, magnification of suffering), and forensic idioms (e.g., one's conscience as a witness, speaking the truth, admission of guilt, statements of hope). Second, the letter displays a coherent core of related rhetorical aims. Paul's theological pen had been pushed by the hand of necessity – some of the Corinthians and Paul's missionary opponents, the so-called *false apostles*, were questioning his ministry conduct and official authoritative status. He failed to visit them when he said he would (cf. 1 Cor. 16.5–7 and 2 Cor. 1.15–17). Furthermore, he had used persuasive rhetoric in his letters when, in fact, he previously disavowed using it (1 Cor. 1.17; 2.1; cf. 2 Cor. 5.11). Finally, he was adjudged unapproved in his financial conduct (2 Cor. 7.2; 11.7–10; 12.14–18) – so much so that his role in delivering the Corinthians' portion of the collection (Paul's special project for assisting the poor in Judea) was in jeopardy (2 Cor. 3.1; 8.20–21; 12.14–18; 13.6–8). Paul became liable to the same criticisms he made of some of the Corinthians: He is worldly (1 Cor. 3.1, 3; see also 2 Cor. 1.17b; 10.2) and unapproved (1 Cor. 11.19, 28; see also 2 Cor. 13.3–7).

Because of these charges of inconsistency and his diminishing credibility, Paul in 2 Corinthians defended his past actions of writing rather than visiting (2.1–11; cf. 7.2–16), explained his intentions and involvements in the collection efforts (chaps. 8–9), and argued that God is active in and through his *persuasive* preaching of the gospel to call the Corinthians to the greater glory of the new covenant (chaps. 3–6; see esp. 5.11). However, this latter deliberative emphasis relates to Paul's disclosure of the dual function of the letter in 12.19. Although Paul affirmed that the Corinthians have *perceived* (δοκέω) that he had been *defending himself* (ἀπολογέο-μαι) *all along* (πάλαι) through whole discourse, he also *speaks in the sight of God for their upbuilding* (οἰκοδομή). This *upbuilding* was for the purpose of Paul's imminent arrival at Corinth (12.14, 21; 13.1, 10). The letter prepares for his arrival in at least four ways: (1) by defending his previous decision not to visit when planned, but writing a letter instead (1.12–2.11); (2) by exhorting them to a lifestyle befitting the salvation offered in the gospel (5.20–7.3; 12.19–13:1); (3) by securing their complete confidence and cooperation in the collection for Jerusalem (chaps. 8–9; 12.14–18) as a sign for restored relationships with himself; and (4) by creating relational space for himself with the Corinthians by refuting his opponents (10.1–12.13).

In the end, Paul argues that the Corinthians should have commended him (12.11; cf. 3.1; 5.12). Instead, Paul must *commend himself* to them (3.1; 4.2; 6.4; 12.12) just as his antagonists had (5.12; 10.12). Paul must refute both (some of) the Corinthians and his missionary rivals (10.1–11.15) while undermining their basis of boasting by showing that he is boast-worthy (1.14; 5.12; 11.23–30; 12.12) in that he exemplifies *through his weakness(es)* the true object of boasting, the power of God in Christ (11.16–12.10).

Problems and solutions to the unity of 2 Corinthians

A starting point to affirm the rhetorical unity of 2 Corinthians involves a consideration of why 2 Corinthians is under *trial* in the first place.[1] On the one hand, 2 Corinthians is mysteriously not explicitly cited in the extant writings of the earliest church fathers – the letters of Ignatius of Antioch, Polycarp, and 1 Clement – but is first mentioned in the mid second century in Marcion's canon – nearly a century after its composition (Furnish, 1984, pp. 29–30). This opens the door for speculation about what form 2 Corinthians originally had. On the other hand, there is absolutely no evidence in the textual tradition that 2 Corinthians is a composite letter. The church fathers nevertheless assumed the unity of the letter. These external arguments, however, have not been judged heavier than the well-documented and much-discussed literary and logistical/chronological problems, which are summarized below.

First, there are disjunctions in thought between 2.13 and 2.14 and then between 7.4 and 7.5. Furthermore, when one reads continuously from 2.13 skipping directly to 7.5, no disjunction is arguably present, suggesting that two letter fragments were spliced together and that 2.13/14 and 7.4/5 are observable seams (see Welborn, 1996). Second, the section 6.14–7.1 contains dissimilar language and theology to Paul's own, thus raising suspicions not only about its position in the letter, but also about its being from the hand of Paul at all. One also can easily read from 6.13 to 7.2, suggesting more seams (see Duff, 1993). Third, the material in chapter 8 is oddly repeated more or less in chapter 9. Such repetitiousness may be better accounted for if each chapter is taken as a separate letter (see Betz, 1985). Finally, there are drastic changes in tone within 2 Corinthians

---

[1] Advocates of the unity of 2 Corinthians have used judicial terminology to describe their efforts (see Stephenson, 1965; Bieringer, 1994a). Consider especially the statement made at the end of Bates' defense of the letter's unity (1965–66, p. 68): "Here then the case for the defence rests."

as a whole, most notably at 10.1. Interpreters rightly ask, how can 2 Corinthians 10–13, which are rather harsh in tone and ironic, be found within the same letter as the reconciliatory tone perceived in 7.4–16?

Logistically, any interpreter of 2 Corinthians is challenged to account for Paul's previous Corinthian correspondence (1 Cor. 5.9) and *the letter of tears* (2 Cor. 2.3–11; 7.8–12), the time of Titus' traveling with the brother(s) (2 Cor. 8.6, 17–18, 22; 12.17–18), Paul's various travel plans (1 Cor. 16.5–6; 2 Cor. 1.15–16), and whether there was an *intermediate visit* as might be suggested by 2 Corinthians in the adverbial statements "come *again*" (2.1; 12.21; 13.2) and "coming a *third* time" (12.14; 13.1; cf. 13.2).

Although the literary problems are weightier, any proponent of the unity of 2 Corinthians must explain both literary and logistical difficulties. However, one can stress the difficulties and perceived inconsistencies or attempt to reconcile them. In the current debate, the partition theorists claim the high ground, despite the many excellent arguments resolving these literary problems in favor of the unity of large portions (chaps. 1–7 or chaps. 1–9) or all of 2 Corinthians (see the discussion in Long, 1999, pp. 1–42). The conclusion one draws from this scholarly exchange is that, if unified, *2 Corinthians addresses a complex rhetorical situation.* If this is the case, then Paul may have drawn upon ancient rhetoric to meet this dynamic exigency. Therefore, *ancient rhetoric* may very well be the means by which to understand the letter's unity.

Advocates of the unity of 2 Corinthians (or large sections of it) have contributed to understanding the unity of Paul's argumentative rhetoric. However, they have failed to convince the scholarly community, apparently for lack of conclusive evidence. What evidence would be conclusive? Those advocating various partition theories have helped to determine parameters for making a successful argument for the letter's unity in at least two ways: by presenting clearly defined problems that need resolution (as summarized above) and by delimiting the type of form-critical methodology that can conclusively argue in favor of the letter's unity. The question that Hans Dieter Betz raises in his commentary on 2 Corinthians 8 and 9 (1985) – how one can argue conclusively for or against the unity of the letter – is entirely appropriate. He rightly argues it is from formal and literary considerations.

Such evidence does exist, and it comes in the form of Greco-Roman rhetorical theory and practice. I agree completely with the apt methodological observation of Frank W. Hughes (1991, pp. 246–47) (but not with his partition theory):

The major difficulty that partition theories pose for those who accept them is that such theories often seem to be quite arbitrary. How does one show that the existence, long ago, of one theoretically reconstructed letter fragment is more plausible than some other theoretical fragment, or, for that matter, than the canonical form of 2 Corinthians? An assumption of this study is that rhetorical criticism could help to confirm or refute the results of theories of partition or interpolation.

In this respect Margaret Mitchell's *Paul and the Rhetoric of Reconciliation* (1991) is commendable. Mitchell performs the rhetorical form-critical work called for by Betz with respect to 1 Corinthians. She argues convincingly that 1 Corinthians is a unified letter exemplifying deliberative rhetoric. Consequently, her work has ended the basis to generate partition theories for 1 Corinthians (some of which involved 2 Corinthians). What Mitchell has accomplished for 1 Corinthians, I hope to do for 2 Corinthians.

Proponents of the rhetorical unity of 2 Corinthians

The proponents of the unity of 2 Corinthians have a negative and positive task: to dismantle the problematic assumptions and conclusions of partition theories and to construct persuasive proposals for the letter's unity (Hester, 2002, pp. 276–77). Today there is a growing minority of scholars who argue for the unity of 2 Corinthians on rhetorical grounds, and each has contributed to this dual task.

Niels Hyldahl (1973) has written an excellent review and critique of partition theories in the course of setting forth a very plausible understanding of the exigency facing Paul in 2 Corinthians. He pursues the simplest solutions to these complex logistical and chronological issues. Among his laudable conclusions are that *the letter of tears* is 1 Corinthians and that Paul made no intermediate visit. Betz's (1985, pp. 32–35) claim that Hyldahl does not provide enough substantial evidence and argumentation is simply unfounded. It is unfortunate that Hydahl's careful work has not been more thoroughly engaged. However, Hyldahl's treatment of the *rhetoric* of the text is weak (only 1.1–11 is identified as the *prooemium*).

The studies of Frances M. Young and David F. Ford (1987), Frederick W. Danker (1991; although cf. 1989, p. 19), and Paul W. Barnett (1997) represent important steps towards a more complete rhetorical analysis of 2 Corinthians. Their efforts have been primarily to give an account of chapters 10–13, which they typically understand as the *peroratio* (cf. Witherington, 1995, pp. 350–51). However, this conclusion is not supported by comparison with extant speeches. Additionally, the rhetorical disposition of the remainder of the letter is left unexplained (Young and Ford, pp. 27, 37–40) or is not accounted for in their thematic outlines of the letter (Danker, pp. 27–28; Barnett, pp. 17–19).

More positively, these works have contributed to understanding the rhetorical situation and emphasizing the importance of the genre of 2 Corinthians. Danker has directed interpreters to see parallels with Demosthenes' *On the Crown* and to consider the importance of benefaction and finances in the letter. Young and Ford understand 1 Corinthians to be *the letter of tears*, and Paul has probably made an intermediate visit before writing 2 Corinthians, which is a letter of self-defense in the tradition of Demosthenes' *Second Letter* (pp. 27–59). Young and Ford argue that Paul was criticized in terms of his worldliness, spiritual credentials, financial matters and patronage, and eloquence (pp. 50–53). Thus, Paul offers an *apologia in absentia* (p. 27). Herein lies the key to affirming the letter's unity (p. 54). Both Danker and Young and Ford correctly focus our attention on the apologetic tradition. However, the task of correlating 2 Corinthians to the broader forensic theory and practice still remains to be completed.

The more recent rhetorical contributions of Ben Witherington III (1995), Jerry McCant (1999), and J. D. Hester (Amador) (2000; 2002) have also advanced the case for unity. Witherington has written a historical-rhetorical commentary on 1 and 2 Corinthians. Although 1 Corinthians receives substantially more attention than 2 Corinthians (253 versus 150 pages), his discussion of the rhetorical situation and dispositional structure of 2 Corinthians is groundbreaking. Witherington argues that 2 Corinthians is a unified letter evidencing the disposition of a forensic speech (pp. 335–36). He admits, as others have noted, that deliberative argumentation is found within 2 Corinthians (esp. chaps. 8–9), but that this is not "characteristic of the letter as a whole" (p. 333 note 23; cf. pp. 43–44). Furthermore, the exigency that Paul met is one calling for reconciliation. The obstacles to reconciliation – the Corinthians' dabbling with idols, Paul's failed travel plans, patronage issues, matters of integrity – were exploited by certain opponents (pp. 339–43). As a result, "it appears that the Corinthians felt they had the right to judge Paul and his message and were evaluating him by the same criteria by which popular orators and teachers were judged. Paul disputed this right . . . and sought to make clear that he was answerable only to God" (p. 47). Because of this, 2 Corinthians takes the form of an apology of Paul's apostleship.

While I affirm Witherington's historical-rhetorical approach and conclusion about the forensic nature and unity of 2 Corinthians, I understand
the letter not as a *general defense* of Paul's apostleship, but as a specific
defense of his manner of preaching, ministry practice, and itinerant intentions. At stake is an understanding of the nature of Paul's apology. It is
not enough for Paul to argue that he is answerable only to God (*contra*
Witherington); there is every indication that Paul offers a *real defense* to
the Corinthians in order to secure their goodwill and future relations with
them (see my discussion in Chapter 7).

Furthermore, Witherington does not equate 1 Corinthians with *the letter
of tears* (which Witherington believes is simply lost); he also believes that
Paul made an intermediate visit. These conclusions ultimately undermine
the unity of the letter by complicating the logistical and chronological
framework and by not acknowledging the central issue of Paul's defense –
his failure to revisit Corinth (1.17; cf. 12.14, 21; 13.1, 10, and 1 Cor.
4.18). Finally, I believe that a better accounting of the letter's disposition
is possible, particularly concerning the *partitio* and *peroratio* (see my
discussion in Chapter 8).

Although a large step in the right direction, in the end Witherington's
work does not provide a conclusive case for the rhetorical unity of the
letter, because very little support from ancient sources – handbooks and
speeches – is used to establish that 2 Corinthians conforms to ancient
apologetic practice.[2] The question remains whether and to what extent
2 Corinthians actually displays features in adherence to forensic theory
and practice.

McCant (1999) presents a very thoroughgoing and provocative case
that 2 Corinthians is an apologetic forensic parody (p. 19) unified around
several well-documented themes (see pp. 21–22). In 2 Corinthians 12.19,
McCant argues that Paul "disclaims self-defense," which functions as "a
subversion of anticipation" and thus points to Paul's use of parody (p. 15).
McCant's attention to style and intertextuality is notable, although parody
is seen as Paul's primary literary mode. Parody is not restricted to the
fool's speech in chaps. 11–12, but extends to the whole letter (McCant
outlines chaps. 1–7 as "A Parodic Defense of Behavior"; chaps. 8–9 as

---

[2] Witherington is well aware of the provisional nature of his own proposal: "Study of
the rhetorical form of Paul's letters is a discipline still being reborn, and any results that we
come up with will necessarily be tentative and subject to further correction" (p. 39). I, too,
cannot claim to account fully for the rhetoric of 2 Corinthians; my proposal will no doubt
enjoy the revision of others. Furthermore, it was not within the scope of Witherington's
commentary to perform an analysis such as M. Mitchell (1991) performed. Conversely,
Mitchell must disclaim her own work as not being a commentary (p. vii), which is certainly
the same caveat I must offer.

"A Parody of Benefaction"; and chaps. 10–13 as "A Parodic Defense of Authority") and even back into 1 Corinthians 4 and 9 (p. 26). Paul used parody to confront the Corinthians' "relational tautness" and the "tension" created by "[a]n offending member of the church and Paul's failure to keep a promise and visit the Corinthians . . ." (p. 26). This parody is most evident as Paul has become prosecutor (see pp. 163–64) and educator, who "wants to 'build up' the Corinthians by helping them understand the true nature of apostleship. Apostleship is a critical issue for Paul" (p. 17).

Critical for McCant is the view that we cannot discover the charges against Paul. He argues (p. 163):

> The difficulty for the interpreter of 2 Corinthians is that, if they ever existed, we do not have the prosecutor's charges. If the Corinthians made charges, we do not know what they were. What Paul tells us probably reflects the general situation at Corinth, but it is impossible to formulate the Corinthian "charges." All we have is Paul's parodic defense and surely he is capable of some distortion, misrepresentation and bias.

Moreover, McCant maintains that there are no missionary opponents; in fact, he calls for a moratorium on this area of research in 2 Corinthians and claims that it is based largely on mirror-reading (pp. 17–18, 26).

If McCant is correct to identify 2 Corinthians formally as a defense (p. 13), I would fundamentally disagree with his reading of 12.19 and his broader understanding of the rhetoric of the letter. First, McCant does not consider the relevance of ancient *stasis* theory, which would help delineate the charges and Paul's response to them. Second, no accounting for the disposition of the letter is provided. Third, like Witherington, McCant ascribes to an intermediate visit and a lost letter of tears (pp. 26–27) and emphasizes that Paul's apostleship more generally is the issue, *rather than specific charges*. Fourth, this latter view is related to the most problematic feature of McCant's thesis, namely, *that all of 2 Corinthians is parodic*. I would grant that 2 Cor. 11.1–12.10 contains increasingly parodic features; but I would question its presence in chap. 10 and earlier altogether. What Paul is engaged in is a challenge–response scenario within a culture of honor and shame (Watson, 2002). It seems implausible that Paul would subject the Corinthians to such thoroughgoing parody (thirteen chapters!) in order to educate them. How irritating! And principally such a parody would be completely unfounded, since according to McCant's reconstruction there is only "tension" and no specific charges, criticisms, or opponents of Paul (although McCant, p. 32 entertains "charges" concerning Paul's failed visit and sent letter based upon 2 Cor. 1.12–2.11). Indeed, if there were no charges, then what defense is there for Paul to parody?

Fifth, McCant is right to observe Paul's tactic of playing the prosecutor. However, this does not support his parodic view of 2 Corinthians, since counter-accusation is a common rhetorical *topos* befitting a defense. Particularly, in the case of 2 Corinthians this tactic seems completely justified since Paul critiques the Corinthians' poor moral conduct as the basis for his determination not to visit (2.1–5) as he had originally planned (1.15–16; cf. 1 Cor. 16.5), the failure of which is precisely the charge he is responding to (1.17).

Finally, in 2 Corinthians 12.19 there is no contrast of thought between the Corinthians' perception of Paul defending himself and his speaking before God in Christ. The later statement is a forensic *topos* in which a litigant reminds the jury that he speaks in the full awareness of God and thus indicates confidence in his own case (see Cic. *Inv.* 1.23, 101; Quint. *Inst.* 6.1.34; *Rhet. Her.* 1.7; see also my discussion of 12.19 in Chapter 8.9). Also in 12.19 Paul acknowledges that everything (τὰ πάντα), *even his perceived defense*, is for their upbuilding. Thus, 12.19 discloses the dual function of the letter, apology and moral formation, not its comprehensively parodic character. In the end, McCant's reading of 2 Corinthians does not offer a compelling case for the unity of 2 Corinthians, since it is not able to take at face value its judicial dimensions.

Hester has performed both the negative (2000) and the positive tasks (2002) while making a case for the unity of 2 Corinthians. He emphasizes *inventio* rather than historical reconstructions (2000, p. 94) and uses "a rhetorical theory of dynamic argumentation" (2002, p. 294) which is greatly dependent on Chaïm Perelman and Lucie Olbrechts-Tyteca's theory of argumentation (1969) (p. 278). Although this may give Hester added interpretive resources by which to analyze and describe Paul's argumentation, it also requires readers to be conversant with modern discourse and rhetorical categories. He, too, holds to an intermediate visit (2000, p. 98).

In my estimation, Hester's main contributions are (1) confronting the assumptions of modern historical-criticism regarding decisions to partition 2 Corinthians because of its *perceived inconsistencies* and *illogic*, decisions which impose a particular modern linear rationality onto a dynamic argumentative text (2000, pp. 93–94); and (2) understanding the rhetoric of the text through attention to aspects of argumentative shifts in relation to the argumentation of the whole. For example, although not following an ancient disposition schema for outlining the text, Hester rightly observes that Paul has distributed his narrative material (2002, pp. 278–80). Also, Paul's repetitiveness and shift of argumentation at 9.1 is due to employing a *paralepsis* figure which "functions to downplay the rhetor's concerns just mentioned . . . by playing up the confidence he feels" (2002, p. 290). Hester (2000, p. 109) summarizes his arguments: "All the 'seams,' non-sequiturs and formalist deviations have been, in every case, easily explained by reference to common rhetorical practices and the strategic needs of Paul to address the argumentative situations arising from his relationship to the Corinthian community."

Hester offers a much more sophisticated rhetorical understanding of the invention of the argumentation and themes of 2 Corinthians. However, he does not entertain a consideration of the genre of 2 Corinthians as a whole (he deems chaps. 10–13 an "apostolic *apologia*"; 2000, pp. 95–97). Thus, the results of his arguments will remain inconclusive for the unity of the letter on historical grounds. In other words, the inventive and argumentative features observed in the text by Hester must have some warrant in the historical-cultural milieu. To enter into Paul's milieu requires a consideration of literary genre, something which Hester does not fully address. The best way to argue *conclusively* for the letter's unity, I argue, must be within the discipline of ancient rhetorical criticism and involve a rigorous genre analysis of the letter.

This survey indicates that three fundamental issues face the proponents of the unity of 2 Corinthians. The first is determining the rhetorical exigence of the letter in terms of charges and opponents. Are there any charges against Paul? If so, what precisely are these charges? Who are bringing these charges? Are they some of the Corinthians and/or Paul's missionary rivals? The second issue concerns how Paul addressed this exigence. What manner or means did Paul employ? Is he thoroughly parodic? To what extent is he truly apologetic by drawing on the forensic tradition? The third issue is the method and manner by which 2 Corinthians can be shown to be a unity. Should we emphasize invention, argumentation, style and figures, genre, or disposition? My view is that actual charges were issued by real opponents from within and without and that the best method to demonstrate the unity of 2 Corinthians is historical rhetoric working with generic features of ancient apology.

The historical-rhetorical method of this study

The classicist Donald A. Clark (1957), after surveying ancient rhetoric, concluded with the following remarks:

Although these precepts of ancient rhetoric are designed primarily to train boys and young men to win audiences by addressing them orally in public, we must recall that from the earliest times, these precepts also guided those who addressed the public in writing. The epistles of St. Paul and Seneca, whether read aloud to groups or passed from hand to hand in manuscript, derive their structure and style from the same precepts of rhetoric as do the speeches of Demosthenes or Cicero.

New Testament interpreters have for too long neglected this field of study. In an impassioned plea Walter A. Jennrich (1948) pointed out the "modern neglect of [ancient] rhetoric" and argued that biblical exegetes should pay more attention to rhetorical influences ("artistic form" and "style") in NT texts. Fortunately this trend is steadily changing.

Epistolary criticism applied to 2 Corinthians has proven itself of little use for arguments for the unity of the letter (White, 1986, pp. 136–39; and Belleville, 1989, who restricts her analysis to chaps. 1–7; although see Olson, 1976, who works with all of 2 Corinthians). This is due to its reliance on documentary letters as a basis of comparison. The method is not able adequately to account for the main body of Paul's letters – where the literary problems of 2 Corinthians are found. Since Paul's letters are to be seen rather as rhetorical documents (see Chapter 6), one must turn to ancient rhetorical conventions and genres.

Although often appealed to, what is lacking in New Testament scholarship is a thorough examination of ancient apology as a distinct genre. Thus, the first task of this monograph is to survey forensic speech. The basis for arguing that 2 Corinthians conforms to apology involves consideration of four features of forensic discourse: invention (argumentation and themes), style, disposition, and exigency. These four areas are justifiable on the basis of modern genre theory. M. M. Bakhtin (1986, p. 60) maintains that "All three of these aspects – thematic content, style, and compositional structure – are inseparably linked to the *whole* of the utterance and are equally determined by the specific nature of the particular sphere of communication." Here one can see the generic interdependence of the first three features (thematic, style, disposition) on the last, the exigency or "the particular sphere of communication" (cf. Cambell and Jamieson, 1978, pp. 19–25; Conley, 1979, pp. 47–48). Additionally, each generic component relates broadly to the *officia* of ancient rhetoric as found in Aristotle, Cicero, and Quintilian (excepting memory and delivery) (see Wisse, 1989, pp. 77–80).

Invention (εὕρεσις/*inventio*) involved pre-considerations when developing a speech thematically (see Watson, 1988, pp. 14–20). As Malcolm Heath (1997, p. 89) explains, "In rhetoric it designates the discovery of the resources for discursive persuasion latent in any rhetorical problem." Invention involves types of argumentation and their construction. An instrumental tool of invention was *stasis* theory.

Stylistics (λέξις/*elocutio*) concerns the analysis of 2 Corinthians at the microlevel in terms of tropes and figures of speech (for an overview see Rowe, 1997; in Paul see the fine study of Spencer, 1998). Admittedly, this feature of 2 Corinthians plays less of a role in this study. Of the three types of orator, forensic orators were generally least interested in style (see Arist. *Rhet.* 3.12.5).

Disposition (διάθεσις/οἰκονομία/τάξις/*dispositio*/*compositio*) concerns the design or arrangement of the speech as a whole at the macrolevel in terms of the sections of the speech, such as *prooemium*, *narratio*, *partitio*, etc. Furthermore, disposition concerns the function of these sections for the overall aims of the rhetorical piece to meet the demands of the exigency (for an overview see Wuellner, 1997). The disposition of forensic rhetoric will be carefully surveyed in Chapter 5, since it plays a critical role in affirming the compositional unity of 2 Corinthians.

Finally, a consideration of exigency, which is understood here to mean *rhetorical situation*, is to account for the *perceived* or *actual* historical circumstances that necessitated and gave rise to Paul's letter. Using Lloyd F. Bitzer's terminology (1968, p. 6; for a minor critique, see Stamps, 1993), technically, the rhetorical situation comprises exigency, audience, and constraints: It involves "a complex of persons, events, objects, and relations presenting an actual or potential exigence which can be completely or partially removed if discourse, introduced into the situation, can so constrain human decision or action as to bring about the significant modification of the exigence." Bitzer differentiates between exigencies, some of which are unchangeable and therefore non-rhetorical, and rhetorical situations, which of necessity have an exigence that can be changed.

Determining the rhetorical situation is a preliminary consideration when doing rhetorical work. As Aristotle (see Conley, 1979, pp. 47–48) and many others have argued (Pogoloff, 1992, pp. 91–95), the rhetorical situation initially determines the genre of the writing. Interpretively, the problem that needs solution (exigency), whether conceived as a historical or literary construct, needs to be deduced from the rhetorical piece itself (see Schüssler Fiorenza, 1987, p. 391).

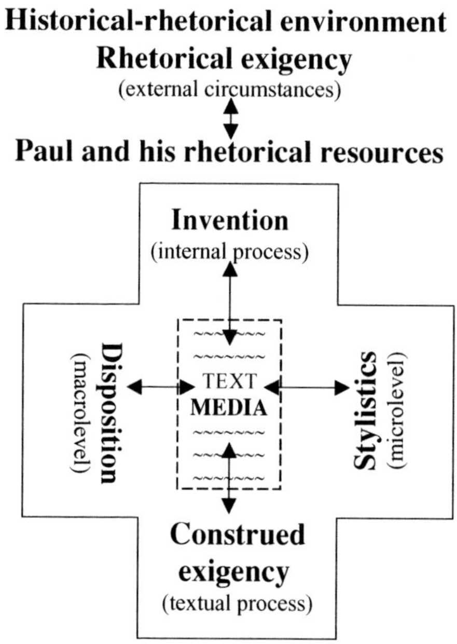

Historical-rhetorical environment
Rhetorical exigency
(external circumstances)

↕

Paul and his rhetorical resources

Invention
(internal process)

Disposition
(macrolevel)　←　TEXT
MEDIA　→　**Stylistics**
(microlevel)

Construed
exigency
(textual process)

Figure 1.1　The four rhetorical features of texts

These rhetorical features – invention, disposition, stylistics, and exigency – are depicted in Figure 1.1 (cf. Robbins, 1996b, p. 21).

To interpret the text is to investigate these rhetorical features. We cannot know for certain the rhetorical exigency that led to Paul's decision to write 2 Corinthians as an apology. However, what we have is Paul's *construed exigency* as a textual phenomenon that is capable of our careful exploration. Critical for this study is an analysis of Paul's *construed exigency* (see Chapter 7) in an attempt to understand the actual *rhetorical exigency*.

After introducing the extant forensic literature in Chapter 2, I conclude by correlating the generic features of forensic discourse in terms of exigency, invention, disposition, and media. Next, I survey each forensic feature respectively in Chapters 3–6. Chapter 6 also serves as a transition to discuss the forensic rhetoric of 2 Corinthians by setting forth preliminarily the view that 2 Corinthians is an *official apologetic letter*.

This leads to the second task of this study, in which I investigate the rhetorical exigency, disposition, and invention of 2 Corinthians respectively in Chapters 7–9. Throughout these chapters I hope to show that 2 Corinthians is a unified piece. One can account for the literary and logistical problems on the basis of the rhetorical exigence facing Paul, his invention of a line of defense and suitable arguments, and his thoughtful arrangement. What I hope will become evident is that the horizons of 2 Corinthians and ancient forensic rhetoric are significantly overlapping and that this was Paul's precise intention. I shall conclude this study in Chapter 10 by offering a summary of findings and reflecting on the nature of Paul's theology as rhetorically conditioned.

PART 1

A survey of ancient forensic discourse

2

THE ANATOMY OF A GENRE: SOURCES, NATURE, AND FEATURES OF FORENSIC RHETORIC

2.1   Sources for forensic rhetoric and theory

Greco-Roman rhetoric has been surveyed quite sufficiently (see Blass, 1962; Kennedy, 1963, 1972, 1980, 1983, 1989, 1994; Anderson, 1999, pp. 35–127). The major branches of oratory formalized and recognized in antiquity include forensic/dicanic/judicial (λόγοι δικανικοί), deliberative/demegoric/political (λόγοι δημηγορικοί), and epideictic/encomiastic/demonstrative (λόγοι ἐπιδεικτικοί). Several significant works exist that specifically treat forensic rhetoric, but they fail to give a comprehensive delimitation of the boundaries of this genre (Volkmann, 1885, pp. 33–293; Kennedy, 1963, pp. 125–52; J. Martin, 1974, pp. 15–166; Lausberg, 1998; Neumeister, 1964; Stroh, 1975; Vitanza, 1993).

Scholars have commonly traced *handbook rhetoric* to Corax and Tisias of Sicily in the fifth century BC (Pl. *Phaedr.* 272e–274a; Arist. *Soph. Elench.* 183b32; Cic. *Brut.* 46; Quint. *Inst.* 3.1.8–18). Corax is credited with defining rhetoric as the art of persuasion (πειθοῦς δημιουργός), devising probability argumentation, and naming the sections of forensic speeches (B. Smith, 1921, pp. 18–21; cf. Hinks, 1940; Kennedy, 1959; Goebel, 1983). However, the reconstruction of these early stages of rhetorical theory is currently debated (see Goebel, 1983; J. Poulakos, 1990; Cole, 1991; Schiappa, 1991, 1999; Enos, 1993).

Despite the paucity of direct evidence, we know that forensic oratory initially developed because of various social and political factors (Smith, 1921, pp. 13–16). First, a need arose in Sicily during the aftermath of the overthrow of the tyrants (466 BC) for citizens to reclaim lost property through litigation (see Freese, 1926, pp. viii–ix). Second, the use of courts increased in Athens shortly thereafter (Gagarin, 1994, p. 59; cf. Kennedy, 1963, pp. 27, 260). Significantly, two other branches of oratory developed in Athens at this time: epideictic oratory in the form of ceremonial speeches offered during the Persian War and deliberative oratory in the form of political speeches within the context of the renewed Athenian democracy (see Usher, 1990, pp. 1–2).

For my purposes, there is ample information to study the form and character of forensic rhetoric through extant Greco-Roman handbooks, speeches, letters, and educational exercises. These works are catalogued below. Searches of many Greek texts were conducted using the *Thesaurus Linguae Graecae* Disk D by the TLG Project, University of California, Irvine. Also, English, Greek, and Latin citations from ancient sources are taken from the LCL editions of any particular Greek or Latin author, unless so stated.

Rhetorical handbooks

The loss of many theoretical works known in antiquity is regrettable. Many speech technicians, e.g., Corax and Tisias, are reported to have written textbooks on rhetoric (or τέχναι) by the end of the fifth century BC (see Freese, 1926, pp. vii–xvi). Aristotle wrote a lost work entitled Συναγωγὴ Τεχνῶν ("Collection of Rhetorical Arts") devoted to surveying these manuals. However, these textbooks likely treated forensic oratory and its proper disposition (Arist. *Soph. Elench.* 183b23, 36 and Cic. *Brut.* 46–48).

The extant theoretical works, rhetorical handbooks, and exercises treating forensic rhetoric used in this study include the following: **Greek**: **Plato's** *Phaedrus* (Pl. *Phaedr.*); **Aristotle's** *Rhetorica* (Arist. *Rhet.*) and *Topica* (Arist. *Top.*); **Anaximenes'** *Rhetorica ad Alexandrum* (Anax. *Rhet. Al.*); **Hermagoras'** *De Inventione* (Hermag. *Inv.*); **Aelius Theon's** *Progymnasmata* (Theon *Prog.*); **Roman**: **Cicero's** *Brutus* (Cic. *Brut.*), *De oratore* (Cic. *De Or.*), *De Inventione Rhetorica* (Cic. *Inv.*), *De Optimo Genere Oratorum* (Cic. *Opt. Gen.*), *Orator ad M. Brutum* (Cic. *Or. Brut.*), *Partitiones Oratoriae* (Cic. *Part. Or.*), and *Topica* (Cic. *Top.*); the **unknown author** of *Rhetorica ad Herennium* (*Rhet. Her.*); and **Quintilian's** *Institutio Oratoria* (Quint. *Inst.*).

Forensic speeches

Thousands of speeches circulated in some form during antiquity. However, only a fraction have survived (for an extensive listing, dating, and classification of extant speeches see Ober, 1989, pp. 341–49). A number of these speeches contain lacunae of various sizes, which limits their usefulness for this study (e.g., Demades' *On the Twelve Years*). Many speeches are too lacunate to include below (e.g., many of Hyperides').

Interestingly, there are only four sets of accusation and defense speeches for the same case: three involve actual cases (Dem. 19 and Aeschin. 2; Aeschin. 3 and Dem. 18; and Lys. 6 and Andoc. 1) and one is fictitious (Antisthenes' *Odysseus* and *Ajax*). The following forensic speeches are categorized as either model, accusatory, defensive, mixed, as letters, in histories, or in comedies.

Model speeches

These include **Alcidamas'** *Odysseus in Response to the Defense of Palamedes* (Alcid. *Od.*); **Antiphon's** *Tetralogies* (Antiph. 2, 3, 4); **Antisthenes'** *Ajax* (Antisth. *Aj.*) and *Odysseus* (Antisth. *Od.*); **Gorgias'** *Defense of Palamedes* (Gorg. *Pal.*); and finally **Isocrates'** *Antidosis* (Isoc. 15), a mixed piece expressed as a self-defense in a mock trial intended for educational purposes.[1] The distinction between model speeches and actual published speeches is somewhat specious because published speeches were used themselves as models and exemplars (cf. Isoc. 15.55, 87). For this reason there is debate over how accurately the published version matched the delivered version (Too, 1995, p. 81 note 19).

Accusation speeches

Aeschines' *Against Ctesiphon* (Aeschin. *In Ctes.*) and *Against Timarchus* (Aeschin. *In Tim.*); **Ps.-Andocides'** *Against Alcibiades* ([Andoc.] 4); **Antiphon's** *Against the Step Mother* (Antiph. 1); **Apollodorus'** *Against Timotheus* ([Dem.] 49), *Against Polycles* ([Dem.] 50), *Against Callippus* ([Dem.] 52), *Against Nicostratus* ([Dem.] 53), *Against Neaera* ([Dem.] 59); **Cicero's** *In Catilinam* (Cic. *Cat.*), *In Pisonem* (Cic. *Pis.*), *In Sallustium* ([Cic.] *Sal.*), *In Vatinium* (Cic. *Vat.*), and *In Verrem* (Cic. *Verr.*); **Demosthenes'** *De Falsa Legatione* (Dem. 19), *Against Leptines* (Dem. 20), *Against Medias* (Dem. 21), *Against Androiton* (Dem. 22), *Against Aristocrates* (Dem. 23), *Against Timocrates* (Dem. 24), *Against Aristogeiton I* (Dem. 25), *Against Aristogeiton II* (Dem. 26), *Against Aphobus I* (Dem. 27), *Against Aphobus II* (Dem. 28), *Against Aphobus III* (Dem. 29), *Against Onetor I* (Dem. 30), *Against Onetor II* (Dem. 31), *Against Zenothemis* (Dem. 32), *Against Apaturius* (Dem. 33), *Against Phormio* (Dem. 34), *Against Lacritus* (Dem. 35), *Against Pantaenetus* (Dem. 37),

---

[1] Gagarin (1994, p. 59) would include "also Prodicus' speeches by Vice and Virtue in *The Choice of Heracles*, and the *agones* of tragedy and comedy (Jason and Medea, Clytemnestra and Electra, the stronger and weaker *logos*, etc.), which take the form of a quasi-legal debate between two opposed positions."

Against Nausimachus (Dem. 38), *Against Boeotus I* (Dem. 39), *Against Boeotus II* (Dem. 40), *Against Spudias* (Dem. 41), *Against Phaenippus* (Dem. 42), *Against Macartatus* (Dem. 43), *Against Leochares* (Dem. 44), *Against Stephanus I* (Dem. 45), *Against Stephanus II* (Dem. 46), *Against Evergus* (Dem. 47), *Against Olympiodorus* (Dem. 48), *Against Conon* (Dem. 54), *Against Callicles* (Dem. 55), *Against Dionysodorus* (Dem. 56), *Against Eubulides* (Dem. 57), and *Against Theocrines* (Dem. 58); **Dinarchus'** *Against Demosthenes* (Din. 1), *Against Aristogiton* (Din. 2), and *Against Philocles* (Din. 3); **Hyperides'** *Against Athenogenes* (Hyp. 3); **Isaeus'** *On the Estate of Pyrrhus* (Isae. 3), *On the Estate of Nicostratus* (Isae. 4), *On the Estate of Dicaeogenes* (Isae. 5), *On the Estate of Philoctemon* (Isae. 6), *On the Estate of Astyphilus* (Isae. 9), and *On the Estate of Aristarchus* (Isae. 10); **Isocrates'** *Trapeziticus* (Isoc. 17), *Against Callimachus* (Isoc. 18), *Against Lochites* (Isoc. 20), and *Against Euthynus* (Isoc. 21); **Lycurgus'** *Against Leocrates* (Lycurg. *Leoc.*); and **Lysias'** *Against Andocides* (Lys. 6), *Accusation of Calumny against Fellow Members of a Society* (Lys. 8), *Against Theomnestus I* (Lys. 10), *Against Theomnestus II* (Lys. 11), *Against Eratosthenes* (Lys. 12), *Against Agoratus* (Lys. 13), *Against Alcibiades I* (Lys. 14), *Against Alcibiades II* (Lys. 15), *On the Property of Eraton: Against the Treasury* (Lys. 17), *Against the Corn-Dealers* (Lys. 22), *Against Pancleon* (Lys. 23), *On the Scrutiny of Evandros* (Lys. 26), *Against Epicrates and his Fellow Envoys* (Lys. 27), *Against Ergocles* (Lys. 28), *Against Philocrates* (Lys. 29), *Against Nicomachus* (Lys. 30), *Against Philon: On his Scrutiny* (Lys. 31), and *Against Diogeiton* (Lys. 32).

Defense speeches

Aeschines' *On the Embassy* (Aeschin. *Leg.*); **Andocides'** *On the Mysteries* (Andoc. 1); **Antiphon's** *On the Murder of Herodes* (Antiph. 5) and *On the Chorus Boy* (Antiph. 6); **Cicero's** *Pro Archia* (Cic. *Arch.*), *Pro Balbo* (Cic. *Balb.*), *Pro Caecina* (Cic. *Caecin.*), *Pro Caelio* (Cic. *Cael.*), *Pro Cluentio* (Cic. *Clu.*), *Pro Cornelio* (Cic. *Corn.*), *Pro Rege Deiotaro* (Cic. *Deiot.*), *Pro Flacco* (Cic. *Flac.*), *Pro Fonteio* (Cic. *Font.*), *Pro Lege Manilia* (Cic. *Leg. Man.*), *Pro Ligario* (Cic. *Lig.*), *Pro Marcello* (Cic. *Marcell.*), *Pro Milone* (Cic. *Mil.*), *Pro Murena* (Cic. *Mur.*), *Pro Plancio* (Cic. *Planc.*), *Pro Quinctio* (Cic. *Quinct.*), *Pro Q. Roscio Comoedo* (Cic. *Q. Rosc.*), *Pro Rabirio Perduellionis Reo* (Cic. *Rab. Perd.*), *Pro Rabirio Postumo* (Cic. *Rab. Post.*), *Pro Sexto Roscio Amerino* (Cic. *Rosc. Amer.*), *Pro Scauro* (Cic. *Scaur.*), *Pro Sestio* (Cic. *Sest.*), *Pro Sulla* (Cic. *Sull.*), and *Pro Tullio* (Cic. *Tul.*); **Demades'** *On the Twelve Years* ([Demad.]

Dōdek); **Demosthenes'** *On the Crown* (Dem. 18), *Against the Special Plea of Zeonthemis* (Dem. 32), *For Phormio* (Dem. 36), and *On the Trierarchic Crown* (Dem. 51); **Hyperides'** *Defense of Lycophron* (Hyp. 1) and *Defense of Euxenippus* (Hyp. 4); **Isaeus'** *On the Estate of Cleonymus* (Isae. 1), *On the Estate of Menecles* (Isae. 2), *On the Estate of Apollodorus* (Isae. 7), *On the Estate of Ciron* (Isae. 8), *On the Estate of Hagnias* (Isae. 11), and *On Behalf of Euphiletus* (Isae. 12); **Isocrates'** *Concerning the Team of Horses* (Isoc. 16) and *Aegineticus* (Isoc. 19); **Lysias'** *On the Murder of Eratosthenes* (Lys. 1), *Against Simon* (Lys. 3), *On a Wound by Premeditation* (Lys. 4), *For Callias* (Lys. 5), *Before the Areopagus: Defense in the Matter of the Olive-Stump* (Lys. 7), *For the Soldier* (Lys. 9), *Before the Council: In Defence of Mantitheus at his Scrutiny* (Lys. 16), *On the Confiscation of the Property of the Brother of Nicias: Peroration* (Lys. 18), *On the Property of Aristophanes: Against the Treasury* (Lys. 19), *For Polystratus* (Lys. 20), *Defense against a Charge of Taking Bribes* (Lys. 21), *On the Refusal of a Pension to the Invalid* (Lys. 24), and *Defense against a Charge of Subverting the Democracy* (Lys. 25); **Plato's** *Apologia Socratis* (Pl. *Ap.*); and **Xenophon's** *Apologia Socratis* (Xen. *Ap.*).

Mixed speeches

Andocides' *On his Return* (Andoc. 2) is an apologetic demegoric speech. **Gorgias'** *Encomium of Helen* (Gorg. *Hel.*); **Alcidamas'** *On the Writers of Written Discourses or On the Sophists* (Alcid. *Soph.*); and **Isocrates'** *Busiris* (Isoc. 11) are display pieces and mixtures of each speech type.

Speeches as letters

The following are examples of speeches written in letter form. **Apologetic forensic literary letters:** Demosthenes' second letter, *Concerning his own Restoration* (Dem. *Ep.* 2) and **Plato's** *Third Letter* (Plat. *Ep.* 3). **Apologetic demegoric literary letters:** Isocrates' *To the Rulers of the Mytilenaeans* (Isoc. *Ep.* 8), **Plato's** *Seventh Letter* (Plat. *Ep.* 7), **Demosthenes'** *Concerning the Sons of Lycurgus* and *On the Slanderous Attacks of Theramenes* (Dem. *Ep.* 3 and *Ep.* 4). **Deliberative parenetic letters:** Isocrates' *To Demonicus* (Isoc. 1), *To Dionysius* (Isoc. *Ep.* 1), *To Philip, I and II* (Isoc. *Ep.* 2 and 3), *To the Children of Jason* (Isoc. *Ep.* 6), and *To Archidamus* (Isoc. *Ep.* 9); **Plato's** *Eighth Letter* (Plat. *Ep.* 8); **Cicero's** *Pet.*; **Sallust's** *Epistulae ad Caesarem Senem de Re Publica* (Sal. *Rep.*); **Pliny's** *Epistle* 8.24; and *Socraticorum Epistula* 30 (Anderson, 1999,

pp. 121–26; see also M. Mitchell, 1991, pp. 22–23). **Forensic epideictic letters: Pliny's** *To Ruso* (Pliny 9.19), which is a brief, playful letter
defending one Virginius Rufus' self-made epitaph against another man,
who declined having one made; also **Pliny's** *To Lupercus* (Pliny 9.26),
which is Pliny's defense of his style of oratory.

Forensic speeches within historical accounts (mostly defensive)

Dionysius of Halicarnassus' *Roman Antiquities* (Dion. Hal. *Ant. Rom.*)
9.29–32; **Livy's** *Ab Urbe Condita* (Liv.) 3.45.6–11; 26.30.11–31.11;
38.47–49; 39.36.7–37.17; 40.9.1–15,16; 42.41–42; 45.22–24; **Q. Curtius
Rufus'** *History of Alexander the Great* (Curt.) 6.10.1–37; 7.1.18–2.11;
Flavius Josephus' *Wars of the Jews* (Joseph. *Bel.*) 1.617–40 and *Antiq-
uities* (Joseph. *Ant.*) 16.91–126; the **Apostle Paul's** defense speeches in
Acts 21.27–22.29; 24.1–23; 26.1–32; and **C. Cornelius Tacitus'** *Annales*
(Tac. *Ann.*) 6.8; 13.21; 16.21–35 (Veltman, 1978, pp. 243–56, who also
discusses defense speeches in Herodotus, Thucydides, Xenophon, and
Appian). More speeches could be located, especially accusatory ones,
within ancient historical narratives (for deliberative speeches see M.
Mitchell, 1991, pp. 21–22; for speeches in Thucydides see West, 1973).

Speeches within comedies

Forensic: Aristophanes' *Nubes* (Ar. *Nub.*) 1353–90, 1399–1452 and
Vespae (Ar. *Vesp.*) 907–30, 950–79; **Deliberative: Aristophanes'** *Aves*
(Ar. *Av.*) 467–626; *Ecclesiazusae* (Ar. *Eccl.*) 171–240, *Lysistrata* (Ar.
Lys.) 507–97, 1124–61, *Nubes* (Ar. *Nub.*) 961–1023, 1036–1104, *Thes-
mophoriazusae* (Ar. *Thesm.*) 383–432, 466–519, and *Vespae* (Ar. *Vesp.*)
548–630, 650–724; **Mixed forensic/deliberative: Aristophanes'** *Acharnenses* (Ar. *Ach.*) 496–556 (Murphy, 1938, pp. 69–113).

How ought one use these sources? Stephen M. Pogoloff (1992, p. 93)
has aptly stated that "too much rhetorical criticism employs the ancient
handbooks as if they offered rigid generic formulas." To avoid this criticism, my analysis draws heavily upon the forensic speeches themselves.
Nevertheless, it is still necessary to consult the rhetorical handbooks to
describe *stasis* and topical theories. However, this does not detract from
the analysis below, since the theorists were informed by studying actual
speeches or their own production of them (cf. Quint. *Inst.* 5.10.120–21).
Thus, from these sources one is able to understand the diversity and
distinctness of forensic oratory.

2.2 Profusion of forensic rhetoric in Greco-Roman cultures

Rhetoric's power, both in the manner of expression (spoken and written) and in the purpose of its idealizing content and pragmatic application, gave it an abiding resilience. This is no less true for forensic oratory, which remained vigorous from its inception in the fifth century BC through the first century AD. This can be seen in at least five ways: (1) the proliferation of written speeches, (2) the theoretical developments in rhetorical handbooks that primarily involved forensic rhetoric, (3) the flexibility of forensic rhetoric in terms of both hybridization with epideictic and deliberative subgenres and the mixture with other genres (history, drama, and epistolography), (4) the existence of forensic schools in Rome, and (5) the dissemination of forensic rhetoric during the second sophistic movement in Greco-Roman education.

Proliferation of written speeches

The number of forensic speeches published by various logographers as advertisement of their services was quite enormous (Worthington, 1993, esp. p. 67 note 8). From 420 to 320 BC there were dozens of orators and logographers, most now unknown, producing a plethora of speeches. Eventually there was the selection of the best orators to be emulated (Gagarin and MacDowell, 1998, p. xvi note 16); hence, the development of the canon of the ten Attic orators. This canonization likely occurred in the third or second centuries BC under the impetus of library cataloguing at Alexandria (R. M. Smith, 1995; *contra* Douglas, 1956; cf. R. W. Smith, 1974, pp. 13–19); if not, then certainly by the first century BC (Worthington, 1994, pp. 244–63). Alexandria, because of its library's practice of procuring books, became a repository for published speeches, which allowed for their systematic study by Dionysius of Halicarnassus in the first century BC and Hermogenes of Tarsus in the second century AD (Gagarin and MacDowell, 1998, p. xvi). The imitation of the fifth- and fourth-century Greek orators was axiomatic for Hellenistic education (Wallace and Williams, 1998, pp. 96–97; R. W. Smith, 1974, pp. 122–30; Anderson, 1999, p. 79). One poignant example of this datum is R. W. Smith's (1974, pp. 124–26) listing of sixteen Greek authors, mostly orators, in papyri from Egypt dating from the third century BC to the fifth century AD, which "provides evidence of wide-spread use of and interest in speech models or treatises."

Furthermore, at the end of the first century BC, Dionysius of Halicarnassus wrote many essays analyzing the style of Isaeus, Isocrates,

Lysias, Aeschines, Thucydides, Hyperides, Demosthenes, and Dinarchus. His contemporary Caecilius of Calacte wrote a piece, no longer extant, *On the Style of the Ten Attic Orators* (Usher, 1974, pp. xxiii–xxvii, 3). In Theon's *Progymnasmata*, quotations of forensic orations are cited as examples: eight different speeches of Demosthenes (speeches 18–24, 30), two from Aeschines (*In Ctes.* and *In Tim.*), and one speech each from Isaeus, Lycurgus, and Hyperides. Dio Chrysostom (*Or.* 18.11) recommended that Demosthenes, Lysias, Aeschines, Hyperides, and Lycurgus be studied for emulation. Quintilian mentioned many Greek orators (e.g., Demosthenes, Isocrates, Aeschines, Andocides, Antiphon, Hyperides, and Lysias) and was especially fond of Cicero, quoting from his speeches profusely (see Little, 1951, vol. 1, pp. 167–200).

Theoretical handbooks and developments in forensic rhetoric

The handbooks by Hermagoras, Cicero, Quintilian, and the author of *Rhetorica ad Herennium* treated either exclusively or primarily forensic rhetoric. As Clark (1957, pp. 140–41) notes, "As judicial rhetoric was the earliest of the three kinds, it remained the most important in the forum and the schools and occupies the greatest space in ancient textbooks." This is not to say that the other branches of oratory disappeared or were not treated in handbooks. We have Philodemus' treatise on rhetoric (first century BC) espousing epideictic rhetoric. Eventually epideictic did supplant forensic as the dominant mode; but forensic rhetoric was flourishing still in the first century AD.

Furthermore, theoretical developments in rhetoric were primarily related to forensic oratory (see Arist. *Rhet.* 1.1.11), most notably the parts of the speech and *stasis* theory. The first technical treatises covered disposition (Kennedy, 1959, p. 172). Plato and Aristotle resisted this emphasis. After Aristotle, the most significant contributor is Hermagoras, whose comprehensive system of invention (*stasis* theory) influenced later theorists such as Cicero and Quintilian (Kennedy, 1963, pp. 318–21; cf. Nadeau, 1959).

The flexibility of forensic rhetoric

Despite the fact that rhetoric, and particularly forensic oratory, had been treated with suspicion, scorn, and even ridicule virtually from its inception,[2] its practitioners demonstrated its versatility for use in entertainment, legal and state matters, education, and letter writing. Forensic rhetoric was flexible enough to merge with rhetorical subgenres (deliberative and epideictic), and even influence various genres and written forms (published speeches, letters, drama, and history).

For example, Gorgias' *Encomium of Helen*, produced at the end of the fifth century, is a display speech, the title of which is misleading. Rather than being an epideictic speech in praise of Helen, it is a defense of her actions (*Hel.* 8; Innes and Winterbottom, 1988, p. 4 note 2; MacDowell, 1982, p. 12). In addition to this rhetorical mixture, one-third of the speech is devoted to Gorgias' theory of the nature of λόγος (8–14). It would seem that Gorgias used the medium of a defensive/encomiastic speech to promote his epistemological views. In the final analysis, though, we wonder how seriously Gorgias should be taken, since the discourse ends by calling the whole speech a game (παίγνιον – 21, the very last word; see MacDowell, 1982, p. 16).

Gorgias was not alone in publishing fictitious speeches treating mythological, legendary, and heroic figures. Alcidamas (fifth/fourth century BC) wrote *Odysseus* and *Ajax*. Isocrates also produced *Helen*, which advanced his educational ideology (see T. Poulakos, 1989). Other speechwriters from this period could be named (e.g., Antisthenes, ca. 445–ca. 360 BC) who wrote on these and other mythological or heroic figures. One favorite topic was the defense of Socrates (or his accusation, as Polycrates is credited in Isoc. 11.4). George A. Kennedy (1963, p. 149 note 40) lists in addition to the *Apologiae Socratis* by Plato and Xenophon those by Lysias, Theodectes, Demetrius of Phaleron, Zeon of Sidon, Plutarch, Theo of Antioch, and Libanius. We know that such display pieces were normally distributed (cf. Isoc. 11.1–2 and 15.55, 87). These pieces were propagandistic, promoting the philosophy of the particular teacher (Goldstein, 1968, pp. 119–26).

A very interesting work is *Busiris* by Isocrates (436–338 BC), another pupil of Gorgias. The *Busiris* (ca. 390 BC) is a didactic piece that criticizes Polycrates of Cyprus (fifth/fourth century BC) for his display piece entitled *Defense of Busiris*, a mythical king of Egypt. Isocrates chastised Polycrates for having written not a defense, but rather an accusation (5). Thus, Isocrates proceeded to demonstrate by example how Busiris should

---

[2] For example, it has too many parts in its speech (Plato; Aristotle). It feigns true knowledge and wisdom (Plato). It can persuade against the truth (Isocrates; Aristophanes' *Frogs*). It has too many simplistic rules and pays not enough attention to argumentation (Aristotle). It is easily confused with proper education (Isocrates' *Against the Sophists*; *Antidosis*).

have received praise and a defense (τὸν ἔπαινον καὶ τὴν ἀπολογίαν ποιήσασθαι – 9; cf. 44). The mixture of subgenres is not difficult to recognize: epideictic (eulogistic content), deliberative (persuasive context; urging Polycrates to write better speeches), and defensive (in mode of expression and form). All these purposes converge in 11.44:

> Although the subject admits of many arguments for the amplification of my theme of eulogy and defence, I believe it unnecessary to speak at greater length; for my aim in this discourse is not to make a display to impress others, but to show for your benefit how each of these topics should be treated, since the composition [τὸν λόγον] which you wrote may justly be considered by anyone to be, not a defence [ἀπολογίαν] of Busiris, but an admission [ὁμολογίαν] of all the crimes charged against him.

Note the play on words.

Particularly notable are the formal features of *Busiris* merging forensic rhetoric with ancient epistolography. On the one hand, the disposition of *Busiris* is markedly forensic: *prooemium* (1–3), *narratio* (4–8), *prothesis* (9), *probatio* (10–29), *refutatio* (30–48; 44–48, which also contains admonitions), and *peroratio* (49–50). On the other, Isocrates sends *Busiris* as a letter to Polycrates: "concerning those suggestions, however, by which at the present time I might be of service to you, I have thought I should advise you by letter [ταῦτα δ' ὠήθην χρῆναι σοὶ μὲν ἐπιστεῖλαι], though concealing my views, to the best of my ability, from everyone else" (2). Whether this is in fact how the discourse was transmitted, or a device feigning humility, is not clear. One can observe the merger of epistolary, rhetorical, and propagandistic concerns (see Chapter 6.3–4 below).

Forensic rhetoric's pragmatic flexibility is observed in Andocides' *On his Return*, which is technically a demegoric (i.e. deliberative) speech. It was delivered to the Athenian assembly (ἐκκλησία) at the end of the fifth century. However, it is apologetic in purport; Andocides is attempting to persuade the Athenian council to allow him to return after having been exiled. To accomplish this task, Andocides must amplify his own services and show how he sacrificially gave of himself and his goods for the state. The speech does not contain ἀπολογία or κατηγορία or their cognates. However, it does contain language of wrongdoing in the context of opponents (5.8; 6.2, 5; 17.9, 10, 11; 19.4, 7; 24.5; 25.2; 27.4, 6). From his perspective, justice was at stake (5.4; 7.7; 12.6; 17.10; 18.3; 19.10; 22.4, 5; 24.9). Moreover, the speech was carefully designed according to forensic speech practice: *prooemium* (1–9), *narratio* (10–16), *divisio/partitio*

(17–18), which outlined the topics of both his *money* and his own *person* offered to the state, *probatio* (19–26), which treated his *monetary* gifts and request for pardon (19–23) followed by a focus on his *body* and *personal* actions (24–26), and *peroratio* (27–28), which contains disparaging remarks about his opponents. This speech illustrates how apologetic discourse could suitably function within deliberative settings.

Forensic rhetoric and oratory also influenced Greek tragedy and drama in the fifth and fourth centuries in various ways. Michael Lloyd (1992, pp. 34–35) discusses critical features of Euripides' *agon* scenes (i.e. verbal and argumentative clashes between main characters) in which the speeches are self-consciously given, the points carefully outlined, forensically arranged, and refutations offered point by point. G. Xanthakis-Karamanos (1979, pp. 66–68; cf. Gagarin, 1994, p. 47) argues that the characters are portrayed less in terms of ἦθος and more in terms of διάνοια, i.e. expounding rationalistic arguments. Furthermore, there are more dramatic debates (ἀγῶνες λόγων) accompanied by the prosaic rendering of tragic expressions "resembling ordinary diction, as used in the Assembly or the lawcourts" (Xanthakis-Karamanos, 1979, p. 68; cf. Gagarin, 1994, p. 59). Charles T. Murphy (1938) demonstrates that forensic rhetoric was also influential in the disposition and argumentation of the ἀγῶνες in many of the comedies of Aristophanes (ca. 450–385 BC). In fact, within Aristophanes' *Acharnenses* (425 BC) is found a masterful speech by Dicaeopolis defending himself to the chorus and the Lacedaemonians to the Athenian audience (496–556). The speech is both forensic and deliberative (Murphy, 1938, pp. 100–101). Murphy (pp. 101–104) discusses at length the speech's disposition, which even includes a refutation section.

The same is true for historical writing, which is amply seasoned with forensic elements in the political speeches. Christopher Carey (1994b, esp. p. 34) demonstrates this for Thucydides. Michael Gagarin shows how often the deliberative speeches in Thucydides are paired as "in the manner of a legal dispute" (1994, p. 59). In the Hellenistic period forensic rhetoric's influence on history writing is particularly seen through the influence of *stasis* theory (see Hall, 1997).

Epistolography likewise could merge with rhetoric (Stirewalt, 1993, pp. 9, 15–16, 20–24; Costa, 2001, pp. xi–xii). Isocrates gives a fine example of a written speech that was "dispatched," in order to provide admonition *To Demonicus* (ca. 374 BC). It is sent to him as a written document: "I have dispatched [ἀπέσταλκα] to you this discourse [λόγον] as a gift, in proof of my good will toward you and in token of my friendship for Hipponicus" (2.2; cf. 5.1). Exhortations are found in 9–11. Other epistolary speeches have epistolary introductions (Isoc. *Ep.* 1–3, 6, 9; Dem. *Ep.* 1, 2; Pl. *Ep.* 3, 7, 8). These examples of epistolary oratory were not anomalous.[3] The apologetic letter will receive direct attention in Chapter 6.2.

These examples illustrate that formalized forensic rhetoric not only displayed great variety in its own manner of expression, mixing with epideictic and deliberative subgenres, but also gained a prevailing influence in Greek literature broadly speaking.

Forensic schools in Rome

Competing schools of forensic rhetoric flourished in the Roman Empire. Kennedy (1994, p. 160) relates the dispute in Rome during the first century BC between Apollodorus of Pergamum and his former student and competitor Theodorus of Gadara concerning "the structure of a judicial oration." Then, during Claudius' reign, forensic orators could once again charge fees for their services, which attests to the vitality of forensic oratory (Kennedy, 1972, p. 437).

Greco-Roman education in the second sophistic movement

The second sophistic movement, beginning sometime in the second century BC and extending well into the new millennium, invigorated interest in rhetoric (Enos, 1980; cf. Kennedy, 1994, pp. 234–35). Bruce W. Winter (1993a, p. 64) relates Philo's evaluation of the movement: "Philo [*Agr.* 143] laments that, in the early decades of the first century, city after city was being won over by these orators and the whole world was honouring them." At the end of the first century AD, Dio Chrysostom bemoans the proliferation of professional sophists and their disciples at the Isthmian games (*Or.* 8.9). This certainly affected Corinth in the mid first century AD (Winter, 1997, pp. 116–125; Litfin, 1994, pp. 140–46). Winter (1997, p. 144; cf. Witherington, 1995, pp. 349–50) argues, "There can be no doubt, then, that sophists and their students were prominent in Corinth and played an important role in the life of the city."

Furthermore, the practice of formal rhetoric was guaranteed by its continued use in political and judicial settings. Juridical fervor peaked in

---

[3] See also the partial list in Chapter 2.1 under "Speeches as Letters." For more deliberative letters, see M. Mitchell, 1991, pp. 22–23; cf. West (1973, pp. 7–15), who cites four examples of speeches sent as letters as recorded in Thucydides' historical account: Pausanias' letter to Xerxes (1.128.7), Xerxes' letter to Pausanias (1.129.3), Artaxerxes' letter to the Spartans (4.50.2), and Phrynichus' letter to Astyochus (8.50.2).

Rome during the early empire (Parks, 1945, pp. 52–60). For this reason, forensics continued to be seen as necessary to rhetorical education (see Kennedy, 1963, pp. 268–73).

Concerning the extent and influence of rhetorical education in Greco-Roman cultures, so much has been said that hardly any mention is required (see, e.g., Clarke, 1968; S. Bonner, 1977; Heath, 1995, pp. 11–18). C. D. N. Costa (2001, p. xi) states, "This period, especially the Imperial age, was the time of the dominance of the sophists and rhetors, the professional teachers and practitioners of rhetoric, who were profoundly influential in the political and educational life especially in the cities of the Greek East." Palestine was greatly affected by its influence (Mack, 1990, pp. 25–31; Kinneavy, 1987, pp. 56–91; Kurz, 1980, pp. 192–94). It should be emphasized that education in Rome was especially enamored with Greek rhetoric (Clarke, 1968, pp. 10–15; Enos, 1972, pp. 37–38; 1975; 1977, pp. 4, 7–8). Kennedy (1963, p. 22) argues,

> Roman education, after primary training at the hands of the *grammaticus*, was even more dominated by rhetoricians than was Greek. Athletics and music were almost ignored, and the other disciplines of the liberal arts were decidedly auxiliary to the one great training in speech, which was most characteristically developed in the declamation of *suasoriae* and *controversiae*. The practice of these exercises, even in Cicero's time and much more in the age of the elder Seneca, was not simply a schoolboy exercise but a social grace, cultivated by all educated people for their delight and amusement. The world was a rhetorician's world, its ideal an orator; speech became an artistic product to be admired apart from its content or significance.

This implicates that first, Greek orators and forensic rhetorical theory were highly valued as resources for study and imitation, and second, such an emphasis would likely exist outside of Rome across the entire empire.

It is instructive to consider the importance of declamation exercises (see Russell, 1983; S. Bonner, 1969; Winterbottom, 1984) and *progymnasmata* (Butts, 1986; Anderson, 1999, pp. 72–77; Kennedy, 2003). Declamations consist in fictitious speeches ostensibly to persuade a judge or an assembly to adopt a certain course of action. They involved real-life scenarios and concurrent legal terminology (see Crook, 1995, pp. 63–67), but are technically epideictic. Professional rhetoricians delivered declamations throughout their entire lives, which often led to rivalries among the best-known declaimers for public consumption (Russell, 1983, pp. 74–86).

Quintilian (*Inst.* 3.8.55–56; cf. 3.8.58–70) also states that

> in scholastic declamations the fictitious themes for deliberative speeches are often not unlike those of controversial speeches and are a compromise between the two forms, as for instance when the theme set is a discussion in the presence of Gaius Caesar of the punishment to be meted out to Theodotus; for it consists of accusation and defence, both of them peculiar to forensic oratory. But the topic of expediency also enters the case.

Once again, forensic rhetoric's versatility is evident. Furthermore, Quintilian (*Inst.* 4.2.28–30) relates that often the declaimers followed the school rhetorical training too rigidly, and thus always included a statement of facts after the *exordium*. Such a statement attests to the continued importance of speech disposition. Kennedy (1997, pp. 44–45) argues that in execution, declamation was precisely in line with the early rhetorical tradition (e.g., Gorgias, Isocrates).

Concerning the *progymnasmata*, Aelius Theon (*Prog.* 2.144–153; trans. Butts, 1986) argues that the final stages of instruction consisted in the imitation of complete orations and an understanding of their construction:

> Consequently, just as one may introduce these exercises to the mind of the young students, it is necessary, in the same way, that what follows be in agreement. Therefore, in addition to what has been said, the teacher himself, after composing some refutations and confirmations in an especially brilliant way, must also instruct his young students to recite them, so that once they have been molded in accordance with the treatment of those, they can imitate them. When they have become competent in writing, one must detail for them the order of the subject-headings and arguments, and indicate as well the proper place for digression, amplification, and all the other items. Also, one must make clear the character of the problem.

Theon described the instructor's introduction of theories of disposition, and his last remark concerning "the character of the problem" is likely referring to a consideration of *stasis* theory.[4]

---

[4] This paragraph comes at the end of the second book, entitled "On the Education of Young Students" in which also is "On the Use of the Progymnasmata by the Ancients."

Theon maintained that, although the *progymnasmata* were beneficial for the rhetorical craft (τὴν ῥητορικὴν δύναμιν) and especially forensics (*Prog.* 1.25–33), they had a broad application across literary genres. He says: "For these exercises are, so to speak, the foundation stones for every form of writing" (*Prog.* 2.141–42). Thus, R. Dean Anderson (1999, p. 77) is correct to argue that the value of Theon's *Progymnasmata* is not limited to oratory, but rather extends to literature in general, especially literary letters:

> Such exercises formed the practice in the building blocks of speeches generally (of whatever genre) and such material (e.g., instances of χρεῖαι, προσωποποιΐαι, or extended comparisons – συγκρίσεις) can, not infrequently, be found built into the speeches and other forms of literature of the time. In this respect a knowledge of the προγυμνάσματα may be helpful in terms of the analysis of literary letters.

In Chapter 6, I hope to show the rhetorical influence on ancient letter writing. There I argue that the apologetic letter was a viable genre. Thus, Anderson's suggestion will provide justification for analyzing Paul's letters rhetorically, if indeed it can be shown that Paul has written an apologetic letter.

2.3   Written or spoken rhetoric: oratory and orality

As argued above, oratory from its formal origins was conveyed in a written medium for various ends, despite the fact of its essential oral nature. This affirmation is critical for developing an appropriate framework for viewing Paul's epistles as speeches sent as letters. Richard L. Enos (1984, p. 78; cf. Loubser, 1995, p. 62) has an extended discussion treating this topic and concludes: "The unity of oral and written expression was so inextricably bound in ancient discourse that its oneness was an unquestioned presumption upon which theories of rhetoric were developed."

Perhaps the most renowned debate on this topic was by Alcidamas and Isocrates. These sophists vigorously debated whether rhetoric should be conceived of as an oral or written discipline (see Van Hook, 1919; for the debate in the first century AD see Winter, 1997, pp. 205–206). Both educators were bitterly opposed to the other's philosophy of rhetoric.

The *problem* (πρόβλημα), argues Butts (1986, p. 182 note 38), is equivalent to πρόθεσις and is a "quasi-technical term of rhetoric taken from dialectic (see Arist. *Top.* I.11) used to denote the 'subject' of any oratorical undertaking." In order to arrive at this subject, a student employed *stasis* theory as proposed by Hermagoras.

Alcidamas espoused extemporaneous speech; Isocrates written speech. The enmity is seen in several works, beginning with Isocrates' *Against the Sophists* (ca. 390 BC), in which, as LaRue Van Hook (1919, p. 89) explains, "he attacked the principles and methods employed by his rivals in the profession. Three classes of sophists are censured: (1) the Eristics; (2) the teachers of rhetoric; (3) the writers of 'arts of rhetoric.' Alcidamas belonged primarily to the second class attacked." This challenge was met rather directly by Alcidamas when he wrote *On the Writers of Written Discourses* or *Concerning the Sophists* (ca. 385 BC). This work, taking the form of a written (ironically!) accusation (*Soph.* 1), advances the notion through a series of contrasts that the extemporaneous approach to speech is superior to a written one. Alcidamas (*Soph.* 14; trans. Van Hook, 1919, pp. 91–94) argues:

> I think that for this reason also we must hold written speeches in disesteem, that they involve their composers in inconsistency; for it is inherently impossible to employ written speeches on all occasions. And so, when a speaker in part speaks extemporaneously, and in part uses a set form, he inevitably involves himself in culpable inconsistency, and his speech appears in measure histrionic and rhapsodic, and in a measure mean and trivial in comparison with the artistic finish of others.

The speech follows a discernible disposition and is cogently argued: *prooemium* with *prothesis* (1), *probatio* (2–28), *refutatio* (29–33), and *peroratio* (34). The *refutatio* is rather interesting, since Alcidamas addresses, among other anticipated criticisms, why his speech is in written form, a fact that greatly undermines his entire argument. Nevertheless, Isocrates' view on the matter was favored by posterity (e.g., Aristotle) and Alcidamas was little esteemed on matters of style by later critics (Van Hook, 1919, p. 91; Aristotle in *Rhet.* 3.3 classifies Alcidamas' style as "frigid"). In the Roman period, Enos' view (1984, p. 78) that "the publication of such forms of rhetoric as forensic argument, which was implicitly intended for both hearing and publication" indicates the utter unity of written and oral rhetoric. This is true despite the increased emphasis on extemporary public declamations in the first century AD (Winter, 1997, p. 206).

Thus, even though rhetoric was written, this did not remove the desire to preserve an oral, fresh style as opposed to a contrived, artificial one. As much as Isocrates and Alcidamas disagreed whether rhetoric should be oral or written, in fact they shared the view that rhetorical art should be "hidden" (Edwards and Usher, 1985, pp. 9–10). The common understanding of rhetoric as an "art concealing the art of rhetoric" is found throughout the rhetorical tradition (for a list of ancient sources expressing this notion see [Cicero], trans. Caplan, 1954, pp. 250–51 note a; cf. Kennedy, 1997, p. 44). Generally speaking, Cicero (*De Or.* 2.156) rightly expresses this widespread concern: "any suggestion of artifice is likely to prejudice an orator with the judiciary: for it weakens at once the credibility of the orator and the cogency of his oratory." As applied to invention, consider also Cicero's sentiments (*De Or.* 2.177; see also Arist. *Rhet.* 3.2.1–5; and *Rhet. Her.* 4.10 regarding the selection of examples): the "handling [of invention material] should be diversified, so that your hearer may neither perceive the art of it, nor be worn out by too much monotony." One's style (Cic. *Inv.* 1.25; Cic. *Or. Brut.* 38; and Cic. *Part. Or.* 19) and delivery (Cic. *Brut.* 139 and Quint. *Inst.* 1.11.3) should not be visibly artificial. The same is true for disposition with respect to the *divisio* (*Rhet. Her.* 1.17), the *narratio* (Quint. *Inst.* 2.5.7; 4.2.57), and the *peroratio* (Cic. *Brut.* 139; Cic. *Inv.* 1.98). If the apostle Paul followed this universal dictum, it would complicate attempts to discern rhetorical disposition in his letters. Recent studies on the Book of Acts and specifically Paul's speeches within Acts would indicate that he is at least depicted as using Greco-Roman rhetorical theory (see Satterthwaite, 1993; Winter, 1991b, 1993b; on Luke's reliance on *stasis* theory see Jolivet, 1999).

2.4   Features that identify forensic discourse

All forensic oratory is founded upon the universal phenomenon of accusation and defense, with the ultimate concern being justice and equity. It is the universal notion of justice that governs and unites the myriad of forensic speeches, despite their unique circumstances and the ulterior motives of litigants. This universal phenomenon in turn attracted the attention of the forensic theorists, who were inspired to mull over, systematize, and codify the observed oratorical methods and persuasive means.

What are the defining and distinguishing characteristics of Greek forensic discourse in terms of its setting, content, and form? Kennedy's survey of Greek oratory (1963, pp. 25–52; cf. 261–63) involves five distinctive features: (1) a court setting involving litigants; (2) the presence of a narration of facts; (3) a refutation of the opponent; (4) *ethopoiia* (the articulation of the character of the speaker); and (5) the theme of justice. Similarly, Fred Veltman's (1978, p. 252) typology of defensive speeches within historical writings (specifically, "trial episodes") includes these features: (1) a trial scene with charges mentioned, (2) the speech identified as an apology, (3) direct address, (4) the speech addressing the charges, and (5) use of rhetorical questions. These observations are helpful, but a more specific and detailed typology may be offered.

There are at least twelve features that can be categorized as relating to forensic exigency, invention, and disposition. Some of these features are unique to or distinctive of forensic discourse; others are typical or common features that are found elsewhere. Additionally, forensic discourse is found in various types of media and with various intentions, whether delivered in person or written, whether a localized or broad distribution, whether published as addressing a real or fictitious situation, whether intended as philosophical propaganda or as an educational piece. Strictly speaking, the media of forensic discourse do not represent features, but rather typical ways in which the discourse would be implemented and brought into action for particular purposes. Thus, these twelve features with types of media are:

Exigency

1   Alleged wrongdoing in the past
2   A judicial setting, with jury and with litigants (defendant and accuser)
3   A formal designation or recognition that the speech is a defense/apology or accusation

Invention

4   Essential issue(s) or *stasis* theory
5   Inartificial proofs: use of witnesses, other physical evidences, and laws
6   Artificial proofs: *pathos*, *ethos*, and *logos*
7   Topics for forensic argumentation

Disposition

8   Discernible rhetorical disposition
9   *Narratio*
10 *Partitio*
11 *Refutatio*
12 Self-adulation

Media

13   Oral or written rhetoric
14   Revision, circulation, and distribution
15   Real or fictitious situation
16   Philosophical propaganda or educational piece

The next four chapters will treat each of these in turn.

3

FORENSIC EXIGENCY

3.1   Alleged wrongdoing in the past

Forensic rhetoric essentially consists in someone formally accusing an individual or the state with a wrongdoing (Arist. *Rhet.* 1.1.1–6). Cases were accordingly either public (δημόσιος) or private (ἰδιωτικός). The scope of such alleged injustices range from homicide to citizenship, from misconduct against the state to failure to repay a personal debt (see Carey, 1997; Alexander, 1990). The terms denoting the wrongdoing varied, but included words like ἀδικία (*injustice* – Din. 3.20.2), ἀδίκημα (*crime* – Din. 1.4.1; 8.5; 22.6; 23.2; 27.3; 55.3; 55.8; 60.3; 60.6; 108.7; Din. 2.5.8; 17.3; 22.7; Din. 3.8.1; 11.2; 15.4; 17.2), πρᾶγμα (*deed, crime* – Lycurg. *Leoc.* 63.2; 66.2; 67.4; 90.5; 91.2; 112.6; Din. 1.88.4; 89.2), ἁμαρτία or ἁμάρτημα (*fault, sin* – Din. 1.18.2; 57.5; 60.2). The formal charge could be designated by αἰτία (*charge, accusation* – Aesch. *Leg.* 5.3; Din. 1.6.2; 30.7; Dem. 18.4.9; Hyp. 1.*Fr.*IV; IVb3.4; Lys. 16.9.1).

In numerous instances, however, another critical dimension to the allegations existed. Accusations were also formulated for political purposes, to malign the character of the accused in order to weaken their testimony in another legal case or to render them and their proposed political policies undesirable (Hunter, 1990). Whenever beneficial, this underlying motivation was exposed (or even manufactured) by the accused as a defensive measure. Hyperides' *Defense of Euxenippus* is such an example. Here the charge against Euxenippus is exposed as personally motivated by Polyeuctus (the accuser), against whom Euxenippus had prevailed in an earlier decision (18). Also the defendant in Antiphon 6.33–36, 49–50 argues that the charges were brought forth simply to thwart an impeachment case presented by the defendant. Carey (1997, p. 5; cf. Goldstein, 1968, pp. 117–19) further describes this complex situation: "Above and beyond the overtly and unambiguously political use of the courts, one finds politicians using non-political cases to harry their rivals and those associated with them, by bringing actions themselves, by using agents to prosecute, or by appearing as witness or supporting speaker in court." Thus, to bring someone to trial could be a means to achieve character assassination by discrediting the name of a defendant and his associates. Winter (1991a, p. 566) describes the personal dimension of this succinctly: "Litigation caused personal enmity and litigation was used to aggravate personal enmity." Thus, whenever there is a claim to wrongdoing, the actual *cause* of the allegations may in fact lie outside the particular charge at hand.

3.2 Judicial setting

Allegations would call for a verdict. The *judicial setting* concerns the judicial procedures and jargon, judges/jury, and the litigants, both accuser and defendant or their advocates. Important differences existed between Greek and Roman systems of justice. Despite the differences, however, Kennedy (1968, p. 419; cf. Anderson, 1999, p. 86) contends that "the rhetorical tradition is essentially a unity." Thus, the respective judicial procedures need not detain us here (see Bonner and Smith, 1930–38; Lavency, 1964; Wolf, 1968; Soubie, 1973, 1974; R. W. Smith, 1974, pp. 58–72; MacDowell, 1978; E. Harris, 1994; Carey, 1997, pp. 1–4, 242–43).

In Greek, the *case* or *trial* may be designated by various terms depending on one's viewpoint. A common designation is πρᾶγμα (*matter*), which may refer to the case itself including its arguments (e.g., Antiph. 6.8.1; Lycurg. *Leoc.* 11.2, 5; 13.2; 29.9; 149.3; Dem. 19.242.6; 32.13.1; Din. 1.7.2; 48.9; 105.2; Hyp. 1.IVb.3.1, 9.2; Hyp. 4.11.9). The whole case from the perspective of litigants is an ἀγών (*contest*) (e.g., Andoc. 1.105.8; [Andoc.] 4.2.5; Antiph. 5.85.6; 6.3.1; Isae. 3.24.4; 6.2.7; 8.34.5; Isoc.17.1.1; 18.33.4). Since justice is at stake, not surprisingly the term δίκη may refer to the verdict rendered or the lawsuit itself (e.g., Dem. 32.2, 9,10; Xen. *Ap.* 24).

In Athens the jury/judges (δικασταί) were ordinary citizens selected to render verdicts. Approximately 6,000 jurors were selected for this service annually. Private suits required anywhere from 201 to 401 judges, depending on the sum of money involved. In public suits, multiples of 500 were possible. The qualifications for being a δικαστής changed with time; typically, any male citizen over thirty years of age was eligible. One person, the κριτής, was selected to preside, but otherwise had no special voice. Thus, knowledge of Athenian law and rhetoric possessed by the average male citizen – eventually selected for jury service – was more extensive than one might otherwise think (Carey, 1997, pp. 5–7; MacDowell, 1978, pp. 33–40).

To a great degree the courts functioned in support of various political procedures, one of which was the formal evaluation of men being considered for service as public officials (see Arist. *Ath. Pol.* 55 and 59). This evaluation involved a *dokimasia* trial (MacDowell, 1978, pp. 167–72; Adeleye, 1983; Hunter, 1990, pp. 311–14; Carey, 1997, p. 5). Persons, if scrutinized and accused of being ineligible for serving in public office, could offer a defense. This is the setting for Lysias' 16th and 25th orations (the accusations are Lys. 26 and Lys. 31).

In Athens the litigants typically spoke for themselves twice, alternating with the prosecution, which initiated the sequence. It became advantageous with the development and systematization of rhetorical techniques to hire a speechwriter (*logographos*). Antiphon was reportedly the first (Photius *Lex.* 486a7–11; Plutarch *Mor.* 832c–d cited in Gagarin and MacDowell, 1998, p. xi note 7). We have many extant examples of such speeches by Antiphon, Lysias, and Demosthenes (see Lavency, 1964, pp. 26–31).[1] An alternative was to learn from the rhetoricians and their τέχναι (*technical manuals*). Kennedy (1959, p. 174) argues, "If the prospective litigant could not buy a whole speech and could not afford or had not the time to study with a sophist, he could turn to a rhetorician and learn from him in a single lecture, or by reading a written summary of his lecture, the necessary parts of a speech and the chief features of each part." Kennedy maintains that these early forensic τέχναι treated the parts of the speech or what later became known as τάξις (*disposition*). This had practical benefits for easy instruction.

Occasionally a litigant would use an advocate, as was common in Roman forensic practice (Kennedy, 1968, pp. 419–26; Gagarin, 1997, pp. 9–10). Roman custom held that a patron would advocate. John A. Crook (1995, p. 3) discusses the basic relation of advocacy to rhetoric: "Ancient advocates employed and were masters of rhetoric: for some observers that is the most important and obvious fact about them. Rhetoric was then regarded as the theoretical foundation of forensic practice."

Finally, forensic oratory extended beyond real cases into the construction of fictitious cases of legendary figures (Alcid. *Od.*; Antisth.

---

[1] Lavency's work is the standard treatment of this phenomenon in ancient Greece. He helpfully tabulates the speeches of the speechwriters. Lavency designates whether the speeches were written for a litigant (defendant or accuser), or given by a supporter (συνήγορος) in conjunction with the litigant's speech (defendant or accuser), or spoken for oneself (independently or supplementing another primary speaker who was speaking on his behalf).

Aj. and *Od.*; Antiph. 2, 3, 4; Gorg. *Pal.* and *Hel.*; Isoc. *Bus.*). Many
fictitious speeches were constructed around infamous political figures
like Socrates. Eventually, such literary constructions became customary
as educational exercises (see Theon. *Prog.*).

This flexibility of forensic discourse caused the Greek dramatists to
include in their comedies and tragedies paired speeches resembling a
judicial setting involving accusation and defense (Gagarin, 1994, p. 59;
Lloyd, 1992, esp. pp. 34–35; Xanthakis-Karamanos, 1979; C. T. Murphy,
1938). Furthermore, epistolary forensic discourses were sent as letters and
would generate the judicial setting (Andoc. 2; Dem. *Eps.* 2, 3, 4; Isoc. 15;
Ep. 8; Pl. *Eps.* 3, 7). This was particularly the case when the *defendant*
was in exile (Andoc. 2; Dem. *Eps.* 2, 3; Isoc. *Ep.* 8) and/or had come under
particular scrutiny, as was the case for Isocrates, who wrote *Antidosis* as
a mock trial to defend his reputation (Isoc. 15; cf. Pl. *Eps.* 3, 7). See my
discussion of apologetic letters in Chapter 6.2.

3.3   Designation as defense or accusation

Part and parcel of the exigency is the fact that a plaintiff will *accuse* and
the accused *defend*, therefore using these titles to describe the discourse.
One may argue that the use of such designations falls under *invention*
rather than *exigency*. If we are talking about how the designations *defend*
or *accuse* are used to advance the argument, then possibly so. As Heath
(1995, p. 11) indicates, "Classifying one's speech was therefore a crucial
foundation for invention." However, I have in mind simply the recognition, even before the invention process starts, that one was engaging in
defense or accusation.

A distinctive feature of forensic speeches is the *formal recognition on
the part of the speaker* (or logographer) that the speech is either a *defense*
(ἀπολογία; ἀπολογέομαι) or *accusation* (κατηγορία; κατηγορέω). The
pairing of these terms is found repeatedly in Aristotle (*Rhet.* 1.3.3; 1.3.9;
1.10.1, *passim*). Such terms may be included within the speech title or are
assumed by the use of the prepositions πρός (*against*) and ὑπέρ (*on behalf
of*) with a person's name, e.g., "[An accusation] Against Demosthenes."

Typically, the writer would self-consciously use these terms within the
speech. Thus, κατηγορία is used in the accusation speech at Dinarchus
1.114.1: "I have now played my full part in assisting the prosecution
[κατηγορία] and have shown regard for nothing but justice [δίκαιος] and
your interests [συμφέρω]." See also κατηγορέω in Dinarchus 1.48.8;
105.4; 113.4; ἀπολογία in Aeschines *On the Embassy* 5.4, 9; Andocides 1.6.9; 8.2; 9.8; Antiphon 3.2.2.5; 3.4.1.2; Dinarchus 1.108.2; 3.4.7;

Isaeus 11.32.6; Isocrates 16.3.5; Xenophon *Apologia Socratis* 1, 4; and ἀπολογέομαι in Andocides 1.6.2, 4; 1.7.15; Antiphon 2.2.4.2; 2.4.3.2; 3.2.1.7; 5.90.4; and Dinarchus 1.108.6, 113.4; 3.3.7 (cf. Isoc. 15.8.8; 15.13.2; 15.321.3; Lycurg. *Frag.* 3; Din. *Fr. passim*).

These formal designations are found with more frequency at the beginning and ending of speeches. In addition to Dinarchus 1.114.1 (above), consider also the following examples in which κατηγορέω or ἀπολογέομαι is found within the *peroratio*.

> And first of all I pray and beseech the gods to save me, and then I beseech you, who hold the verdict in your hands, before whom I have defended myself [ἀπολελόγημαι] against every one of the accusations [πρὸς ἕκαστον τῶν κατηγορημένων], to the best of my recollection; I beg you to save me.
>
> (Aesch. *Leg.* 180.1–3)

> All the charges [ἐκ τῶν κατηγορηθέντων] which I can remember, gentleman, I have answered [ἀπολελόγημαι]; and for your own sakes I think you should acquit me.   (Antiph. 5.85.1)

> Now, I have made my accusation [κατηγόρηκα] to the best of my ability.   (Lys. 14.46.1)

> But I really see no need for me to be so very particular in rebutting [ἀπολογούμενον] each one of the statements that he has made, and to weary you any longer.   (Lys. 24.21.1–2)

These terms were not necessary to convey the idea of defense or accusation. For example, consider the concise statement: "Well, gentleman of the jury, you have heard virtually all that I had to say on my own behalf [ὑπὲρ ἐμαυτοῦ εἰπεῖν]" (Hyp. 1.IVb.19.1; cf. Lys. 18.24.1).

Once a judicial setting was established, the litigants would consider how best to construct their case. We turn now to consider typical and distinctive features of forensic invention.

4

FORENSIC INVENTION

4.1   Essential issue and *stasis* theory

The first concern when preparing an accusation or defense speech is determining the basic issue(s) upon which the case turns. Christoff Neumeister (1964, p. 15; cf. Volkmann, 1885; J. Martin, 1974; Lausberg, 1998) begins his consideration of the characteristics of forensic oratory in Cicero with these remarks:

> Der Gegenstand einer Gerichtsrede ist die causa, der juristische Fall. Jede causa enthält eine Frage (quaestio), etwa: "Hat Milo den Clodius ermordet?" Der Ankläger behauptet: "Er hat ihn ermordet", der Verteidiger entgegnet: "Nein, er hat es nicht getan." Die Behauptung des Anklägers und die abstreitende Gegenbehauptung des Verteidigers bilden einen Widerspruch (controversia), der nach Auflösung verlangt. Er ist gleichsam das dynamische Prinzip, das den ganzen Gerichtsprozeß in Bewegung bringt. Gleichzeitig gibt er der causa die logische Struktur, bestimmt, in der Terminologie der Rhetorik gesprochen, ihren status.
>
> [The object of a court-speech is the *causa*, the legal case. Each *causa* contains a question (*quaestio*), something like: "Has Milo murdered Clodius?" The accuser claims: "He has murdered him"; the defender replies: "No, he has not done it." The claim of the accuser and the denying counter-claim of the defender form a contradiction (*controversia*) that afterwards requires resolution. This is the dynamic principle that brings the whole court-process in movement, as it were. Simultaneously as it gives the *causa* the logical structure, it decides, in the terminology of spoken rhetoric, its status.]

Reflection upon these dynamics – case, question, opposing arguments – resulted in the development of *stasis* theory. Many have surveyed ancient theories of *stasis* in classical (Dieter, 1950; Nadeau, 1959, 1964; Braet, 1987; Heath, 1994, 1995) and biblical fields (Watson, 1988, pp. 9–13; T. Martin, 1995; Peterson, 1998, pp. 32–38).

Hermagoras of Temnos (fl. ca. 150 BC) offered an extensive treatment of *stasis*, although elements of the theory are detectable earlier. Aristotle's *Rhetoric* contains glimpses into this early development (1.13.1–19; 3.15.1–8; 3.17.1–2; see Thompson, 1975), as do Plato and Isocrates before him (Gaines, 1985, p. 160). After Hermagoras the theory is articulated and developed in the *Rhetorica ad Herennium*, in Cicero (both early to mid first century BC), Quintilian (late first century AD), Hermogenes of Tarsus (mid second century AD), and many others in between. Quintilian's discussion on *stasis* is particularly relevant, since he is comprehensive in scope and conversant with many major and minor figures in the rhetorical schools earlier than his own time (see Holtsmark, 1968).

When two parties disagree, each having respective causes, a rhetorical situation emerges. Quintilian quotes Isocrates defining a cause as "some definite question concerned with some point of civil affairs, or a dispute in which definite persons are involved" (*Inst.* 3.5.18). When one evaluated a rhetorical situation, the first step was to determine the basic issue of contention. Heath (1994, pp. 116–22) discusses the various definitions of *stasis* that were debated: (1) *stasis* is the initial proposition of the defense (Hermagoras); (2) *stasis* is the conflict of the initial propositions of prosecution and defense; and (3) *stasis* is the question that arises from the conflict of initial propositions. Cicero (*Inv.* 1) proposed both (2) and (3). Quintilian dismisses (1) and (2) (*Inst.* 3.6.4–6, 13–19) and arrives at a modified version of (3) (*Inst.* 3.6.5, 20–21) where *stasis* is determined from the question that arises from the conflict of initial propositions.

Despite these differences, Ray Nadeau (1964, p. 375) rightly argues, "Both ancients and moderns . . . are in substantial agreement that a *stasis* or issue, whenever and however it occurs, takes the form of a question which focuses the contrary views of proponents and opponents." Importantly, we can observe in the extant speeches statements of issue in the form of questions and functioning as the *prothesis* (see Chapter 5.3).

Among the various theoreticians there was unity amidst variety when delineating the possible types of *stases* (see Quint. *Inst.* 3.6.80). Issues were typically divided into two types: rational and legal (*rationale genus* and *legale genus*). There are three rational issues or questions: whether a thing is, what it is, and of what kind it is. These pertain to conjecture (στοχασμός, *constitutio coniecturalis*), definition (ὅρος, *constitutio definitiva* or *proprietas*), and quality (ποιότης or κατὰ συμβεβηκός, *constitutio qualitas* or *generalis*) respectively. As far as we can tell, the earliest forensic speeches were written without *stasis* theories. However, ancient (and modern) interpreters have analyzed them according to the classification above. For example, ancient editors of Isaeus' speeches inserted an argument summary (ὑπόθεσις) identifying the issue. Richard Volkmann (1885, pp. 58, 70–73, 79) identifies examples of speeches that revolve primarily around matters of fact (Antiph. 1, 6; Isae. 3–9, 12; Lys. 3; Cic. *Rosc.*, *Amer.*, *Sull.*, *Planc.*, *Clu.*), definition (Isae. 1; Lycurg. *Leoc.*), and quality (Cic. *Pro Milone*).

Quintilian (*Inst.* 3.6.83) argued that the most honorable *stasis* for a defendant was quality. Brian K. Peterson (1998, p. 35; cf. *Rhet. Her.* 1.18–25) provides a helpful summary of the *constitutio qualitas*:

> Within these four *stases*, it is in the area of "quality" that Hermagoras' system becomes the most developed . . . In forensic oratory, Hermagoras outlined two major divisions for the *stasis* of quality. The first could be called "justification" (ἀντίληψις; Quintilian 7.4.4; *De Inv.* 1.15, 2.60), in which no wrong is admitted, but it is claimed that the action which is being prosecuted is in fact honorable. The second major division within the *stasis* of quality can be called "defense" (ἀντίθεσις; Quintilian 7.4.7; *De Inv.* 1.15, 2.69), in which the wrong is admitted but punishment is countered on some other grounds. This position is further broken down into four subtypes: 1) Counter-charge (ἀντέγκλημα; Quintilian 7.4.8), in which one accuses the person that the opposition is trying to vindicate; 2) Counter-plea (ἀντίστασις; Quintilian 7.4.12), which insists that some benefit was rendered by this act, or at least that it resulted in a lesser evil; 3) Shifting blame (μετάστασις; Quintilian 7.4.13), either blaming some other person or some thing (such as another law); 4) Plea for leniency (συγγνώμη; Quintilian 7.4.17), a "last resort" asking for mercy because the act resulted from ignorance, accident or over-riding necessity.

Legal procedure or jurisdiction (μετάληψις, *constitutio translatio*), i.e., whether the case is legally sound, was sometimes treated as a fourth issue (Peterson, 1998, pp. 33–34). Typically, however, legal questions were classified separately, although acknowledged to be subordinate and classifiable under the three *stases* (see Quint. *Inst.* 3.6.88). There are four subheadings relating to issues of law: (1) word and intent of a law (*scriptum et voluntas*); (2) contradictory laws (*leges contrariae*); (3) applying a law to a case when the law does not specify such an application (*collectio*); and (4) ambiguous law (*ambiguitas*) (Holtsmark, 1968, pp. 364–65; Watson, 1988, p. 13).

The importance of understanding the issue cannot be underestimated. Quintilian (*Inst.* 3.6.21) quotes Hermagoras on this subject and gives his own opinion:

> Hermagoras calls a *basis* that which enables the matter in question to be understood and to which the proofs of the parties concerned will also be directed. My own opinion has always been that, whereas there are frequently different *bases* of question in connexion with a cause, the *basis* of the cause itself is its most important point on which the whole matter turns.

Quintilian (*Inst.* 3.6.92) argued that there may be different *stases* upon which to build a case. However, he advised choosing the one basis that allowed for the greatest argumentative force. Thus, when constructing a case, it is good to focus on the one *stasis* upon which the case will stand or fall (*Inst.* 3.6.9). In order to decide which *stasis* is central, one needed, if limited to only one line of argument, to ask what it would be (*Inst.* 3.6.10). In the end, "every kind of case will contain a *cause*, a *point for the decision of the judge*, and a *central argument*" (*Inst.* 3.6.104).

Heath (1995, p. 23) maintains that "issue-theory is . . . only a part of the equipment needed by a rhetorician – and not the most advanced and demanding part. But identifying the issue and working through its division provides a firm underlying structure of argument, without which all subsequent elaborations would be ineffective." Theon's *Progymnasmata* (2.144–53; see Butts, 1986, p. 182 note 38) likely indicates that *stasis* theory was taught at the secondary level of education; however, it was certainly required at the tertiary level. At the secondary level a *grammatikos* would take students through the elementary *progymnasmata* consisting of retelling a story or developing brief arguments for or against a law, etc. At the tertiary stage a *rhetor* taught, among other subjects, the composition of declamations, both of a deliberative (*suasoria*) and forensic type (*controversiae*) (see Anderson, 1999, p. 75).

Nadeau (1964, p. 367) tentatively suggests that such a high level of education was in existence already in the fourth century BC. Nevertheless, at the start of the first century BC this was fully in place (Anderson, 1999, p. 73). Already in the second century Hermagoras was analyzing the determination of the point to be judged (κρινόμενον) by examining the interchange between the prosecutor and defendant. Heath (1994, p. 117; cf. Braet, 1987, pp. 81–83) argues that the schematic exchange of Table 4.1 found in Cicero (*Inv.* 1.18–19) is most likely from Hermagoras.

Table 4.1 *Hermagorean exchange for determining the main issue and arguments*

"P" is the prosecutor, "D" the defendant, and "J" the judge.

P1	*intentio*; κατάφασις	You killed your mother.	Indictment
D1	*depulsio*; ἀπόφασις	I killed her justly.	Defense
J1	*quaestio*; ζήτημα	Did he kill her justly?	Question
D2	*ratio*; αἴτιον	For she killed my father.	Excuse/reason
P2	*infirmatio rationis*; αἴτιον	But your mother should not have been killed by you, her son; her crime could have been punished without your committing a crime.	Rebuttal
J2	*iudicatio*; κρινόμενον	Was it right for Orestes to kill his mother because she had killed his father?	Point of judgment
D3	*firmamentum*; τὸ συνέχον	My mother's disposition . . . was such that her children above all were bound to exact the penalty.	Foundation or supporting argument

Significantly, throughout *De Inventione* Cicero gives other examples of this process for the purpose of applying *topoi* to the creation of arguments (e.g., 2.73, 79, 87; cf. Cic. *Top.* 95 and *Part. Or.* 103). Nadeau (1959, p. 71) maintains that "the system of Hermagoras, which first appeared in the second century B.C., remained current for approximately three centuries in spite of revisions and the publication of rival systems." The ancient authorities disagreed on terminology of such an exchange and precisely where the essential *stasis* is to be found (e.g., arising from the first conflict of causes [J1] or the second [J2]). However, the fact that such a method was circulating, being discussed and refined after its inception, is significant for analyzing any discursive controversy in this era, especially Paul's letters.

It is fitting to end this section by looking at several examples from the Attic orators who show sophistication towards the dynamics of issue determination.[1] First, we may consider the late-fifth-century speeches by

[1] For other examples, see Volkmann, 1885, pp. 47–48, 58–67, 69–70, 73, 81–84, 86; for various approaches for defense in Aristophanes akin to later *stasis* theory, see Murphy, 1938, pp. 96–97.

Antiphon. In *Against the Step Mother* the litigant discloses the statement of the issue when addressing the jury at 1.21.1: "Consider now how much more just my request is than my brother's." This claim is substantiated through numerous examples in 1.21–30. In *On the Murder of Herodes* the essential issue is stated just after the *narratio* in 5.25: "Those are the facts; now consider what is probable [τὰ εἰκόντα]" (my translation). The proof section (5.25–73) is devoted to working out various probabilities to demonstrate the innocence of the defendant. (The noun εἰκός and its cognates are found throughout this section at 25.2; 26.5, 6, 10; 27.7; 28.4; 37.2; 43.1; 45.9; 48.9; 49.3; 50.6; 59.2; 60.4; 63.6; 64.5; 65.4, 6; 66.2; 68.3; 73.2; and 74.2.)

Hyperides in *Against Athenogenes* (written for a certain Epicrates – 330–342 BC) understood the case to turn on the question of whether Athenogenes' agreement signed by Epicrates was just. This is indicated just after the *narratio* in the statement of the prosecution's cause and the *prothesis* (Hyp. 3.13):

> Well, gentlemen of the jury, you have heard the facts in detail. But Athenogenes will presently tell you that in law whatever agreements one man makes with another are binding. Yes, my friend, just agreements. But if they are unjust, the opposite is true: the law forbids that they be binding. I will quote the laws themselves to make this clearer to you.

The main issue of law and the nature of the agreement arises in dialogue with the cause/argument of the opponent. Thus, Hyperides must first relate what the laws say about unjust agreements and then attempt to demonstrate that Athenogenes deceived him, hence showing that the agreement was unjust and therefore unlawful and not binding (14–27).

Similar acuity is seen in Dinarchus' *Against Demosthenes* (323 BC). The *narratio* comes to a halt with a question at the end of paragraph 6: "Will that council then . . . be powerless now to administer justice over the money credited to Demosthenes?" Dinarchus answered his own question dryly: "It will; for the council has told lies against Demosthenes. This was the crowning argument in his [Demosthenes'] case." Once again the issue of the case was determined in conversation with the opposing argument, in this case stated also in the form of a question. The main issue here is whether or not the council that brought the charges against Demosthenes was credible. The issue shapes the speech to such an extent that Dinarchus must admit in the end that he has presented in effect an *apologia* for the council (Din. 1.108.2).

4.2 Inartificial proofs: use of witnesses, other evidences, and laws

The goal of invention is to find all the possible means of persuasion given a specific case (Arist. *Rhet.* 1.2.1). *Stasis* theory helped determine the issue and most important lines of argumentation. Moreover, the rhetorical theorists understood the types of arguments to fall under two general categories: inartificial proofs (ἄτεχνοι; *inartificiales*) and artificial proofs (ἔντεχνοι; *artificiales*) (*Rhet.* 1.2.2; cf. Anax. *Rhet. Alex.* 7.17–25; see Watson, 1988, pp. 14–20; Carey, 1994a). Artificial proofs will be treated in the next section.

Inartificial proofs included the use of witnesses (μάρτυρες; μαρτυρίαι; *testes*; *testimonia*), testimony from torture (βάσανοι; *tormenta*), informal agreements (*pacta conventa*), contracts (συνθῆκαι; συγγραφαί), laws (νόμοι), previous court decisions (*praeiudicia*; *res iudicatae*), rumors (*rumores*), documents (γραφαί; *tabulae*; *scripta*), and oaths (ὅρκος; *iusiurandum*). Aristotle (*Rhet.* 1.2.2) lists witnesses, tortures, and contracts. Aristotle provides further elaboration on laws (1.15.3–12), witnesses (recent versus ancient; 1.15.13–19), contracts (1.15.20–25), tortures (1.15.26), and oaths (1.15.27–33). Anaximenes designates as supplemental (ἐπίθετοι – 7.1428a.23–25; 14.1431b.9) and elaborates the opinion of the speaker (δόξα τοῦ λέγοντος – 14.1431b.10–19), evidence from witnesses (15.1431b.20–1432a.11), torture (16.1432a.12–33), and oaths (17.1432a.34–1432b.4).

Cicero (*De Or.* 2.26.116; cf. *Part. Or.* 2.6) includes a list reflective of the Roman system of government and justice: "documents, oral evidence, informal agreements, examinations [*quaestiones*], statutes, decrees of the Senate, judicial precedents, magisterial orders, opinions of counsel, and whatever else is not produced by the orator, but is supplied to him by the case itself or by the parties." Quintilian lists (*Inst.* 5.1.2; cf. *Rhet. Her.* 2.13.19) and then discusses inartificial proofs in terms of decisions of previous courts (5.2), rumors (5.3), evidence from torture (5.4), documents (5.5), oaths (5.6), and witnesses (5.7).

Especially noteworthy is that Cicero (*Part. Or.* 2.6) lists types of divine evidences (*testimonia*) that include oracles (*oracula*), auspices (*auspicia*), prophecies (*vaticinationes*), and answers of priests, augers, and diviners (*responsa sacerdotum, haruspicum, coniectorum*). There are a few paramount examples of such appeals in antiquity. Socrates (in Xen. *Apol.* 14) relates the prodigious oracle from Delphi given to him to the effect that no human was more free, upright, or temperate than himself. To lessen the force of his own oracle, Socrates immediately relates that the lawgiver

Lycurgus of Lacedaemon received a more favorable oracle in that he was deified. Quintilian (*Inst.* 5.11.42; cf. Carey, 1994a) knows this tradition of Socrates' oracle; he also relates Cicero's use of divine testimony (in Cic. *Lig.* 6.19). The distinction that Quintilian makes between supernatural evidence (*divina testimonia*) and divine arguments (*divina argumenta*) is interesting: "When such arguments [appealing to the gods] are inherent in the case itself they are called supernatural evidence [*divina testimonia*]; when they are adduced from without they are styled supernatural arguments [*argumenta*]" (*Inst.* 5.11.42). When analyzing a speech, it is difficult to determine whether evidence is external or internal to the case; the inclusion of the former would technically fall under artificial proof. On these ambiguities, see Carey (1994a, pp. 95–96).

Watson (1988, p. 14) rightly argues that "Inartificial proofs mainly belong to judicial rhetoric." Inartificial proofs carry considerable weight because they "depend principally upon authority" (Cic. *Top.* 24). The primary responsibility of the orator was to determine the facts of the case (Quint. *Inst.* 5.1.2). "What happened?" "Are there reliable witnesses?" "Are there reliable documents?" "Is there any way to prove the case one way or another using *hard* evidence?" Conversely, the skill of interrogation was necessary for handling witnesses and direct evidence (Quint. *Inst.* 5.7.8–37).

The extant forensic speeches provide numerous examples of inartificial proofs. Testimony from torture is cited in Isocrates 17.13–17, 27, 54, in which a litigant is denied unrestricted access to a critical slave as a witness; this fact becomes a major focus of the litigant's argument (cf. Antiph. 1.6–12; Isae. 8.10–14, 29, 45). In Isocrates 21.4 it is lamented that such evidence is lacking because of the circumstances (cf. Andoc. 1.22, 30, 64; Lys. 4.12–17 and *passim*; Lys. 7.34–37; Dem. 37.40, 42, 51; 45.16, 61, 62; Lycurg. *Leoc.* 28–34 and *passim*, 112; cf. Volkmann, 1885, pp. 178–90).

Arguably the two most forceful inartificial proofs were laws and testimony. Aristotle in the opening of his *Rhetorica* (1.1.7–9) argued that laws should delimit the extent of the litigants' arguments as much as possible. Cicero (*Top.* 95) likewise attributes great importance to law: "But since there should be no firmer foundation than law in settling disputes, we must be careful to summon the Law as our helper and witness." There are two examples of cases where laws were recited in the *prooemium* to indicate the severity of the case and to gain the attention of the jury (Dem. 32.1; Isoc. 18.2–3). Additionally, in many other forensic orations, laws and their interpretations play a significant role (e.g., Aeschin. *In*

Tim. 4–37; Alcid. *Od.* 11; Andoc. 1.70–100; [Andoc.] 4.34–38; Dem. 19.70–71, 131–33; Isae. 8.43; Isae. 10.10; Hyp. 3.14–17; Hyp. 4.5–10; Lycurg. *Leoc.* 111–40; Lys. 3.40–43). The continued importance of laws for forensic cases is attested by the distinct development of the legal issues in *stasis* theory, as noted above.

Similarly, Quintilian (*Inst.* 5.7.1) attributed testimony the highest place of honor for a case: "It is, however, the evidence [*testimonia*] that gives the greatest trouble to advocates." As the strongest evidence, he advised supplying testimony early. Likewise, credible testimony ought to be used to debunk the testimony used by the opponent (*Inst.* 5.7.3–4). In forensic speeches, witnesses confirm events critical to the case, especially within narratives (Carey, 1994a, p. 95; see Alcid. *Od.* 7; Antiph. 5. 20, 22, 24; Antiph. 6.15; Andoc. 1.18, 28, 46, 69; Dem. 32.13; Isae. 10.7; Isoc. 17.12, 15, 16; Isoc. 18.8, 10; Lycurg. *Leoc.* 20, 23, 24; Lys. 3.14, 20; Lys. 7.10; Lys. 10.5; Lys. 16.8; Lys. 17.2, 3). Similarly, testimony is found in the *probatio* (e.g., Antiph. 5.28, 30, 35, 56, 61; Isoc. 17.32, 37, 41; Lys. 17.9; Din. 1.27), the *refutatio* (Andoc. 1.123, 127; Din. 1.52; Isoc. 18.54; Pl. *Apol.* 31c.2), the self-adulation section (Antiph. 5.83; cf. Pl. *Apol.* 34b), and in the *peroratio* (Isae. 3.80; Isae. 8.42; Isoc. 17.52). Indeed, testimonies may be distributed throughout entire speeches (Aeschin. *In Tim.* 50, 65, 67, 100, 104, 115; *Leg.* 19, 44, 46, 55, 68, 85, 86, 107, and *passim*; Isae. 2.5, 16, 34, 37; Isae. 3.7, 12, 14, 15, 37, 43, 53, 56, 76, 80; Isae. 8.11, 13, 17, 20, 24, 27, 42). No examples of testimony in the *prooemium* were found (laws are recited there in Dem. 32.1 and Isoc. 18.2–3).

A notable idiom involves the use of γνώσεσθε ("You will know . . .") to alert the jury of evidence from witnesses or contracts (e.g., [Dem.] 53.21; [Dem.] 59.89.3; Dem. 23.159.9, 174.7; Dem. 29.50.4; Dem. 36.55.8; Dem. 45.27.9; Dem. 58.36.10; Isae. 3.6.7, 12.4; Isae. 6.50.5; Isoc. 18.19.5; Lys. 17.9.2) or to prepare them for the reading of laws (Dem. 20.88.6, 95.1; Dem. 24.41.6; Dem. 43.62.1, 71.4; Dem. 46.14.2; Dem. 58.10.8; Isae. 3.42.4; Isae. 6.48.5; Isae. 11.11.2). However, γνώσεσθε is not infrequently used to introduce argumentative material, as in Isocrates 18.52: "But when you have heard only one of the acts which he has committed [πεπραγμένων] you will readily recognize [γνώσεσθε] the general run of his villainy [πονηρίαν]" (see also Aesch. *In Ctes.* 195.1; Andoc. 2.22.1; Antiph. 6.41.3; Dem. 18.150.5; Dem. 45.2.7; Dem. 48.46.2; Isae. 8.15.2; Isoc. 15.37, 217, 240; Isoc. 17.40; Lys. 1.39.2; Lys. 19.19.1; in deliberative speeches see Isoc. 6.29.1; Isoc. 8.50.6; 81.5).

Figure 4.1   Relation of *ethos*, *logos*, and *pathos* in persuasion

4.3   Artificial proofs: *pathos*, *ethos*, and *logos*

Although judicial rhetoric is fundamentally concerned with laws and evidence, litigants needed to supplement these with reasonably constructed artificial proofs (ἔντεχνοι). As Cicero puts it, "one kind [of evidence is] made up of things which are not thought out by himself . . . the other kind is founded entirely on the orator's reasoned argument" (Cic. *De Or.* 2.116). Such reasoned arguments were necessary to secure a favorable verdict because the bases for reconstructing the *truth* (from evidence, laws, etc.) was either unavailable, questionable, or untrustworthy.

Aristotle was the first to elaborate artistic proof as consisting in *logos*, *pathos*, and *ethos* (*Rhet.* 1.2.3–6). Although technically Aristotle did not regard *pathos* as an aspect of the rhetorician's art (Wisse, 1989, p. 18), he developed a theory of emotion and discusses it quite extensively (*Rhet.* 2.1–11). Aristotle's triad was not stringently followed (May, 1988, p. 3); the Stoics particularly shunned *pathos* as a means of persuasion (Solmsen, 1941, pp. 178, 189–90; cf. Wisse, 1989, pp. 80–83). However, Cicero later treated them together as a coherent system (*Or. Brut.* 2.115; cf. Quint. *Inst.* 5.12.9–13).

As a starting point, it is instructive to reproduce (in slightly modified form) a diagram by Jakob Wisse (1989, p. 6) that describes the relation of *pathos*, *ethos*, and *logos* to the speech event (see Figure 4.1). Wisse warns against separating the elements too sharply. For instance, the *ethos* of the speaker often affects the *pathos* of the audience (1989, pp. 7–8). As a result, these questions must be pondered: How are we to understand *pathos*, *ethos*, and *logos*? How is each attained in a speech itself and its delivery? What examples do we have in extant speeches of *pathos*, *ethos*, and *logos*?

Pathos as an artificial proof

Some understanding of *pathos* in oratory can be gained from the rhetorical handbooks. Watson (1988, pp. 15–16) summarizes them aptly:

Pathos (πάθος, *adfectus*) is emotion and, as a means of proof, is arousal of the emotion of the audience for or against both the matter at hand and those representing it [Arist. *Rhet.* 1.2.3, 5; Cic. *De Or.* 2.42.178, 44.185–87; *Or. Brut.* 37.128; Quint. *Inst.* 6.2.20–24]. The rhetor seeks to elicit positive pathos for his own case and negative pathos for his opponent's case [Arist. *Rhet.* 2.1.8–2.17.6; Cic. *De Or.* 2.44.185–87, 51.52; Quint. *Inst.* 6.2.25–36]. Proofs using pathos include the rhetor perceived as a good man (rather than being a good man as with ethos), asseveration or positive and earnest affirmation, and giving an element of character and supporting it with a plausible reason [Quint. *Inst.* 5.12.9–13].

Watson's summary of *pathos* again suggests how *pathos* is related to *ethos*. But how is *pathos* achieved? The basic means to establish *pathos*, according to Aristotle, is simply to understand how emotions work: e.g., what makes one angry, the types of people with whom one gets angry, and what occasions give rise to anger (*Rhet.* 2.1.8–2.2.27; for a listing of emotions discussed in *Rhetorica*, see Wisse, 1989, pp. 66–67).

In the rhetoricians after Aristotle the discussion of how to arouse the emotions is either spurned (e.g., Hermagoras and other Hellenistic rhetoricians) or subordinated to speech components: the *prooemium* and the *peroratio* (Cic. *Inv.* 1.22, 100, 106–109; Quint. *Inst.* 4.1; 6.1). The basic method is description and amplification (Cic. *Inv.* 1.53.100; *De Or.* 2.43.182; Quint. *Inst.* 6.2.23; 8.4.9). In Cicero's earlier work, *De Inventione* (1.16.22), the sources for "good will" (*benevolentia*) in the *prooemium* are one's own person, the opponent(s), the jury, and the case itself. With respect to two subsections in the *peroratio*, the *indignatio* (against an opponent) and *conquestio* (lament), Cicero provides lists of commonplaces to assist arousing feelings of hatred and pity respectively (Cic. *Inv.* 1.53.100–59.109). In Cicero's later work (*De Or.* 2.182–214; *Or. Brut.* 128–33) Friedrich Solmsen (1941, pp. 178–79) contends that there is a recovery of the value of emotional arguments, arguably because of Cicero's experience in the courts. In *Orator ad M. Brutum* 132, Cicero encourages appeals for mercy and the use of fiery language, citing Demosthenes' *De Corona* (294) as an example of the latter. Similarly, Quintilian argues that orators need to feel the emotions for themselves through visualization in order to convey it to the hearers (*Inst.* 6.2.26–31). This procedure aids in the graphic and emotional description of events (*Inst.* 6.2.32–36). Finally, Quintilian advocates using humor to rid the judge of ill feeling (*Inst.* 6.3).

Carey (1994b; cf. DiCicco, 1995, pp. 113–64) has surveyed the use of *pathos* in the Attic forensic speeches in some detail. He states (p. 27), "The speaker will often use the *prooemium* to lay claim to qualities which the audience will respect, or stress the disadvantages of his situation as a claim to sympathy." Examples of *captatio benevolentiae* are numerous: a display of modesty (Dem. 54.1), suffering present dangers (Lys. 19.1), having been terribly wronged (Dem. 45.1), or appeals to inexperience in speaking or in the legal system (Antiph. 1.1; Isae. 10.1; Dem. 41.2; Pl. *Apol.* 17a.1–18a.6). *Pathos* in the *prooemium* could not only gain the goodwill of the audience, but also help remove hostility against oneself (Dem. 45.6; Antiph. 1.1–4; Lys. 32.1; Isae. 1.6; Dem. 39.1; Dem. 41.1–2; Dem. 48.1; Dem. 57.1–6; for other examples, see Carey, 1994b, pp. 28–29).

The use of *pathos* can be found throughout the *narratio*, *probatio*, and *refutatio* (Dem. 37.52–53; Dem. 45.77; Lys. 16.20). Often there is recourse to smashing the character of the opponents (Aeschin. 1.40), sometimes by introducing information outside the case (called a διαβολή) ([Dem.] 53.4–18; Dem. 54.3–6; Lys. 3.5–9; see esp. Carey, 1994b, p. 32). The opposite of this is to invoke a sense of gratitude for services/benefactions performed by oneself or one's family (Lys. 3.47; Lys. 18.27; Lys. 20.30; Isae. 4.27; Isae. 7.37–41; [Dem.] 50.64).

With respect to the *peroratio*, there are numerous examples of appeals for mercy or its equivalent. For example, consider Isaeus 2.42: "I beg you all, gentlemen, and beseech and entreat you to pity me and to acquit the witness here" (cf. Antiph. 2.2.13 [cf. 2.4.4]; Lys. 4.20; Lys. 9.22; Lys. 20.35–36; Cic. *Mil.* 37.101–103; *Quinct.* 31.95–99; *Rosc. Amer.* 53.154). Just prior to the *peroratio* an appeal for mercy is made in Lysias 19.53. Not surprisingly, the opposite appeal is made in prosecution speeches (Antiph. 1.27; Dem. 25.100–101; Lycurg. *Leoc.* 150.10; Lys. 32.19). One could also display one's family (especially children!) during the speech's *peroratio* to illicit pity (e.g., Lys. 20.35; Hyp. 4.41; Cic. *Rosc. Amer.* 53.153; cf. Dem. 19.310). Socrates refuses this procedure (Pl. *Apol.* 30b, 43c–d), and Andocides has no family to help him (1.148–149). Cicero also relates several such experiences (Cic. *Or. Brut.* 131), and Quintilian seems in favor of it (*Inst.* 4.1.28; 6.1.30–31, 33). Aristophanes parodies such incidents in *Vespae* 969–78 (cf. 567–571; cited in Murphy, 1938, pp. 83, 99).

Ethos as an artificial proof

As I turn to consider the importance of *ethos*, once again Watson's summary of this particular matter is helpful (1988, pp. 14–15):

Ethos (ἦθος) is moral character and conduct, the course of life [Arist. *Rhet.* 1.2.3–4; 1.8.6; Cic. *De Or.* 2.43.182–84; Quint. *Inst.* 6.2.8–17, who conflates *ethos* and *pathos*]. It ". . . is related to men's nature and character, their habits and all the intercourse of life . . ." [Cic. *Or. Brut.* 37.128]. As a means of artificial proof, the rhetor seeks to show his own and his client's ethos in the best light and his opponent's in the worst. Ethos is an ethical proof based on the demonstration through the speech of the rhetor's goodness, goodwill, and moral uprighteousness, all of which enhances the persuasiveness and perceived truth of the message. Ethos was often considered the most effective means of proof [Arist. *Rhet.* 1.2.4; Quint. *Inst.* 4.1.7; 5.12.9].

The speaker' authority and credibility are at stake. Isocrates in his *Antidosis* (279–80) makes the point that a person's "honorable reputation" makes his or her words more persuasive, and not simply the specific use of probabilities, proofs, and other means of persuasion. How are they perceived as oriented to the truth (Wisse, 1989, p. 7)?

The basic methods to achieve this are simple: through disclosure of unknown meritorious deeds with witnesses, recollection of such known deeds, or the positive portrayal or defense of oneself and one's client (Kennedy, 1963, pp. 136–37). Aristotle believed that the orator should convey three attributes: good sense (φρόνησις), virtue (ἀρετή), and goodwill (εὔνοια) (*Rhet.* 2.1.5–7). Service in the military and/or for the state, success in commerce, and piety towards the gods reflected good character (see, e.g., Antiph. 5.81–84; Lys. 16.9; Lys. 19.55–59).

The speechwriters Lysias and Isaeus became renowned for their ability to convey one's character persuasively (Kennedy, 1963, pp. 136, 144; Carey, 1994b, pp. 40–43). For instance, Lysias 19.53 displays a strong sense of *ethos* (in addition to *logos* and *pathos*):

> If, therefore, our statements are deemed to be reasonable and the proofs that we have adduced satisfactory, gentlemen of the jury, show your pity by all manner of means. For, grievous as was the weight of this slander, we expected to conquer with the help of truth: but if you should altogether refuse to entertain our plea, we felt ourselves without a single hope of deliverance. Ah, by the Olympian gods, gentleman, choose rather to deliver us with justice than to ruin us with injustice; and believe that those men speak the truth who, though keeping silent, show themselves throughout their lives self-respecting and just.

Appealing to the truth, mentioning the slander of opponents, invoking the gods, and relying on one's just conduct are to be noted. In this same speech, the speaker furnishes documents to show his father's services to the state and provides witnesses to his father's character (57–59). Friends were regularly called forward to attest to one's character, as Andocides does at the end of his defense (1.150; cf. Pl. *Apol.* 34b).

Another feature of *ethos* is the common claim to "speak the truth." This affirmation is seen above. The expression "to speak the truth" (τἀληθῆ λέγειν or its equivalent) is common enough to be considered an idiom for forensic oratory: e.g., Aeschin. *Leg.* 2.3 (οἱ τἀληθῆ λέγοντες); 107.6 (ἀληθῆ λέγω); Andoc. 1.72 (τἀληθῆ εἰρήσεται); Dem. 19.146, 176 (ταῦτ᾽ ἀληθῆ λέγω); Dem. 32.31 (ἐρεῖν τἀληθῆν); Isoc. 15.43 (κατειπόντι τὴν ἀλήθειαν); Isoc. 17.15.7 (τἀληθῆ . . . λέγειν); 17.54.4 (τἀληθῆ λέγουσιν); Lys. 16.21.1 (τὰ γὰρ ἀληθῆ χρὴ λέγειν); 24.15.3 (ἀληθῆ λέγειν); Pl. *Apol.* 17b.5 (τἀληθῆ λέγοντα); 18a.5 (τἀληθῆ λέγειν); 20d.5 (πᾶσαν ὑμῖν τὴν ἀληθείαν ἐρῶ); 31c.3 (τἀληθῆ λέγω).

Logos as an artificial proof

Essentially, in forensic oratory reliance on *logos*-based argumentation took three forms: example, probability, and deductive arguments, which may be understood to include *enthymemes*, *epicheiremes*, and elaborations (Watson, 1988, pp. 16–20; Hellholm, 1994, pp. 127–38). Quintilian (*Inst.* 5.9.1) lists "indications [*signa*], arguments [*argumenta*] or examples [*exempla*]." Under *signa* he includes probabilities (εἰκότα) and sure signs (τεκμήρια); the latter have a definite conclusion and are not technically, so he argues, artificial proofs (*Inst.* 5.9.3–7). Furthermore, his treatment of *argumenta* focuses primarily on the *enthymeme*. Aristotle argued for three types of arguments: examples, *enthymemes*, and *enthymemes* with maxims (*Rhet.* 1.2.8; 2.26.5). Aristotle subsumed the probability under enthymematic argumentation, maintaining that *enthymemes* are constructed often on probabilities (εἰκότα).

The goal of *logos*-based argumentation is to prove "what is not certain by means of what is certain" (Cic. *Inv.* 1.32.53; Quint. *Inst.* 5.10.8). Quintilian (*Inst.* 5.10.12–13) lists four certainties upon which arguments are constructed: (1) "those things which we perceive by the senses," (2) "those things about which there is general agreement, such as the existence of gods," (3) "those things which are established by law or have passed into current usage, if not throughout the whole world, at any rate in the nation or state where the case is being pleaded," and (4) those "things

which are admitted by either party . . . or is not disputed by our adversary."
These items represent what may be called a *rhetorical epistemology*.

Examples

Examples (παραδείγματα; *exempla*) are inductive in nature and can be
drawn from several sources: "from history, fables, comparisons, fictions
of poets, and judgments" (Watson, 1988, p. 16). Of these, history (which
sets a precedent) and the judgments of authoritative persons or councils
carry considerable weight (Cic. *Inv.* 1.30.47–49). Aristotle advised using
examples after an *enthymeme* because then the example takes on the force
of a witness. If one has several examples, however, then it is possible to
use them in succession before an *enthymeme* (*Rhet.* 2.20.9). Although
examples are important for deliberative oratory, they are fairly common
in forensic oratory (Arist. *Rhet.* 2.20.8; see also, e.g., Antiph. 1.21–30,
106–109; Dem. 19.276; Xen. *Apol.* 20; Quint. *Inst.* 5.11; Cic. *Clu.* 27.75;
Mil. 4.9; *Mur.* 2.4). The *refutatio* may, for example, recall events from
the opponent's deplorable history in the military (e.g., Lys. 19.45–52; see
Natali, 1989; and Fiore, 1986, pp. 26–100).

Probability

Probability argument (εἰκός) concerns what seems likely, plausible, or
probable given a set of circumstances or evidences (*signa*/σημεῖα) (Quint.
Inst. 5.10.15–16). Probability arguments gain their strength from cumula-
tive evidences: A bloodstain is not significant unless a murder has taken
place. Furthermore, if the bloodstain is found on the murder victim's
enemy, a stronger probability emerges (Quint. *Inst.* 5.9.8–10). Some form
of εἰκός may be used, but need not be. Gagarin (1994, p. 66 note 10) makes
a distinction between explicit and implicit probability arguments. In the
latter, the concept of probability can be expressed in the form of a question
(Why would I do that?) or a statement (I would not do that).

While it is true that (early) sophists often championed the argument
from probability and are often so criticized (starting with Plato), the use of
probability argument did not replace the use of evidences (Gagarin, 1994,
pp. 46–68). Essentially, orators turned to probability when evidence was
debatable or lacking (Gagarin, 1994, p. 53). Thus, one finds deliberate
distinctions being made between the facts and probability (e.g., Antiph.
5.26 and Lys. 3.37.1). Demosthenes (22.22–23) also evaluates the types
of proofs and means of persuasion, mentioning specifically probability
and witnesses, which he considers the best. There are numerous examples

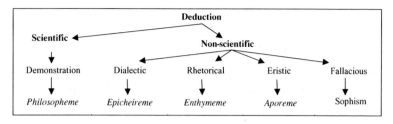

Figure 4.2   Aristotle's types of deductive argumentation

of probability arguments found in forensic speeches (Antiph. 2.2.6, 4.8; Alcid. *Od.* 10; Gorg. *Hel.* 5, 7; *Pal.* [*passim*]; Isae. 4.18.4; Isae. 6.11.4; Isae. 8.14.1; Lys. 19.53; in Dinarchus generally, see Worthington, 1992, p. 217; on the early development of probability argumentation, see Hinks, 1940, pp. 63–65; and B. Smith, 1921).

Deductive arguments

Various descriptions of deductive argumentation in the extant rhetorical works around the time of the apostle Paul have been found (Eriksson, 1998, pp. 53–62; Alexandre, 1999, p. 76). Since most practitioners of rhetorical criticism of the NT are more familiar with the term *enthymeme*, it would be helpful to distinguish demonstrations (ἀποδείξεις), *enthymemes* (ἐνθυμήματα), and *epicheiremes* (ἐπιχειρήματα) as presented in Cicero and Quintilian and in view of Aristotle's thoughts on the matter, since Aristotle's system of argumentation provided the seedbed for later developments (see Cic. *Inv.* 1.61, and Dilts and Kennedy, 1997, pp. ix–x). It is possible to represent Aristotle's classifications of deductive argumentation (*Top.* 8.162.a16; Thompson, 1975, pp. 11–16) (see Figure 4.2).

One can see the generic relationship of the *epicheireme* to the *philosopheme* (demonstration) and the *enthymeme*. Brad McAdon (2001, p. 145) has recently shown how Aristotle conceived demonstration, dialectic, and rhetoric as different aspects of deduction (συλλογισμός) for different settings – "scientific investigation from first principles, dialectic for questioning and answering within some kind of preexisting format, and rhetoric for supplying a means of persuasion." Demonstration involved the pursuit of knowledge within a specific field, whereas dialectic and rhetoric were open to all fields of knowledge. Obviously, the setting for each type of argumentation which Aristotle envisioned was quite distinct: Demonstration had no audience; dialectic involved educated peers and a master/teacher; and rhetoric an untrained civic audience (McAdon, 2001, p. 150). Purportedly, the Greek Stoics, who wanted more precision in their argumentation, preferred the *epicheireme* form, and eventually it is embraced by the early Cicero as described in *De Inventione* (Church and Cathcart, 1965, pp. 141, 147; cf. Thompson, 1975, pp. 40–41). It is important to consider the change in audience envisioned by Cicero (and Quintilian), who describe the *epicheireme* as a more rigorous argumentation form for use in the presentation of speeches.

Quintilian's survey reveals disagreement on how to define and conceptualize these different types of arguments (*Inst.* 5.10.1–8); some exasperation may be detected when he concludes his survey by merging *epicheireme*, demonstration, and *enthymeme* as arguments adducing "uncertain things from what is certain" (*Inst.* 5.10.1, 8). Thomas M. Conley (1984; cf. Kraus, 2002) has shown the variability of the concept of the *enthymeme* in ancient theory and practice. Quintilian's accounting reveals the same for the *epicheireme* (*Inst.* 5.10.4–6; see Kroll, 1936). However, a relatively clear picture emerges that the *epicheireme* should be understood as a middle position between the scientific syllogism (demonstration) and the rhetorical syllogism (*enthymeme*); in fact, Aristotle defines the *epicheireme* as the dialectical deduction (*Top.* 8.162.a16). As such it merges rhetoric and philosophy (Kroll, 1936, p. 3). Consequently, Quintilian (*Inst.* 5.14.27–28) warns against extensive use of *enthymemes* or *epicheiremes* in speeches:

> For a speech of that character would resemble dialogues and dialectical controversies rather than pleadings of the kind with which we are concerned, and there is an enormous difference between the two. For in the former we are confronted with learned men seeking for truth among men of learning; consequently they subject everything to a minute and scrupulous inquiry with a view to arriving at clear and convincing truths.

Demonstration

The demonstration is a "clear proof" (*evidens probatio*; Quint. *Inst.* 5.10.7) using established and widely accepted premises to arrive at a logically valid conclusion (Arist. *An.Post.* 1.2.71b17–25). Here, the notions of validity (with respect to premises) and causality (in terms of a *derived* conclusion) are critical (see Thompson, 1975, pp. 40–44).

Enthymeme

Syllogisms are rare in rhetoric because audiences accept unstated premises or conclusions (Arist. *Rhet.* 2.22.3). The syllogism consists of a major premise and minor premise followed by a conclusion drawn from them both. Quintilian gives the following example: "Virtue is the only thing that is good, for that alone is good which no one can put to a bad use [major premise]; but no one can make a bad use of virtue [minor premise]; virtue is therefore good [conclusion]" (*Inst.* 5.14.25). Each premise may be accompanied by a supporting proof, or the premise may be self-standing (thus, a τεκμήριον – Arist. *Rhet.* 1.2.17–18) and in need of no explicit support.

More common are rhetorical syllogisms called *enthymemes* (ἐνθύμηματα). However, the variability of the concept of *enthymeme* in ancient use and theory in addition to its particular Roman form in the time of Paul must inform our discussion (Conley, 1984; Kraus, 2002). I shall provide a brief account of *enthymeme* in Aristotle before summarizing the excellent survey of Roman enthymematic argumentation in the first centuries by Manfred Kraus (2002).

Aristotle argued extensively for the use of the *enthymeme* in rhetorical argumentation (*Rhet.* 1.2.8–22; 2.20–24; cf. *Top.* 1.1), even though his discussion and examples may not easily convey a precise definition of the *enthymeme* (see Ryan, 1984; McAdon, 2001; cf. Thompson, 1975, pp. 68–77). Aristotle distinguished two kinds of *enthymeme*: demonstrative (δεικτίκα) and refutative (ἐλεγκτικά) (*Rhet.* 2.22.13–17), of which there are many types. Whereas demonstrative syllogisms are used to arrive at scientific knowledge or ἐπιστήμη in which a fact and its causes are clearly demonstrated (thus termed an ἀπόδειξις), the use of an *enthymeme* is to achieve *persuasion* (πίστις) in regard to some decision on the basis of probable causes or signs (see Kurz, 1980).

In practice each syllogistic element need not be present (Arist. *Rhet.* 2.22.1–2; Quintilian calls the *enthymeme* an *imperfectus syllogismus* [*Inst.* 5.10.3; 5.14.2]). Moreover, in contrast to demonstration, the premises need only to be probable and credible and are often based upon the opinions and actions of people (see Quint. *Inst.* 5.14.14; cf. Eriksson, 1999a, pp. 104–5). However, Aristotle encouraged the basing of argumentation upon certainties when that suited the argumentative needs (*Rhet.* 1.2.14; 2.22.3; see Kennedy, 1963, p. 97, and Thompson, 1975, pp. 69–71). If the *enthymeme* is constructed on the basis of causes or probable causes (εἰκότα), then it is classified as the type *rationes essendi*, i.e. providing the reasons/causes for the existence of a fact. If the *enthymeme* is constructed on the basis of signs (σημεῖα), then it is of the type *rationes cognoscendi*, i.e. providing the reasons for acknowledging a fact's existence (McBurney, 1936 [1994], pp. 173–77). Thus, from the certainty of the premise, whether based upon a sign or probable cause, the certainty of the conclusion follows. If the *enthymeme* is built upon a "sure sign" (τεκμήριον), then it is irrefutable, even though it may not fully explicate all the causal relationships, as would a syllogism or a group of syllogisms (*sorites*) (Arist. *Rhet.* 2.25.14; see also Kurz, 1980, p. 178).

Typically, the *enthymeme* is recognized by a premise with its supporting reason and a conclusion. Causal conjunctions such as "because" or "therefore" may indicate an *enthymeme* (for the types of Greek connectives, see Moores, 1995, pp. 36–37). Sometimes a "maxim" is found, either as the premise or the conclusion (for Aristotle's discussion, see *Rhet.* 2.20.1; 2.21; cf. DiCicco, 1995, pp. 229–35). It is often difficult to spot an *enthymeme*, as John D. Moores (1995, p. 34) argues: "The enthymematic character of the mode in which reasoning is presented is, in fact, something which quite often can perfectly appropriately remain unperceived by both the one who formulates it and the recipient for whom it is addressed."

Kraus (2002) surveys the *enthymeme* in the two centuries surrounding the apostle Paul. Kraus discusses many examples of its use as a figure of speech (*contrarium*) in early Roman theory, as a argument constructed "from incompatibles as a Stoic syllogism" in Cicero's *Topica*, as an argument from incompatibles in Cicero's speeches (e.g. *Balb.* 12; *Caecin.* 43–44; *Mil.* 41, 79; *Quinct.* 38–39, 45, 62, 76; *Rosc. Amer.* 113), and as arguments based upon consequents and upon incompatibilities in Quintilian (*Inst.* 5.14.1–3). Significant is Kraus' assessment (p. 105) that "It is not unreasonable to search for *enthymemes* of the Ciceronian type even in New Testament texts. And indeed arguments of this kind are not infrequent, for example, in Paul's letters." He discusses Romans 2.21–23 as nicely arguing from incompatibles (cf. 1 Cor. 10.21–22; Rom. 8.32).

Epicheireme

Aristotle defined the *epicheireme* as the "dialectical deduction" (*Top.* 8.162.a16). It combines features of both the demonstration and the *enthymeme*. Quintilian basically considers it along with *enthymeme* to be a variation of a complete syllogism (*Inst.* 5.10.1–7). It is a syllogistic deduction often from only probable or credible premises (like *enthymemes*) to a causally derived conclusion (like demonstrations). This much is

Table 4.2 *Comparison of Greco-Roman argument patterns*

Epicheireme or *ratiocinatio* Cic. *Inv.* 1.57–77 (cf. Quint. *Inst.* 5.14.5–32)	**Deductive argument** *Rhet. Her.* 2.28	**Amplification of a theme** *Rhet. Her.* 4.56-57 (cf. Theon and Hermogenes)
1 major premise; *propositio*	1 thesis; *propositio*	1 theme expressed
2 proof of major premise; *propositionis adprobatio*	2 reason; *ratio* (causal basis)	2 reason added
3 minor premise; *adsumptio*	3 proof of the reason; *ratio confirmatio*	3 theme is expressed in new form with or without reasons
4 proof of the minor premise; *adsumptionis adprobatio*	4 embellishment; *exornatio*	4 argument from the contrary 5 argument by comparison 6 argument from example
5 the conclusion or what is proved; *complexio*	5 résumé; *complexio*	7 conclusion

certain from the description in Cicero (*Inv.* 1.67; see also Solmsen, 1941, pp. 170–71) and Quintilian (*Inst.* 5.10.5–6; 5.14.5–6).

Cicero called the *epicheireme* argument *ratiocinatio*. In form it included up to five elements related to a syllogism, each premise having its own proof (Cic. *Inv.* 1.57–77). Cicero allowed for the flexibility of the five elements (*Inv.* 1.62, 64, 66, 70). He attributes this five-part argument to Aristotle and the Peripatetics (*Inv.* 1.61). Although critical of Cicero's isolation of distinct proofs (which Quintilian converges with the premises), Quintilian is in basic agreement concerning the form (*Inst.* 5.14.5–9; cf. 5.14.10–32). The author of *Rhetorica ad Herennium* (2.28) also presents a deductive argumentative pattern similar to Cicero's with an additional element, *exornatio* (embellishment of a premise). It is possible that Quintilian (*Inst.* 5.14.6) was aware of this line of argumentation, since he mentions the *exornatio*. Furthermore, in *Rhetorica ad Herennium* an inductive argumentative pattern is presented for the amplification of a theme. These complete argument structures are summarized in Table 4.2 (Alexandre, 1999, p. 76).

The simplicity can be deceiving since Cicero presents a rather convoluted and lengthy example of a five-part *ratiocinatio* (*Inv.* 1.68–69). So also does the author of *Rhetorica ad Herennium* (2.28–30).

Variation was allowed (Cic. *Inv.* 1.76; Quint. *Inst.* 5.14.10–13). The author of *Rhetorica ad Herennium* (2.28, 30) allows for the embellishment and résumé to be dropped. Furthermore, there was some confusion as to the exact formulation of *epicheiremes* (Quint. *Inst.* 5.10.1–8; for discussion see McBurney, 1936 [1994], pp. 186–87; Solmsen, 1941, p. 170). Quintilian (*Inst.* 5.10.4) admits at one point that "it would however, in my opinion, be truer to say that it is not our handling of the subject, but the thing itself which we attempt which should be called an ἐπιχείρημα, that is to say the argument by which we try to prove something and which, even if it is not yet stated in so many words, has been clearly conceived in the mind." He affirms Cicero, who argues that the ἐπιχείρημα is a "reasoning" (*ratiocinatio*). One might readily infer from this that the execution of an epicheirematic argument would not do justice to its formulation in the mind of the speaker.

Despite one's evaluation of these patterns of argumentation, it is apparent that in the Hellenistic period such patterns were common and circulating in various forms (Long, 2002 and 2003). The following four argument units from Dio Chrysostom's forty-sixth oration, entitled *Delivered in his Native City prior to his Philosophical Career* (ca. AD 80), are examples. In Prusa at this time a grain shortage caused an enraged mob to attack Dio's properties, since he was a grain dealer. People suspected him of withholding desperately needed grain, or worse yet, of favoring the rich over the poor in the matter. The following day Dio presented this apologetic oration to the public as the local officials decided upon the best course of action. In 46.3–4, Dio presents two argument units, citing the examples of his father and grandfather as benefactors of the city, thus establishing grounds for evaluating himself more favorably. See Table 4.3.

It is not enough to rely on the deeds of his forefathers. In 46.7–9, Dio addresses his own conduct among the citizens of Prusa. See Table 4.4. Both 46.3–4 and 46.7–9 contain two units that can be arranged according to the argument patterns described in *Rhetorica ad Herennium* and Cicero. Whether or not Dio intentionally formulated these units in conformity with rhetorical argument patterns, his argument progresses from premise to proof to conclusion. Often γάρ is used to provide substantiation of a claim or premise. Also, οὖν marks a conclusion. One must also observe the "interlocking" of argument sections. For example, the conclusion of the second argument unit recapitulates the content of both the first and second units; and the conclusion to the fourth unit functions as the initial premise for the next argument unit starting at 46.9.

Table 4.3 Epicheirematic *argumentation in Dio Chrysostom 46.3–4*

Epicheireme	
Premise A	Now with reference [περὶ μὲν γάρ] to my father, there is no need for me to tell whether he was a good citizen,
Proof A	for [γάρ] you are always singing his praises, both collectively and individually, whenever you refer to him, as being no ordinary citizen.
Premise B	You should know, however [μέντοι], that these words of praise of yours are of no use to him
[Proof B]	[implied – for you now show violence to me];
Minor conclusion	on the other hand [ἀλλ'], when you give your approval to me, his son, then you have been mindful of him too.
Deductive argument	
Thesis	Again, no one could say of my grandfather either [καὶ περὶ τοῦ πάππου δέ] that he disgraced the city or that he spent nothing on it out of his own means.
Reason	For [γάρ] he spent on public benefactions all that he had from his father and his grandfather, so that he had nothing left at all, and then he acquired a second fortune by his learning and from imperial favour.
Proof of reason	Moreover [καὶ τοίνυν], it is plain that he asked for no favour for himself, though held in such great friendship and esteem, but rather that he guarded and husbanded for you the goodwill of the Emperor.
Embellishment	But [δέ] if anyone thinks it foolishness to remind you of goodwill and nobility on the part of your own citizens, I do not know how such a man can wish to be treated well himself.
Conclusion for both movements	Being descended, then [δή], from such forbears, even if I were an utter knave myself, yet surely on their account I should merit some consideration instead of being stoned or burned to death by you.

Although this fascinating facet of rhetorical argumentation deserves more attention, enough has been said here for comparison with Paul's patterns of expression.

4.4   *Topoi* of forensic argumentation

A treatment of forensic invention would be incomplete without a consideration of rhetorical *topoi* (τόποι/*loci/sedes argumentorum*). *Topoi* are places from which to construct an argument. Judicial rhetoric

Table 4.4 Epicheirematic *argumentation in Dio Chrysostom 46.7–9*

Epicheireme	
Premise A	46.7–9 And [καί] pray consider what sort of citizen I am in other respects also, comparing me with whom you please – of all whom you do not consign to the flames.
Proof A	For example [μὲν γάρ], though I have real estate, all in your territory too, yet none of my neighbours, whether rich or poor – and many of the latter class are my neighbours too – has ever lodged complaint against me, either justly or unjustly, alleging that he was being deprived of something or being evicted.
Premise B	[δέ] Nor am I either over clever as a speaker or, if I may say so, poorest of all in that art.
[Proof B]	[Dio had already received training as a rhetor, so people would have known that he was not the poorest speaker.]
Conclusion	Well, then [οὖν], is there any one whom I have injured by my words, by causing trouble for any one who loves peace and quiet or by contriving some outrage against him? Or have I placed anyone in jeopardy touching his estate, pretending that it belongs to Caesar, or have I as advocate played false to any one?

Epicheireme	
Premise A	Again [καὶ μήν . . . γε], no man is more blameless than I am in connexion with the present shortage.
Proof A	[γάρ] Have I produced the most grain of all and then put it under lock and key, raising the price? Why, you yourselves know the productive capacity of my farms – that I rarely, if ever, have sold grain, even when the harvest is unusually productive, and that in all these years I have not had even enough for my own needs, but that the income from my land is derived exclusively from wine and cattle.
Premise B	Nay but [ἀλλ'], some one may claim, though I lend money, I am unwilling to supply it for the purchase of grain.
Proof B	[οὔκουν] There is no need for me to say anything on that score either, for [γάρ] you know both those who lend money in our city and those who borrow.
Conclusion and premise for next section: 46.9	What is it, then [οὖν], which I might do to relieve you from your distress but which I refuse to do, or what is it that makes you feel towards me as you do?

fundamentally concerns justice (δίκη) and equity (*aequitas*), and *topoi* were conceived in light of these (Cic. *Top.* 91; *Part. Or.* 98). Appeals to justice, in which some form of the Greek root δικ* is found, are very common.[2] The gods favor justice and oversee the justice process, and thus the voting jury ought to likewise (Andoc. 1.31–33; Lycurg. *Leoc.* 97; Lys. 19.64; Lycurg. *Leoc.* 1.91–97; Lys. 19.54; Cic. *Clu.* 7, 202).

To assist in the development of arguments most suitable to justice and equity, rhetoricians developed extensive treatments of various notions of *topoi*. These include (1) commonplace *topoi*, (2) *topoi* associated with the different *staseis*, (3) *topoi* pertaining to persons and actions, and (4) argumentative *topoi*. It would be tedious and unnecessary to show how these *topoi* are incorporated into actual speeches, since this has already been done and they permeate all oratory (see Palmer, 1934, and DiCicco, 1995, pp. 188–241). In this respect, we are reminded of Quintilian's observation that all aspects of the theory of invention and *topoi* as found in the rhetorical handbooks are dependent on the orators (*Inst.* 5.10.120–21):

> For the discovery of arguments was not the result of the publica-tion of text-books, but every kind of argument was put forward before any rules were laid down, and it was only later that writ-ers of rhetoric noted them and collected them for publication. A proof of this is the fact that the examples which they use are old and quoted from the orators, while they themselves discover nothing new or that has not been said before. The creators of the art were therefore the orators, though we owe a debt of gratitude also to those who have given us a shortcut to knowledge.

Thus, my task here is to recapitulate the various topical systems in order to ascertain and evaluate which systems a student of rhetoric in the first century may have encountered.

The summarization of the rhetorical topical systems is made difficult because the notion of *topoi* was not uniform among the theorists (see

[2] For example, Gorg. *Pal.* 2; *Hel.* 21. Consider in Lycurgus' *Against Leocrates* alone the number and variation of occurrences: ἀδικῶς – 30.2; 113.1; ἀδικέω – 5.1; 6.3; 10.4; 26.8; 59.8; 78.7; 114.7; 116.5; 119.2; 122.7; 126.11; 126.12; 127.7; 129.4; 134.2, 7; 141.7; ἀδίκημα – 2.2; 6.5; 8.2; 9.1; 9.6; 9.7; 28.3; 32.4; 35.8; 36.1; 52.3; 52.8; 66.4; 79.7; 97.3; 124.9; 125.8; 126.6; 146.8; 147.2; 148.3; ἀδικία – 78.5; 117.4; δίκαιος – 1.1; 6.2; 10.9; 11.1; 12.1; 12.2; 13.1; 13.6; 20.9; 28.1; 29.6; 34.1; 35.5; 35.7; 46.5; 51.9; 52.2; 54.1; 75.6; 114.5; 128.6; 131.1; 134.5; δικαίως – 1.5; 3.6; 13.6; 31.7; 49.8; 63.4; 67.1; 76.9; 88.7; 89.2; 93.6; 98.3; 100.1; 122.5; 135.3; 138.4; 144.1; 146.9; 149.2; δίκην – 91.7; 126.10. This speech is a specimen in this regard.

Ochs, 1969, pp. 419–20; Huseman, 1965 [1994]). Another difficulty is where *topoi* should be considered in the invention process: Is this during the determination of *stasis* or afterwards in the formation of arguments? (See Anderson, 1999, pp. 98–105.)

Aristotle distinguished between general *topoi* (τὰ κοινά or *koinoi topoi*), special *topoi* (εἴδη or ἴδια), and formal argumentative *topoi* (τόποι ἐνθυμημάτων) (Cope, 1867, pp. 128–29, and McBurney, 1936 [1994], p. 179). There are four general *topoi* that all orators are *obliged* to employ: possibility or impossibility (δυνατὸν καὶ ἀδύνατον), past and future fact (τὸ γεγονὸς καὶ τὸ μέλλον), the greater or lesser degree (τὸ μᾶλλον καὶ ἧττον), and amplification or depreciation (τὸ αὔξειν καὶ μειοῦν) (*Rhet.* 2.19). Aristotle never clearly relates the "universals" to the special or formal *topoi* (*Rhet.* 2.18.3–5; 2.19.27), but Richard C. Huseman (1965 [1994]) believes them to be general headings for the formal *topoi*. I am inclined to agree with Edward M. Cope (1867, pp. 128–129; cf. McBurney, 1936 [1994]), who argues that they are a distinct type of *topoi* but related to the special and the argumentative *topoi*. Aristotle's point is that the general *topoi* apply across all fields of knowledge.

The special *topoi* (εἴδη or ἴδια) are concerned with the specific nature of a particular subject. Aristotle discusses special *topoi* with reference to ethics and politics, two subjects closely connected to rhetoric (*Rhet.* 1.2.21; see Cope, 1867, pp. 124–33). For forensic oratory broadly speaking, this entails what is just and unjust (*Rhet.* 1.3.5), an injustice being defined as voluntarily causing injury contrary to written or unwritten law (*Rhet.* 1.10.3). The special *topoi* arise out of a consideration of three things: "first, the nature and the number of the motives which lead men to act unjustly; secondly, what is the mind of those who so act; thirdly, the character and dispositions of those who are exposed to injustice" (*Rhet.* 1.10.2). Aristotle treats these *topoi* in detail (*Rhet.* 1.10–14).

In addition to these specific or material *topoi*, Aristotle develops a system of twenty-eight formal argumentative *topoi* (τόποι ἐνθυμημάτων) (*Rhet.* 2.23). Donovan J. Ochs (1969, p. 425) correctly elucidates their nature: "Aristotle's list of rhetorical [formal] topics, however, is an amalgam of miscellaneous molds into which the topical arguments usually are cast. The title of each *topos* specifies a type of relationship, and the relationship can exist between terms, between propositions, or between past, present, or future events." Often, one of these *topoi* encompasses or is closely related to other *topoi* in Aristotle's system (Palmer, 1934). For example, *topos* 22 can be understood to encompass *topoi* 5, 18, and 26. See Table 4.5, which summarizes and compares Aristotle's formal *topoi*

Table 4.5 *Aristotle's formal argumentative* topoi *and the* loci argumentorum

Basic topical concern for each type of speech		
DELIBERATIVE	FORENSIC	EPIDEICTIC
Goodness	Justice	Virtue
Utility	Injustice	Vice

Aristotle's twenty-eight formal argumentative *topoi* (τόποι ἐνθυμημάτων) as found in *Ars Rhetorica* 2.23 in relation to the *loci argumentorum* in Cicero and Quintilian

1 opposites [*CO, CP, CT, Q*];	15 inward thoughts and outward show
2 inflections/derivatives; *CO, CP, CT, Q*	16 proportional results/analogy; *CT*
	17 identical results of action/decision
3 correlative terms; *CO, CP, CT, Q*	18 altered choices
4 more and less; *CO, CP, CT, Q*	19 attributed motives
5 time; *Q*	20 incentives and deterrents for
6 turning opponent's arguments	people
against him or her	21 incredible occurrences
7 definition; *CO, CP, CT, Q*	22 conflicting facts or actions; *CP, CT*
8 ambiguous terms	23 explaining circumstances/
9 division; *CO, CP, CT, Q*	accusations; *CO, CP*
10 induction	24 cause to effect; *CO, CP, CT, Q*
11 existing decisions/authority; *CO, CT*	25 better course of action
	26 comparing whether actions are
12 from parts to whole; *CP, CT, Q*	contrary
13 simple consequences [*CO, CP, CT, Q*];	27 noting previous mistakes
	28 meaning of names; *CP, CT, Q*
14 crisscross; *CP?*	

CO = Cic. *De Or.* 2.163–73
CP = Cic. *Part. Or.* 2.7
CT = Cic. *Top.* 8–25, 71
Q = Quint. *Inst.* 5.10.53–91; cf. 5.8.5

with Cicero's and Quintilian's.[3] The use of brackets indicates that one should be cautious when comparing Aristotle with Cicero or Quintilian because, as Georgiana P. Palmer (1934) argues, the particular meaning of each in the respective authors may be different.[4]

---

[3] The table, in terms of the names of the *topoi*, is slightly adapted from Huseman (1965 [1994], pp. 198–99). The comparison with Cicero and Quintilian is my own work.

[4] For example, Aristotle's first *topos* of opposites is different than the Roman argument *ex contrario*. The former is concerned with opposites that confirm each other, the latter

James H. McBurney (1936 [1994], p. 180; cf. Ochs, p. 424) insightfully discusses the interrelation of these three types of *topoi* for the formation of a rhetorical argument: "In summary, then, we may say that whereas the speaker goes to the special and general for his premises, he may call upon these 'lines of argument' [twenty-eight formal argumentative *topoi*] for his mode of reasoning. The premises and the line of argument selected will together constitute an enthymeme." Aristotle's threefold topical system marked an advancement in abstraction from his predecessors, who constructed arguments in a clichéd fashion based on commonplaces from actual scenarios – material which, as Solmsen (1941, p. 40) says, "referred invariably to particular subjects in the sense that the orator had his readymade commonplaces for either enhancing or minimizing, say, the trustworthiness of the witnesses, the importance of oaths to be sworn in court, etc."

The influence of both Aristotle's specific *topoi* and general *topoi* for later theorists and practitioners is questioned (Anderson, 1999, p. 42). Michael C. Leff (1983, pp. 28–29) maintains that the *loci ex personis et rebus* in Cicero's *De Inventione Rhetorica* do not have any connection with Aristotle, but rather Hermagoras. However, significant similarities exist in the Roman rhetoricians to posit at least an indirect influence. For example, Cicero (*Inv.* 1.34–43) and Quintilian (*Inst.* 5.10.20, 23–52) both discuss persons and actions topically as did Aristotle (*Rhet.* 1.10.2), although not achieving Aristotle's psychological and philosophical sophistication. Cicero calls these *materia argumentationum* (1.34). For persons, he discusses name, nature, manner of life, fortune, habit, feeling, interest, purpose, achievements, accidents, and speech. For actions, he reviews place, opportunity, time, occasion, manner, facilities, and adjuncts such as similarity, contrary, negative, genus, species, result, and consequence. The last half-dozen or so are quite similar to the *topoi* developed in *Orator ad M. Brutum* and *Topica*, which correspond more closely to Aristotle's general *topoi*. Quintilian (*Inst.* 5.10.20) has a similar approach for persons and actions, which he calls *sedes argumentorum*, although differing in details (5.10.23–52).

Similarities to Aristotle's twenty-eight formal *topoi* are also detected in Cicero's list of *topoi* in *De Oratore* 2.163–73. These *topoi* include

---

with opposites that are contradictory (Palmer, pp. 5–6). The problem with Aristotle is that his definitions and examples are sometimes truncated and/or cryptic (Ochs, pp. 424–25). For a criticism of how interpreters have handled Aristotle's general *topoi* see Palmer (pp. 1–4 and *passim*). However, Palmer is admittedly vulnerable to criticism respecting her understanding of Aristotle's *topoi* in that she relies more upon the examples of the *topos* provided by Aristotle than the description (p. 44).

definition, distribution, connected terms and headings, resemblance, differences, opposites, corresponding circumstances, concurrent circumstances, antecedents, contradictions, causes, effects, and greater/lesser/equal. See also Cicero's praise of Aristotle's keen insight into *topoi* (*Or. Brut.* 2.152, 160). A similar but shorter list is found in *Partitiones Oratoriae* (2.7), which is thought to be an interpolation from *Topica* 8–25, 71, and includes whole/parts, definition, enumeration of parts, etymology, generic/formal relations, similarities, differences, contraries, cause, effect, comparison, greater/smaller/equal, distributions, classes of things, elements and pre-conditions of things, etc. To use these *topoi* one must "examine them and seek for arguments from them all; but we shall use our judgment always to reject those of little value and also sometimes to pass over those that are of general application and not intimately related to the case" (*Part. Or.* 2.8; cf. 2.7; *Or. Brut.* 2.163). Quintilian (*Inst.* 5.10.53–91; cf. 5.8.5), too, has his similar version of argumentative *topoi* (*loci argumentorum*). These include definition to which genus, species, difference and property relate, division, division of time (beginning, growth, and consummation), similarities, consequences, causes, effects, opposite, comparison, part/whole, and greater/lesser/equal. Solmsen (1941, p. 173 note 74) surmises upon these similarities in Cicero: "It is generally and rightly assumed that Cicero borrows the *loci* of the *De orat.* (and similarly those included in the *Topica* and the *Part. orat.*) from a contemporary Academic system which in turn shows Stoic influence."[5]

Stoic influence is evident in yet another form of *topoi* found in Cicero (*Inv.* and *Top.*) and *Rhetorica ad Herennium*, *topoi* more specifically related to the circumstances of the case, i.e. *stasis* theory (conjecture, definition, quality, and legality).[6] By considering specific argumentative scenarios, Cicero and the author of *Rhetorica ad Herennium* reflect Aristotle's predecessors, who constructed (or recorded) commonplaces to meet various scenarios encountered in presenting a case. The origin of topical theory is to be credited to Gorgias and Protagoras according to Cicero (*Brut.* 46–47). A relic of this pre-Aristotelian form of *topoi* is

---

[5] I would question Solmsen's last sentiment, since Cicero charges that the Stoics were not interested in topical theory, only dialectics (*Top.* 6).

[6] These *topoi* related to the *stases* are discussed in Cic. *Inv.* 2.17–42 (conjecture – 14–51; definition – 52–56; legal procedure – 57–61; and quality – 62–115) and *Rhet. Her.* 2.3-6-17 (conjecture – 3–12; legal procedure – 13–18; and quality/juridical – 19–26). Cicero's discussion of *stases* in conjunction with *topoi* in *Top.* 87–90 is one component in his theoretical development of general inquiry or a *thesis* as opposed to a *hypothesis* (a specific case as in oratory) (see Ochs, 1989).

found in Anaximenes' *Rhetorica ad Alexandrum*, which treats commonplaces under the parts of the speech. Anaximenes' discussion treats each
class of speech (defense, accusation, vituperation, etc.) one at a time
while discussing the parts of the speech (*prooemium*, proof, *refutatio*,
etc.) and *topoi* appropriate to each section. It was probably Hermagoras,
and Greek theorists after him, who converted the pre-Aristotelian *topoi*
to the *topoi* presented under the system of *stases* (Solmsen, 1941, p. 173).
However, Cicero attests to the continuation of commonplaces attached to
the sections of a speech, since in his early rhetorical work *De Inventione
Rhetorica* (1.100–109) *topoi* are given for the *peroratio, narratio*, etc.

Finally, it should be said that Quintilian (*Inst.* 2.4.22–32) found the
pre-Aristotelian *communes loci* objectionable (which attests also to their
continued utilization) and refused to subsume *topoi* to *stasis* theory (*Inst.*
5.10.53). However, he admitted the value of *communes loci* as training
devices (*Inst.* 10.5.12–13). Furthermore, as indicated above, Quintilian
expounded a form of the *loci argumentorum*. Leff (1983, p. 34) summarizes Quintilian's complex view: "the *topoi* can enhance native ability and
enlarge the capacity to recognize the argumentative possibilities in any
case whatsoever. The *topoi*, then, are less important as models for producing a type of argument than as exercises for developing the intellectual
faculty of making arguments in general."

My survey would suggest that there are five relatively distinct types
of *topoi*: (1) *loci communes* (commonplaces), which one can employ
for predictable case scenarios for particular sections of a speech (pre-
Aristotle; Anaximenes; Cicero); e.g., how to question witnesses, dep-
recate the opponent; (2) *loci ex statibus*, i.e. *topoi* related to *loci communes* but which were eventually directly associated with *stasis* theory
(Hermagoras; Cicero; *Rhet. Her.*); (3) *loci ex personis et rebus* or specific areas of investigation in relation to why and how people perform
unjust acts (Aristotle) or in relation to persons and the actions involved in
the case (Cicero; Quintilian); (4) *loci argumentorum*, Aristotle's formal
argumentative *topoi* with Cicero's and Quintilian's, which denote basic
logical relations to assist in the analysis of data in preparation for the construction of particular arguments; and (5) Aristotle's four universal *topoi*
or *koinoi topoi*. The movement through these five types is from specific
or pre-formulated considerations to more general, abstract ones.

What form of topical theory was prevalent in the first century around
the Mediterranean basin? This is difficult to determine. After tracking
the *loci ex personis et rebus* in ancient theory, Leff (1983, pp. 24–25)
concludes that it and the *loci ex statibus* are the most important ones.
This is warranted since the Hellenistic schools championed the theory

of *stasis*. Cicero's *De Inventione* and Quintilian (negatively) attest to this, and both are working with Hellenistic sources (see *Inst.* 3.4.29–62; cf. Anderson, 1999, pp. 67–72). Furthermore, the *loci argumentorum* in Cicero and Quintilian is proof of their continued importance in rhetorical theory, whether or not these are derived directly from Aristotle's formal *topoi*. Therefore, when performing a topical analysis in 2 Corinthians, one should give priority to *topoi* associated with *stasis* theory, *loci ex personis et rebus*, and *loci argumentorum*.

For Cicero (*Top.* 96–100), the movement from the *loci ex statibus* to the consideration of the arrangement of the speech was a natural one. In fact, disposition is sometimes treated as a component of invention (*Rhet. Her.* 1.4; Cic. *Part Or.* 3; Quint. *Inst.* 3.3.1–9). Once the status of the case, the evidences, and the types of arguments were determined with the aid of *topoi*, the speechwriter would construct the speech's disposition.

5

FORENSIC DISPOSITION

5.1   Discernible rhetorical disposition

By disposition, I mean the intentional arrangement of the speech according to conventional sections which attempts best to foster favorable attention and persuasion in the audience. Different terms for disposition include *partes*-system, τάξις, arrangement, composition, *collatio*, distribution, division, and organization (Carrino, 1959). George H. Goebel (1983, pp. 201–202) argues that "Disposition is a matter of the end rather than the means – what point you want to make rather than how you make it – and it is no accident that the ancient rhetorical handbooks almost invariably define the main parts of the speech according to the purposes they serve."

It is important to understand, as Goebel's definition indicates, that disposition was an extremely critical component in the rhetorical process. Enos (1985, p. 109) summarizes Cicero's view of the matter: "Throughout his career Cicero saw arrangement as central to composition, believing that invention is localized, that ideas must be appropriate not only to the situation but also to the proper place within the discourse." This is arguably true for the earliest orators and rhetorical theorists.

Nevertheless, disposition as a feature of ancient rhetoric surprisingly is devalued or ignored by current interpreters.[1] There are two reasons for this. First, Plato and Aristotle disparaged speech disposition (Pl. *Phaedr.* 266de–267a; Arist. *Rhet.* 3.13.3, 5; cf. 2.26.5). Both do so explicitly in criticism of the dispositional teaching of Theodorus. Aristotle reduced disposition to two components: *prothesis* and proof (*Rhet.* 3.13.1–3).

---

[1] For example, Worthington finds elaborate chiastic patterns for Dinarchus' speeches, but neglects to consider the parts of the oration; he mentions only introduction/*prooemium* and conclusion (1992, e.g., 27–39, 121, 276, 288, 308, 314, 337–55). Also, Gagarin (1997) merely adopts a tripartite division for the analysis of Antiphon's speeches (introduction, argument, epilogue). For the importance of considering disposition, see Crawford's reconstruction and analysis of Cicero's fragmentary speeches by a consideration of disposition (1994, pp. 94–98).

72   *A survey of ancient forensic discourse*

(In actuality Aristotle allowed for more; see below.) Both Plato and Aristotle were responding rhetorically to what they considered *sophistic technique* that could be characterized as divorcing skill from the morality of the orator. As good philosophers and rhetoricians, Plato and Aristotle were depreciating the works and theories of others in an attempt to promote their own school of thought.

The devastating result of Plato's and Aristotle's criticism, however, is that modern interpreters have devalued disposition when investigating speeches. This works two ways. Either no investigation of a speech's disposition is performed at all (e.g., Worthington, 1992) or, if it is, it is ancillary to the rhetorical analysis. For example, John T. Kirby (1990, pp. 113, 116) argues: "*Dispositio* has to do with the arrangement of the various portions of a speech. On a superficial level this is the most obvious method of rhetorical analysis . . . [But] A more sensitive mode of analysis is needed for rhetorical criticism."

The second reason for depreciating disposition is the widespread assumption that disposition theory and practice developed according to an evolutionary model – simple to more complex. Typically, the legendary Corax and Tisias are deemed to have developed a rather simple theory of only three or four distinct speech sections. Kennedy (1959) maintains that Corax developed three sections: introduction, ἀγών, conclusion. To this, Kennedy argues (pp. 177–78), Tisias (with his forensic concern) would have added a narration. The notion that the earliest dispositions were simple rather than more complex is fallacious in itself and is based upon the spurious and multiform accounts of Corax's disposition as found in the *Prolegomena Rhetorices* (in Rabe, 1931). Goebel (1983, pp. 172–73, 238–65) has presented a very strong case that these accounts are unhelpful for reconstructing the disposition theory of Corax and Tisias, since they date from the first or second century AD or much later (*contra* Hamberger, 1914, and Wilcox, 1943).

There is substantial evidence that the earliest theories of disposition were more sophisticated than three or four sections (see Goebel, 1983; cf. Walz, 1832–36 and Hamberger, 1914, p. 38; B. Smith, 1921, p. 20). Our earliest accounts for disposition theory can be found in a variety of theoretical works and display pieces – model speeches, dialogues, and rhetorical handbooks. We have Alcidamas' *Odysseus in Response to the Defense of Palamedes* (possibly spurious), Antisthenes' *Ajax* and *Odysseus* (400–360 BC), Antiphon's *Tetralogies* (mid fifth century BC), Gorgias' *Defense of Palamedes* and *Helen* (both late fifth century BC),[2]

[2] The Greek texts of the speeches of Alcidamas, Antiphon, Antisthenes, and Gorgias can be found in Blass (1908). English translations of Gorgias and Antiphon can be found in Sprague (1972).

Plato's *Phaedrus* (early fourth century BC), and Aristotle's *Rhetorica* (ca. 330 BC). Antiphon's *Tetralogies* – theoretical court speeches depicting prosecution and defense and rebuttal and counter-rebuttal and exemplifying probability arguments in particular – are likely older than Gorgias' *Palamedes* and *Helen* (Ober, 1989, p. 342). Their authenticity is disputed and therefore only could help confirm our findings.[3]

Therefore, a good starting point to discuss early theories of disposition – as Mark A. Smeltzer (1996, 1997) has done – is Gorgias' *Defense of Palamedes*. After this I shall investigate other early display pieces, then consider Plato and Aristotle.

Gorgias' speech is a theoretical piece, as Goebel argues (1983, p. 173), because "the *Palamedes* is ostentatiously divided into its component parts, and it is clear that one of his purposes in writing was to illustrate his idea of the ideal judicial disposition." This mock trial pits Palamedes, the defendant, against Odysseus, who claimed that Palamedes attempted to betray the Greeks to the Trojans. The *Defense of Palamedes* contains the following structure (Goebel, 1983, pp. 147–54, 175–82):[4]

1   Introduction: 1–3

2   *Narratio*: 5. Here truncated as Palamades argues "I do not know how anyone could know what did not happen [τὸ μὴ γενό-μενον]."

3   Thesis statement or *Partitio*:[5] 4–5. The introduction is ended by a series of questions about the nature of the case (4). These questions lead to the thesis statement (5). This thesis outlines (in order) the two sections of the main argument which follows: "I shall prove by a double argument that he [Odysseus] does not speak the truth; for had I wanted to do such things, [A] I couldn't have, and had I been able, [B] I wouldn't have wanted to."

4   Proof of argumentation: A = 6–12; B = 13–21. The first section demonstrates that it was impossible for Palamedes to have carried out treachery. The second section considers possible

---

[3] Goebel (1983, pp. 15, 16, 144; so also Gagarin, 1997, pp. 8–9; *contra* Sealey, 1984) argues that they are authentic on the grounds of marked similarity of probability argumentation and thus concludes that they are representatives of the development of Athenian rhetorical theory prior to Gorgias' influence.

[4] I have used Goebel's headings, but have added one ("Thesis statement and *partitio*") and combined the last two (appeal to mercy and summary) into the heading "Conclusion". Also, the English translations given for *Palamedes* are from Goebel, except the narration section and a portion of the self-adulation at 32, which contains Kennedy's English translation found in Sprague (1972).

[5] The existence of a *partitio* at 5 is acknowledged by Innes and Winterbottom (1988, p. 4), but they fail to notice how the questions at 4 prepare for and contribute to the development of how Palamedes presents his argument.

motivations for such treachery and their improbability as well as considering the loss that would have occurred had Palamedes betrayed the Greeks. Goebel summarizes these as means and motive respectively.

5   Against the accuser (πρὸς τὸν κατήγορον), possibly including a counter-attack: 22–27. Goebel argues that this section of a speech is technically called τὰ πρὸς τὸν ἀντίδικον (the matters against the opponent). Following this is the next section of the speech, in which the defendant relates his virtuous life to the judges.

6   About the defendant's character (περὶ ἑαυτοῦ) or self-adulation: 28–32. "I should like, judges, to address to you some words about myself [περὶ ἐμαυτοῦ], which are, though they appear boastful, true, and though they would be intolerable under other circumstances, appropriate to a defendant. I shall offer you an audit and account of my past life" (28). Then at 32 Palamedes states: "To be sure, it is not for me to praise myself, but the present occasion requires me to make my defense in every possible way since I have been accused of these things."

7   Conclusion: 33–37.[6] Here Palamedes makes sure that the judges understand the gravity of making an error and its consequences for themselves and the rest of Greece. There is an opportunity to appeal for mercy (33) and to summarize the speech (τὸ ὑπομ-νῆσαι – 37), but both are deemed unnecessary. Palamedes states that he normally would have included both if addressing common people.

Two sections of *The Defense of Palamedes* are notable: "concerning one-self" and "against the accuser." Regarding the latter, Goebel (1983, p. 174) argues "that Gorgias and Antiphon share essentially the same scheme of disposition, whose most characteristic feature is a section, between proof and epilogue, directed πρὸς τὸν ἀντίδικον. In later theory this comes simply to mean 'refutation.'"

---

[6] Innes and Winterbottom (1988, p. 4) maintain that the epilogue begins with the statement in 33: λοιπὸν δὲ περὶ ὑμῶν πρὸς ὑμᾶς ἐστί μοι λόγος, ὃν εἰπὼν παύσομαι τῆς ἀπολογίας ("For the rest, my speech is to you and about you; when I have said this I shall end my defense"). I concur. Goebel (p. 37) argues conversely that there are two distinct sections: an exhortation to the judges (called – πρὸς τοὺς δικαστὰς περὶ ἑαυτῶν), possibly including an appeal for mercy (33–36) and a potential summary (called – τὸ ὑπομνῆσαι). However, it is better to understand both as parts of the concluding section of the speech, since Palamedes phrases it this way. See discussion below of extant speeches.

A look at the display speeches *Helen* by Gorgias and those by Alcidamas and Antisthenes, both purported pupils of Gorgias (Freeman, 1946, pp. 356–57), provides further support for the contention that earlier disposition theory was more complex than is generally assumed. Of particular interest are the narratives, thesis statements, and refutations. See Table 5.1

All the speeches have discrete introductions, with the possible exception of Antisthenes' *Odysseus*. All have narrative sections, although in Antisthenes' *Odysseus* the narrative material is dispersed throughout the speech. Likewise, in Alcidamas' *Odysseus* the main argument is an extended narration of events (τὰ πράγματα/τὰ γενόμενα). All have a clear thesis statement. Moreover, the thesis statement in *Helen* has four argument heads which are clearly marked throughout the main argument (τὸ πρῶτον [6] . . . τὴν τετάρτην αἰτίαν [15]; "The first . . . the fourth reason"). The thesis in Alcidamas' *Odysseus* is divided along the material relating to Palamedes' father and to Palamedes. Two speeches refute the argument and malign the character of the other litigant. The section on self-adulation is not explicitly seen in these speeches, but elements are still present. Antisthenes' Odysseus boasts about himself throughout the defense, especially in the conclusion. Likewise, Helen's divine lineage and beauty are narrated before the thesis statement. Alcidamas' Odysseus magnifies the folly of Palamedes in view of his own moral maxims, which essentially functions as self-adulation. If Gorgias had developed a theory of seven sections for a judicial speech already by the end of the fifth century, then one must consider whether these or similar sections are to be found in actual forensic speeches of the fifth and fourth centuries.

Plato and Aristotle also give testimony to multiple sections of a forensic speech. In the course of deriding Theodorus' misguided focus on speech sections, Socrates in *Phaedrus* (266de–267a) lists *prooemium* (προοίμιον), narrative statement (διήγησις) with evidence/testimonies (μαρτυρίαι), confirmation (πίστωσις) as characterized by positive proofs (τεκμήρια), additional confirmation (ἐπιπίστωσις) as characterized by probabilities (εἰκότα), refutation (ἔλεγχος), additional refutation (ἐπεξέλεγχος), and recapitulation (ἐπάνοδος) for "reminding the audience summarily of each point at the end of the speech" (τὸ ἐν κεφαλαίῳ ἕκαστα λέγεις ὑπομνῆσαι ἐπὶ τελευτῆς τοὺς ἀκούοντας περὶ τῶν εἰρημένων). Since the sections are numbered, Plato presumably gives them in the same order as they could have been found in a forensic speech. There is an essential correspondence with the sections and ordering in Gorgias' *Palamedes* except for omitting the *prothesis* and self-adulation sections.

Table 5.1 *Comparison of the disposition of the speeches of Gorgias, Alcidamas, and Antisthenes*

Speech Section	Gorgias' *Helen*	Alcidamas' *Odysseus*	Antisthenes' *Ajax*	Antisthenes' *Odysseus*
Introduction	1–2	1–4	1	1a
Narration	3–5	5–11 with witnesses	2–4 "Still the event (τὸ πρᾶγμα) really took place,"	(dispersed)
Thesis statement	6a She did what she did by (a) chance or necessity; (b) force; (c) speech; or (d) love.	12 "I will prove that [a] his father and [b] Palamedes were responsible for what happened (τὰ πράγματα) . . ."	5a "but as it is, the difference between us is tremendous."	1b "I have done more good to the army than all of you put together."
Main argument	6b–19 These four points are explicitly taken up in the very same order.	13–21 – the events (τὰ γενόμενα) explained about his father (13–16) and Palamedes' failure (17–21)	5b–6 – how the two are different	1c–10 – how Odysseus has done more good
Refutation		22–28		11–13
Self-adulation		While slandering Palamedes, Odysseus offers several moral maxims (27–28).		(found throughout; see conclusion)
Conclusion	20–21	29	7–9	14

The handbooks by Anaximenes of Lamsacus (ca. 380–320 BC) and Aristotle are extremely helpful. They represent two differing schools with respect to disposition (see also Kennedy, 1963, pp. 117–24). On the one hand, Anaximenes places tremendous importance on structuring the parts of a speech. This is seen in the fact that for each subgenre (dissuasive and persuasive, vituperative and eulogistic, accusatory and defensive) a specific discussion of arrangement and argumentative strategies is given. On the other hand, *superficially* Aristotle is more cynical of disposition than Plato because he reduces it to two sections and places its discussion last in his rhetoric. However, Aristotle shows even more remarkable similarities with Gorgias on the actual sections and ordering of a speech.

Aristotle begins his final treatment of disposition (*Rhet.* 3.13–19) by arguing that only two speech sections are necessary; the statement of the case (πρόθεσις) and its proof (πίστις) (3.13.1–4). A *prooemium* and epilogue also are begrudgingly granted as befitting a speech (3.13.4). However, Aristotle systematically (and with seemingly restrained delight) discusses the sections of the speech in the same order as Gorgias. Additionally, each section is elaborated according to deliberative, epideictic, or forensic settings. His discussion of disposition for forensic speeches may be summarized as follows:

1 *Prooemium*: προοίμιον (3.14.1–15.15). Ideally, "the most essential and special function of the exordium is to make clear what is the end or purpose of the speech" (3.14.6). "In the exordium we should state the subject [πρᾶγμα], in order that the question to be decided may not escape notice" (3.19.4). In the case where the audience is less than ideal, then "The defendant, when about to introduce himself, must remove all obstacles, so that he must first clear away all prejudice" (3.14.7). At a later point, Aristotle provides many ways by which to excite or remove prejudice from the standpoint of either defendant or accuser (3.14.15).

2 Narrative: διήγησις (3.16.1–11). Typically most suitable for forensic speech (3.13.3), the narrative should be as long or short as necessary; however, in the defense it need not be too long (3.16.6): "one should only mention such past things as are likely to excite pity or indignation" (3.16.7). Emotional appeals are increased by mentioning what is most typical of yourself or your adversary (3.16.10). Most importantly, the narrative should be constructed so as to show the virtue of the speaker: "you should incidentally narrate anything that tends to show your own virtue . . . or the wickedness of your opponent" (3.16.5). "And the narrative should be of a moral character, and in fact it will be so, if we know what effects this. One thing is to make clear our moral purpose; for as is the moral purpose, so is the character, and as is the end, so is the moral

purpose" (3.16.8). Finally, Aristotle indicates that the *narratio* should be
introduced at various points in the speech, and not necessarily only at the
beginning (3.16.11).

3 Proofs: πίστεις (3.17.1–12). Foremost, the proofs should correspond
to *the point of dispute*. *Enthymemes* are suited to forensic speeches and
examples to deliberative speeches. But, *enthymemes* should neither be
amassed (3.17.6) nor conceived for every point (3.17.7). Furthermore, if
one desires to arouse emotions or develop an ethical character, one should
not use *enthymemes*, "for demonstration involves neither moral character
nor moral purpose" (3.17.8). Instead, the orator should use moral maxims
in both the narrative and the proof (3.17.9).

4 *Refutatio*: ἔλεγχον (3.17.13–15). Aristotle discusses this section
under "proofs" (3.17.16); yet it is treated distinctly. "The refutation of
the opponent [τὰ πρὸς τὸν ἀντίδικον] is not a particular kind of proof;
his arguments should be refuted partly by objection, partly by counter-
syllogism" (3.17.14). Typically, the speaker should present proofs first,
then dismantle the opponent's arguments. However, if the opponent's
points are varied, then one should refute them first (3.17.15).

5 About the defendant's character: περὶ αὐτοῦ (3.17.16–17). One might
question whether Aristotle sees this as a distinct section. Indeed, he also
discusses questions (3.18.1–6) and joking (3.18.7) before moving to consider the epilogue. However, one may argue that Aristotle envisioned this
self-adulation (περὶ αὐτοῦ) as a distinct section of the speech, since he
correlates it with the refutation of one's opponent (3.17.10; cf. 3.14.7).
Specifically, Aristotle discusses the practice of Isocrates in *Address to
Philip* (4–7) and the *Antidosis* (132–39, 141–49), in which Isocrates "puts
compliments on his [own] composition into the mouth of an imaginary
friend" (Freese, 1926, p. 460 note c). Aristotle's last piece of advice is to
use moral maxims, which are the equivalent of *enthymemes* (3.17.17).

6 Epilogue: ἐπίλογος (3.19.1–6). "The epilogue is composed of four
parts: to dispose the hearer favorably towards oneself and unfavourably
towards the adversary; to amplify and depreciate; to excite the emotions
of the hearer; to recapitulate" (3.19.1). The summary may involve a comparison of the points made by the speaker and the opponent (3.19.5). The
style of the epilogue should be such that it is rapid, with no connecting
particles (3.19.6).

Compared with Gorgias, the speech sections and terminology are
remarkably similar, especially the *refutatio* (τὰ πρὸς τὸν ἀντίδικον) and
self-adulation (περὶ αὐτοῦ). What remains a mystery is where Aristotle
envisioned that the πρόθεσις should be placed. The term is used sparingly
(only in 3.13) in reference to the aim of the speech, i.e. that which must be

proved. It may belong in the *prooemium* (as it is often with Anaximenes), since this is where Aristotle indicates that the case (πρᾶγμα) should be clearly stated (3.19.4). Wherever placed, the function of Aristotle's *prothesis* is similar to Gorgias' *partitio*. The point of surveying Plato and Aristotle in conjunction with Gorgias is to demonstrate that forensic disposition theory was quite advanced early on and included as many as seven sections.

There is little need to elaborate at length what the remaining rhetorical theorists say with respect to the number and ordering of the speech sections, for the rhetorical tradition is quite uniform, with only slight variations (see Anderson, 1996, pp. 58–59; Lausberg, 1998, pp. 122–23). The author of *Rhetorica ad Herennium* advocates six sections: *exordium, narratio, divisio, confirmatio, confutatio,* and *conclusio* (1.4). Cicero in *De Inventione Rhetorica* 1.19–109 and *De Oratore* 2.80 (cf. *Or. Brut.* 122–27) argues for seven: *exordium, narratio, partitio, confirmatio, reprehensio, digressio,* and *conclusio.* Quintilian (*Inst.* 11.3.1–9) advocates five: *prooemium, narratio, probatio, refutatio,* and *peroratio,* since the *partitio* is technically not a section but a feature of speeches (*Inst.* 3.9.2–3).

It is instructive to investigate the disposition of *On the Mysteries* (399 BC) by Andocides, *Antidosis* (353 BC) by Isocrates, and Demosthenes' famous *On the Crown* (330 BC). These speeches deserve special attention as specimens exhibiting the full power of forensic apology in diverse settings. Andocides' speech is an apology to the Athenian jury addressing formal accusations (see Lys. 6); Isocrates' speech is a written apology addressing floating criticism; Demosthenes' speech defends his honor against formal accusations before the Athenian jury (Aeschin. *In Ctes.*).

Gagarin and MacDowell (1998) consider Andocides' *On the Mysteries* one of the most effective forensic speeches ever written. It is a masterful piece of self-defense delivered to clear Andocides of the stigma of allegedly attempting to subvert the Sicilian expedition some fifteen years earlier. At that time, the night before the Athenian navy set sail, the statues of Hermes (the god of travel) were defaced. Andocides and his friends were suspected of this and other religious impieties, specifically, the mocking of the Eleusinian Mysteries. Andocides confessed to some crimes to clear his family name. Later a law written by Isotimides was put into effect that barred those incriminated in acts of impiety from participating in the public life of Athens. Thus Andocides went into exile. From afar he wrote and sent to the assembly *On his Return* (ca. 408 BC) – but this speech failed to secure his safe return. Then, under the amnesty of

Table 5.2 *The disposition of Andocides'* On the Mysteries

  I *Prooemium* 1–7

 II *Partitio* 8–9

III Series of small relatively complete speeches (A–D) 10–139. Narrative
    material is distributed in the speech.

    A Defense against impiety and being an informer
      1 *Partitio* 10
        (a) No impiety towards Mysteries
        (b) Not an informer
      2 *Narratio = probatio* 11–28
        (a) 11–18 – No impiety
        (b) 19–28 – Not an informer (accusers' words false)
      3 *Peroratio* 29–33
        (a) 29a Uses the same language as in 10
        (b) Move to attack accusers 29b–30
        Appeal to the gods and final plea to justice 31–33

    B Defense against charges relating to the Hermae affair
      1 *Partitio* 34a on Hermae and Informants
      2 *Narratio = probatio* 34b–69
      3 *Peroratio* 70a

    C Defense against the use of Isotimides' law
      1 *Proemium* 70b (brief)
      2 *Narratio* 71 the origin of Isotimides' law
      3 *Prothesis* 72 law is void
      4 *Probatio* 71–91 Andocides' view of the law
      5 *Refutatio* 92–100 accuser's misuse of laws
      6 *Peroratio* 101–102
        (a) Vivid characterization of his accuser 101
        (b) Plea for acquittal 102
          i Importance of acquittal 103–105
          ii Digression on historical precedent 106–109

    D Defense of secondary charge; olive branch on altar
      1 *Proemium* 110
      2 *Narratio* 111–12
      3 *Partitio* 113–14
      4 *Probatio* 115–16
      5 *Refutatio* 117–39 (functions for whole speech)
        (a) Attack on Callias 117–31
        (b) Attack on Agyrrhius 132–36
        (c) Attack on Cephisius 137–39

 IV Self-adulation 140–45
    A Appeal to ancestors' past 140–43
    B Appeal to his own past 144–45

  V Final *peroratio* 146–50 If condemned to death, no one of Andocides'
    family is left. Friends called up.

403, he returned to Athens. Not three years later he was accused of another impiety and an argument was put forward that the law of Isotimides was still applicable to him. Lysias' extant work *Against Andocides* is one of the speeches from the prosecution. Andocides prevailed nevertheless with *On the Mysteries*. The arrangement of the speech reveals a flexible disposition in which several smaller relatively complete speeches are worked into one whole. Michael Edwards (1995, p. 15) argues why such an elaborate schema was necessary:

> The complex nature of the charges against him and their history meant that Andocides was faced with the problem of making, in effect, three separate defences in one long speech. The matter of the Mysteries (415), the question whether the decree of Isotimides was nullified by the amnesty of 403, and the olive branch affair just before the trial. Andocides deals with each of these in turn, and what might have been a very difficult speech for the jurors to follow is in fact well-ordered and for the most part clear.

I would add that a fourth defense was required, one relating to charges with respect to the defacing of the Hermae. See Table 5.2.

Edwards' arrangement is: *prooemium* (1–10), narration (11–18), proof (19–33), narration/proof (34–70), discussion of laws (71–91), *refutatio* (92–100, 101–109, 110–16, 117–31, 132–36, 137–39), and epilogue (140–50). This is problematic for the following reasons.[7] Edwards does not take seriously enough the self-stated outlining of the whole speech at 8 where Andocides contemplates how to proceed with the details of the case in view of the charges. He then hypothetically outlines the speech in inverted order ("Should I start with the end? . . ."). Furthermore, in 8 Andocides explains that the *narratio* is a critical part of his entire argument; thus, we observe the *narratio* woven through the speech with the respective charges.

Andocides' speech ostensibly follows a disposition schema similar to Gorgias' (*contra* Gagarin and MacDowell, 1998, p. 100). It displays all the sections that are seen in Gorgias, especially *narratio*, *partitio*, *refutatio*, and self-adulation. The final two sections (140–45, 146–50),

---

[7] Gagarin's and MacDowell's (1998, p. 101) outline is even less satisfactory: introductory remarks (1–10), events of 415 BC regarding Mysteries (11–33) and the mutilation of Hermae (34–70), the decree of Isotimides and why the events of 405–403 BC make them no longer valid (71–91), attacks on prosecutors and motive of Callias (92–136), which includes an effective rebuttal of the secondary charge about the suppliant-branch (110–16).

Table 5.3 *The disposition of Isocrates'* Antidosis

I Introduction to the mock-trial format (1–13)
II *Prooemium* (14–16)
III *Narratio* (17–29)
IV *Divisio* and *partitio* (30–32)
A Isocrates' oratory led to injustices;
B Isocrates' education made large sums of money from pupils
V *Probatio* (33–195)
A Answer to charges (33–139), which contains a related *refutatio* (88–100) followed by an extensive defense of the honorable deeds of Timotheus, one his students (101–39);
B Isocrates' wealth and the results of his education for men and the benefits to Athens (140–95)
VI *Refutatio* (196–319)
VII *Peroratio* (320–21)

which recall Andocides' family and his own deeds, create a tremendous amount of *ethos/pathos* for Andocides.

Isocrates championed the rhetorical education of Greece and later Rome posthumously (cf. *Against the Sophists*; Kennedy, 1963, p. 271). He is responsible for the remarkable and extraordinary piece *Antidosis* (353 BC), named from the legal term related to a trial Isocrates had just lost regarding property and his financial responsibility to Athens. This work, written in the form of a mock defensive speech, is an accounting of his life's work. As a part of his defense Isocrates recites portions of many of his speeches (51–88). It is masterfully constructed with a discernible forensic disposition (cf. R. Bonner, 1920, who only identifies a *prooemium* at 13–28). The *narratio, divisio* and *partitio*, and *refutatio* are effectively crafted. See Table 5.3.

Demosthenes' *On the Crown* has received special attention from NT interpreters because of its relevance for understanding Pauline rhetoric generally (Hughes, 1989) and 2 Corinthians in particular (e.g., Danker, 1991; Peterson, 1998, p. 88; cf. for Galatians Brinsmead, 1982, p. 43). The disposition of the speech is given here in Table 5.4, but see my discussion of its various elements below.

5.2   *Narratio*

The *narratio* or statement of the facts affords the orator an opportunity to prepare for the rest of the arguments. In a real sense the argument begins with the *narratio*. Typically, the rhetoricians believed that the *narratio*

Table 5.4 *The disposition of Demosthenes'* On the Crown

I *Proemium* (1–8)
II Preliminary *refutatio* (9–16)
III *Narratio* (17–52)
IV *Divisio* and *partitio* (53–58)
  A The entry of false statements about Demosthenes' words and deeds
     into public records,
  B The crowning of one liable to audit, and
  C The proclamation of the crown in the theater rather than the
     council-house or assembly
 V *Probatio* (59–121)
  A Demosthenes' words and actions (59–109); transition (110);
  B The audit (111–19); and
  C The proclamation (120–21)
  D Summary and transition (122–25)
VI *Refutatio* (126–296)
VII Self-adulation (297–320)
VIII *Peroratio* (321–23)

---

should be "lucid, brief, and clear" (Quint. *Inst.* 4.2.31; see also Watson, 1988, p. 21 note 198). There were disagreements about the necessity of each of these points according to differing Greek schools. Quintilian (*Inst.* 4.2.31–33) discusses the schools of Aristotle, Isocrates, and Theodorus. I have also already presented Aristotle's view that the *narratio* should promote the character of the orator and can be distributed throughout the speech.

Additionally, the extant forensic speeches provide evidence for at least three formal features that deserve special attention. First, the *narratio* may be demarcated not infrequently with some form of πράσσω/πράγμα ("I act/do"; "deed"), διηγέομαι/διήγησις ("I narrate"; "narrative"), or γίνομαι ("I happen"). Thus, one finds reference to τὰ πράγματα ("the deeds/actions"), τὰ πεπραγμένα ("the things that have been done"), or τὰ γενόμενα ("the things that have happened"). Theon (5.1–2; trans. Butts, 1986) introduces his chapter devoted to *narratio* with the following statement: "A narrative [διήγημα] is an explanatory account of matters which have occurred or as if they have occurred [πραγμάτων γεγονότων ἢ ὡς γεγονότων]." Notice that all three technical terms are found; thus, students would have learned appropriate terminology to introduce or conclude a *narratio*. Quintilian (*Inst.* 4.2.21–22) may be aware of this practice since he encourages prefacing the *narratio* with recognizable statements.

Such words can be found at the beginning or marking the end of the *narratio* or both. For example, Isocrates 17.3: "I shall relate the facts to you from the beginning as well as I can" (ἐξ ἀρχῆς οὖν ὑμῖν, ὅπως δύν-ωμαι, διηγήσομαι τὰ πεπραγμένα); and at 17.24: "Well, all the facts in the case I have told you as accurately as I could" (Τὰ μὲν οὖν γεγενημένα, ὡς ἀκριβέστατα οἷός ἦν, ἅπανθ᾿ ὑμῖν εἴρηκα). Demosthenes 32.4–13 also introduces the narrative in 3.4 by relating "what has been done" (τὰ πεπραγμένα) and ending with "this is the matter [πρᾶγμα] by which you are to cast your votes" (13.1) (see also Alcid. *Od.* 5; Antisth. *Aj.* 2; Dem. 18.17, 50; Isoc. 16.10).

Second, γάρ typically demarcates the beginning of the *narratio* (e.g., Alcid. *Od.* 5; Andoc. 2.20.3; Antisth. *Od.* 2.4).[8] Third, the narrative typically follows the *prooemium*, can vary considerably in length, and is often confirmed with testimony of persons or written documents (Quint. *Inst.* 4.3.1). We also should keep in mind Aristotle's view that the *narratio* should show the *ethos* of the orator.

I will illustrate these points with a few examples (see also Alcid. *Od.* 5–11; Antiph. 5.20–24; Dem. 19.9–16; Din. 1.4–6; Hyp. 3.1–12; Isoc. 16.4–9; Isoc. 17.3–23; Lycurg. *Leoc.* 16–34; Lys. 3.6–20; Lys. 7.4–10; Lys. 16.4–8; in Aristophanes see *Nub.* 1354–76 and *Vesp.* 910–14). Antiphon's *Against the Stepmother* (422–411 BC) involved a wrongful death case initiated by the deceased man's son against his stepmother and stepbrother. Poisoning was suspected. The speech arrangement is as follows: *prooemium* (1–4), *refutatio* (5–13 – the step-brother's refusal to have slaves interrogated), *narratio* (14–20 – a "true account of what happened" [περὶ δὲ τῶν γενομένων πειράσομαι ὑμῖν διηγήσασθαι τὴν ἀλήθειαν] at the end of 13). Here the *narratio* follows a *refutatio*.[9] This flexibility is not unique.[10] We have just observed Andocides' need to spread the narrative across the entire speech. This was a favorable tactic in later theory (Kennedy, 1963, p. 147; e.g., Isoc. 16.4). It is also common to employ narrative material in the *probatio* (e.g., Antiph. 6.11–15; Isoc. 18.5–12) or *refutatio* (e.g., Antiph. 6.41–46).

---

[8] While discussing Demosthenes' speech *Against Androiton*, Kennedy (1963, p. 219) says that γάρ is the typical word used to introduce the narration. So also Edwards and Usher (1985, p. 80), who argue that "later orators such as Lysias preferred *gar* (as 1 *Caed. Erat.* 6, 10 [= Lys. 1] *Theom.* 4 [= Lys. 10])."

[9] Cf. Hyp. 4.14–15, where this narration is after the *probatio* (5–13) and just prior to the *refutatio* (16–32).

[10] Cf. Antiph. 5, which has the following structure: *prooemium* (1–8), the *refutatio* (9–19), *narratio* (20–24), etc.

5.3 *Partitio*

The *partitio* is simply a *prothesis*, although having more than one argument head. The Latin term *divisio* is related to *partitio*, but indicates that the main heads of the argument are prepared in view of the opposing position. The author of *Rhetorica ad Herennium* (1.17) describes the *divisio* as having two parts. The first contains the points of agreement and disagreement between litigants arising out of the narrative. This is followed by a distribution, which is made up of two parts: the enumeration and the exposition. The enumeration involves telling how many points one will make. The exposition is the giving of the points to be discussed. No more than three points are recommended. Cicero (*Inv.* 1.31) indicates that the *partitio* can take two forms: points of agreement and disagreement with a stated problem, or "the matters which we intend to discuss are briefly set forth in a mechanical way." In theory *partitio* heads should be explicit – but in actual speeches this is the exception rather than the rule. Commonly the *partitio* is much less obvious (at least to modern readers).

A special relationship existed between the *partitio*/*divisio* and *stasis* theory as rhetorical theory developed (see Chapter 4.1). Heath (1995, p. 21), discussing *stasis* theory in relation to Hermogenes, argues: "Identifying the issue of the case is the first step; next one proceeds to the division, and it is here that the standard heads come in. Each issue comes with a prepackaged outline of the most effective strategy for handling it." Heath (p. 23) continues, "[I]dentifying the issue and working through its division provides a firm underlying structure of argument, without which all subsequent elaborations would be ineffective." Such a practice is discerned in Quintilian (*Inst.* 3.9–11), who discusses the preliminary stage of analyzing the case according to *stasis* theory and discovering the heads of the argument.

There are several distinctive features pertaining to how a *partitio* is formulated, how it is to be recognized, and how it functions within a speech. First, it typically follows the *narratio* as is later recognized by the rhetorical theorists, although sometimes coming after the *prooemium*. If there is no narration section, then the *partitio* follows the *prooemium* (see, e.g., Isoc. 18.4 and Pl. *Ap.* 18a.7–9).[11]

---

[11] See also C. Murphy (1938, p. 82), who, after observing often the same in Aristophanes (although Murphy finds *prothesis* following the *narratio* in *Lys.* 551–4 and *Eccl.* 209–11), explains that "A full *narratio* or διήγησις seldom occurs and Aristophanes never uses the regular phrase of the orators to introduce a *narratio* . . . This omission need cause no surprise, as we usually know the antecedent facts from the play itself; the orators regularly omit the διήγησις if the facts are known."

Second, the *partitio* is often formulated dialectically in view of the conflict with the opponent because the end of the *narratio* often contains the point of issue to be judged (e.g., Andoc. 1.8, 10, 72, 113–14; Antisth. *Aj.* 3; *Od.* 3–4; Dem. 18.53–58; Din. 1.6; Hyp. 3.13; Isoc. 16.10–11; Lys. 16.9). Quintilian (*Inst.* 4.2.132; cf. *Rhet. Her.* 1.17) argues: "As regards the conclusion of the *statement of facts*, there is a controversy with those who would have the statement end where the issue to be determined begins . . . This rule can always be observed by the prosecutor, but not always the defendant."

Third, rhetorical questions are sometimes found immediately preceding the *partitio* or within it. This use of questions, which calls the audience to a higher degree of attention, can prepare for the issue of the case to be determined and the heads of the main argument of the speech (e.g., Alcid. *Od.* 12; Andoc. 1.8; Antisth. *Od.* 3–4; Din. 1.6; Din. 3.4; Gorg. *Pal.* 4). We must remember that the *stasis* of the case was often articulated as a question (see Chapter 4.1).

Fourth, the *partitio* can contain many argument heads (see examples below). *Rhetorica ad Herennium* recommends three at most (1.17). Quintilian (*Inst.* 4.5.3) belittles such a view, "since the case may quite conceivably require more." The extant forensic speeches that I have surveyed show from one point (a *prothesis*) to five argument heads.

Fifth, as Cicero (*Inv.* 1.33) argues, these elements usually outline in the same order the *probatio*. Quintilian (*Inst.* 4.5.28) agrees: "the worse fault of all is to treat your points in an order different from that which was assigned them in your *proposition*." Also in the speeches the *partitio* does not outline the *refutatio* or self-adulation (although see Cic. *Inv.* 1.33). A pragmatic explanation of why the *partitio* relates only to the *probatio* may be that the *refutatio* was constructed with hearsay just prior to the delivery of the speech. This is particularly true for the defense (cf. Quint. *Inst.* 5.13.3). Also, the *refutatio* typically contains many diverse and separate arguments not easily outlined.

Sixth, in actual speeches the *partitio* is subtle and is not always easily discerned (e.g., Isoc. 16.10–11). On the other hand, Quintilian (*Inst.* 4.5.22; cf. 4.5.26) and the other theorists argue that the *partitio* should be rather obvious:

> it [the partition] will, if judiciously employed, greatly add to the lucidity and grace of our speech. For it not only makes our arguments clearer by isolating the points from the crowd in which they would be otherwise lost and placing them before the eyes

of the judge, but relieves his attention by assigning a definite limit to certain parts of our speech.

However, after recalling Cicero's mocking of Quintus Hortensius' counting the heads with his fingers, Quintilian (*Inst.* 4.5.24) states: "For there is a limit to gesture, and we must be specially careful to avoid excessive minuteness and any suggestion of articulated structure in our *partition*." To aid the listener, usually key words/themes are used which are then found in the corresponding section in the *probatio*, either explicitly introducing the section or simply being found in greater concentration within it. Typically a new section is demarcated by some explicit statement or obvious shift in topic.

A few examples of partitions at this point will help demonstrate these features (for other partitions see Alcid. *Od.* 12; Dem. 19.3–8; Din. 1.7; Din. 3.5; Hyp. 4.4–5; Isoc. 16.10–11; Isoc. 17.24; Isoc. 18.4; Lyc. *Leoc.* 35; Lys. 3.21; Lys. 7.11; Lys. 16.9). Antiphon's defense speech *On the Chorus Boy* (422–411 BC) contains a *divisio* in 7 followed by a *partitio* in 8 immediately after the *prooemium* (1–6):

> 7 My own attitude to my defence, gentlemen, is very different from that of my accusers to their prosecution. They, on their side, allege that their object in bringing this action is to discharge a sacred duty and to satisfy justice; whereas they have in fact treated their speech for the prosecution as nothing but an opportunity for malicious falsehood, and such behaviour is the worst travesty of justice humanly possible. Their aim is . . . to blacken me . . . 8 But I consider that indeed [A] I should first be judged concerning the charge itself, and [B] then relate to you everything that happened [τοῦ πράγματος κρίνεσθαι, καὶ διηγήσασθαι ἐν ὑμῖν τὰ γενόμενα πάντα].[12] Afterwards [ἔπειτα], if you so desire, [C] I shall be pleased to answer the remaining accusations made, as they will, I feel, turn to my own credit and advantage.

The defendant in 8 outlines the probation: (A) since the prosecution is only concerned with slandering the defendant, he needs to be judged

---

[12] On the preferred reading of κρίνεσθαι (to be judged) rather than the suggested ἀποκρίνεσθαι (to reply), see Gagarin, 1997, p. 227. The corresponding section in which the defendant clarifies and isolates the present charge of murder in 9–10 (thus showing that he needs to be judged on the specific charge) proves the importance of considering oratorical disposition, since in this case it may help resolve text-critical questions. I have used my own translation at the beginning of 8.

on the specific charge (πρᾶγμα) (9–10); (B) the defendant will recount what happened (11–15; notice the narration with witnesses embedded within the *probatio*) with respect to the specific charge (πρᾶγμα) (16–19), and (C) the defendant must reply to the other accusations (20–32). A rather brazen *refutatio* section follows the *probatio* (33–46). Transitions between argument movements are detectable.

Andocides' *On his Return* (an apologetic demegoric speech; ca. 408 BC) gives the heads of the main argument after the *narratio* (10–16) as follows: 18b "But he is most worthy of praise who dares both [A] his money and [B] himself." The *probatio* takes up each of these headings sequentially: A = 19–23, money and request for pardon; B = 24–26, his bodily sacrifice and personal actions.

So also Pseudo-Andocides' *Against Alcibiades* (late fourth century?) contains a *partitio* after the brief *narratio* (8) with four headings: 9–10 the orator is going to discuss Alcibiades' misdeeds with respect to: (A) state, (B) family, (C) other citizens, (D) foreigners. This is confirmed by the treatment of each of these in the same order (11–23): (A) 11–12, he was a poor statesman (13a is a transition); (B) 13b–15, he mistreated his wife; (C) 16–19, he evidenced poor conduct towards fellow citizens; (D) 20–23, he mistreated foreigners, specifically Taureas (20–21) and the Miligian Woman (22–23). After this follows the *refutatio* (24–38).

Demosthenes' *On the Crown* provides a very nice example of a *partitio* after the *narratio*. Demosthenes, after reciting the charges, indicates that he will treat the charges in the same order (53–58): (A) the entry of false statements (about Demosthenes' words and deeds) into public records; (B) the crowning of one liable to audit and (C) the proclamation of the crown in the theater rather than the council-house or assembly. The *probatio* in 59–121, which immediately follows, maintains this same order: (A) Demosthenes' words and actions (59–109); transition (110); (B) the audit (111–19); and (C) the proclamation (120–21). This proof section is followed by a brief summary and transition to the *refutatio* (122–25).[13]

[13] Contrast this with the view of Usher (1993, pp. 17–18), who sees only a *prothesis* in *On the Crown*. From my research I have concluded that Demosthenes' uses of partitions in his other speeches are not as standard as in *On the Crown*. For example, in Dem. 32.2 the division is in the midst of the *prooemium* (1–3): (A) His case is not valid in court (οὐκ εἰσαγώγιμον) (2.6) and (B) he hopes to reveal his plan and his evil (πονηρίας) (2.7). The *probatio*, denoted as "teaching the other things" (13), follows the *partitio* in inverted order: (B) 14–19 – Zenothemis refused to be put out of possession, in order to sail back to Sicily; thus, Zenothemis should be punished as an evil man (πονηρός – 18.4); (A) 20–23 – He has no basis for a plea (εἰσαγώγιμον – 22.2, 4; 23.5; 24.1; cf. 1.1, 6). Another variation is seen in Dem. 19, in which five heads are repeated three separate times in the *partitio* (3–8) after the *prooemium*; yet these headings are not presented in any apparent order in the *probatio* (17–66). Later theoreticians would have frowned on this.

These partitions are not as clearly stated as one might want them to be. In fact, interpreters show little concern to identify them at all, or identify them only minimally (see Gagarin, 1997, pp. 225, 227; Gagarin and MacDowell, 1998, pp. 76, 141–42, 159–61). Yet, when identified, these partitions greatly assist navigating the speech and would supply evidence to answer broader interpretive questions.

5.4   *Refutatio*

Cicero (*Inv.* 1.78) maintains that "The *refutation* is that part of an oration in which arguments are used to impair, disprove, or weaken the confirmation or proof in our opponents' speech." Despite this, Quintilian (*Inst.* 5.13.2) advises against appeal to the emotions! The purpose of this section is fourfold: (1) to question the credibility of the opponents' case by directly countering their arguments; (2) to attack the opponents by generally painting a bleak portrait of them politically and ethically; (3) to anticipate any opposition to one's own arguments; and (4) to answer related criticism or personal attacks. The sources for refutative material might be some informant or simply the trial process, in which "the speechwriter had the opportunity of hearing the evidence and some of the main arguments of his opponents on as many as three occasions before the trial" (Edwards and Usher, 1985, p. 10; they refer readers to Harrison, 1968–71, vol. 2, pp. 64–66, 94–105, 131). The occasions are when the case is handed to an arbitrator, at the preliminary hearing, and when the defendant submits a special plea.

There are several distinctive features of a *refutatio*. First, the *refutatio* normally follows the *probatio*, usually with some obvious demarcation, such as a change in topic and tone (e.g., Antiph. 6.32–33; Isoc. 17.44).[14] Second, there is a higher concentration of references to the opponent(s) and their arguments, sometimes by way of anticipation. For example, consider Isocrates 18.13 (cf. 18.35–36; Antisth. *Od.* 11–13): "I learn that Callimachus not only intends to speak falsely in the matter of his complaint, but will also deny that the arbitration took place, and that he is prepared to go so far as to assert that he never would have entrusted an

---

[14] However, consider Lycurgus' speech *Against Leocrates*, in which each point in the *probatio* is followed immediately with refutative material: *prooemium* (1–15); *narratio* (16–34); *partitio* (35). He has condemned himself as a traitor of the (A) city/fatherland, (B) gods, and (C) laws; *probatio* given in order, but each section immediately followed by a corresponding *refutatio*: (A) 36–54 how Leocrates betrayed his country, (B) 75–89 how Leocrates betrayed the gods with respect to sacred arms (75–78), oaths (79–82), and oracles (83–89), and (C) 111–34 how Leocrates betrayed the customs/laws; *refutatio* (A′) 55–74, (B′) 90–110, and (C′) 135–40; *peroratio* 141–50.

arbitration to Nicomachus, whom he knew to be an old friend of ours."
Third, many diverse topics are treated, all of which pertain to discrediting
the opponent(s) in some way (e.g., Isoc. 17.45–52; 18.13–57). Fourth,
the use of harsh language to describe the opponent is typical (e.g., Alcid.
Od. 22–28; Antisth. *Od.* 13; Isoc. 18.47–57; Lys. 3.44–45). However,
derogatory comments directed towards the opponents are usually sprin-
kled throughout the speech (e.g., in the *partitio*, Dem. 18.10–11; after the
narration, 18.50–52; Isoc. 16.22–23). Fifth, the *refutatio* is also an opportunity to anticipate or repulse arguments to be made against your own
speech/person. Thus, statements like "perhaps you will say in response
that . . ." are not uncommon (e.g., Dem. 19.72, 80, 88, 147, 158, 182;
25.42; Din. 1.48, 61, 89, 91; Hyp. 1.13).

Additionally, certain refutative strategies are typical. For example, one
can turn the opponent's own argument against him. This is seen in Hyperides 3.23–33 when the accuser, who claims that the defendant has acted
unlawfully, is shown to be lawless himself (cf. Antiph. 6.42). One also
can claim that one's opponent is inconsistent. For example, Dinarchus
(1.48) anticipates that his opponent Demosthenes will insist that he is
inconsistent because previously Dinarchus had been convicted by the
council and resisted its accusation, but now Dinarchus is defending the
council and accusing Demosthenes. Likewise, Dinarchus accuses Demosthenes of inconsistency (1.91–104). One can accuse one's opponent to be
mighty or clever in speech (e.g., Dem. 20.146; Isoc. 15.5; Pl. *Ap.* 17b1–
4). Aeschines (Aesch. *In Ctes.* 174; cf. *Leg.* 114) attacks Demosthenes
to this extent: "But as regards his good judgment and power of speech
[λόγου δύναμιν], how does it stand with him? Eloquent of speech [δεῖνος
λέγειν], infamous of life." Finally, one could use indefinite expressions
like "such" or "some" (τις or τινες) when addressing one's opponents or
some potential objection (e.g., Aesch. *In Tim.* 141.3; Dem. 19.229–31,
293–95, 306; 20. 56; 25.40, 43; 54.35.4; see also Murphy, 1938, p. 85,
who cites this example in comedy: Ar. *Ach.* 540 [ἐρεῖ τις]).

These features may be illustrated in more detail by looking at two
refutations (for others see Alcid. *Od.* 22–28; Andoc. 1.92–100, 117–39;
Antiph. 5.9–19; Antisth. *Od.* 11–13; Dem. 18.126–320, which involves
substantial *synkrisis*; 19.67–168; Din. 1.48–104; Hyp. 1.IVb.8–13; Hyp.
3.28–33; Hyp. 4.16–32; Isoc. 16.42–44; Isoc. 17.45–52; Isoc. 18.13–57;
Lyc. *Leoc.* 55–74, 90–110, 135–40; Lys. 3.44–45; Lys. 16.19–20; Pl.
Ap. 28a4–34b5). In Pseudo-Andocides' *Against Alcibiades*, the *refutatio*
(24–38) begins with the statement "some [τινες] dare to say that the like
of Alcibiades has never been before." This attempts to repel any critique
of his critique of Alcibiades in the preceding *probatio*. Furthermore, the

accuser in 25 explicitly anticipates Alcibiades' argument: "I imagine that Alcibiades will make no reply to this [his past misdeeds], but will talk instead of his victory at Olympia, and that he will seek to defend himself on any grounds rather than those on which he has been charged." Later in the *refutatio* (34) the accuser criticizes Alcibiades' family: "Indeed, not even Alcibiades himself would venture to maintain that they, the worst miscreants of their time though they were, did not have more regard for decency and honesty than himself; for no one in the world could frame an accusation which would do justice to his misdeeds." Such venom is typical.

In Antiphon's defense speech *On the Chorus Boy* the defense begins the *refutatio* section (33–46) with several first-person remarks: "I will go further. I will prove that my accusers here are the most reckless perjurers and the most godless scoundrels alive; that they have earned not only my own hatred, but the hatred of everyone of you and of your fellow-citizens besides, by instituting this trial." One's opponents are often lambasted for the need to go to trial in the first place.

5.5   Self-adulation

This section contains speech concerning oneself (περὶ ἑαυτοῦ) in an attempt to ameliorate the jury. It is therefore the most relevant for the defendant. Lysias (12.38; cf. Quint. *Inst.* 11.1.17–18, 22–23; and Murphy, 1938, p. 97) attests to the common practice of relating one's heroic deeds when defending oneself against accusations:

> And note that he [this particular accused man] cannot even resort to the expedient, so habitual among our citizens, of saying nothing to answer the counts of the accusation, but making other statements about themselves [περὶ δὲ σφῶν αὐτῶν] which at times deceive you; they represent to you that they are good soldiers, or have taken many vessels of the enemy while in command of war-ships, or have won over cities from hostility to friendship.

According to Cicero (*Inv.* 1.97; cf. Quint. *Inst.* 9.2.55), Hermagoras reportedly recommended a digression possibly involving "praise of oneself":

> Hermagoras puts the digression next [after the *refutatio*], and then finally the peroration. In this digression he thinks a passage should be introduced unconnected with the case and the

> actual point to be decided; it might contain praise of oneself [*sui laudem*] or abuse of the opponent, or may lead to some other case which may supply confirmation or refutation not by argument but by adding emphasis by means of some amplification. If anyone thinks this is a proper division of a speech, he may follow Hermagoras' rule . . . I am of the opinion that praise and vituperation should not be made a separate part, but should be closely interwoven with the argumentation itself.

Although the later rhetorical theorists (*Rhetorica ad Herennium*; Cicero, Quintilian) do not promote the praise of oneself *as a distinct section*, they tacitly acknowledge its value. Quintilian (*Inst.* 11.1.17–18, 22–23) discusses Demosthenes' and Cicero's need for self-praise out of self-defense.

Evidence indicates that such a section could be a complement to the *refutatio* (see Cic. *Inv.* 1.97). It shows the orator's favorable character, deeds, accomplishments, devotion, piety, or whatever, especially in view of the contrary claims of the opponent(s). In Plato's *Apology* the *refutatio* (28a4–34b5) becomes increasingly more concerned with Socrates' good character, so that at the end he appeals to his bravery, dreams, oracles of the gods (cf. 2 Cor 12.1–10!), and his beneficial instruction to students (cf. Isoc. 15.101–95). So also does Demosthenes' *On the Crown* contain self-praise concerning his own policies, conduct, and reputation as a statesman (e.g., 160–79; cf. 297–305) in the midst of the *refutatio* in contrast with Aeschines (126–296) (cf. Kennedy, 1963, pp. 233–34). Likewise, after Demosthenes moves specifically to speak of his honorary deeds (297–305), he returns to compare himself with Aeschines to denigrate him severely (307–14). Demosthenes' use of *synkrisis* comes to a climax near the end of his honorable deeds section (319–20):

> You must compare me with the orators of to-day; with yourself, for instance, or anyone you like: I exclude none. When the commonwealth was at liberty to choose the best policy, when there was a competition of patriotism open to all comers, I made better speeches than any other man, and all business was conducted by my resolutions, my statutes, my diplomacy. Not one of you ever put in an appearance – except when you must needs fall foul of my measures. But when certain deplorable events had taken place, and there was a call, not for counsellors, but for men who would obey orders, who were ready to injure their country for pay, and willing to truckle to strangers, then you and your party were at your post, great men with gorgeous equipages. I was

powerless [ἀσθενής; cf. 2 Cor. 12.9–10!], I admit; but I was still the better patriot.

At 321, when talking about the qualities of the good citizen, Demosthenes remarks that he could apply this concerning himself (περὶ ἐμαυτοῦ) without offense.

Key phrases that can help identify this section are ὑπὲρ ἐμαυτοῦ, "on my behalf" or περὶ ἐμαυτοῦ, "concerning myself." The distinction between the two is that the former may be more acutely *defensive* in nature, since the expression ἀπολογέομαι ὑπὲρ ἐμαυτοῦ ("I defend on my behalf") is found, e.g., in Din. 1.48. In this regard, consider also the statements of Isaeus and Andocides (cf. Antiph. 2.4.11). Isaeus (10.1) argues in the *prooemium*, in the midst of a *captatio benevolentiae*, "But, as it is, we are not on equal terms; for they are both able speakers [λέγειν δεινοί] and clever plotters, so that they have often pleaded before you on behalf of others, whereas I, so far from speaking on behalf of another, have never before pleaded on my own behalf [ὑπὲρ ἐμαυτοῦ] . . ." In the *peroratio* of his self-defense, Andocides (1.148) bemoans his desperate situation: "For after all, whom can I produce here to plead for me [ὑπὲρ ἐμαυτοῦ]? My father? He is dead. My brothers? I have none. My children? They are still unborn."

An example of these features is found in Hyperides' *Defense of Lycophron* (ca. 333 BC). After giving the *refutatio* (8–13), the orator in 14 turns to talk about himself: "So Ariston may say whatever he pleases, gentlemen of the jury, and invent lies against me, but surely your verdict upon me must be based, not on the slanders of the prosecutor, but on a review of the whole of my life." He contends for his good character and links himself to Athens by way of activities, social status, and honors (16–18). The conclusion to this section is signaled at the transition to the *peroratio*: "Well, gentleman of the jury, you have heard virtually all that I had to say in my own defense [lit. "concerning myself"]" (ὅσα μὲν οὖν ἐγὼ εἶχον, ὦ ἄνδρες δικασταί, ὑπὲρ ἐμαυτοῦ εἰπεῖν, σχεδὸν ἀκηκόατε) (cf. the use of ὑπὲρ ἐμαυτοῦ in Antiph. 2.2.13 immediately after the honorable deeds section in 2.2.12; so also Lys. 16.20, which uses the expression ὑπὲρ τῶν ἐμαυτοῦ πραγμάτων).

This example of self-adulation is no isolated instance (e.g., Andoc. 1.140–45; Antiph. 2.2.12; Dem. 18.297–323; Isoc. 18.58–65; and Lys. 7.30–33).[15] In Antiphon's defense speech *On the Murder of Herodes* the defendant offers extended discussions of his father's services to the

---

[15] Hyp. 4.33–37 is another example of self-adulation, although modified uniquely for the circumstances. After scattered references to the defendant's good character

city (74–80) and concerning himself (81–84). On his own behalf, the defendant argues that the signs from the gods (τὰ σημεῖα τὰ ἀπὸ τῶν θεῶν) are favorable to him and supplies witnesses to attest to this fact (83–84; cf. 2 Cor. 12.1–4, 9–10). This material is placed immediately before the *peroratio* (85–96).

Lysias' *On the Property of Aristophanes: Against the Treasury* (388 BC) provides yet another example of self-conscious discussion "concerning oneself." The defendant argues, "I propose next to tell you briefly about myself [περὶ ἐμαυτοῦ]" (55). The defendant then turns to his father's benefactions (56):

> So much let me say regarding myself [περὶ ... ἐμαυτοῦ]: as to my father [περὶ δὲ τοῦ πατρός], since he has been treated as guilty in the accusations, forgive me if I mention what he has spent on the city and on his friends; I do this not for vainglory [οὐ γὰρ φιλοτιμίας ἕνεκα], but to bring in as evidence the fact that the same man cannot both spend a great deal without compulsion and covet some of the public property at the gravest risk.

Another example, which also shows the close relation this section has with *refutatio*, comes from Demosthenes' *On the False Embassy*, an accusation speech against Aeschines (343 BC). After a lengthy and sustained *refutatio* that covers many points (67–168), Demosthenes introduces (169) and compares (174) his own good conduct with that of his opponents, Aeschines and Philocrates.

Three other features of forensic self-adulation should be mentioned. First, it may be that the whole speech is devoted to self-praise and thus no distinct self-adulation section is found. For example, the *dokimasia* speech of Lysias 16 was offered in a scrutiny trial for a public office (see esp. 16.9). So also Odysseus' case with Ajax has no need of a distinct self-adulation, since the main argument espouses his own heroic actions, which benefited even Ajax (Antisth. *Od.* 6–10).

Second, a litigant might find it expedient to laud the exploits of others to bolster his own case. For example, in Isocrates 16, a son repeatedly recounts his father's favorable exploits and civic service (22, 36, 39, 41). In his *Antidosis*, Isocrates avoids direct praise of himself by relating the many honorable accomplishments of Timotheus, one of his students (101–39; see R. Bonner, 1920).

throughout the *refutatio* (16–32), Hyperides, before the *peroratio*, praises not himself but Athens, who protects and justly rules over her citizens, especially those of wealth and means.

Third, it is not uncommon to mention one's good deeds in contrast to the opponent's misdeeds within the *peroratio*. A final bravado is clearly seen in [Andocides] 4.41–42 in the midst of the *peroratio*, in which the opponent is once again vilified. Also, if we are not to understand Demosthenes' *On the Crown* as having the honorable deeds section extending virtually to the end, then a final bravado is also found in 321–23. The purpose of this final boast, it would seem, is to end the speech with a heightened sense of *ethos/pathos* (cf. Antiph. 2.2.12; Dem. 45.85). A defendant might also capitalize on the opportunity afforded in the *peroratio* by calling up family and friends to speak on his behalf. Cicero orchestrates precisely this in support of Cluentius' good reputation (*Clu.* 196–98). Such "boasting" and practices were parodied in Greek and Roman comedy (see Murphy, 1938, pp. 76–77).

5.6   Conclusion

Forensic disposition has not been adequately appreciated as a heuristic tool to study ancient forensic speeches. My contention is that the early and widespread concern for disposition within forensic speeches was in relative conformity with later forensic theory. Four critical sections for forensic speeches were identified and investigated: *narratio, partitio, refutatio,* and self-adulation.

The arrangement in actual speeches shows variation and versatility. This is not surprising, as Quintilian (*Inst.* 2.13) explains, because the circumstances of the unique case must dictate the ordering and inclusion of the various speech sections. My survey illustrates a tension between employing different possible sections and yet doing so only as would assist in achieving a favorable verdict. Certainly, not every speech displays a well-defined or uniform arrangement. My research has, however, led me to the conclusion that an orator's use of disposition is not overtly obvious. This may reflect a concern to avoid the appearance of using sophistic artifice, as C. Joachim Classen (1992, p. 343) argues:

> On *dispositio* rhetorical theory may be consulted, but extreme caution is called for, as has been pointed out. Perhaps the most useful aspect which practical oratory can illustrate is that the best orator disguises his knowledge of the theory, that he alters accepted patterns and adjusts them to the particular case and his intention. Thus not what conforms to the rules, but what seems at variance with them often proves most instructive of the interpretation.

The theoretical notions articulated by Classen may account for why interpreters have not always detected, sought after, or agreed on the disposition
of a given speech. Nevertheless, if one can perceive a disposition schema,
then one may better understand how the argumentative parts function
within the whole speech.

6

APOLOGETIC LETTERS

6.1   Introduction: the problem of Paul's letters and epistolary speeches

Many interpreters, such as Jan Lambrecht (1989), Dennis L. Stamps (1992, 1995; cf. 1999), Classen (1992), Jeffrey T. Reed (1993), Stanley E. Porter (1997a, 1997b, 1999), Anderson (1996, 1999), and Philip H. Kern (1998), question the applicability of ancient rhetoric to Paul's epistles and typically favor modern universal rhetoric or discourse theory (cf. Black, 1989, 1990).

These interpreters have raised many significant questions and arguments. First, *Paul did not use rhetorical terminology in the technical senses that truly corresponded to rhetorical meanings* (Anderson, 1996, pp. 122–23, 253–55 *contra* Fairweather, 1994; cf. Black, 1990, pp. 63–64, who questions Betz, 1985). Second, *the choice of rhetorical species for individual letters is difficult to determine and therefore unhelpful, since scholarly opinions conflict* (e.g., for Galatians see Kern, 1998, pp. 120–66). Third, *a foreign structure is imposed on the letters with considerable variation from one rhetorical critic to the next* (Porter, 1997b, pp. 539–61; Kern, 1998, pp. 90–119). Fourth, *Paul's letters do not correspond to the appropriate venue associated with the respective species*, e.g., the courtroom or assembly (Kern, 1998, pp. 16, 18, 29–33, 204–208). Fifth, *the rhetorical handbooks are used almost exclusively as a basis for analysis of Paul's letters*, when in fact, there were other rhetorics circulating, such as philosophical rhetoric, epistolary rhetoric, diatribe, synagogue homily, and common conversation (Kern, 1998, pp. 12–30; cf. Winter, 1997, p. 240). Sixth, *the existence of an "apologetic letter" genre is questioned* (Kern, 1998, p. 33; cf. Hansen, 1989, pp. 25–27). Finally, *epistles and oratory were clearly distinguished in antiquity, so one should not confuse genres* (Classen, 1992, p. 342; Reed, 1993, pp. 292–324; Stamps, 1995, pp. 142–48; and Porter, 1997b, pp. 566–67).

These questions and methodological concerns should be welcomed, since biblical scholars are still attempting to understand Greco-Roman rhetorical practice and theory and its relevancy to the NT. On the one hand, the second, third, and fourth items above call ancient rhetorical critics to use ancient sources with greater care, clarity, and consistency when interpreting biblical materials. Specifically, rhetorical analyses must establish a suitable occasion and venue and explore invention and disposition through a careful genre analysis using suitable parallels for comparison.

On the other hand, many of these concerns are unjustified because of the nature and profusion of ancient Greco-Roman rhetorical theory (as discussed in Chapter 2). One major tenet, for example, was to hide rhetorical artifice (see Chapter 2.3), so that we should not expect Paul to flaunt his knowledge of theory through using technical terminology. Also, it is no longer possible to assert a rigid dichotomy between ancient epistles and oratory (see Chapter 2.2 and below; cf. Malherbe, 1988, pp. 2–7; Stowers, 1986, p. 34; and Long, 1999, pp. 50–54, 59–63, 162–64). Apologetic letters were used, circulated, studied, and imitated. Extant examples provide us with excellent analogies for 2 Corinthians (see Chapter 6.2 below).

What kind of letter is 2 Corinthians?

To answer this question, one must consider the ancient epistolary tradition. M. Luther Stirewalt (1993) reviews ancient epistolography according to its settings (normative, extended, and fictitious) and letter types (official, personal, technical, essay, school exercise, and entertainment). Normative settings may involve the "official letter" or the "personal familiar letter" (pp. 6–15) in which "actual correspondence" between parties has occurred (p. 2). Extended settings are those in which the contents of the letter are shared with the extended receiving community or are for public consumption generally. Stirewalt (p. 3) explains, "Under these influences extended settings provide the contexts in which writers publicize non-epistolary topics for a group of people, identified or unidentified, and known or assumed to be interested. Such activity is represented by letters on technical and professional subjects and for propaganda." Stirewalt (pp. 15–20) includes here "letter-writing on professional and technical subjects" and the "letter-essay." Finally, Stirewalt (p. 3) summarizes, "In fictitious settings the writer impersonates another and composes a message in that person's name." Categories for this setting include "the letter for school exercise" and "letters for entertainment" (pp. 20–25).

Typically, interpreters have studied Paul's letters as personal letters (i.e. documentary or non-literary) rather than official literary letters. This is so despite John White's (1986, p. 3) caveat concerning the omission of literary letters from his study in the introduction to his collection of documentary letters: "Nor is their exclusion [i.e. the exclusion of official literary letters] intended to suggest that they are irrelevant to the study of early Christian letters. The use of rhetorical techniques, especially in the theological body of Paul's letters, indicates that a knowledge of these traditions is quite relevant to the study of early Christian letters."

White's (1971, 1986) analyses of Paul's letters as personal letters evidences mixed results (see Church, 1978; cf. White, 1971). Of all the letters analyzed by White as personal letters, 2 Corinthians is the most convoluted and perplexing (1986, pp. 136–39). For example, 2 Corinthians 1–7 (which White takes as unified) is an extremely confused composition. White (p. 136) states:

> We anticipate the initiation of the body-middle of II Corinthians in 1:13, since the body-opening section concludes with the background item in 1:12. But the section of the letter that extends from 1:3–22 actually bears all the marks of a body closing section. Indeed, we find two additional body closing sections [1.23–3.4; 7.3–16] in the first seven chapters of II Corinthians!

Likewise, Linda L. Belleville (1989) seeks to justify her conclusion that 2 Corinthians 1–7 is a letter of apologetic self-commendation on epistolary grounds. However, Belleville's proposal is untenable because she must argue that the "background period" extends from 1.8 to 5.21, which she admits (pp. 55–56) is "quite long." Furthermore, her treatment of 7.3–16 as the conclusion of the letter is problematic (pp. 149–50, 155). Lastly, Belleville (pp. 157–59) creates a new epistolary category (apologetic self-commendation) in order to account for the fact that Paul is writing a letter of commendation for himself. Although Belleville commendably recognizes the apologetic nature of chapters 1–7, this recognition is best accounted for when one understands all of 2 Corinthians as an official apologetic literary letter in an extended setting.

The failure to recognize distinct conceptions of letters in antiquity has caused confusion among some interpreters of Paul. For example, Stamps (1995, p. 143) summarizes Demetrius' *On Style* (first century BC or AD) as if Demetrius' were the only conception of letters in antiquity:

> Demetrius clearly distinguishes letters from oration. As opposed to oration, letters should not: (a) imitate conversational style (226); (b) be too long or stilted in expression (228); (c) employ certain types of ornamental devices or arguments (229, 231,

232); (d) address certain topics (230). Hence, with regard to style, Demetrius clearly distinguishes letter writing from anything oratorical.

However, Demetrius is self-consciously concerned *only* with personal letters (*Eloc.* 230–32; cf. Stirewalt, 1993, p. 3 note 4). If one compares Paul's letters to the type of letter described in Demetrius' *On Style*, they are different in several ways. His letters are longer, averaging 2,500 words and ranging from 355 to 7,101 words when compared with the greatest letter writers in his day; Cicero's letters average 295 words, ranging from 22 to 2,530 words; and Seneca's letters average 955 words, ranging from 149 to 4,134 words (Achtemeier, 1990, p. 22). Paul's letters are, moreover, more complex and contain extensive argumentation through examples, elaborations, *enthymemes*, and *epicheiremes* (see Robbins, 1996a, pp. 56–57; Eriksson, 1999a, 1999b; Long, 2002, 2003, and Chapter 9 below). Furthermore, Paul's consistent use of direct address, questions, and occasional diatribe style suggests an oral style rather than a letter style such as Demetrius advocated (see esp. Loubser, 1995, p. 64).

Demetrius (*Eloc.* 234) distinguished the personal letter from the letters of Thucydides, Plato, and Aristotle (see *Eloc.* 225, 228, 234). The latter are official letters, letter-essays, or letters treating technical subjects which Demetrius (*Eloc.* 234) describes as more like a "treatise" (σύγγραμμα) than a letter. Ancient literary critics treated such letters "under the canons of oratory" (Goldstein, 1968, p. 99, cites Dion. Hal. *Thuc.* 42 and *Dem.* 23; cf. Dem. *Eloc.* 228, 234). Thus, Demetrius' *On Style* describes only one kind of letter, the personal letter, and his concern to distinguish it from these other types indicates that these other types were well known in his day.

However, if Paul's letters are not personal letters, then one is left with three choices: official correspondences, technical letters within a philosophical school, or letter-essays, which are a subset of the technical letter (Stirewalt, 1993, p. 18). It is difficult to classify the Pauline epistles as letter-essays because they address acute local circumstances rather than envision a "far extended setting" (Stirewalt, p. 18), with Romans being a possible exception (see Stirewalt, 1993, p. 18 note 55; and Aune, 1991). To decide between the official letter in a normative setting and the technical letters associated with philosophical schools in an extended setting is much more difficult. The former has more in its favor.

Concerning the technical letters, the letter collections of Plato, Isocrates, Aristotle, Epicurus, and the major philosophical schools incorporated rhetorical forms and were to be studied and "used for instruction, propaganda, and controversy" (Stirewalt, p. 17). Although White (1986, pp. 218–19) hesitates to view Paul's letters as philosophical, a fruitful avenue of research in Pauline studies recently is to understand Paul and his communities within this philosophical school context (e.g., Malherbe, 1989; Glad, 1995; cf. Costa, 2001, p. xv). Also, Paul's exhortative argumentation (e.g. 1 Thessalonians 4–5; 1 Corinthians 5–6) has an epitomic quality not unlike what one finds in Plutarch or the second century AD Stoic Hierocles (see Long, 2002).

More generally, however, Paul's letters function like official letters, especially 2 Corinthians. Although Paul broadens the addressees in 1.1 to include the entire region of Achaia (which suggests an extended setting), he speaks to a particular set of issues and problems in a normative setting calling the Corinthians to reform morally and to finish their collection project. The official letter was well suited for "the governance of communities" (Stirewalt, 1993, p. 10). Often involved were letter couriers, who would relay orally the mind of the official more directly to supplement the official letter (Stirewalt, p. 9). With the Corinthians, Paul did precisely this, sending Titus, Timothy, and others to carry his letters, relaying additional instructions and information (1 Cor. 4.17; 16.10–11; 2 Cor. 2.12–13; 7.6–16; 12.16–18). Finally, like the technical letter, the official letter was rhetorically conceived and addressed diverse venues. Stirewalt (p. 9) explains, "in dealing with the city state, the popular assembly, and public forensic activity, the official administrative, diplomatic letter was a rhetorical product." In Chapters 7–9 I shall attempt to marshal considerable evidence that Paul has composed an official apologetic letter.

6.2   Apologetic letters: forensic and demegoric

Ever since Betz's commentary on Galatians (1979), the question remains whether there was an established apologetic letter form in antiquity (see Hansen, 1989, pp. 25–27). Since Betz and Bernard Brinsmead (1982; see discussion in Long, 1999, pp. 160–61) failed to provide a rhetorical analysis of an ancient apologetic letter, the methodological move to analyze Paul's letters using Greco-Roman rhetorical theory has remained tenuous (although see Hughes, 1989, pp. 47–50; and M. Mitchell, 1991). Kern (1998, p. 33) argues "Despite assertions to the contrary, we still lack examples of the apologetic letter when understood as an epistle crafted around a classic oration." Betz (1972, p. 40) had earlier regretted the fact that little work had been done on ancient letters. My investigation of apologetic letters below will include a review of Demosthenes' apologetic letters, several analyses of apologetic letters written by Isocrates, Plato, and Demosthenes, and finally a consideration of forensic letters in the theoretical work *Epistolary Types* by Pseudo-Demetrius.

Demosthenes' apologetic letters

The work of Jonathan A. Goldstein, *The Letters of Demosthenes* (1968), which investigates the authenticity of the Demosthenean letter corpus, is paramount in this discussion. He aptly summarizes the character of the collection: "Whether the letters had a spurious origin as propaganda or as rhetorical fictions, the aim of the author would be to present a defense of Demosthenes' career, a simulated self-defense" (p. 97). Goldstein (p. 98) defines apology according to this criterion: "A work can be called an apology provided its content throughout aims at presenting a defense in answer to accusations against a certain person or group of persons or at overcoming or preventing opinions adverse to them."

In order to confirm the authenticity of Demosthenes' letters, Goldstein (pp. 31–34) considers three possible genres: apologetic demegoric letters, propaganda, and self-apology in a court setting.[1] He concludes that Demosthenes' letters are authentic apologetic demegoric letters that were addressed to the Athenian assembly; however, they are "open letters" for wider consumption (pp. 99–100). Goldstein (p. 98; cf. Sykutris, 1931, pp. 200–202) argues, "The use of the open letter is nothing unusual in self-apology. In fourth-century Athens the open letter, like the published oration, was a favorite vehicle for this and for other propagandistic purposes." Also notable is his observation that the implementation of forensic rhetorical features was instrumental in the formation of these literary genres. Concerning propaganda, Goldstein (p. 102) argues, "When, as often, Athenian brochures of polemical propaganda adopted one of the forms of public oratory, literary form followed real life, and the genus that was chosen was almost without exception the forensic genus." Goldstein (p. 117; cf. pp. 119, 124–25) continues: "Study of the avenues used by the Athenians to press their private and political antagonisms will show how even attacks on the reputation of dead men were deliberately put into the forensic arena and how purely propagandistic or rhetorical polemics inevitably chose the form of a speech to a court."

---

[1] Goldstein also proposes four alternative genres, if the letters are inauthentic: (1) rhetorical exercises; (2) part of a historical novel; (3) works by a rhetorical historian or biographer; (4) political propaganda pieces composed after his death similar to Plato's *Apology* and Isocrates' *Archidamus*. These possibilities are dismissed quickly because of their length and historical specificity, among other reasons.

According to epistolary conventions, Demosthenes' letters would have been classified, in distinction to personal letters (*litterae familiares*), as official letters (*litterae negotiales*) (Goldstein, p. 99). The fourth-century AD rhetorician Julius Victor makes this distinction, indicating that official letters are more weighty (*gravis*) and employ rhetorical precepts (*oratoria praecepta*) (Goldstein, p. 99 note 10). If Goldstein is correct about the authenticity of Demosthenes' apologetic demegoric letters, then we have the existence of apologetic literary letters in the fourth century BC. This is new literary territory (Goldstein, p. 127). This fact is one basis for arguing for the letters' authenticity, since the rhetorical schools and propagandists would have more likely written a fictitious court scene or a pure apologetic letter. For my discussion, it is significant that Demosthenes' letters were known and studied in the second century AD by Hermogenes and even earlier (Goldstein, pp. 211–57).

It is not strange that a demegoric speech made to the assembly could be apologetic. There were several conditions that might necessitate this: (1) "to come to the aid of the distressed, whether private individuals or city-states" (Anax. *Rhet. Alex.* 34 as cited in Goldstein, p. 101); (2) the report of an unsuccessful embassy; (3) the decision to entrust or to continue to entrust a military campaign to a general; or (4) the proposal to grant public honors to a person who was met with opposition (Goldstein, pp. 101–102). Orators delivered such speeches in the public assemblies utilizing forensic rhetorical techniques and strategies.

Before considering examples of demegoric and forensic apologetic literary letters, it is helpful to consider Goldstein's criteria for distinguishing between them. He (pp. 103–20) admits that it may be difficult because each genus could be used in different venues. For example, an address to the assembly is not decisive to determine a demegoric speech, since a forensic oration could on occasion be so delivered (Lys. 26). The distinctions between future–past and justice–expediency are also not decisive (pp. 103–104). Of the criteria developed, the most critical are noted by an asterisk. See Table 6.1.

On the basis of these criteria, Goldstein determined that Demosthenes' *Epistles* 2–4 are apologetic *demegoriae*. However, this conclusion does not diminish their apologetic import or purpose.

Analyses of several apologetic letters of Isocrates, Plato, and Demosthenes

Several official apologetic letters exist that are organized with a discernible disposition. The apologetic demegoric letters include Isocrates'

Table 6.1 *Differentiating apologetic demegoric and apologetic forensic speech*

Apologetic demegoric	Apologetic forensic
addressed to assembly	addressed to judges
concerned with expediency	concerned with justice
future orientation	past orientation
*dispersed narrative	*narrative relating to charges
*no charges or accusations formally recounted	*statement of accusations/charges
*laws or policy to be made	*violation of laws
proof by examples	proof by *enthymemes*
*public interest/motivation	*personal interest/motivation
*shorter, more modest speeches	*longer, more flamboyant speech
*restrained personal attack, no names given	*abusive personal attack

To the Rulers of the Mytilenaeans, Demosthenes' *Third* and *Fourth Letter*, and Plato's *Seventh Letter*. Possibly Demosthenes' *Second Letter* is apologetic demegoric; however, because Demosthenes mentioned charges against himself (2–3, 14), is concerned for his own self-interest (13–16), and denies any wrongdoing (16), I would argue that it is an apologetic forensic letter (*contra* Goldstein). Plato's *Third Letter* is self-consciously an apologetic forensic letter. Although some would question the authenticity of these letters (Longenecker, 1990, p. civ; Kern, 1998, pp. 32–33; cf. Hansen, 1989, p. 26), this does not limit their relevance in the present discussion, for they still demonstrate the merger of rhetoric and epistolography. A survey of these apologetic letters will confirm the precedent for apologetic literary letters.

First, let us consider Isocrates' *To the Rulers of the Mytilenaeans*, which was written to secure the restoration of Agenor, the music teacher of Isocrates' grandsons, after the overthrow of the democracy. This letter appeals to advantage (4), yet is structured as a defensive speech (see Table 6.2).

Isocrates was not in a courtroom, but presented his argument as if he were. His strategy was to make an appeal for Agenor by presenting a miniature *defense*. His language subtly indicated that justice was at stake. However, Isocrates was cognizant that the Mytilenaean rulers were not conducting a court case, so he must appeal to their benefit. The letter created its own venue in that it called the rulers to a decision independently of any formal court of hearing.

Table 6.2 *The disposition of Isocrates' letter* To the Rulers of the Mytilenaeans

---

   I *Proemium*: 1–2: A *captatio benevolentiae* is present; Isocrates' grandsons had a "hope"; concern for justice

  II *Narratio*: 3: The rulers' policy of restoration, pointing to their proper conduct

 III *Prothesis*: 4: The restoration of these individuals is to the rulers' advantage (συμφέρω)

 IV *Probatio*: 4–6: How Agenor will contribute to the city's great reputation for music

  V *Refutatio*: 7: "Someone [τις] may object" that they be allowed to return only if they are "justly" (δικαίως) entitled to return (Goldstein, p. 151, argues that this begins the epilogue)

 VI *Self-adulation*: 7–9: Isocrates' favorable contributions (7–8) and his association with people who are of good character, such as Agenor (9)

VII *Peroratio*: 10: Self-reflective; summary of letter

The infamous *Seventh Letter* of Plato (354 BC), addressed "to the friends and followers of Dion," exemplifies mixed rhetoric, having deliberative and apologetic characteristics and concerns. Goldstein (p. 126) argues that it is not written as a speech:

> It is possible that the *Antidosis* was a model and a stimulus for Plato's Ep. 7. However, unlike Isocrates, Plato did not feel obliged to write in one of the forms of public oratory. In the *Seventh Epistle* he does present a defense of his own career in the course of giving advice to the adherents of the late Dion, but the work is not written as an oration. A "symbouleutic" composition it may be, but it can hardly be said to be a *demegoria*, as Dionysius of Halicarnassus recognized.

Goldstein's opinion is based largely on the fact that the letter is "longer than any of Demosthenes's demegoriae" (p. 126 note 172). This criterion in itself may be faulty. Plato's manner of expression is simpler and plainer than Demosthenes' probably on account of his philosophy of rhetoric. The letter has a discernible disposition that is centered around the giving of advice. See Table 6.3.

Although the letter is political, many have noted its apologetic force. Glenn R. Morrow (1962, pp. 45–46; cf. Bluck, 1947, pp. 13–20) argues:

> the *Seventh Epistle* is more than a letter of political advice to Dion's party at Syracuse. It is clearly intended for a larger public

Table 6.3 *The disposition of Plato's* Seventh Letter

I *Proemium*: 324a–b: Plato was replying to a letter
II *Narratio*: 324b–330b: how Plato came to be involved with politics and Dion
III *Partitio*: 330c
A Why Plato returned to Syracuse a second time
B Plato will *first* offer advice for present circumstances
IV *Probatio*: 330d–351d (treating *partitio* in inverted fashion)
A 330d–337e: advice offered
B 337e–351e: second visit and its disastrous outcome
V *Digressio*: 340c–344c: self-proclaimed digression (344d) on *truth*
351a–d: praise of Dion's political aspirations
VI *Peroratio*: (352a): self-reflective, summary

than the persons to whom it is addressed, and is also clearly intended to serve as a defense of Plato's relations with Syracuse and of the political philosophy he held. This apologetic purpose is unmistakable, and at times it completely overshadows the professed aim of the letter. For this reason the letter has been looked upon with suspicion, either because of an alleged lack of unity resulting from the attempt to combine in one composition the two purposes of political advice and apology, or because it is felt that the apologetic purpose points to a later attempt by a disciple of Plato to clear the reputation of Plato and the academy.

Morrow's summary of the issue of the literary integrity of Plato's *Seventh Letter* is equally applicable to 2 Corinthians for the same reasons.

Plato's *Third Letter* (if genuine, 356 BC; see Morrow, pp. 88–100) is self-consciously an apologetic forensic letter, which Stirewalt (1993, p. 39) maintains is "built upon the pattern of *The Apology*" and hence likely forged. On the extended setting, Morrow (p. 89) argues,

Like the *Seventh*, this letter is a defense of Plato and is obviously intended for a larger audience than Dionysius, to whom it is addressed. The defense presented in the letter is a double one (316b). Plato, if he is the author, defends himself first against Dionysius' charge that he had discouraged the tyrant from liberalizing the government of Syracuse and resettling the Greek cities in Sicily – policies that were responsible for a great part of Dion's popular strength. Secondly, he is answering the charge, brought by Philistus and others (315e), that he was responsible

Table 6.4 *The disposition of Plato's* Third Letter

  I *Proemium*: 315a–c: Rebuke of Dionysius' position above the gods; a
    weighty beginning
 II *Narratio*: 315d–316a: Recounting rumors and how Plato is
    misrepresented
III *Partitio*: 316b
    A He had good reasons not to participate in Dionysius' politics
    B His advice didn't prevent Dionysius from his purposes of
      resettlement
 IV *Probatio*: 316c–319c
    A 316c–318e: issue of Plato's non-involvement
    B 319a–c: issue of settlement
  V *Peroratio*: 319d–e: Self-reflective, summary of letter, and a final appeal to
    justice (δίκη) and for Dionysius to stop lying and start speaking the truth
    (ἐκ τοῦ ψεύδους εἰς τὸν ἀληθῆν λόγον)

---

for Dionysius' political acts . . . These two charges are closely
related, both of them concerned with Plato's official position and
political aims at Syracuse.

Plato defends himself openly: "But as I just said, I don't need to be
further misrepresented, either to the people of Syracuse or to anyone else
whom these words of yours may influence; rather I need to be defended
[ἀπολογίας] against those earlier charges as well as against these graver
and more malicious ones that have since appeared. Since, then, I am
accused on two counts, I must make a two fold defense [τὰς ἀπολογίας]"
(316a6–b3 – trans. Morrow, 1962). Furthermore, the letter is carefully
arranged. See Table 6.4.

A lengthy *refutatio* and honorable deeds section is absent, although
the *narratio* conceivably serves as a *refutatio*, since various rumors and
lies are addressed. Furthermore, the beginning of the *peroratio* in 319d
contains features consistent with these two complementary sections: Plato
makes a direct appeal not to "slander" and create "lies" against him any
longer (319d) and also briefly states that his own policies were the "best"
ones to follow.

Finally, there are the epistolary speeches of Demosthenes. His *Second Letter* is in the spirit of Andocides' apologetic demegoric speech
On his Return. Demosthenes found himself in a similar situation, but
rather than delivering a speech, he wrote a speech in the form of a letter
entitled *Concerning his own Restoration*. The letter begins with an epistolary introduction: "Demosthenes to the Council and the Assembly sends

Table 6.5 *The disposition of Demosthenes'* Second Letter

I *Proemium*: 1–2: Issue of charges and stirring pity; justice is at stake for his acquittal
II *Narratio*: Incorporated in the *probatio*
III *Prothesis*: 3: Demosthenes has done no wrong
IV *Probatio*: 3–12: Positive arguments in his favor
    3–6: Demosthenes' involvement with foreign affairs was always upright
    7–8: He didn't give in to Philip's monetary offers
    9–11: He was an outstanding statesman
    12: He mentions other honorable deeds (= self-adulation section?)
V *Refutatio*: 13–20: He addresses potential objections
    13–16: He was not one of the friends of Harpalus; he has done no wrong
    17–20: He explains his departure from Athens
VI *Peroratio*: 21–25: Self-reflective; summary of his appeal for acquittal when they vote

greetings" (ΔΗΜΟΣΘΕΝΗΣ ΤΗΙ ΒΟΥΛΗΙ ΚΑΙ ΤΩΙ ΔΗΜΩΙ ΧΑΙΡΕΙΝ). Goldstein (p. 157) contends that "the argument of Ep. 2 is far simpler [than *Ep.* 3]. His case was now manageable enough for him to write a relatively straightforward composition which bears considerable resemblance to the ordinary forensic-epideictic genre of self-apology, doubtless repeating much of the defense which he had given at his trial." The letter has a discernible disposition. See Table 6.5.[2]

Although Goldstein argues that this letter is an apologetic *demegoria*, important considerations support its classification as a forensic epistolary apology. Demosthenes begins with the assertion that the charge brought against him by the "fatherland" was false (2). Throughout the letter he claims to have done no wrong (1.2; 3.2; 9.4; 16.3; 24.1) and calls "upon the gods and heroes to bear testimony" to this fact (16.4). He too, like Andocides, must recall his beneficial actions for the state (3–12), even at the risk of envy (4). In his current circumstances he experiences various troubles (13; 17.5; 25) and only wants relief from them (21). Thus, he hopes to persuade the officials to vote in his favor to secure his safe return (23), despite the efforts of his accusers (25). Thus, Demosthenes' *Second Letter* is more essentially a self-apology than are his *Third* and *Fourth Letters*, which are apologetic *demegoriae*. For a rhetorical analysis

---

[2] My analysis is similar to Goldstein's (p. 160; cf. p. 163), although he sees 3 as a *partitio*, not a *prothesis*. This presents problems in his analysis, as he must explain why one head is not treated. Because of this, Goldstein is not able to see how 13 is the beginning of refutative arguments.

of these remaining letters, see Goldstein (pp. 133–57, 173–76, 211–34, 247–51).

Apologetic letters in Pseudo-Demetrius' *Epistolary Types*

The epistolary theorist Pseudo-Demetrius in *Epistolary Types* treats apologetic letters. Although its dating is debatable, the first century BC is typically suggested (Stowers, 1986, p. 34; cf. Malherbe, 1988, p. 4). Raymond F. Collins (1996) has demonstrated Paul's familiarity with the epistolary tradition represented by Pseudo-Demetrius through his use of the technical term for letters of recommendation (or συστατικαὶ ἐπιστο-λαί) in 2 Cor. 3.1. So, an investigation of *Epistolary Types* may shed light on Paul's apology.

What relationship the twenty-one letter types described in *Epistolary Types* has with rhetorical theory is disputed. However, a close examination of the accusing/defending letters in Pseudo-Demetrius demonstrates that indeed there is a very close relationship. The description of the accusatory and defensive types (17 and 18) is given here in full using Malherbe's translation (1988). However, I have supplied a disposition analysis of the example letters. See Figure 6.1.

Pseudo-Demetrius constructed these examples in view of forensic rhetoric. Stanley K. Stowers (1986, p. 167), after reiterating that apologetic letters answer charges through argumentation and contain a narration, concludes "These features are suggested in Demetrius' model [apologetic] letter." After a survey of forensic rhetoric, more specific reasons can be offered. First, both letter descriptions use the characteristic formal designations for forensic speech types: "accusation" and "apology" (Stowers, 1986, p. 166). Second, both letter examples evidence a disposition that corresponds to a forensic speech. The *narratio* in both is begun with γάρ and in the apologetic letter the *narratio* is concerned to assert that nothing has happened, using γίνομαι, which is characteristic of a forensic *narratio* (see Chapter 5.2). Also the *peroratio* in both letters summarizes the argument. Third, in both examples the writer makes counter-accusations, which is an argumentative topic particularly relevant to forensic rhetoric (see Chapter 4.1 and 9.2). Fourth, in the apologetic letter technical argumentation is found. The letter purports to offer a demonstration (ἀπόδειξις). Also, a probability argument in the form of a conditional sentence is used: "if I had at any time spoken against other people to you, I would also have spoken against you to others."

The exact relation of Pseudo-Demetrius to the broader epistolographic tradition as described by Stirewalt (1993) is curious. White (1986,

Defensive letters

(17) The accusing type [κατηγορικός] is that which consists of an accusation of things that have been done beyond the bounds of propriety. For example:

prooemium: It was not pleasant for me to hear what was being said against me,

narratio: for [γάρ] it was at variance with my upright conduct.

prothesis: On the other hand, you, too, conducted yourself badly when you placed yourself in the hands of the man who was speaking against me, even though you knew him to be a slanderer and liar.

probatio: Speaking in general, you continue to cause (me) grief [λυπεῖς], for you have as friend someone whom you know to be an enemy of all men. Nor have you weighed [δοκιμάζω] this one fact, that the man who brings accusations against (absent) people while he is with you and others, is likely to do the same thing against you.

peroratio: Him, therefore [οὖν], I blame because he does this, but you (I blame) because, although you seem to be intelligent, you nevertheless have no discrimination with regard to the friends you keep.

(18) The apologetic type [ἀπολογητικὸς] is that which adduces, with proof [μετ' ἀποδείξεως], arguments which contradict charges that are being made [τὰ κατηγορούμενα]. For example:

prooemium: Fortune has served me well by preserving for me important facts to be used in the demonstration [πρὸς τὴν ἀπόδειξιν] of my case.

narratio: For [γὰρ] at the time that they say I did this, I had already sailed for Alexandria, so that I happened neither to see nor meet the person about whom I am accused. Since [δὲ] there has been no disagreement [μηδεμιᾶς γενομένης] between you and me, it is absurd for you to accuse someone who has wronged you in no way.

prothesis: But those who brought the accusation appear themselves to have perpetrated some foul deed,

Figure 6.1 The disposition of Pseudo-Demetrius' accusatory and defensive letters

probatio:	and, suspecting that I might write you something about them, they (took care) to slander me in anticipation. If you have believed their empty accusations, tell me. On the other hand, if you persevere with me as you should, you will learn everything when I arrive. In fact, one could be confident that, if I had at any time spoken against other people to you, I would also have spoken against you to others.
peroratio:	So [οὖν], wait for my arrival, and everything will be put to the proof, so that you may know how rightly [καλῶς] you have judged me to be your friend, and I may prove you by your actions. I dare say that those who accused us will rather attack each other and choke themselves [refutative remark].

Figure 6.1 (*cont.*)

pp. 202–203) argues that Pseudo Demetrius describes types of persuasion more suitable to the body of the letter than the opening or closing. Similarly, White contends that over half of the twenty-one types correspond to the literary letter tradition rather than the documentary one. Among those listed by White are the accusing and apologetic letters.[3] One concludes that the epistolary tradition represented by Pseudo-Demetrius has been shaped by Greco-Roman rhetorical theory and culture; specifically the accusing and apologetic types by forensic theory and practice.

This ends my treatment of apologetic letters. Whether written for the assembly or as open letters, such letters drew upon all the branches of rhetoric in their construction, most fundamentally forensic rhetoric. Goldstein's treatment of the ancient forms of apology and polemic is helpful to demonstrate this point. Goldstein (pp. 265–66) also argues that Demosthenes' apologetic letters were imitated by the author

[3] White indicates that, if one is "less technical in defining these styles," examples can be found in among the documentary letters (e.g., letter 18 is a good example of the apologetic letter). I have also found two letters of Pliny – a pleader in the second half of the first century AD – that playfully rely on forensic features: Pliny 9.19; 9.26. One in particular is Pliny's self-defense of his ornate style of oratory. Both have a disposition that includes an anticipation/*refutatio*. In 9.19 Pliny is a witness (*testis*) for his deceased client, for whom a defense (*defensio*) is offered by way of comparison. In 9.26 Pliny must give a reply to Lupercus for having judged (*arbitror*) his style to be tumid rather than sublime. As evidence to support his case, Pliny cites Homer and Demosthenes; he then anticipates and refutes Lupercus' criticism of Demosthenes drawn from Aeschines. There is also the self-consciously apologetic fictitious letter of Chion to Clearchus (16 – in Costa, 2001, pp. 118–23), which has a discernible disposition with a distributed *narratio* (1.6–11; 3.28–31; 5.43–52) and a pronounced self-adulation section (4.38–7.75).

Pseudo-Aeschines, who wrote corresponding accusatory and apologetic letters most likely as a school exercise or as propaganda. I concur with Goldstein that this tradition of apology is to be seen within the broader tradition of self-apology evidenced in Andocides' *On the Mysteries* and *On his Return*, the *Apologiae Socratis*, and Isocrates' *Antidosis*. Such works, particularly the latter two, were propagandistic.

6.3   Second Corinthians as a propagandistic apologetic letter

In conclusion I offer some general comments about 2 Corinthians in light of the discussions above on the apologetic letter tradition and ancient propaganda. Second Corinthians is not a personal, documentary letter, for reasons given above: its extended setting, length, extensive argumentation, and lively conversational style. Goldstein's work is helpful for surveying apologetic letters, both of a demegoric and of a purely forensic variety.

On the one hand, 2 Corinthians has features that suggest an apologetic demegoric letter, since it is addressed to the *assembly* (ἐκκλησία) of Corinthian Christians and contains exhortative material (2 Corinthians 6) and deliberative sections concerning the collection (2 Corinthians 8 and 9). On the other hand, Paul addresses charges (1.17), repeatedly denies wrongdoing (7.2; 12.17–18), stresses his good intentions (1.12; 2.17; 4.2; 13.8), explains his financial conduct (8.5, 20–21; 11.7–8; 12.14–18), admits culpability (13.7), but sarcastically asks for forgiveness (12.13). Paul's exhortation and directions about the collection serve his apologetic purpose by contributing to Paul's counter-charges. These and other matters are the focus of Chapters 7–9. Thus, 2 Corinthians is a genuine apology, not in part but in whole (*contra* Betz, 1972, esp. pp. 40–41; Stowers, 1986, p. 173). Paul was working within the well-established Greek tradition of self-apology.

Paul likely understood the propagandistic force 2 Corinthians would carry (on religious and philosophical propaganda see respectively Bowers, 1980; and Aune, 1991, pp. 106–11). It promoted his ministry and defended his right to the Corinthians' allegiance in the collection for the saints. Paul was educating the Corinthians; indeed, he was attempting to build them up (12:19; 13:10). It was an open letter, addressed also to the saints in Achaia (1:1). In this respect, Paul found himself in a situation not unlike Isocrates' when he was under scrutiny and wrote *Antidosis* in response. Isocrates explained the nature of *Antidosis* in 13 as he made the transition to the beginning of the mock trial defense:

I beg you now to listen to my defence [ἀναγιγνώσκετε τὴν ἀπολογίαν], which purports to have been written for a trial, but whose real purpose [βουλομένη] is to show the truth about myself [περὶ ἐμοῦ δηλῶσαι τὴν ἀλήθειαν], to make those who are ignorant about me know the sort of man that I am and those who are afflicted with envy suffer a still more painful attack of this malady; for a greater revenge upon them than this I could not hope to obtain.

But more specifically, *Antidosis* presents a justification of his method of rhetorical instruction and involvement in the legal environment against criticisms of corrupting youth and securing excessive wealth from trial cases (see esp. the *partitio* in 30–32). Thus *Antidosis*, in the form and setting of a forensic speech, was used to defend Isocrates against floating criticism and to promote his model of rhetoric and education. It was a classic piece of propaganda (Goldstein, 1968, pp. 125–26).

Isocrates was *misunderstood* by the Athenian populace. Paul was *scrutinized* by his Corinthian church (13.2–10), and they did not understand him completely (1.13–14; 5.12–13). Isocrates used the form of a defensive speech in *Antidosis* to defend his philosophy effectively and to promote it (see his own comments in 8). For Paul the opportunity had arisen to defend himself (12.19) and eulogize his own work or *to commend himself*, although he was forced to do so (11.16–12.11).

Paul understood the powerful precedence that had been set by the prominent philosophical and political figures Isocrates, Plato, and Demosthenes through published speeches and letters. Nearer to Paul's own day, Cicero published his own speeches as propaganda for circulation in Rome and Greece, which the general public was eager to read (Settle, 1962, pp. 12, 16, 46–54). In fact, Egyptian papyri contain numerous Ciceronian speeches with juxtalinear translations in Greek. The earliest fragment may date to 20 BC, although many date much later (Settle, p. 50). These precedents were testimony to the power of the well-argued and written word.

In the next three chapters, I hope to demonstrate how closely 2 Corinthians conforms to the forensic tradition of self-apology in terms of exigency (Chapter 7), disposition (Chapter 8), and invention (Chapter 9).

PART 2

A rhetorical analysis of 2 Corinthians as ancient apology

Thus far my analysis of forensic discourse indicates that there are several avenues to approach studying 2 Corinthians: exigency, invention, and disposition. The primary focus of Part 2 is to determine to what extent 2 Corinthians conforms to ancient apologetic practice. In other words, it attempts to answer the question: What forensic features are discernible and arguably present in 2 Corinthians? I maintain that the letter is primarily an apologetic work in form and function, despite the fact that it contains encomiastic and deliberative elements. Proof of this comes by way of the extensive analyses presented within the next three chapters.

Here I must remind the reader that this study is constructive in trying to understand 2 Corinthians viewed as a whole. My conclusion regarding the compositional integrity of 2 Corinthians arises from my study of the disposition, invention, and reconstructed exigency. In what order to present my findings is difficult to determine, since the inventive, dispositional, and situational elements are so closely intertwined. Should one begin with the conflict between Paul and his accusers, which eventually resulted in the construction of an epistolary speech? Or should we begin with the end product and the final arrangement of the discourse? These are represented in Figure 7.1.

Construction of discourse			
Paul, Corinthians, and circumstances →	Conflict of causes →	Invention of arguments →	Arrangement of discourse

Deconstruction of discourse			
Arrangement of discourse →	Invention of arguments →	Conflict of causes →	Paul, Corinthians, and circumstances

Figure 7.1 Construction and deconstruction of forensic discourses

My presentation is a compromise. I begin in Chapter 7 by investigating Paul's tumultuous relationship with the Corinthians, resulting in a rhetorical situation involving criticisms, slanders, and charges that necessitated an apology. Then I proceed in Chapter 8 to disposition and in Chapter 9 to invention. The reader should understand that Chapter 7 presupposes certain conclusions reached from my analysis of disposition and invention. Regarding the disposition of 2 Corinthians, my view may be presented summarily as follows:

1   *Prooemium*: 1.1–7
2   *Narratio*: 1.8–16 (distributed at 2.12–13 and 7.2–16)
3   *Divisio* and *partitio*: 1.17–24
4   *Probatio*: 2.1–9.15
5   *Refutatio*: 10.1–11.15
6   Self-adulation: 11.16–12.10
7   *Peroratio*: 12.11–13.10

Regarding invention, Paul treats as a primary criticism that he had failed to revisit Corinth; instead of visiting he wrote a chastising *letter of tears*, namely, 1 Corinthians.

7

THE RHETORICAL EXIGENCY
OF 2 CORINTHIANS

7.1 Introduction to the problem

At the beginning of the epistolary speech *To Dionysius* (2–3; cf. Isoc. *To Philip* 25), Isocrates reflects on the nature of speeches versus letters (for similar sentiments in Pseudo-Demetrius, see White, 1986, pp. 190–91):

> I know, to be sure, that when men essay to give advice, it is far preferable that they should come in person rather than send a letter, not only because it is easier to discuss the same matters face to face [παρὼν πρὸς παρόντα] than to give their views by letter, nor yet because all men give greater credence to the spoken rather than to the written word, since they listen to the former as to practical advice and to the latter as to an artistic composition; but also, in addition to these reasons, in personal converse, if anything that is said is either not understood or not believed, the one who is presenting the arguments, being present [παρὼν] can come to the rescue in either case; but when written missives are used and any such misconception arises, there is no one to correct it, for since the writer is not at hand [ἀπόντος], the defender is lacking.

Using letters could lead to misunderstandings. Paul was painfully aware of this potential (1 Cor. 4.17–19; cf. 5.1–5). He says in 2 Cor. 1.13–14a: "For we write nothing else to you than what you read and understand, and I hope you will understand until the end; just as you also partially did understand us" (NASB).

Of 2 Corinthians, Charles K. Barrett (1973, p. 6) has aptly said, "No one who has made a serious attempt to study the Corinthian situation is likely to feel convinced that he has a monopoly of truth." Barrett reminds us that any reconstruction is tentative. However, there are a number of helpful studies upon which to draw a plausible picture of Paul's predicament as seen in the Corinthian correspondence.

I begin with the observation that Paul was defending himself in 2 Corinthians, as is indicated by 12.19a: "All along you were thinking that we have been defending [ἀπολογούμεθα] ourselves to you" (*contra* McCant, 1999; see Chapter 1 and below). In 2 Corinthians Paul was accused with acting inconsistently by (1) saying that he will visit and then not doing so and writing instead and (2) being worldly, i.e. using worldly rhetoric and underhandedly pursuing financial gain when teaching against these things. Attached to these allegations are suspicions about Paul's motivations, especially respecting his integrity in the collection for the saints.

There is considerable continuity with the criticisms found in 1 Corinthians, where Paul was criticized in comparison with other missionaries (1 Cor. 4.1–5) and, not unrelatedly, with respect to his financial independence, for which he must offer an *apologia* (1 Cor. 9.3). Some Corinthians also criticized his delay in returning to Corinth (1 Cor. 4.18–19; cf. 16.1–10). Furthermore, Paul had instructed the Corinthians to judge certain matters for themselves (1 Cor. 6.1–8) and to approve (δοκιμάζω) persons to accompany him in the delivery of the collection (1 Cor. 16.3). These persons were to have *letters* (ἐπιστολαί) whether from Paul or more likely from the Corinthians. Paul was now subjected to these same requirements: He needed the Corinthians' approval (2 Cor. 13.3–7) and a letter of recommendation (2 Cor. 3.1). The setting of such allegations is analogous to the δοκιμασία trial process by which the Greek city-states would scrutinize their governing officials before entering into official capacities (see Chapter 3.2).

7.2   Formal designation and alleged wrongdoing

Pogoloff (1992) rightly argues that the rhetorical situation constrains the form of a given discourse. In 2 Cor. 12.19 Paul unambiguously indicates that his discourse has been understood by the Corinthians "all along" (πάλαι) as an apology (ἀπολογέομαι) (Young and Ford, 1987, pp. 27–28, 36–40). The initial position of πάλαι (or less likely πάλιν) indicates an emphasis of extent.[1] This implicates that the Corinthians' perception of the import of the letter as an apology encompasses the entire letter.

---

[1] Πάλαι is better supported with ℵ* A B F G *passim* than πάλιν with ℵ² D ψ *passim*. P46 adds an οὐ before πάλαι, thus converting the statement into a question expecting a positive response: "Haven't you understood that we have been defending ourselves to you?" If πάλιν is the original reading, then it may be that 2 Corinthians was understood as another apology in light of the apology offered in 1 Corinthians 9.

This statement in 12.19 occurs in the *peroratio* (see esp. Chapter 8.9). Its scope extends beyond chapters 10–13 (*contra* Betz, 1972) to include all of 2 Corinthians (cf. Barnett, 1997, p. 21, who understands 12.19 as referring to 1.3–2.13 in particular). Such a self-conscious and explicit use of ἀπολογέομαι (or its cognates) in the *peroratio* is typical in forensic discourse (for examples see Chapter 3.3 and 8.9).

What brought Paul into disrepute among the Corinthians so that he must eventually defend himself in 2 Corinthians? Many socio-historical and rhetorical studies have contributed to our understanding of these dynamics: e.g., those of Edwin A. Judge (1960; 1980; 1984), Gerd Theissen (1982), Ronald F. Hock (1980), Stowers (1984), Christopher Forbes (1986), Elisabeth Schüssler Fiorenza (1987), Peter Marshall (1987), Karl A. Plank (1987), Pogoloff (1992), Witherington (1995), and Winter (1997). Pogoloff (1992, pp. 129–72) more recently has argued the importance of rhetoric in this equation, as have Duane Litfin (1994) and Winter (1997). This satisfies Judge's call (1980, p. 215) "to identify the social conventions that marked out the battlefield" between Paul and the Corinthians. It also provides a *missing link* to Theissen's query (1982, pp. 54–57) about the nature of the Corinthian factions. Betz (1986, p. 40) recognizes the importance of "eloquence and knowledge" for understanding the Corinthian situation. He (pp. 32–34) sees the expression "word and knowledge" in 1 Cor. 1.5 as consciously developing Isocrates' and the later Cicero's (e.g., in *De Oratore*) notion of holding rhetoric and philosophy together.

The results of these studies may be initially summarized before further elaboration below. Within the Corinthian correspondence there are two basic criticisms surrounding Paul: social status and religious status. The first was affected by Paul's relatively poor rhetorical skills in vocal delivery (e.g., 1 Cor. 2.1–5; 2 Cor. 10.9–10), refusal to enter into certain patron/client relationships (1 Corinthians 9), and his lowly profession of tentmaking accompanied with humiliating circumstances such as hunger (e.g., 1 Cor. 4.8–16; 9.6–18). In particular, Paul's refusal to accept patronage from the Corinthians while receiving it from the Macedonians (see 2 Cor. 8.4–5; 11.7–9) was cause for enmity between Paul and the Corinthians. The second issue, exacerbated by Paul's refusal to receive financial support, concerned the authenticity of his apostleship (1 Corinthians 4 and 9) and his severe afflictions (2 Cor. 4.7–12; 6.3–5), sometimes at the hands of Jewish authorities (2 Cor. 11.23–25; cf. 6.5), which discredited his claim to have God's approval (see 1 Cor. 4.1, 9; 2 Cor. 1.21; 2.14; 3.5–6; 5.20; 10.13).

The backdrop to 1 Corinthians

To understand the initial shaping of these criticisms of Paul, a look at 1 Corinthians is necessary, particularly chapters 4 and 9. Young and Ford (1987, p. 47; see esp. their appendix pp. 55–57; cf. Theissen, 1982, pp. 44–53; and Litfin, 1994, pp. 151–59) rightly argue "1 Cor. 1–4 and 9 anticipate a remarkable number of themes picked up again in 2 Corinthians."

Some Corinthians were already scrutinizing Paul (1 Cor. 4.3–4; 9.3). In 1 Cor. 4.1–5 he was being examined by comparison with other missionaries, particularly Apollos (Pogoloff, 1992; Witherington, 1995, pp. 83–87). Paul states: "But with me it is a very small thing that I should be judged [ἀνακριθῶ] by you or by any human court. I do not even judge myself [ἐμαυτὸν ἀνακρίνω]" (1 Cor. 4.3). Paul warned them not to judge him prematurely, but to await the Lord's coming when the Lord will manifest (φανερώσει) the intentions of the heart (4.5; cf. 3.10–15). This scenario sheds significant light on Paul's use of φανερόω and derivatives at critical points in 2 Corinthians concerning his own conduct (2.14; 5.10–11; 11.6; cf. 3.3; 4.2, 10–11; 7.12). Obviously, Paul understood that the Corinthians could not wait until the Lord's evaluation; he needed to defend the character and intentions of his own work to them, if he was to have any participation with them in the collection.

At some level Paul had already presented a defense in 1 Corinthians 1–4. Marshall (1987, p. 217) correctly assesses the criticisms: "his lack of status and eloquence" (1.17; 2.1–4), "working for wages" (4.12), "his absence from Corinth" (4.18), "possibly his intimacy with certain of the Corinthians" (1.14, 16), and most critically "his refusal of financial assistance" (9.1–23) (cf. Dahl, 1977, pp. 40–61; Litfin, 1994, pp. 187–201; Winter, 1997, p. 12). Litfin (1994, pp. 151–55, 159–72) argues that these criticisms concern Paul's *modus operandi*, particularly his poor public speaking. Winter (1997, p. 202; cf. p. 181) only adds that, in addition to being an *apologia*, 1 Corinthians 1–4 contains a "censure of Christian admiration for rhetorical skill."

Pogoloff, Litfin, and Winter emphasize rhetoric and social status as key factors for understanding 1 Corinthians 1–4. Pogoloff (1992, p. 274) concludes that the rhetorical situation of 1 Corinthians involves "a narrative in which each of at least two competing groups of patrons and their clients boast that they have the wiser teacher." Pogoloff believes Paul to have been viewed, at least by some of the Corinthians, as a wise man. This particular point is questionable, as the analyses of Litfin (1994, pp. 160–73) and Winter (1997, pp. 179–202) would suggest. Nevertheless, Pogoloff correctly demonstrates the social standing that one could achieve by attaching oneself to another "wise in speech." Pogoloff's narrative reconstruction is quite understandable in view of our knowledge of the second sophistic movement and its emphasis on showy display and appearance (see Judge, 1960, pp. 125–26; Winter, 1993a, pp. 63–64; on outward appearances, see Stowers, 1984, pp. 74–75; on the relationship to ancient παιδεία, see Litfin, 1994, p. 170, and Winter, 1997, pp. 182–84). Witherington (1995, p. 47) rightly argues, "It appears that the Corinthians felt they had the right to judge Paul and his message and were evaluating him by the same criteria by which popular orators and teachers were judged." Paul rejected the association of his gospel presentation with such social conventions (1 Cor. 1.17; 2.1, 4, 13; 1 Thess. 2.1–12; see also Winter, 1993a; and Litfin, 1994, pp. 174–209).

However true it is that rhetoric was an issue in Corinth, we cannot ignore the fact that Paul was criticized also for his refusal of monetary gifts, his lowly manual labor, and his weakness in terms of his appearance, sickness, maltreatment by others, and public scorn (see Hock, 1980). Aristotle (*Rhet.* 2.6.13) maintained that shame comes from sufferings, which lead to "ignominy and reproach." Hock (1980, p. 60) argues: "In the social world of a city like Corinth, Paul would have been a weak figure, without power, prestige, and privilege." Thus, in 1 Cor. 4.6–21 Paul rejects the notion that the Corinthians were independent from him, who had suffered much for their sake (4.8).

His various afflictions and weakness caused serious doubts about Paul and the power of the Spirit in him (Plank, 1987, pp. 20–23). Plank (p. 23) rightly argues, "Assessed by the canons of human power his claim to authority has no backing and collapses with the admission of weakness . . . The criticism of Paul's weakness challenges his authority and thereby urges his apology." A critical canon of power was rhetorical presence. However, Paul's absence from Corinth necessitated that he send rhetorically sophisticated and forceful letters to reestablish his rightful presence in the community (e.g., 1 Cor. 5.1–5).

Additionally, that Paul was subjected to persecution and beatings was an indication of his inferiority. Forbes' (1986, p. 19) assessment of Paul's lists of sufferings in 1 Cor. 4.8–15 and elsewhere is helpful: "It is hardly likely to have inspired confidence in Paul's position, among the status-conscious leaders of the Corinthian church. 'Labours' is of course an entirely respectable topic, but imprisonments and beatings by both the Jewish and Roman authorities, not to mention stonings, are hardly calculated to inspire confidence in the respectability of anyone's position."

To counter such *hybristic criticism*, Paul carefully distributes his spiritual credentials throughout 1 Corinthians (1.17; 2.6–16; 3.9–10; 4.1–21;

12.1–3; 14.20–21, 36–38) and clearly presents his authority in Christ (1.10, 17; 2.2, 16; 4.1, 15; 9.12; 11.1; 15.8–11; 16.24). Particularly, to address the criticism of 4.8, Paul applies sarcasm and appeals to his paternity. In 1 Cor. 4.10 he argues sarcastically, "We are fools for the sake of Christ, but you are wise in Christ. We are weak, but you are strong. You are held in honor, but we in disrepute" (see Marshall, 1987, pp. 181–218; cf. Pogoloff, 1992, p. 224; and Plank, 1987, pp. 34–69, 92). Additionally, Paul insists that he was the *pater familias* (4.14–15) – one who has greatest authority, despite a lowly social status – and they should thus imitate him (4.16). Forbes (1986, p. 14; cf. Marshall, 1987, pp. 249–51) argues that, when faced with status and authority issues in Corinth through offers of patronage, Paul adopted the model of the father–child relationship (1 Cor. 4.14–16; 2 Cor. 6.11–13; 11.2; 12.14–15) and the ambassadorial relationship where Paul represents God (2 Cor. 5.20). We should note that Paul adopts the role of affectionate father, while at the same time offering moral exhortation, in the context of his sufferings related to his work and finances. This indicates that the Corinthians found Paul's failure to receive their gifts to be a rejection of mutual affection and love and their patronage (see Hock, 1980, p. 63; Witherington, 1995, p. 467 note 6). The role of father would also speak to Paul's position as wise teacher, since the language of fatherhood was also a metaphor for the philosopher–pupil relationship (Quint. *Inst.* 2.2.4–5; Peterson, 1998, p. 101 note 145).

In 1 Corinthians 9, Paul again addressed those who were examining him (τοῖς ἐμὲ ἀνακρίνουσιν) (9.3; cf. 4.3), unless this is a fictitious (Martin, 1995, pp. 77–80) or parodic apology (McCant, 1999, p. 26). However, there is ample evidence that Paul was scrutinized, as 1 Corinthians 4 clearly indicates. This issue in 1 Corinthians 9 is that some rejected Paul's initial labor in Corinth. He asks rhetorically in 9.1, "Are you not my work in the Lord?" Paul asserts that he is their apostle (9.2). The matter centered on Paul's financial independence from the Corinthians in order not to have "an obstacle in the way of the gospel of Christ" (9.12). He has rejected an important feature of patronage: remuneration for providing teaching services (Hock, 1980; Witherington, 1995, pp. 21–24, 418–19). This rejection was "quite a severe snub in Greek social terms" (Forbes, 1986, p. 14). Enmity resulted: Some rejected Paul as a legitimate apostle (Marshall, 1987; Theissen, 1982, pp. 40–54; Hock, 1980, pp. 50, 59–62). Furthermore, Hock (1978) has argued that Paul deliberately chose to support himself as a tentmaker, demeaning as this was. Winter (1997, pp. 162–70) argues that it was self-consciously an anti-sophistic measure on Paul's part. Thus, Paul's lowly means of income – a low-status marker – was a further point of humiliation to some of the Corinthians.

Thus, 1 Corinthians reveals that Paul is being examined in relation to (1) other leaders or missionaries respecting his *modus operandi*, particularly his poor oratorical abilities, (2) his lowly status as is indicated by his afflictions and servile occupation, (3) his financial independence, which amounted to his refusal to receive patronage from the Corinthians, and (4) his absence from Corinth. To meet these criticisms Paul constructed a sophisticated rhetorical piece in 1 Corinthians (M. Mitchell, 1991; Witherington, 1995; Eriksson, 1998; *contra* Winter, 1997, p. 201). It included an apologetic section (1 Corinthians 9) within a complete argumentative unit (1 Cor. 8.1–11.1; see Watson, 1989; and Smit, 1996) and other distinct rhetorical units and argumentation such as 1 Corinthians 12–14 (see Smit, 1993) and 1 Corinthians 15 (Watson, 1993; and Eriksson, 1999a).

Concerning 1 Corinthians, Witherington (1995, p. 45) argues, "Rhetoric gave Paul a means to relate to and impress his Corinthian audience." This rhetorical letter, however, made Paul liable to criticism. Winter (1997, p. 201) is right to argue that, if had Paul constructed 1 Corinthians *rhetorically*, he would have been liable to the charge of using that which he condemned. This is, in fact, the case, and explains why Paul must defend his use of persuasion in 2 Cor. 5.11. Some adjudged 1 Corinthians as "weighty and strong" (2 Cor. 10.10), which indicates not only that Paul had rhetorical training, but that he could evidence it when needed (Judge, 1968, p. 37; Winter, 1997, pp. 207–208, 215–26). Thus, Paul might have characterized one of his purposes in writing 1 Corinthians this way: "I wrote you with some rhetorical polish in order that your zeal towards me would be renewed" (cf. 2 Cor. 7.12).[2]

That the Corinthians already audited Paul such that he needed to write 1 Corinthians as he did raises several questions. What is at stake is a proper understanding of the developments between 1 and 2 Corinthians. Is there any continuity between these letters? Or was Paul's defense in 2 Corinthians a distinct development? The relationship between 1 and 2 Corinthians has been greatly obscured because of the historical reconstructions involving an intermediate visit and the letters of tears (see Witherington, 1995, 346–47; and Savage, 1996). A careful investigation of 2 Corinthians in terms of exigency (below) and invention (Chapter 9) would suggest that there was not an intermediate visit (none is recorded in Acts) and that 1 Corinthians is the letter of tears (so Hyldahl, 1973).

---

[2] I have mimicked Pogoloff's (1992, p. 280) manner of summary in his conclusion when he has Paul say of 1 Corinthians, "The problems aroused by my rhetoric I hope I have put right with yet more rhetoric."

Discovering the charges in 2 Corinthians

What were the specific accusations and charges behind 2 Corinthians? We have only one side of the case: Paul's defense. How closely his line of defense matched the actual charges and allegations will perhaps never be known. Young and Ford (1987, p. 55) are correct to conclude "that there is much we cannot know definitely about the occasion of 2 Corinthians, but that the thrust of Paul's argument is clear, provided that we take the text as a unity, and understand its genre as that of an apologetic letter." I shall first review recent reconstructions of the charges by Young and Ford (1987) and Witherington (1995) before offering my proposal.

Despite Young's and Ford's caution about reconstructing the charges, they argue that Paul is liable to criticism in terms of his worldliness, spiritual credentials, financial matters and patronage, and eloquence (pp. 50–53; cf. Savage, 1996, pp. 12, 54–99; and Lane 1982, p. 18). They place Paul's failure to visit under the charge of worldliness, since Paul must argue (so they contend) that he follows God's will, "even if that means not being a good business man and keeping to his schedules" (p. 18). These serious criticisms warranted a serious answer from Paul.

Witherington (1995), working with 2.17 as the *propositio*, argues that the basic charge is that Paul is no apostle, since he refused patronage. Furthermore, Paul was thought guilty of preparing "secretly to bilk the Corinthians of money through his appeal for the collection for the poor Christians of Jerusalem" (p. 371). Rather than an apostle, Paul is a "dishonest schemer" who is to be contrasted with some who accept patronage and have letters of recommendation. Witherington (p. 348) is content with Barrett's list of criticisms against Paul, minus the charge of anti-nomianism: "The charges of being an illegitimate apostle, of lacking the signs of an *apostolos* in his presence and actions, and of dishonesty are, nonetheless, highly probable, and one may add that charge that Paul was no rhetor." This is no slight addition, since each of Paul's three central argument movements in the *probatio* (see Chapter 8.6) begins with an account of Paul's manner of rhetoric (2.17; 4.2, 5; 5.11).

Although the particular charge of defrauding the Corinthians of money through pilfering from the collection is well stated and correct according to my analysis, I find weaknesses with Witherington's overall understanding of the charges. First, to view Paul's apostleship as the main issue may be justifiable (so also Theissen, 1982, p. 54; cf. pp. 40–42, 51–53, 58; Barrett, 1973, p. 30; for chapters 10–13 see Betz, 1972), but this is too general to be of much help for understanding the complex exigency. The term *apostle* in 2 Corinthians is scarce and is used mainly with respect to the *false apostles*.[3] Paul had already defended his status as apostle among the Corinthians in 1 Cor. 4.9; 9.1–5; 15.8–10. In 2 Corinthians, however, Paul's particular conduct was suspect, making him liable to accusations. Thus, we need to understand exactly what the problems were.

A second weakness with Witherington's proposal is that Paul did not make his lack of accepting patronage from the Corinthians a focal argument in 2 Corinthians. Instead, he addressed it in the *refutatio*, as one of several criticisms and in relation to the insinuation of robbery (11.7–9; cf. 8.5 and 12.16–18 in the *peroratio* in terms of financial trickery). Once again, Paul had already answered why he did not accept patronage in 1 Corinthians 9. Some concern persisted (see 2 Cor. 11.7–9; 12.13; but note the intense sarcasm!), especially in the form of suspicions surrounding the collection. However, Paul's refusal of Corinthian patronage was not central to his defense in 2 Corinthians. Finally, Witherington (p. 360; cf. 339–43) does not stress enough the critical charge that Paul had failed to visit the Corinthians when he intended. This theme dominates the opening and closing of the letter (2 Cor. 1.15–17; 2.1–3; cf. 12.14, 20–21; 13.1, 10). This failure should not be listed among "less crucial charges" of "his sternness in the painful letter . . . and his supposed lack of love and concern for the Corinthians" (p. 360). Overall, Witherington's analysis suffers from being too general, carrying over *too directly* the issues of Paul's apostleship and patronage from 1 Corinthians, and not taking seriously the matter of Paul's delayed travel plans. This is partly the result of taking 2.17 as the *propositio*, rather than identifying the *divisio* and *partitio* in 1.17–24. (See my further critique in Chapter 8.5.)

The charges in 2 Corinthians

Within 2 Corinthians, Paul addresses two interrelated charges of inconsistency. Here one must look at the *divisio* in 1.17, where the initial charges are found (Windisch, 1924, p. 64; Malherbe, 1983, pp. 167–68; cf. Bultmann, 1985, p. 39). That 1.17 is the *divisio* introducing the *partitio* is given support by the fact that these charges are reiterated and given more flare in the opening of the *refutatio* in 10.1–11 (see Malherbe, 1983, pp. 167–68 and Chapter 8.7).

---

[3] The word ἀπόστολος is found in reference to Paul only in 1.1. One possible exception is 12.12; but here Paul is talking about the general credentials of an apostle. The term is used of Paul's co-workers (8.23) and the super-apostles (11.5, 13; 12.11). One could argue that Paul's silence on the matter is golden; this really is the underlying charge against him. It seems more likely that he was being charged with specific failures, which, if justified, would prove him to be a phony.

First and foremost, Paul failed to visit the Corinthians (1.17; cf. 2.1–2). In this regard, Paul was considered to have acted lightly (τῇ ἐλαφρίᾳ). Does this charge indicate that the Corinthians judged Paul was trying to avoid a difficult circumstance? In other words, some Corinthians thought that Paul was trying to make things easier for himself. He narrates, however, that by writing rather than visiting he made things eas-ier for the Corinthians (2.1–2) while matters remained dire for himself (1.8–11). This may partially account for Paul's exposé of his afflictions in 2 Corinthians (4.7–10; 6.3–10; 11.23–33). Second, Paul's intentions were worldly (κατὰ σάρκα) (Young and Ford, 1987, p. 18; cf. 10.3–4; 1 Cor. 4.5).

The first charge, failing to visit, appears to have been the catalyst for much of Paul's problem in Corinth. It gained momentum when Paul sent a letter – 1 Corinthians – that chastised the Corinthians on several matters (2 Cor. 2.3–4, 9; 7.8, 12). Paul may have been perceived as pushing the boundaries of propriety, particularly by issuing a grave judgment during the church meeting by evoking his presence while the letter was being read aloud (1 Cor. 5.1–5). The opening remarks of the *refutatio* would confirm this. Some were accusing Paul of writing "weighty" letters while being absent (ἄπων), i.e. instead of "visiting" (10.1, 9–11). In this context we must note that Paul is defending his authority *precisely regarding the Corinthians' morality* (10.5–8; cf. 6.14–7.1; 12.20), just as in 1 Corinthians 4–5.

For an orator to moralize too much in Paul's day was ill advised (Dio Chrys. *Alex.*; *Rhet. Her.* 4.25). Dio Chrysostom (*Alex.* 18–20) argued that philosophers were lacking who would do the work of firm rebuke and correction. Patrick Sinclair (1993, p. 562) explains the nature of this boundary for oratory as seen by the author of *Rhetorica ad Herennium* in relation to the construction of *sententiae* (moral maxims): "He is more concerned with admonishing his reader not to appear to overstep the bounds of social propriety by seeming to dictate morality." When it was necessary to formulate maxims, it was done by drawing upon "generally accepted and objectified statements of Roman morality, especially the laws, rather than being original formulations of his own personal code of moral beliefs" (p. 562). It is noteworthy that Paul's uses of *senten-tiae* in 2 Corinthians are often scripture citations or of a general nature (see Chapter 9.4).

Addressing the charge of failing to visit (and writing instead) is a unifying theme for Paul's defense in 2 Corinthians (1.12–17; 2.1–11; 7.2–16; 10.1, 9–11; 12.20–13.10). Witherington (1995, p. 340) recog-nizes this: "Throughout 2 Corinthians Paul returns again and again to his travel plans." In fact, Paul must admit in 13.7 that he appears to be unapproved (ἀδόκιμος) because he failed to visit (see Chapter 8.9). That such a criticism would necessitate a prolonged *apologia* is not unfounded. Already in 1 Corinthians Paul was aware that some have become arrogant thinking that he was not coming to Corinth (1 Cor. 4.18–21; cf. 11.34; 16.1–12). This criticism required Paul to promise to stay longer when he finally would arrive (1 Cor. 16.5–7; see Marshall, 1987, p. 178). Some Corinthians might easily question whether he truly esteemed them or *worse, whether he had ulterior motives.*

The second charge was that Paul had worldly intentions (1.17b). This is likewise found re-articulated in the opening of the *refutatio* (10.2; Theissen, 1982, pp. 45, 47). Some think that Paul is walking *according to the flesh* (κατὰ σάρκα). Interpreters struggle with the meaning of this expression (see Barrett, 1973, pp. 249–50). Is this a charge of being unspiritual? Or, does it imply that Paul uses worldly methods, such as coercion (1.23) and persuasion (5.11)? Does it imply that Paul is concerned with worldly things, i.e. monetary gain (12.16–18)? A consideration of Paul's use of disposition and argumentation in the next two chapters indicates that he was charged with being *worldly* particularly in respect to rhetoric and monetary gain. Consequently, some questioned Paul's spiritual validity. Paul's afflictions and weaknesses generally would also make people pause when evaluating his spiritual status. The two interrelated dimensions of the charge of worldliness – coercive rhetorical persuasion and pursuit of monetary gain underhandedly – deserve individual treatment.

The charge of using worldly rhetoric

The *narratio* in 2 Cor. 1.8–16 is constructed to address each aspect of the charge of worldliness and his failure to visit (see Chapter 8.4). Paul was accused of being worldly because he used rhetoric in a manipulative and evasive manner (1.12–13), which is reiterated in the *refutatio* at 10.4–6, 9–11. Throughout 2 Corinthians repeated references support this contention (1.12, 17; 2.17; 4.2, 7; 10.3–4; cf. Litfin, 1994, pp. 155–59, 210–12). The Corinthians believed that Paul had used *worldly rhetoric* even while he was speaking so vehemently against it in 1 Corinthians (1.17, 22; 2.1–5, 13). This criticism is indicated first in the *narratio* at 2 Cor. 1.12: "we have behaved in the world with frankness and godly sincerity, not by earthly wisdom [οὐκ ἐν σοφίᾳ σαρκικῇ] but by the grace of God – and all the more toward you." The expression σοφία σαρκική refers to sophistic rhetorical methods that Paul denounced in 1 Cor. 1.17; 2.1, 4, 13 (Pogoloff, 1992, p. 144; cf. Furnish, 1984, p. 128).

The *divisio* of 2 Corinthians at 1.17b also indicates that Paul was accused of using worldly rhetoric: Paul says *yes* and then *no*. This was the standard criticism against those trained in rhetoric. Pogoloff (1992, pp. 144–45) explains: "Such vacillation was a part of the rhetorical training, since such education taught students how to argue any side of a question. This lack of commitment to a particular point of view was often admitted by rhetoricians as a necessary weakness of rhetorical art, and was criticized by philosophers who called for a rhetoric committed to truth alone."

In the *probatio* Paul denied any rhetorical manipulation or motivation with monetary gain attached to it (2.17; 4.2, 5). In view of 2.17 and 4.2 Betz (1986, p. 40) wonders, "Did anyone suspect Paul of being such a sophist and fraud? Paul's words do not give away whether he responds to a direct suspicion, but his strong and somewhat nervous self-defense does not make sense unless there actually was such an accusation." Betz is absolutely correct. What is crippling Betz's observations is his commitment to partition theories, since he understands 2.17 and 4.2 only within the confines of the "first apology" (2.14–6.13; 7.2–4). Thus, Betz is unable to appreciate the significance of 1.12, 17 and 10.9–11 as components of a more complete picture. From 10.9–11 we learn that some were criticizing Paul's letters (including 1 Corinthians) as being "weighty and strong" while his stage presence and λόγος were weak. Concerning 10.9–11 within the so-called *letter of tears* (2 Corinthians 10–13 in Betz's reconstruction), Betz (1986, p. 42; cf. p. 44) argues:

> How did Paul go about defending himself? The challenge was extraordinary, and Paul was aware of it. It was again one of rhetoric: Paul's defense could only be made by the written letter and therefore had to take into account the disadvantages of being absent and having his authority discredited from a distance. His own eloquence, confined to the letter, had to be such that it could prevail over the rhetoric of his opponents which had obviously gained the upper hand. This challenge explains why the letter of tears is, from a literary perspective, such a brilliant piece of text.

In order to separate 1.12 and 17 from chapters 10–13, Betz must devalue their significance. Betz (p. 45) argues that Paul's point about his own fickleness about his plans to visit in 1.17 is "only a minor one in the whole debate about Paul's handling of the word." Furthermore, Paul's denial of using worldly wisdom (σοφία σαρκική) in 1.12 "seems no longer a matter of contention." Betz must pass over the narrative-argumentative value of

1.12 and the importance of 1.17 as the *divisio* in order to ameliorate these verses to correspond to "the letter of reconciliation" (comprising 2 Cor. 1.1–2.13; 7.5–16; 13.11–13 according to Betz).

Paul provides a more substantial answer in 5.11–7.1 to the criticism that he was using worldly rhetoric. Paul persuades people (πείθω), but he was motivated to do so by the "fear of the Lord" (5.11; cf. 1 Cor. 2.4). Furthermore, Paul denied any status seeking associated with this (5.12). What was important for him was the goal of his persuasion: reconciliation between God and the Corinthians (5.19–20; 6.14–7.1) and between him and the Corinthians (6.13; 7.2–4). Paul's persuasion was justifiable, so he pleaded, because it was applied to honorable, God-directed ends, i.e. "the fear of the Lord/God" (5.11; 7.1). It is not the same kind of rhetoric or persuasive speech that he denigrated in 1 Corinthians (1.17; 2.1, 4, 13). The one seeks reconciliation, the other prestige and increased social status.

The charge of financial trickery

Finally, Paul was judged worldly in his pursuit of financial gain. This was a common charge against first-century sophists (Winter, 1997, pp. 28, 49, 95–97, 163–65, 218). In the *refutatio* he denies "robbing churches" (11.8). This may be hyperbolic; however, there appears to have been actual suspicion that Paul was taking "a cut" from the Macedonians' contribution to the collection for the saints (see 8.5; 12.15–18; cf. Malherbe, 1989, p. 115; Savage, 1996, p. 88). Paul describes his dealings with the collection in 2 Corinthians 8 and 9 in such a way that no one could find fault (μωμάομαι) with him (8.20). In 8.5 Paul describes in what manner the Macedonians contributed to the collection: "first they gave themselves to the Lord and to us by the will of God." Reading between the lines, one infers that the Macedonians gave abundantly (8.4) first to the collection, as they had planned, and then, "by God's will," to meet Paul's personal needs. The qualifying phrase, "by God's will" is absolutely critical. Hock (1980, p. 64; 1978, p. 561) argues that the Macedonian gift to Paul was simply to compensate for what he could not earn from his tentmaking. Paul did not manipulate them to give to him; nor did he do it underhandedly by taking a portion from what they contributed to the collection.

Certainly when the Corinthians learned that Paul had received money, possibly by trickery using others (9.5; 12.16–18) (sophists collecting fees through emissaries was not uncommon; Winter, 1997, pp. 218–19) or even committing robbery (11.8), they must have been particularly disturbed, since Paul emphatically argued that he offered his gospel free of charge

(1 Cor. 9.15, 18). Many interpreters favor this scenario. Winter (1997, p. 219) argues,

> The conduct of his financial affairs in 1 Corinthians 9 may have sounded admirable given Paul's lofty theory of a self-supporting apostolic ministry, but there were some who insisted that it did not bear close scrutiny (2 Cor. 12.14–18). Perhaps, they seem to have suggested, some of the money was really not destined for the poor in Jerusalem. This was despite the care Paul took to avoid giving the wrong impression.

Paul, of course, denied such charges emphatically: "We cheated no one" (2 Cor. 7.2; cf. 12.15–18). Dale B. Martin (1995, p. 84) has already suggested a similar situation:

> It may also have been the case that some Corinthians had found out that although Paul told them he refused money from his churches (1 Cor. 9), he had actually been receiving money from other churches, probably even while staying in Corinth (Phil. 4.15–16; 2 Cor. 11.8). We have no way of knowing if Paul was intentionally deceiving the Corinthians on this score, but some of them, not surprisingly, took his actions and words as deceptive. In 2 Corinthians 12:16, for example, he seems to echo Corinthian insinuations that he has taken advantage of them "by guile." In 2:17–18 [*sic*; 12.17–18] he insists that his statements to them have *not* been vacillating or deceptive, implying that some at Corinth have claimed that they were. At any rate, Paul's financial relationship with these Corinthians has caused problems. Those problems obviously relate to status issues, and Paul's insistence that he merely wanted to avoid burdening the Corinthians cannot be the whole story.

I am assured that Paul was not deceiving them in 1 Corinthians; he indicated quite plainly that he wanted no obstacle (ἐγκοπή) to his gospel (1 Cor. 9.12 – see Marshall, 1987, pp. 218–58). Theissen (1982, p. 51) is correct to argue, "What obstacle he has in mind is evident in 1 Thess. 2:5: Paul wants to avoid the suspicion that he works under the cloak of greed (ἐν προφάσει πλεονεξίας) or 'peddles' the gospel as do others (2 Cor. 2:17; cf. 9:5). That is why he works day and night (1 Thess. 2:9)."

As it turned out, at least for a time, Paul's decision not to accept patronage caused problems. Timothy B. Savage (1996, p. 88) argues:

In a society where wealth was a sign of status Paul's insistence on remaining poor would naturally offend his converts. Worst of all, it would force them to bear the ignominy of being associated with an impoverished apostle. Paul deepens the wound by entertaining minor gifts from other churches (2 Corinthians 11:9). Not surprisingly, the Corinthians feel inferior and lash out at their apostle – he is acting unjustly (12:13) and without love (11:11; 12:15b).

Thus, William S. Kurz's evaluation (1996, p. 61 note 32) in light of the patronage question in Corinth is apt: "Paul's eagerness for the completion of the collection (2 Cor. 8–9) complicates this situation. It could appear that he was trying to gain their support without obligating himself to them as their client (see 12:16 and 11:5–15)."

In 2 Corinthians Paul answers the charge about his handling of financial matters. Was he tricking them (πλεονεκτέω) by sending others to Corinth (12.16–18; cf. 7.2)? Certainly not. Paul devotes two chapters to explain the circumstances and approved personnel as "safeguards" for carrying out the collection (Young and Ford, 1987, pp. 22–23). He was sure to add that he had handled the affairs of the collection with the utmost integrity (8.20–21).

Thus, I would maintain that Paul faced two related charges. The first concerned his failure to visit, which was exacerbated when he wrote a rhetorically sophisticated and weighty letter, the letter of tears – 1 Corinthians – calling the Corinthians to obedience and allegiance to himself while at the same time rejecting the mores of sophistic rhetoric. The second charge was that Paul had worldly ambitions. This had two facets: Paul used worldly rhetoric and sought illicit wealth. What allowed these charges to fester was the fact that Paul was absent from Corinth for some time (Litfin, 1994, p. 170). Marshall (1987, p. 276) rightly summarizes: "The hybrists appear to have been successful in persuading the Corinthians that Paul was not to be trusted. He had refused their gifts while accepting them from others. He had behaved inconsistently in a number of matters; most recently, in the many changes that he had made to his travel plans."

Since Paul faced these serious charges, his spiritual credentials were also suspect. Is Paul spiritually legitimate? Is he approved by God or not? Does he belong to Christ? To make matters worse, Paul was weak physically because of his ailments; socially because of his tentmaking; and religiously because of his poor reputation and correction at the hand of the leaders of the synagogue. Paul did not evidence spiritual power in his physical life, especially when being reprimanded by the Jewish and Roman authorities. These "consequential criticisms," although secondary, were detrimental. Thus, an apologetic reply was necessary.

Paul explicitly restates such concerns as criticisms against himself in the *refutatio* (10.1–11.15), even though they have been answered throughout 2 Corinthians. (What distinguishes these criticisms from the charges is that Paul must answer the charges in his *probatio* formally.) First, some accuse Paul of not belonging to Christ (10.7). However, Paul is established in Christ (1.21), forgives in Christ (2.10), preaches Christ (2.12; cf. 2.14, 17; 10.14), and is the aroma of Christ (2.15). He is a minister of the new covenant of Christ and the Spirit (3.2–18). Second, Paul may appear "weak" (10.10; 11.21); however, his afflictions are not to discredit him. God mercifully consoles and delivers Paul (1.3–4; 1.10). Although he bears God's glory in his frail body, a body subjected to various afflictions including worldly punishments (4.7–12; 6.4–10; 11.23–29), he *along with the Corinthians* has received the Spirit that anticipates a future glory (1.22; 5.5). Furthermore, his sufferings are a participation in Christ's sufferings (1.5; cf. 4.10–11; cf. Thrall, 1994, pp. 108–10). Despite Paul's afflictions and any accompanying misunderstandings (6.8–10), he is God's servant persuading the Corinthians to salvation (6.1–7.1). The most significant affirmation of Paul in view of his weakness and suffering comes from the Lord himself: "My grace is sufficient for you, for power is made perfect in weakness" (12.9). This divine *logion* is arguably the climax of the letter.

In view of these criticisms and the two charges expounded above, two further conclusions can be drawn. First, it seems likely that Paul was being subjected to the same criticisms that he made of the Corinthians in 1 Corinthians. Winter (1997, p. 203) has already delineated a likely scenario to account for such a thing taking place. After Paul's critique of sophistic criteria in 1 Corinthians and Apollos' refusal to return to Corinth (1 Cor. 16.12), the angered Corinthians recruited itinerant teachers with similar training in rhetoric. On arrival, these teachers evaluated Paul's letter, 1 Corinthians, and in a defensive posture they mounted a major attack on Paul's weakness, his poor oratorical display. Such criticisms are found in 2 Corinthians.

Thus, in the course of 1 Corinthians Paul chastised them as being fleshly and not spiritual: "And, brothers, I was not able to speak to you as spiritual people, but rather as fleshly people [ὡς σαρκίνοις], as infants in Christ" (1 Cor. 3.1; cf. 3.3). In return some of the Corinthians were counter-charging Paul with conducting himself according to the flesh (see Young and Ford, 1987, p. 50). Similarly, Paul was considered ἀδόκιμος ("unapproved") by some, as is suggested by 2 Corinthians 13.3, 5–7. This criticism probably originated with Paul's own criticism of the Corinthians in 1 Cor. 11.19. Paul argued there that the factions during the assembly of the church were necessary to determine who were approved (δόκιμοι). Furthermore, Paul asked that the Corinthians approve of some (δοκιμάζω) to go along with him in the delivery of the collection (1 Cor. 16.3). Paul likely was accused of being unapproved in his handling of monies; he was thus unapproved for the collection.

It would seem, then, on both counts, that Paul was subjected to his own criticisms. To turn an accusation against its originator is an effective forensic *topos*. For example, among Aristotle's formal argumentative *topoi* it is treated sixth (*Rhet.* 2.23). The tactic of counter-accusation was common. For example, in Antiphon's *First Tetralogy* the defense contends that the prosecution is, in fact, in the wrong. Also, Cicero in *Pro Ligario* accuses the prosecution, who, he argues, was equally or more guilty than the defendant of the same crime. With such a maneuver, some of the Corinthians showed evidence of their own rhetorical education and savvy (see Marshall, 1987, p. 384; cf. Witherington, 1995, pp. 45–47; and Peterson, 1998, p. 61; *contra* Savage, 1996, pp. 20 note 8, 71–72).

The second conclusion to be drawn is that the Corinthian accusers have charged Paul with inconsistency on at least three counts: rhetorical expression, financial support, and his failed itinerary (for others from 1 Corinthians 1–4, see Winter, 1997, pp. 219–20). Such a tactic is another effective forensic *topos*. For example, Aristotle's formal argumentative *topos* number 22 concerns conflicting facts or actions (*Rhet.* 2.23; cf. Cic. *Top.* 8–25 and *Part. Or.* 2.7).

In the first case, he used the *worldly wisdom* of persuasive speech as 1 Corinthians demonstrated to them, *despite his disclaimers to the contrary in that same letter* (1 Cor. 1.17; 2.1, 4, 13). Winter (1997, pp. 207–208; cf. pp. 212–13, 220) argues:

> Did Paul's detractors say, "He might well argue that in his coming to, and conduct in, Corinth he is anti-sophist (1 Cor. 2.1–5) but look at the letters he has written"? Clearly some in the church suspect Paul of operating in a secular fashion (κατὰ σάρκα περιπατούμενος, 2 Cor. 10.2–3), and now level against him the very charge he had voiced against them in 1 Corinthians 3.3, namely, κατὰ ἄνθρωπον περιπατούμενοι. Could Paul defend himself if, having forcefully denounced the use of rhetorical devices in preaching, his own letters betrayed their use? Did his letters conform to the very tradition which he had proscribed for the Corinthians in 1 Corinthians?

Winter's answer is *no* to these latter questions, since he correctly observes (p. 201), "if he had [constructed 1 Corinthians rhetorically], he would have exposed himself to the charge of engaging in what he condemns, given his critique of the sophistic movement and his parody of the rhetorical form in 4.6ff." But, in fact, M. Mitchell's work on 1 Corinthians (1991), not to mention others, has demonstrated that the letter is rhetorically masterful. Thus, Winter's supposition and conclusion are confirmed by the evidence of 2 Corinthians. Winter fails to treat 2 Corinthians as a whole (see pp. 228–30). As a result he does not understand that Paul was answering this very charge in the letter (1.12, 17; 2.17; 4.2; 5.11).

Likewise Forbes (1986, pp. 2, 15; cf. Marshall, 1987, pp. 251–57; Peterson, 1998, pp. 63–64) understands Paul to be under criticism for being inconsistent, but in terms of being a flatterer (κόλαξ). Forbes perceives these criticisms at 2 Cor. 1.17–24 and 4.1–2 with Paul's response to them in 2 Cor. 1.12, 5.11–12, 6.11–12, 7.2–3, and 10.1, 10–11. Paul answers the inconsistency of rhetorical display in 2 Cor. 1.12, 5.11–12, and 10.10–11.

A second inconsistency is that Paul received money from his churches (the Macedonians – 2 Cor. 11.7–9), *which contradicted, so it would seem, Paul's emphatic statements in 1 Cor. 9.15, 18 that he offers his gospel free of charge.* A third inconsistency involved Paul's changed travel plans. Witherington (1995, pp. 340–41; Malherbe, 1983, pp. 167–68) rightly states: "Apparently Paul's opponents were accusing him of saying one thing and doing another in regard to his planned visits, thus proving in their eyes that he was not a true apostle." Thus, the Corinthians found Paul inconsistent in the methods and manner of his ministry with respect to rhetorical expression, financial support, and his failed itinerary.

We can imagine that Paul's accusers attached certain motives to their charges. One facet of rhetorical invention is to consider what motivates someone to commit a crime (Arist. *Rhet.* 1.10–14). Paul's failure to visit could have been construed as motivated by fear of confrontation (cf. 2 Cor. 10.10; 12.20–21). Likewise, Paul's worldliness could be motivated by manipulation, effrontery, and greed. It is greed that could conceivably unite all these together (cf. 2 Cor. 12.13–18).

Already we have noted how the two charges are given answer throughout 2 Corinthians (cf. Danker, 1991, pp. 271–73). However, one can also detect how Paul addressed very pointedly such related motivations. He does not act lightly (τῇ ἐλαφρίᾳ ἐχρησάμην) (1.17a), but acts with boldness (πολλῇ παρρησίᾳ χρώμεθα), unlike Moses (3.12–13), and with authority (χρήσωμαι κατὰ τὴν ἐξουσίαν) (13.10). He knows the "fear of the Lord" (τòν φóβον τοῦ κυρίου), and this is the basis of his persuasion (5.11; cf. 7.1). He is not status-seeking, but commends himself so that the Corinthians can answer those who "boast in outward appearances" (5.12). He is not motivated by money (2.17), nor does he operate by deception (4.2) or trickery (7.2; 12.16–19). Instead, he conducts his ministry openly before God and all (4.2; 5.11; 8.21) and in conformity to the truth (4.2; 5.11; 6.7; 7.14; 11.10; 12.6; 13.8). Furthermore, he works for the good with the collection (1.24b; 8.20–21). Finally, Paul denies any coercion (1.24) or control over the Corinthians (4.5), especially with respect to the collection (9.5, 7). In these and other ways, as are discussed in the following chapters, Paul makes his defense.

Who critiques Paul?

But, who was responsible for generating these criticisms and allegations, and how did Paul learn about them? My analysis above indicates that some of the Corinthians were themselves responsible for the charges and criticisms (so also Savage, 1996, pp. 10–11). However, the situation that eventually *allowed* for Paul to be scrutinized by them was the arrival of other missionaries, perhaps initially Apollos. First Corinthians addressed this initial criticism by calling the Corinthians to unity (1.10; M. Mitchell, 1991) and by attempting to reestablish Paul's authority base within the community (e.g., 1 Cor. 4.1–5, 14, 16–21; 5.1–5; 14.37–38; 15.8–11; cf. Young and Ford, 1987, pp. 47–48). Probably different Jewish-Christian missionaries arrived after Paul's letter (1 Corinthians) was initially well received, so that Paul once again fell into disrepute.

Within the confines of the present work, it is prudent to remain "agnostic" as to the identity of Paul's Jewish-Christian missionary rivals (Young and Ford, 1987, pp. 47–53; Savage, 1996, pp. 3–12). In whatever manner we may conceive of these rhetorical rivals, the strategies of such a group would have been modified after the Jerusalem council and in view of the esteem of sophistic rhetoric in Corinth (Forbes, 1986, pp. 14–15; Witherington, 1995, pp. 346–49; Winter, 1997, pp. 220–21, 235; cf. Barrett, 1973, pp. 6–7, 29–30). As I shall expound in more detail below, it is likely that these missionary rivals received the written endorsement of the Corinthians to take their portion of the collection back to Jerusalem (cf. 1 Cor. 16.3; 2 Cor. 3.1). This would have irritated Paul to no end, providing another reason for writing 2 Corinthians to address the critical matter of the collection in 2 Corinthians 8–9, and to lambaste these meddling missionary rivals in 2 Corinthians 10–11.

Tentative reconstruction of Corinthian correspondences and Paul's travels

We do not know the extent of Paul's knowledge of the developing Corinthian situation. However, by working primarily with evidence in 2 Corinthians supplemented with travel details in 1 Corinthians, I can present the following as a plausible scenario.

In 2 Corinthians Titus gave a report to Paul, one rather favorable (7.6–16). Titus had been in Corinth for some reason, very possibly to deliver 1 Corinthians (cf. Barrett, 1973, pp. 5–11; and R. Collins, 1996, p. 42 note 17). One could speculate that Timothy was responsible for bringing the bad news back to Paul (Kümmel, 1975, p. 210, cited by Barrett, 1973, p. 17), since he was sent to Corinth (1 Cor. 4.17) to arrive after 1 Corinthians was received (1 Cor. 16.10). This would explain why Timothy also co-authored 2 Corinthians with Paul (2 Cor. 1.1). Furnish (1984, pp. 103–104) contends that Timothy is simply co-sender and not co-author. However, if the situation is as I have envisioned it, then Timothy's contribution to the letter would be instrumental for Paul to make a successful defense, since he was the bearer of the deteriorating situation in Corinth (cf. Lane, 1982, pp. 13–15). It may indicate that Timothy and Silas along with Paul were under scrutiny (2 Cor. 1.18–19 – *contra* Furnish, 1984, pp. 103–104).

If 1 Corinthians is the so-called *letter of tears* (2 Cor. 2.4) possibly delivered by Titus and initially causing grief and godly repentance (2 Cor. 7.6–16), it is possible that the effects of this letter turned sour only after Titus had left. Titus probably did not tarry in Corinth, since he would have been eager to report back to Paul, who himself was eagerly awaiting Titus' report (2 Cor. 2.12–13; 7.6). After Titus left, the situation deteriorated, perhaps because of new missionary intruders. Then Timothy arrived, as planned according to 1 Cor. 4.17; 16.10 (Furnish, 1984, pp. 104–105). After catching criticism particularly because he was to remind them of Paul's ways (1 Cor. 4.17), Timothy would have retreated, returning to Paul at a prearranged location in Macedonia.

Paul in the meantime had found Titus in Macedonia and received the initial good news of the Corinthians' favorable response to his letter (2 Cor. 7.6–16). Then quickly and eagerly Paul sent Titus back to Corinth with some brethren in order to prepare for the collection (2 Cor. 8.6, 16–19, 22, 24; 9.5; 12.16–18) and Paul's imminent arrival with Macedonian brethren (2 Cor. 9.3–4; 12.20–21; 13.1–2, 10). Timothy arrived in Macedonia with the bad news only after Titus and the brethren had left. He reported to Paul that some of the Corinthians remained critical of Paul and his co-workers, Silas and himself (2 Cor. 1.19). Paul thought it best to send a defense before arriving himself, lest what he was hoping to avoid – a grievous visit (cf. 2 Cor. 2.1) – would result. This apology is none other than 2 Corinthians. This would indicate that less than a year elapsed between the writing of 1 and 2 Corinthians (cf. Witherington, 1995, pp. 346–47, who holds to more than a year to allow for an intermediate visit and the lost letter of tears). In my estimation, this scenario best accounts for the narrative details available in both Corinthian letters when taken as unified compositions.

7.3   Court setting

Young and Ford (1987, p. 27) are certainly right when they argue that "the law-court metaphor pervades his dealings with the Corinthians, and while he purports to be disinterested in their judgement in view of the final judgement of God, clearly he is anxious to convince them as well." Witherington (1995, p. 47; cf. Betz, 1972, p. 14; and, Litfin, 1994, p. 153) argues that 2 Corinthians is Paul's reply to the Corinthians' self-appointed right to judge him: "Paul disputed this right, especially in 2 Corinthians, and sought to make clear *that he was answerable only to God*" (italics mine). I find the latter notion extremely problematic for this simple reason: For Paul to have continued relations with the Corinthians, he must convince them that they do not understand him fully (2 Cor. 1.12–14) and that he has not wronged them in any way (7.2; 12.13; 13.1–7). A real apology was required.

In what legal or quasi-legal venue was 2 Corinthians received? There are several possibilities, if 1 and 2 Corinthians are considered jointly. First, some Corinthians were apparently self-appointed *judges* over Paul and other leaders (1 Cor. 1.11–13; 3.3–23; 4.1–5; 9.3). This was due in part to sophistic influence, where disciples vigorously rallied around their respective teachers. Furthermore, Witherington (1995, p. 47) argues that "most relished the opportunity to be judge and jury, like the crowds in the Roman arena passing final judgment over whether a combatant deserved to live or die. In a culture where public reputation was of great importance, a crowd could make or break the career of an orator." Second Corinthians could enter under this venue, since Paul addresses *some* in the *refutatio*, presumably his accusers (10.2, 7; cf. 3.1; 8.20; 11.16), who are also critical of his rhetorical abilities (10.9–11; 11.6). Betz (1986, p. 41) rightly observes regarding the criticism in 10.10: "The statement looks like a summary from an evaluation report about Paul's performance as an apostle, especially his facilities with the word."

Furthermore, the Corinthians doubted Paul's approval (δόκιμος) as Christ's representative (2 Cor. 13.3, 6–7). In 1 Cor. 16.3 Paul directs the Corinthians to approve (δοκιμάζω) of some to accompany him with the collection to Jerusalem. No details of the approval process are provided. However, in 2 Corinthians Paul was scrutinized over financial matters (11.7–9), especially pertaining to the collection (12.16–18). The Corinthians were scrutinizing leaders in a way analogous to the δοκιμασία trials (see Chapter 3.2).

Second, a quasi-legal setting is found in 1 Cor. 5.3–5. Paul pronounced a judgment against *the immoral one*, but even more upon the assembled congregation (see G. Harris, 1991).

Third, Paul exhorted the Corinthians to judge matters among themselves in 1 Cor. 6.1–8 (on types of dispute settlement, see Derrett, 1991; on social status and court cases, see Pogoloff, 1992, pp. 200–201; and, Winter, 1991a). Paul hoped for some form of internal arbitration. Alan C. Mitchell (1986, pp. 208–209) concludes, "We believe Paul's answer to the problem of litigation among Corinthian Christians was to propose the option of private arbitration available to them under Roman law." One Christian leader was daring (τολμάω – 6.1) to bring another one to court out of personal enmity arising from allegiances to missionaries, such as Paul (Winter, 1991a, pp. 567–68). This was done, Winter (1991a, p. 568) argues, "because of the established nexus between the various branches of oratory, i.e., declamation and forensic oratory, at the highest level of παιδεία and therefore in the life of secular Corinth." In 2 Cor. 10.2 Paul threatens *to be daring* (τολμάω) against those accusing him of worldly living. Is he deliberately recalling 1 Cor. 6.1–8, so that his letter should be seen in such a court setting?

Fourth, we might ask whether Paul's letter created its own venue. Is the court under which Paul submits his case *merely a divine one*, as Witherington (1995, p. 47) argues? The evidence does not support this conclusion. Although Paul makes appeals to God's favorable opinion of himself to bolster his case (e.g., 2 Cor. 1.3–4, 10, 23; 2.17; 3.5; 4.2, 6; 5.18; 12.9), Paul expects the Corinthians to render a decision about him (1.17; 3.1; 5.12; 10.1–11; 12.13, 15–19; 13.3, 6–7). Paul argues, "Since God views me favorably, so should you!" He wronged no one (7.2) and asked to be forgiven one wrong in particular (12.13).

Considering these options, Paul's apologetic letter likely created its own venue, much like the apologetic demegoric letters surveyed in Chapter 6.3. Additionally, Paul sent 2 Corinthians into a situation of scrutiny, in order to answer the charges and criticisms of some Corinthians. These Corinthians would be the prosecution; Paul and Timothy the defense; and the remaining saints in Corinth and in Achaia would be the jury (1.1) (cf. Andrews, 1995, pp. 275–76).

Importantly, Paul's inclusion of Achaia as the recipients is not a redactional addition (*contra* Windisch, 1924, p. 288) or secondary (*contra* Furnish, 1984, p. 106), for Paul's handling the collection with integrity certainly involved them (9.2; cf. 11.10). Margaret E. Thrall (1994, p. 85) rightly argues that "Paul's comprehensive form of address [to include Achaia] might be intended to ensure that all these other people should have the opportunity of hearing his response to the Corinthians' apparent misunderstanding – if not actual criticism – of the character of his ministry."

A more specific court setting may be in mind: the scrutiny of officials. Mario M. DiCicco (1995, pp. 245–46) argues that 2 Corinthians has significant parallels

> to the *scrutinium* or δοκιμασία in the Greek political system whereby public officials were required to submit to an examination before taking office to determine their worthiness. They had to be approved by an examining body before assuming their duties. Likewise they had to undergo an examination (εὔθυνα) at the end of their term to determine their conduct while in office.

DiCicco (p. 246) maintains that Paul sought for approval on the basis of his visions and miracles (12.1–12). However, Paul's statements in 13.2–3 would rather indicate that his approval (δοκιμή) is based upon his firm moral handling of the Corinthians.

Whether or not this *dokimasia* setting can account for Paul's use of the language of approval in 13.1–7 (δόκιμος, δοκιμάζω, and δοκιμή) is still open for consideration. We have scant evidence of the continuation of such trials, which is not surprising, since the Roman system of government supplanted the traditional functions of the Greek city-states. Nevertheless, it is not inconceivable that the importance of such language outlived and transcended its original setting in some sense (see Philo *In Flac.* 130; *Virt.* 68; and *Spec. Leg.* 157).

In 1 Corinthians Paul used the terms δόκιμος, δοκιμάζω, and δοκιμή in reference to the evaluation of leadership. The Corinthians were evaluating various leaders (1.11–14; 3.3–23), even Paul himself (4.3). To stop such factitious evaluations Paul argued that each leader's work would be tested (δοκιμάζω) at a later time, judgment day (3.13; cf. 4.5). Furthermore, Paul argued in 11.19 that the factions within the Corinthians are necessary, so that the truly approved (δόκιμοι) may become manifest (φανεροί). Indeed, it is necessary for each of the Corinthians to test himself or herself (δοκιμαζέτω) before partaking of the Lord's Supper (11.28). Finally, Paul admonishes the Corinthians to approve of some (οὓς ἐὰν δοκιμάσητε) to go along with him in the delivery of the collection (16.3). These approved persons were to have *letters of recommendation*, presumably from the Corinthians (δι' ἐπιστολῶν) (see R. Collins, 1996, pp. 41–42).

Is this possibly why Paul is under scrutiny in 2 Cor. 13.1–7, because he has been suspected of mishandling money, especially the collection (8.5, 20–21; 11.8; 12.16–18)? Is this why Paul must object to the notion that he needed letters of recommendation to or *from* the Corinthians (3.1)? Indeed, this would resolve the puzzle of Paul having letters *from* the Corinthians (see Thrall, 1994, pp. 220–21).

When one considers Paul's use of δοκιμάζω and related forms in 2 Corinthians 8–9, these suggestions are intriguing. The Macedonians, when under the test of affliction (ἐν πολλῇ δοκιμῇ θλίψεως), were able to give abundantly (8.2). In 8.7–8 Paul wants the Corinthians to contribute to the collection; he is *testing* (δοκιμάζων) their love by the diligence of others, that is, the Macedonians. To assist in the offering, Paul sends along with Titus a brother whom Paul *has often approved* (ἐδοκιμάσαμεν ἐν πολλοῖς πολλάκις) (8.22). Finally, the Corinthians give glory to God by their *approval* of the ministry of the collection (διὰ τῆς δοκιμῆς τῆς διακονίας ταύτης) (9.13).

There are two occurrences of this word family where the correlation with the collection is debatable. In 2.9 Paul argued that he sent the letter of tears (1 Corinthians) in order that he might know their character (δοκιμή) in terms of obedience. In 10.18 Paul contended that "it is not those who commend themselves that are approved [δόκιμος], but those whom the Lord commends." Both of these references may, however, be understood in light of the collection. Second Corinthians 2.9 indicates that the Corinthians' obedience is a part of their approval; but Paul understands their complete obedience to involve their contribution to the collection (9.13). His point in 10.18 is generalized (cf. 10.17), so that it may be applicable to various aspects of Paul's ministry, including his participation in the collection.

It is reasonable to conclude that Paul was facing a scrutiny trial, brought upon him by charges of inconsistency and extortion respecting the collection. The Corinthians were unwilling to support Paul in the collection and had, instead, approved of his rival missionaries, who were to take their portion of the collection. Very likely, Paul became victim of his own accusations. He had argued that some of the Corinthians were unapproved (1 Cor. 11.19); yet some could argue that Paul had proved himself unapproved by his inconsistent intentions and suspicious fiscal policies.

Little would Paul have expected that the scrutiny process he encouraged in 1 Cor. 16.3 *would result in his own scrutiny*, thus requiring the apology of 2 Corinthians.

It would be procedurally inadequate for Paul to argue that *only God's court is what matters*, true as this is in an ultimate sense (cf. 1 Cor. 4.4). No, Paul was required to defend himself for all of Achaia to see. Throughout 2 Corinthians, Paul repeatedly stressed that what he did was manifest to all people (1.12; 4.2; 5.11; 8.20–21; 11.6; cf. 4.10–11; 5.10). God knows him; but the Corinthians, too, needed to know him completely (1.13) and in their consciences (5.11). If the Corinthians failed in their knowledge, then they risked being found unapproved by God by failing to support Paul's position in the collection.

7.4   Conclusion

A consideration of the rhetorical exigency leads us to a number of significant conclusions and intriguing possibilities. Paul was the recipient of serious accusations. These accusations relate to criticisms that he had issued earlier against the Corinthians: He himself is worldly and unapproved. Additionally, Paul was liable to the charge of inconsistency on three counts: (1) his denial of sophistic rhetoric, yet forceful use of rhetoric in 1 Corinthians; (2) his failure to visit when he said he would; and (3) his financial duplicity, receiving money from Macedonians and possibly even pilfering from the Macedonian portion of the collection for the saints, after denying patronage from the Corinthians. Paul's role in the collection came under particular scrutiny. Simultaneously, his missionary rivals won the Corinthians' approval to take their portion to the Jerusalem church. Paul was now lacking a letter of recommendation from the Corinthians.

Paul's absence precipitated charges and criticisms against him. His opponents within and rivals from without capitalized on this situation. To malign another in his or her absence was a common and effective strategy. Pseudo-Demetrius' accusatory letter (17) indicates that this scenario was common; a friend is displaced by another who belittles him in his absence. This strategy was also a political tactic. Something similar happened to Dinarchus when in his absence he (and the council's report) was discredited concerning the Harpalus Affair (324 BC) (Din. 1.53).

This raises the question, however, of why Paul did not return to Corinth to squelch his opposition. First, Paul supplies his own reasons: He had a fruitful ministry in Asia Minor (1 Cor. 16.9) and he sent a letter (1 Corinthians; with Titus) and Timothy to convey his personal presence (1 Cor. 5.1–5) and to represent him (1 Cor. 4.17; 16.10; 2 Cor. 7.5–16).

Second, J. Duncan M. Derrett (1991, p. 23; cf. Witherington, 1995, p. 340–41) argues: "Paul adopted the policy of 'wait and see.' If his work was successful, in spite of interference from rival missionaries, such difficulties might not arise. He rated his 'begetting' of his converts very highly." Additionally, Paul desired not to make a grievous visit (2 Cor. 2.1–3); he delayed coming to avoid a confrontation with a community in which he had initially spent eighteen months and left on such favorable terms. He did this to *spare them* (2 Cor. 1.23; 13.2). Thus, given his fruitful ministry in Asia, Paul decided to wait and avoid direct confrontation, and sent letters and representatives instead.

However, Paul's strategies backfired. Counter-accusations were made and gained ascendancy; if unanswered, they would discredit Paul as God's minister of the collection. Thus, a situation developed analogous to the scrutiny trials of public officials in the Greek city-states. Paul's official status as overseer of the collection was questioned. Although a venue of evaluating missionaries generally (or Paul specifically) already existed (1 Cor. 4.1–5), Paul's apology in 2 Corinthians created its own venue to address the charges and floating criticisms leveled against him. How Paul organized his apology (Chapter 8) and developed a line of defense and suitable types of arguments (Chapter 9) are the subjects of the next two chapters.

8

THE RHETORICAL DISPOSITION OF 2 CORINTHIANS

8.1   Introduction

The arrangement of 2 Corinthians according to the sections of a forensic speech is evidence for the letter's unity. The sudden shifts and changes in tone are best explained by Paul's deliberate arrangement according to the tradition of ancient apology. He was following well-trodden forensic paths to win a favorable verdict. The criticisms and charges against Paul were serious and injurious to his collection efforts. Thus, he provided the Corinthians with a recognizably apt apology, but one that would fortify their obedience (12.19–13.1).

8.2   Discernible disposition

Practitioners of forensic rhetoric arranged speeches into sections to ensure maximum impact in presentation. Second Corinthians exhibits the following arrangement:

I Epistolary opening (1.1–2)
II *Prooemium* (1.3–7): Assurance of hope expressed. Also, three critical themes are introduced: affliction/suffering and comfort, the mutuality between Paul and Corinthians, and abundance.
III *Narratio* (1.8–16) with disclosure statement (1.8) and also distributed (2.12–13 and 7.2–16):
 A 1.8–11 (*pathos*)
  1 verses 8–10, "deadly peril" versus God's deliverance; "the sentence of death"
  2 verse 11, Corinthian financial assistance anticipated in the collection
 B 1.12 (*ethos*) Paul has acted in holiness and sincerity; he is not worldly. This concern is found throughout the letter (2.17; 4.2; 5.16; 6.7–10; 7.2; 8.20–21; 12.16–17).
 C 1.13–16 (*logos*)

       1 1.13–14 Corinthians' complete knowledge of Paul; the letter's general goal is to clarify *who Paul is* when absent and present.

       2 1.15–16 Paul's plans to visit both on his way to Macedonia and then from Macedonia before going to Jerusalem with the entire collection

IV   *Divisio* and *partitio* (1.17–24) (outlines the entire *probatio*):

    A 1.17 Did Paul make his plans to come to Corinth lightly?

    B 1.18–20 The affirmation of the preaching of Paul *et al.* and the glory of God in Christ

    C 1.21–22 Paul *et al.* are established with the Corinthians; they, too, are sealed by God and receive the deposit of the Holy Spirit.

    D 1.23 God is a covenantal witness for Paul; he has a good reason for not coming, namely, to spare the Corinthians in view of their moral failings.

    E 1.24 Paul doesn't lord over their faith; he is a co-worker for their joy in the collection.

V   *Probatio* (2.1–9.15):

    A 2.1–11 Paul explains why he didn't visit the Corinthians, i.e. disciplinary problems.

       Narrative transition: 2.12–13 Paul's brief account of his travels and search for Titus

    B 2.14–3.18 God's triumph in Christ, the giving of the Spirit through the preaching of Christ by Paul *et al.* and the greater glory of the new covenant in Christ

    C 4.1–5.10 Paul's and his associates' ministry of suffering in the life of the Spirit

    D 5.11–7.1 God's reconciliation and Paul's covenantal exhortation to end idolatrous behavior

       Narrative transition: 7.2–16 Finding Titus and their joint confidence in the Corinthians

    E 8.1–9.15 Paul's work: the collection and the Corinthians' faith

VI   *Refutatio* (10.1–11.15): Change of tone; Paul addresses and offers various criticisms.

VII   Self-adulation (11.16–12.10): Paul speaks (foolishly) about his honorary deeds and piety, i.e. his proper conduct (11.16–21); his lineage (11.22); his superior work displaying weakness (11.23–31); his prodigious spiritual experiences (12.1–7, cf.

12.12); and finally his divine affirmation and oracle from Christ (12.8–10).

VIII *Peroratio* (12.11–13.10): Summarizes letter in inverted order: Paul's boasting and opponents (12.11–13), financial integrity (12.14–15, i.e. the collection) and Titus/brethren (12.16–18), exhortation (12.19–13.3), Paul's defense of ministry and seeming "failure" (13.4–7), final self-affirmations regarding truth and building up the Corinthians (13.8–10). The language throughout contains various emotional appeals (urging, parent/child, fearing, warning, etc.).

IX Epistolary closing (13.11–13).

A sequential look at each section will provide an opportunity to justify this arrangement. This will allow, furthermore, for two other types of observations. First, I can enumerate other forensic features such as idiomatic themes and expressions, especially in the *prooemium, probatio,* and *peroratio*, since I did not treat these as distinct sections for forensic speeches in Chapter 5. Second, one can begin to observe important features of Paul's rhetorical invention in comparison with previous and concurrent forensic practice and theory. These observations anticipate the next chapter on rhetorical invention in 2 Corinthians.

8.3 *Prooemium*: 1.3–7

The purpose of the *prooemium* (or *exordium* and *principium*)[1] is "to make the audience attentive, well-disposed, and receptive to the speech that follows" (Watson, 1988, p. 21).[2] Cicero (*Inv.* 1.20; cf. Quint. *Inst.* 4.1.40–41) argued that five types of cases and corresponding *exordia* existed: honorable (*honestum*), difficult (*admirabile*), mean (*humile*), ambiguous (*anceps*), and obscure (*obscurum*). Paul's case was ambiguous (*anceps*) because, as Cicero (*Inv.* 1.20) explains, "the point for decision is doubtful, or the case is partly honourable and partly discreditable so that it

---

[1] προοίμιον (Arist. *Rhet.* 3.13.1414b.3; Pl. *Phdr.* 266d51; Anax. *Rhet. Alex.* 28.1436a.32; Quint. *Inst.* 4.1.1); *prooemium* (*Rhet. Her.* 1.6; Quint. *Inst.* 3.9.1); *principium* (Cic. *De Or.* 2.315; *Rhet. Her.* 3.16; Quint. *Inst.* 4.1.1); *initium* (Cic. *Part. Or.* 8.27); *exordium* (Cic. *Inv.* 1.14.19; *Rhet. Her.* 1.4; Quint. *Inst.* 4.1.1). These references are cited by Watson, 1988, p. 20 note 191.

[2] Watson (p. 21 note 197) also supplies these references: Arist. *Rhet.* 3.14.1415a.7; Anax. *Rhet. Alex.* 29.1436a.33ff.; Cic. *Inv.* 1.20; Cic. *Orat.* 122; Cic. *Part. Or.* 28; Cic. *Top.* 97; *Rhet. Her.* 1.4, 6; Quint. *Inst.* 4.1.5, 37, 41, 50–51; cf. Cic. *De Or.* 1.143; 2.80; Cic. *Orat.* 50; Quint. *Inst.* 4.1.61–62; 4.2.24; 10.1.48.

engenders both good-will and ill-will."[3] If the case is partly honorable/ discreditable, then the litigant must win the goodwill of the audience to make the case seem honorable (*Inv.* 1.21; cf. *Rhet. Her.* 1.6; Quint. *Inst.* 4.1.41).

Paul crafted 1.3–7 (five sentences) as the *prooemium* (Kennedy, 1984, p. 87). Quintilian (*Inst.* 4.1.62) contests the view of some theoreticians who argued that the length of the *exordium* should be restricted to four sentences. The *prooemium* proper does not include 1.8–11 (*contra* Hyldahl, 1973, pp. 289, 293, 295, who views 1.1–11 as the *prooemium*; cf. Furnish, 1984, pp. 121–25; Danker, 1989, pp. 32–38, 1991, p. 267; Thrall, 1994, p. 99; Barnett, 1997, pp. 18, 83). Rather the disclosure formula introduced with γάρ at 1.8 begins the *narratio* (Kennedy, 1984, p. 87).

How does 1.3–7 make the audience well disposed, attentive, and receptive? Cicero (*Inv.* 1.23; cf. *Rhet. Her.* 1.7) argues that one does so by including themes that are "important, novel, or incredible" or that relate to all persons, the state, the audience, famous persons, or the immortal gods. Paul strengthens his case by introducing God, who provides consolation and pity for Paul and the Corinthians (1.3–4), and who is "the father of mercies" (ὁ πατὴρ τῶν οἰκτιρμῶν). Paul situates the Corinthians' view of Paul *within the context of God's merciful concern for them all*. Paul's opening corresponds to other forensic *prooemia* that emphasize the gravity of a case by appealing to the gods (e.g., Antiph. 1.3.6; Antiph. 6.3, 5; Din. 3.1; Isae. 2.1; Isoc. 18.3.3; Lycurg. *Leoc.* 1–2; Lys. 13.3; for prayers in the *exordia* of deliberative orations, see M. Mitchell, 1991, p. 195 note 56).

One might also secure goodwill, according to Cicero (*Inv.* 1.22; cf. Cic. *De Or.* 2.231; *Rhet. Her.* 1.8; Quint. *Inst.* 4.1.13), from one's own person by describing acts and services, relating one's difficulties/misfortunes, and employing "prayers and entreaties with a humble and submissive spirit." The author of *Rhetorica ad Herennium* (1.8) expresses nearly the same sentiment: "likewise [we win goodwill] by setting forth our disabilities, need, loneliness, and misfortune, and pleading for our hearers' aid, and at the same time showing that we have been unwilling to place our hope [*noluisse spem habere*] in anyone else." Paul, too, expresses his hope in 1.7 (see below).

---

[3] If one wants to analyze Paul's *exordium* as some do, deciding upon a direct approach (*principium*) or subtle approach (*insinuatio*), Paul uses the direct approach here (Quint. *Inst.* 4.1.42). The subtle approach was used when the judge was terribly biased against the pleader.

Paul reveals his own piety by affirming the blessedness of God (1.3).[4] Such an affirmation indicates Paul's own favorable estimation by God, since he is the recipient of God's consolation (see Fitzgerald, 1988, pp. 154–55). Furthermore, Paul embodies the suffering of Christ (1.5) through his own afflictions (1.4–7). Implicit in such references are Paul's services for the Corinthians, which are later repeatedly related in the *peristasis* catalogues (4.8–9; 6.4–10; 11.23–28; 12.10). He thus establishes a link of mutuality and service for himself, his co-workers, and the Corinthians. Specifically, this mutuality involves mutual comfort through mutual suffering (1.5–7), an argument that anticipates 2 Corinthians 6 through association with Isa. 49.1–13 (Lane, 1982, p. 20). The theme of mutuality, as John T. Fitzgerald (1988, esp. p. 150) has rightly argued, unites the first nine chapters of 2 Corinthians.

The character Odysseus similarly accentuates mutuality and "shared dangers" in the *prooemium* (1–2) of Antisthenes' fictitious defense *Odysseus*. So also does Mantitheus in his scrutiny case (Lys. 16.3). Mutuality was expected between citizens and their city-states. Andocides (*On his Return*) and Demosthenes (*Concerning his own Restoration*) argue for their acquittal on this basis in their apologetic demegoric speeches. In his epistolary defense Demosthenes (*Ep.* 2.20; cf. 22, 24) pleads: "from here I look across the sea every day to my native land, toward which I am conscious in my heart of feeling an attachment as strong as I pray that I may enjoy on your part [ὅσης παρ' ὑμῶν εὔχομαι]." Likewise, Demosthenes ends his *prooemium* in *On the Crown* (8): "I must therefore renew my appeal to the gods; and in your presence I now beseech them, first that I may find in your hearts such benevolence towards me as I have ever cherished for Athens . . ." Demosthenes here magnifies his piety. Similarly, within the self-adulation section (62–65) the accuser in Isocrates' *Against Callimachus* reiterates his services to the state and in no uncertain terms expresses his expectation of a favorable verdict in return. Thus, Paul employed a common forensic theme in mutuality to achieve a favorable outcome in his case.

Yet another way to secure goodwill is from the audience "if it is shown in what honourable esteem they are held and how eagerly their judgment and opinion are awaited" (Cic. *Inv.* 1.22; cf. *Rhet. Her.* 1.8). Paul highly esteems the Corinthians in 1.7: "Our hope for you is unshaken; for we know that as you share in our sufferings, so also you share in our consolation." The exact significance of 1.7 is debated (see Furnish, 1984, p. 121;

---

[4] Thrall (1994, pp. 98–99) has some difficulty in explaining why Paul does not use a thanksgiving in 2 Corinthians. However, there is tremendous rhetorical significance, as indicated above and below, in the substitution of the benediction in its place.

and Thrall, 1994, pp. 112–13). Does it imply that the Corinthians are suffering currently or *will* suffer? What kind of suffering is involved? Paul's expression of "sure hope" (ἐλπὶς βεβαία) in 1.7 should be understood within the context of forensic theory as recommended in *Rhetorica ad Herennium* 1.8 (quoted above; cf. Quint. *Inst.* 6.1.3). Additionally, within forensic practice numerous instances abound of litigants expressing hope (ἐλπίς or ἐλπίζω) of gaining a favorable outcome from the jury.

For example, the defendant in Isaeus' *On the Estate of Ciron* (383–363 BC) at the end of the *prooemium* (5) states: "It is a difficult task, therefore, gentlemen, for one who is wholly without experience of litigation, when such important interests are at stake, to contend against fabricated stories and witness whose evidence is false; yet, I have great hopes from you [ἀλλὰ πολλὰς ἐλπίδας ἔχω καὶ παρ᾽ ὑμῶν]." Demosthenes, too, in *Against Aphobus I*, writes "Yet nevertheless, I have strong hopes [πολλὰς ἐλπίδας ἔχω] that I shall obtain justice in your court" (2.6). The end of the *prooemium* of Antiphon 6.5 connects hope with the defendant's innocence: "Most things in human life depend on hopes [ταῖς ἐλπίσιν]; and if a man is impious and goes against what is due to the gods, he deprives himself of the greatest benefit a man can have, hope itself [καὶ αὐτῆς ἂν τῆς ἐλπίδος]. No one would dare to set aside the verdict once given, confident that he is not liable to it" (trans. Morrison in Sprague, 1972). Isocrates' statements at the end of the *narratio* in *Antidosis* (28; cf. 167–68, 198, 322) link his *hopes* to a correct knowledge of himself in view of slanderers:

> Yet I am not utterly discouraged because I face so great a penalty; no, if you will only hear me with good will, I have many hopes [πολλὰς ἐλπίδας ἔχω] that those who have been misled as to my pursuits and have been won over by my would-be slanderers will promptly change their views, while those who think of me as I really am will be still more confirmed [βεβαιότερον] in their opinion [translation slightly adjusted from LCL].

In Lysias' *On the Property of Aristophanes: Against the Treasury* (53.8) the pleader argues that the jury's favor is his only hope of salvation (ἐλπὶς . . . σωτηρίας). Isocrates, in his letter *To Dionysius* (3), imitates such language: "[S]ince you are to be the judge [κριτής] in this matter, I have great hope [πολλὰς ἐλπίδας] that I shall prove to be saying something of value." More generally, *hope* is related to the outcome of the case ([Andoc.] 4.24.6; Dem. 32.31.1; Dem. 33.28.6; Dem. 58.60.8; Isae. 7.32.4; Isae. 11.9.10; Lys. 8.2.4; and Lys. 14.21.9, 43.4; cf. Antiph. 5.35; Lys. 6.3; Lys. 19.8; Dem. 25.5; Dem. 29.1.7; Dem. 57.2.2; Dem. 58.1.3).

As indicated above, both the accuser and defender may express hope. Intriguingly, Paul uses ὑπὲρ ὑμῶν rather than using παρ' ὑμῶν ("from you"). If ὑπέρ means "with respect to you" (as it does in 2 Cor. 7.4, 14; 8.24; 9.2–3), then 1.7 should be understood as Paul's hope regarding the Corinthians' *evaluation of him*. This would be paraphrased as follows: "I have unwavering hope in your opinion of me, since, just as you are willing to join in and accept my sufferings, so too will you be encouraged." In this case, Paul is asking the Corinthians to embrace his afflicted state (despite criticisms against him) and accept his explanation of failing to visit on account of his dire circumstances. Just as Paul called the Corinthians to embrace him despite his lowly state in 1 Cor. 4.8–16, so now Paul's defense is secured if the Corinthians become participators (κοινωνοί) in his suffering.

However, if ὑπέρ carries the sense of "for" or "on behalf of" (as in 2 Cor. 8.16; 9.14), then Paul is expressing his hope that the Corinthians will *themselves* fare well in the trial (!): "I have unwavering hope on your behalf." It may be that through double entendre Paul is subverting the trial setting according to a "true rhetoric" (see Given, 2001). Typically, the defendant is liable to the charge by the accusation that he or she has no hope (e.g., Quint. *Inst.* 6.1.3). Here, Paul the defendant is expressing hope for the Corinthians, presumably acting as prosecution (!). As shall be seen, especially in Chapter 9, Paul employed the defensive strategy of counter-charge, so that in the course of the letter the Corinthians found themselves on trial, too. The ambiguity of the expression ὑπέρ ὑμῶν suggests the dual nature of 2 Corinthians as a defense and counter-charge.

The expression of hope in 1.7 correlates thematically with three other occurrences of ἐλπίζω throughout 2 Corinthians:

1.13–14 – For we write you nothing other than what you can read and also understand [ἐπιγινώσκετε]; I hope [ἐλπίζω] you will understand until the end [ἕως τέλους ἐπιγνώσεσθε] – as you have already understood us in part [ἐπέγνωτε ἡμᾶς ἀπὸ μέρους] – that on the day of the Lord Jesus we are your boast even as you are our boast.

5.11 – Therefore, knowing the fear of the Lord, we try to persuade others; but we ourselves are well known [πεφανερώμεθα] to God, and I hope [ἐλπίζω] that we are also well known [πεφανερῶσθαι] to your consciences.

13.6 – I hope [ἐλίζω] you will find out [γνώσεσθε] that we have not failed.

These references are significant because *they are unlike any other references of* ἐλπίζω *in Paul's letters.* Each pertains to knowing Paul. Paul's
self-expressed hope (ἐλπίζω) typically involves his travel plans or spend-
ing time with persons (Rom. 15.24; 1 Cor. 16.7; Phlm. 1.22; 1 Tim. 3.14)
or his intentions to send Timothy to persons (Phil. 2.19, 23). Otherwise,
the verb is used in didactic material (Rom. 8.25; 1 Cor. 13.7; 15.19; 1 Tim.
6.17). Furthermore, each reference contains *the idea of knowing Paul in
an evaluative sense.* Paul is expressing his hope that the Corinthians will
judge him favorably just as God has and will do (1.14; 5.11).

Forensic orations contain uses of ἐλπίζω that correspond to Paul's use
in 2 Corinthians (see Antiph. 6.4.8; Isae. 8.1.4; Lys. 7.39.3). Lysias' defensive speech (despite the title) *Against Simon* (2.5) contains the following
remarks in the *prooemium*: "Now if it were any other court that was to
make a decision upon me, I should be terrified by the danger, considering
what strange machinations and chances occur at times to cause a variety
of surprises to those who are standing their trial; but as it is before you that
I appear, I hope [ἐλπίζω] to obtain justice." Consider also Demosthenes'
Against Medias (4) in the *prooemium*: "but my hope [ἐλπίζω] is that the
more the defendant has pestered you with his solicitations . . . the more
likely it is that I obtain justice." Most significant are the statements made
in the *prooemium* of the scrutiny trial of Lysias' *In Defense of Mantitheus*
(2): "For I have so strong a confidence in myself that, if there is anyone
who is inclined to dislike me, I hope [ἐλπίζω] that when he has heard me
speak of my conduct in the past he will change his mind, and will think
much better of me in the future." The language of accurately knowing the
defendant is precisely what we find in 2 Corinthians; Paul was engaged
in a scrutiny trial of sorts.

Paul's *prooemium* in 1.3–7 conforms rather nicely to various general
descriptions of the *exordium*. For example, Cicero (*Inv.* 1.25) recommends that the "*exordium* ought to be sententious to a marked degree and
of a high seriousness, and, to put it generally, should contain everything
which contributes to dignity, because the best thing to do is that which
especially commends the speaker to his audience." The themes of 1.3–7 –
the blessedness of God, the sufferings of Christ, salvation, affliction and
comfort – all contribute to the seriousness and dignity of 1.3–7. Also, in
De Oratore 2.318–19 Cicero recommends that the content of the *exordium*
should be drawn from "the very heart of the case" or "the most essential part of the defence"; this was completed only after one settled the
argumentative *topoi* and disposition. M. Mitchell (1991, pp. 194–97)
argues that Paul so crafted the *exordium* in 1 Corinthians (1.4–9). Second Corinthians 1.3–7 likewise contains vocabulary that is distributed

Table 8.1 *Significant vocabulary in 2 Cor. 1.3–7 throughout 2 Corinthians*

θλῖψις/θλίβω "affliction"	παράκλησις/παρακαλέω "comfort/exhortation"[a]	περισσεύω (and cognates) "abounding"
θλῖψις (1.4², 8; 2.4; 4.17; 6.4; 7.4; 8.2, 13); θλίβω (1.6; 4.8; 7.5)	παράκλησις (1.3–5, 6², 7; 7.4, 7, 13; 8.4, 17); παρακαλέω (1.4³, 6; 2.7, 8; 5.20; 6.1; 7.6², 7, 13; 8.6; 9.5; 10.1; 12.8, 18; 13.11)	περισσεύω (1.5²; 3.9; 4.15; 8.2, 7²; 9.8², 12); περισσοτέρως (1.12; 2.4; 7.13, 15; 11.23²; 12.15); περισσός (2.7; 9.1; 10.8); περισσεία (8.2; 10.15); περίσσευμα (8.14²); ὑπερπερισσεύω (7.4)

Note: [a] On the dual significance of παράκλησις as "comfort" in 1.3–7 and "appeal" later in the letter, see Witherington, 1995, p. 339.

throughout the speech, as is shown in Table 8.1 (see Kurz, 1996, p. 53, and R. Martin, 1986, p. 54).

God's favorable view of Paul in 1.3–4 also extends through the entire discourse (1.9–10, 12, 18, 20, 21–22, 23; 2.14–17; 3.4–5; 4.2, 6–7; 5.1, 5, 11, 18–21; 6.1, 4, 7; 7.6; 8.5; 11.11, 31; 12:1–10). These themes, moreover, should arouse the emotions (Cic. *De Or.* 2.324); certainly Paul's sublime treatment of suffering and afflictions (1.4–6) accomplishes this. These sufferings are recorded as *peristasis* catalogues in 4.8–9; 6.4–10; 11.23–28; 12.10 (see the excellent treatment of Fitzgerald, 1988, pp. 3, 148–201). As I shall argue in Chapter 9, Paul's recollection of his sufferings and afflictions function as *topoi* in his line of defense according to the *stasis* of quality.

To conclude an *exordium*, Quintilian (*Inst.* 4.1.76–79; 4.2.47) argues a rhetor should offer a statement of intention (*principium*) as a transition to the narration. This transition should not be too abrupt; otherwise, the listeners will be confused. Paul's expression of hope (1.7) suitably concludes the *prooemium* and prepares for the *narratio*.

8.4   *Narratio: 1.8–16; 2.12–13; 7.2–16*

A distinctive need for forensic oratory is to narrate events of a case briefly, clearly, and plausibly (Cic. *Inv.* 1.28; cf. Arist. *Rhet.* 3.16.6; Quint. *Inst.* 4.2.31; *Rhet. Her.* 1.14; Theon *Prog.* 5.39–40). Aelius Theon (*Prog.* 5.4–11) argues that there are six components necessary for the narrative (διήγησις) in the *progymnasmata*: person(s), their action(s), place, time, manner of action, and the reason for these. With the manner of action, *intentionality* is critical, in addition to whether the act was performed out of ignorance, chance, or necessity (*Prog.* 5.32–34; cf. Cic. *Inv.* 1.41).

The *narratio* begins the litigant's argument by showing how the events *really ought to be understood*. Its goal is to persuade the jury (Quint. *Inst.* 4.2.21). In practice, the *narratio* is sometimes demarcated with a beginning and ending formula. Aristotle recommended that it positively portray the character of the orator (*Rhet.* 3.16.5; cf. Quint. *Inst.* 4.2.125) and that it be distributed throughout the oration (*Rhet.* 3.16.11; cf. Cic. *Inv.* 1.30).

In 2 Corinthians the *narratio* begins in 1.8–16 and is distributed in 2.12–13 and 7.2–16 (cf. Barnett, 1997, p. 18, and Hester, 2000, p. 98; 2002, pp. 284–89). In addition to Paul's use of direct address in 1.8 (ἀδελφοί), there are several considerations that lead one to this conclusion.

First, Paul appropriately uses γίνομαι to describe the situation with which he begins the *narratio*. Paul wants the Corinthians to know about *his affliction which occurred in Asia* (ὑπὲρ τῆς θλίψεως ἡμῶν τῆς γενομένης ἐν τῇ Ἀσίᾳ). Additionally, Paul employs a disclosure formula that expresses a desire to alleviate ignorance in 1.8: "For we do not want you to be ignorant" (Οὐ γὰρ θέλομεν ὑμᾶς ἀγνοεῖν). Belleville (1989, pp. 145–48) rightly understands the transition here. The similarity with Alcidamas' introduction to the *narratio* in his *Odysseus* (5) is notable: "For surely indeed even you yourselves know what sort of danger we were in" (Σχεδὸν μὲν γὰρ ἴστε καὶ αὐτοὶ ἐν οἵῳ κινδύνῳ ἐγενόμεθα).

Paul's use of ἀγνοέω corresponds to forensic usage. Isocrates states within the *narratio* of *Antidosis* (19.4–5): "I think you know well enough that [οἶμαι δ'ὑμᾶς οὐκ ἀγνοεῖν ὅτι] time and again in the past Athens has so deeply repented the judgments which have been pronounced in passion." Consider also Apollodorus' *Against Neaera* (59.92.1–2) to introduce narrative material: "I will mention only those which you all remember: Peitholas the Thessalian, and Apollonides the Olynthian, after having been made citizens by the people, were deprived of the gift by the court. These are not events of long ago of which you might be ignorant [ταῦτα γὰρ οὐ πάλαι ἐστὶ γεγενημένα, ὥστε ἀγνοεῖν ὑμᾶς]." Similar statements to οἶμαι δ' ὑμᾶς οὐκ ἀγνοεῖν are found in other speeches (Isoc. 4.37.4, 174.1, 299.2; Dem. 20.167.8; Dem. 21.1.3; Dem. 36.62.4; Dem. 38.28.10; Dem. 39.22.5; Dem. 45.44.10; Isae. 7.45.10; Isae. 8.46.5; Isae. 11.36.6).

Quintilian (*Inst.* 4.2.22) recommended the use of noetic expressions (e.g., "to know") to prepare for the *narratio*: "we shall for instance use phrases like . . . 'you are not ignorant how this matter stands' [*Illud quale*

Table 8.2 *Verb tense in 2 Cor. 1.8–16*

Verse	Past-tense indicative verb forms	Present-tense indicative verb forms
1.8	ἐβαρήθημεν "we were weighed down"	
1.9	ἐσχήκαμεν "we have/had received"	
1.10	ἐρρύσατο "God rescued" ἠλπίκαμεν "we have hoped"	[ῥύσεται (twice) future – "God will save"]
1.12	ἀνεστράφημεν "we behaved"	ἐστίν "this is (our boast)"
1.13		γράφομεν "we are writing" ἀναγινώσκετε "you are reading" ἐπιγινώσκετε "you know" ἐλπίζω "I hope" [ἐπιγνώσεσθε "you will know"]
1.14	ἐπέγνωτε "you knew"	ἐσμεν "we are (your boast)"
1.15	ἐβουλόμην "I was wanting"	

sit, tu scias] and so on." Paul uses disclosure formulae throughout his letters (see Furnish, 1984, p. 112; and, Barnett, 1997, p. 83). They often introduce narrative material in these contexts (Gal. 1.11; 1 Cor. 12.1; 2 Cor. 8.1; Rom. 1.13; Phil. 1.12) or occur in the midst of narrative material (Col. 2.1). Disclosure formulae are also found elsewhere in Paul's letters (Rom. 11.25; 1 Cor. 10.1; 1 Thess. 4.13). Paul's use of such disclosure formulae is apropos according to rhetorical practice and theory.

A second consideration why one should understand 1.8 as initiating the *narratio* is the conjunction γάρ (the first occurrence in 2 Corinthians) (Kennedy, 1984, p. 87). The use of γάρ to introduce a *narratio* is also seen at Gal. 1.11 and 1 Cor. 1.11; 15.3. At Romans 1.13 there is no γάρ (but rather δέ) with the disclosure formula; but a γάρ is found at Rom. 1.11, which anticipates the *narratio*. In Phil. 1.12 one finds δέ to introduce the *narratio*. Instead of γάρ in Col. 1.9–2.3, one finds διὰ τοῦτο to introduce the *narratio*.

Two other factors indicate that 1.8–16 is the *narratio*: its strong ethical tone (1.12) and orientation to the past, for which see Table 8.2.

The past tense is interrupted momentarily only to make ethical assertions (1.12) and argumentative points (1.13–14), which support Paul's claims about *his past intentions to visit in 1.15–16*, upon which he bases his line of defense and *partitio* in 1.17–24. Thus, 1.12 should not be seen as the thesis statement for the letter (*contra* Fitzgerald, 1988, pp. 148–53;

cf. Hester, 2000, p. 111); rather it relates to the universal general purport of apologetic speech, as noted above, *for the defendant to be properly known and understood.*

There are three other features in the *narratio* of 2 Corinthians that are typical of forensic orations more generally. The first is the use of witnesses to confirm past events. Paul in 1.12 (cf. 1.23; Rom. 9.1–2) invokes his conscience as a testimony (τὸ μαρτύριον τῆς συνειδήσεως ἡμῶν) of his past intentions. He appears to be following the advice articulated in Quintilian (*Inst.* 5.11.41): "Conscience is as good as a thousand witnesses."

The second forensic feature is found in 1.9 pertaining to Paul's reference to receiving a "sentence of death" (τὸ ἀπόκριμα τοῦ θανάτου – cf. 1 Cor. 4.9). This expression, whether having a specific referent to some actual pronouncement against Paul or merely a judicial word picture, graphically portrays the seriousness of Paul's circumstances (ἀπόκριμα is extremely rare; in Joseph. *Ant.* 14.210 ἀποκρίματα are Roman senatorial decrees; LSJ s.v. indicates that it is equivalent to κατάκριμα, "condemnation"). Many forensic speeches involve cases in which a sentence of death would be administered if the defendant were found guilty. A testimony of this is found in Hermogenes' statement of concern to Socrates before his trial (Xen. *Apol.* 4): "Do you not see, Socrates, how often Athenian juries are constrained by arguments to put quite innocent people to death, and not less often to acquit the guilty, either through some touch of pity excited by the pleadings, or that the defendant had skill to turn some charming phrase?" Defendants often remind the jury of this grave prospect of death when, if convicted, they will suffer death (Hyp. *Lyc.* IVb.20; cf. Andoc. 1.146–50; [Andoc.] 4.9; Din. 3.2, 5, 16; Hyp. 4.14; Xen. *Apol.* 25). Sentiments not entirely different from receiving a "sentence of death" are found in Alcidamas' *Odysseus* 8, "capital charge" (περὶ θανάτου κρίνειν), Lysias 13.39, "when sentence of death had been passed on them . . ." (Ἐπειδὴ . . . θάνατος αὐτῶν κατεγνώσθη), and Dinarchus 3.21, "the accused has already condemned himself to death" (οὗτος μὲν γὰρ αὑτοῦ πάλαι θάνατον κατέγνωκε). In Xenophon's *Apology* 27, Socrates was born *sentenced to death by nature* (κατεψηφισμένος ἦν μου ὑπὸ τῆς φύσεως ὁ θάνατος). Consistent with this concern, Paul mentions death repeatedly in 2 Corinthians (3.7; 7.9–12; 6.8b–9; 7.10; 11.23; cf. 4.16–17; 5.1–2, 4, 8, 10).

The third feature is Paul's use of the verb ἐπιγινώσκω in 1.13 (cf. 13.6): "For we write you nothing other than what you can read and also understand; I hope you will understand [ἐπιγνώσεσθε] until the end [ἕως τέλους]." This sentiment has curious counterparts in the extant forensic speeches. A very near parallel is found in Lysias 19.11 at the end of narrative material: "Nevertheless, even in these circumstances, you will easily perceive [γνώσεσθε] that the accusations are not true; and I request you with all the insistence in my power to give us a kindly hearing to the end [διὰ τέλους], and to deliver the verdict that you may esteem best for you and most agreeable to your oaths."

There are several examples of the future form γνώσεσθε in forensic speeches to prepare the audience for argumentation. Consider the statement made within the narration (extending from 3–23) in Isocrates 17.19: "as you will learn [γνώσεσθε] as my story proceeds." In some instances (particularly, it seems, with Isaeus' inheritance cases) γνώσεσθε is used to introduce the proof section or arguments within it. Thus, the litigant in Isaeus 1.8 says: "You will understand [γνώσεσθε] their shamelessness and greed better when you have heard the whole story. I will begin my narrative at a point which will, I think, enable you most readily to understand the matter in dispute." Also the pleader in Isaeus 11.7 submits: "I must state the facts from the beginning; for you will thus recognize [γνώσεσθε] my claim as next-of-kin and see that my opponent has no title to the succession."

Thus, Paul's statement in 1.13 prepares for the decision that the Corinthians will need to render concerning Paul and his associates. It is not surprising, then, that this very same concern occurs at the end of the apology in 13.6 – a verse which also combines the idea of hope with a future form of (ἐπι)γινώσκω in relation to the Corinthians' evaluation of Paul. For an extensive discussion of ἐπιγινώσκω at 13.6 in relation to forensic orations, see below under 8.9.

The end of the *narratio* is signaled by a pair of rhetorical questions specifically relating to the charges against Paul and leading to the *partitio*. Quintilian (*Inst.* 4.2.132) discusses disagreement among rhetoricians whether an orator should conclude the *narratio* "where the issue to be determined begins." He thinks that this is more possible for the prosecution than the defense. Paul, however, is able to construct the *narratio* to his liking, bringing it to conclusion with a statement of the issue and a *partitio*.

How does this *narratio* support Paul's apology in 2 Corinthians? First, it begins to answer charges and criticisms he faced. In response to the criticism that he is weak, Paul narrated that God delivered him and will do so again (1.8–11). In response to the charge of relying on worldly rhetoric and pursuits of monetary gain, Paul asserted that he acted with integrity and speaks plainly and understandably (1.12–14). The expressed mutual eschatological boast here in 1.14 has correspondence with the mutual boasting in relation to his handling of the collection with utmost integrity

(8.24; 9.2–3; see immediately below). Finally, to answer the charge that he failed to visit when planned, Paul narrated his good intentions with respect to these plans (1.15–16).

Second, the narrative advances the critical theme of mutuality. Belleville (1989, p. 149) argues respecting 1.8–11, "Paul imparts the information that he does, not primarily for its 'news' content but to establish right at the start a basis for mutuality between the Corinthians and himself, and to show the impact that this mutuality has on the church universal." This mutuality develops into mutual boasting eschatologically in 1.14. This mutual boasting culminates in Paul's discussion of the collection in 2 Corinthians 8 and 9 (Fitzgerald, 1988, p. 150). Fitzgerald (p. 153), speaking only of 2 Corinthians 1–7, observes correctly: "Two themes which flow through the letter are thus the integrity of Paul and the mutuality between Paul and the Corinthians." This summation adequately expresses the primary concerns for 2 Corinthians.

In addition to the initial narration section (1.8–16), 2 Corinthians contains two other relatively distinct narrative segments: 2.12–13 and 7.2–16. This is not to say that no other narration of past events is given. In fact, 2 Corinthians has numerous references to past events, hardships, heroic deeds, and the like.[5] The nature of this narrative material provides an epideictic dimension to the discourse (see Arist. *Rhet.* 3.16.1–3) as well as positively contributing to Paul's apologetic purposes (Fitzgerald, 1988, pp. 158–60). These later narrative sections describe past events relevant to the case.[6] More will be said about 2.12–13 and 7.2–16 in my discussion of the *probatio* below. Suffice it to say that these sections demonstrate the import of the initial *narratio*; namely, while Paul was traveling, he was utterly concerned for the Corinthians and their restoration to him, and he was still boasting about them.

We have every indication that Paul was skilled at composing forensic narrations. He understood how to demarcate and aptly convey his narrative material. Within the initial controlling narration (1.8–16) are found several distinctive phrases or ideas (e.g., the expression of hope, the use of conscience as a witness, death sentence, future knowledge) that intriguingly have verbal correspondence with forensic speeches. This narrative

[5] The term πρᾶγμα is found in the narration at 7.11 with respect to some legal action or matter involving the Corinthians. This more than likely refers to the "grievance" (πρᾶγμα) that Paul discusses in 1 Cor. 6.1. See Chapter 9.

[6] Barnett (1997, p. 18) includes 2.3–13; 7.5–16; 8.1–6, 16–23; 9.2–5; 11.11–12.10 as narrative sections. Hester (2000, pp. 110–11) also finds a distributed *narratio* throughout 2 Corinthians in 1.15–16; 2.12–13; 7.5; 8.1–2; 9.1. At a certain point it becomes unhelpful to include every historic reference under the category of narration. Rather, these narrative elements need to be understood as argumentative components.

material, moreover, is brief and emphasizes Paul's ethical character and dire circumstances and establishes positive and mutual *pathos* with the audience. Finally, Paul has masterfully woven narrative sections throughout 2 Corinthians in support of his *ethos*.

8.5   *Divisio* and *partitio*: 1.17–24

After the *narratio* one expects a *divisio* (points of agreement and disagreement) and a thesis statement. These are complementary, since the orator develops the statement in conjunction with the charges in the case. If the thesis contains several heads, then it is called a *partitio*. Many possible or typical features of the *partitio* were noted in Chapter 5.3. It typically follows the *narratio*, is dialectically formulated (possibly with questions), contains several heads that outline the *probatio* in the same order, and is sometimes subtle, although key terms and ideas help to identify and confirm the headings in the *probatio*.

The *divisio* and *partitio* for 2 Corinthians is 1.17–24. It follows and arises out of the *narratio* in view of explicit criticisms and is articulated very pointedly with questions in 1.17 (NASB): "Therefore, I was not vacillating when I intended to do this, was I? Or what do I purpose, do I purpose according to the flesh, so that with me there will be yes, yes and no, no *at the same time*?" Thrall (1994, p. 140) argues thus concerning 1.17,

> Paul now introduces a conclusion (οὖν) which his readers (or some of them) had drawn from their knowledge of the [travel] plan he has just outlined, coupled with their further knowledge that he had so far failed to carry it to its completion. They should not have drawn this conclusion, as he indicates by using a rhetorical question expecting a negative answer. Nevertheless, they had charged him with acting in a light-minded or irresponsible fashion when he had formed the intention described in vv. 15–16.

Unknowingly, Thrall describes well a classic *divisio* with a *partitio* in which charges were articulated (cf. McCant, 1999, pp. 32–33).

When looking closely at 1.17–24 in light of the subsequent argumentation, I have discerned that these verses contain partition heads corresponding to distinct sections in 2 Corinthians 2–9 through the use of key words and themes (see Table 8.3).

These correspondences in the *probatio* are surprisingly subtle. Paul did not say, "First, I will talk about . . . Second, I will discuss . . ." (see *Rhet. Her.* 1.17 and Cic. *Inv.* 1.31–33). However, this clarity was not necessary,

Table 8.3 *Partition headings in 2 Cor. 1.17–24*

Partition head and conjunction	Key term(s) and theme(s)	Corresponding section in the *probatio*
1.17 = Paul's intentions are inconsistent and worldly. He didn't come to Corinth. **conjunction:** initiated with οὖν	**Terms:** come (ἐλθεῖν) 1.15–16 intention (βούλομαι/βουλεύομαι) 1.15–17 **Themes:** (1) lightness (ἐλαφρία); (2) "worldly" (κατὰ σάρκα)	*2.1–11* = **Terms:** come (ἐλθεῖν) 2.1, 3 (cf. 2.12–13) intention (ἔκρινα ἐμαυτ*ῷ* τοῦτο . . .) 2.1 **Themes:** (1) Paul not wanting to be heavy (2.5 – ἵνα μὴ ἐπιβαρῶ); (2) Paul knows Satan's schemes or νοήματα (2.11; cf. 3.14; 4.4; 10.5; 11.3); thus, he is not worldly
1.18–20 = God confirms the preaching of Christ by Paul, Timothy, and Silas, for the Corinthians to the glory of God. **conjunction:** initiated with δέ	**Terms:** word (λόγος) 1.18; Christ preached (Χριστός κηρυχθείς) 1.19–20; glory (δόξα) 1.20 **Themes:** (1) The preaching of Paul, Timothy, Silas through God in Christ to the Corinthians. (2) In Christ, all God's promises are fulfilled.	*2.17–3.18* = **Terms:** word of God (τὸν λόγον τοῦ θεοῦ) 2.17; Christ (Χριστός) 3.14; Christ = Lord (κύριος) 3.16–18; Lord = Spirit (πνεῦμα) 3.6, 8, 17–18; glory (δόξα) 3.7–11, 18 **Themes:** (1) God leads Paul, Silas, Timothy in Christ. The Corinthians are God's proof of the word of Paul, Silas, and Timothy, since the Spirit is given. (2) The greater glory of the new covenant through Jesus Christ

1.21-22 = Paul and his associates are established also with the Corinthians; they are sealed by God and receive the deposit of the Spirit.

conjunction: initiated with δέ

Terms: God "gives down deposit of the Spirit" (δοὺς τὸν ἀρραβῶνα τοῦ πνεύματος) 1.22
Theme: This gift applies to both Paul and Corinthians, i.e. they share a mutuality in the Spirit.

4.1-5.10 =
Terms: God "gives us the down deposit of the Spirit" (ὁ δοὺς ἡμῖν τὸν ἀρραβῶνα τοῦ πνεύματος) 5.5;
Theme: Paul suffers, but Corinthians have life (4.12; 5.11); but both have same Spirit (4.13); both await glory (4.14; 5.10).

1.23 = God is called to testify for Paul; he did not come to Corinth in order to spare them.

conjunction: initiated with δέ

Term: Corinth (Κόρινθον) 1.23
Theme: God as testifier of covenantal faithfulness

5.11-7.1 =
Term: Corinthians (Κορίνθιοι – 6.11)
Theme: God with Paul, the ministry of reconciliation, and God's new covenant people called to be holy (5.18–20; 6.2, 6.14–7.1)

1.24 = Paul, his co-workers and the Corinthians' faith

conjunction: asyndeton

Terms: co-workers (συνεργοί); Corinthians' joy (χαρά) and faith (πίστις) 1.24
Theme: Paul is not forceful or coercive, but works for joy and to secure the Corinthians' faith.

8.1-9.15 = Titus is Paul's partner and co-worker (συνεργός) 8.23; joy (χαρά) 7.4, 13; 8.2; rejoice (χαίρω) 7.7, 9, 13, 16; cf. 2.3; Corinthians' faith (πίστις) 8.7
Theme: Paul cites example of Macedonians and their joy (chapter 8) and encourages the faith of the Corinthians (8.7) and their participation in the collection (chapter 9).

as my survey of extant forensic speeches has shown (see Chapter 5.3). Even within rhetorical theory, however, one may find articulated a subtle approach to the presentation of the *partitio*. Quintilian (*Inst.* 4.5.5; cf. 4.5.6–28) approved of this tactic when necessary. My analysis of extant forensic speeches indicates that the form of the *partitio* depended on circumstances and the author's preferences. We may reasonably postulate that Paul preferred a subtle approach typically, as this is the case in his other letters (for Gal. 2.14–21, see Betz, 1979, and Brinsmead, 1982; for 1 Thess. 3.11–13, see Jewett, 1986, pp. 74–78, and Hughes, 1990, pp. 103–104; for Rom. 1.16–17, see Enderlein, 1998; for 1 Cor. 1.10 see M. Mitchell, 1991).

Others interpreters offer alternative proposals for the *propositio* or *partitio* (for 1.12, see my discussion under *narratio* above). Kennedy (1984, pp. 87–89; cf. Witherington, 1995, p. 335 note 27) understands 2.14–17 as the *propositio*. Kennedy argues that 2.17 contains three heads: (A) "sincerity," (B) (commissioned) "from God," and (C) "in the sight of God we speak in Christ." These, Kennedy argues, are based upon the general concern for peddling (καπηλεύω, "sell deceitfully") the word of God. Kennedy (p. 89) maintains that these heads are treated "in an interlocking order (*synchysis*)" and outlines the *probatio* as follows:

> B "as commissioned by God" 3:4–4:1
> A "as men of sincerity" 4:2–6
> B "as commissioned by God" 4:7–12
> A "as men of sincerity" 4:13–5:10
> C "In the sight of God we speak in Christ" 5:11–6:13.

However, taking 2.17 as the *prothesis* is problematic for several reasons. First, it fails to take account of the *divisio* at 1.17, articulated with questions, which contains the statement of the initial charge. Second, it assumes that 2 Corinthians 7–9 are not a part of the *probatio*. Third, it breaks from the general principle that the *propositio/partitio* outlines the *probatio* in the same order as it is presented. Fourth, the heads are nearly unrecognizable as heads, since specific terms do not help delimit the sections corresponding to the three heads. If one tracks the specific Greek terms in 2.17 through 2 Corinthians, then one can see how problematic it is to take 2.17 as the *partitio* to arrive at the sections that Kennedy proposes: (A) εἰλικρινεία, "sincerity" (1.12; cf. same theme in 4.2); (B) ἐκ θεοῦ, "from/by God" (3.5; 5.1, 18); (C) κατέναντι θεοῦ ἐν Χριστῷ λαλοῦμεν, "in the sight of God we speak in Christ" (12.19); if we treat these items separately we have κατέναντι θεοῦ (12.19; cf. ἐνώπιον τοῦ θεοῦ, 4.2; 7.12); ἐν Χριστῷ (3.14; 5.17; 5.19; 12.2, 19); λαλοῦμεν (λαλοῦμεν in 4.13; 12.19;

other forms of λαλέω in 7.14; 11.17, 23; 12.4; 13.3). Kennedy must insert key terms such as "commission" into 2.17 to arrive at argument sections in the *probatio*. The fact that certain themes are repeated can be accounted for on other grounds. For example, the notion of "sincerity" in 2.17 and then (thematically) at 4.2–6 is due to an intentional argumentative pattern in which Paul initiates new argumentation in the *probatio* with the mention of rhetorical practices/terms accompanied with notions of commendation. So, 2.17–3.1 introduces the argument section 2.14–3.18; 4.2 introduces the argument section 4.1–5.10; and 5.11–12 (πείθω) introduces 5.11–7.1. See my discussion of the *probatio* below.

Similarly, Witherington (1995, p. 335 notes 27–28 and pp. 360–74) understands 2.17 as the *propositio*. He argues (pp. 372–73) that 2.17 introduces the principle of *synkrisis* which functions to prepare for a positive comparison (with Moses in 3.1–6.13) and a negative one (with his opponents in 2 Corinthians 10–13). However, this general theme of comparison does not do justice to the particular content of Paul's argumentation in 2 Corinthians 3–9. I maintain that 2.14–17 prepares for the particular argument in 2.14–3.18 about the nature of God's affirmation of Paul's and his associates' word for glory (cf. 1.18–20). Witherington (p. 371) rightly appeals to Quintilian (*Inst.* 4.4.8) to understand the *propositio* as being derived from the charges of the accusers (hence a *divisio*). The question is, Where is the primary charge found? I maintain that 1.17 is the locale (see Thrall, 1994, p. 140, quoted above). Witherington (p. 360) acknowledges this, but considers Paul's "possible dishonesty about his travel plans, his sternness in the painful letter . . . and his supposed lack of love and concern for the Corinthians" to be "less crucial charges."

There is an additional reason for treating 1.17–24 as a *partitio*. Young and Ford (1987, p. 18; cf. 103, 106; cf. Hester, 2002, p. 85 and other commentators who treat 1.18–22 as a digression) are not alone when they say "the sequence of thought in 1.15–22 is not easy to discern." In many ways 1.17–24 is rather discordant, as Thrall's (1994) close reading of the text reveals.

First, there is an alternation from singular to plural referents (1.17→1.18–22) and back again (1.18–22→1.23) and once again from singular to plural (1.23→1.24). Thus, Paul's rhetorical questions concerning his personal inconsistency in 1.17 (singular) are followed by a reference to God's confirmation of his, Timothy's, and Silas' preaching at Corinth in 1.18–19 (plural). Thrall and others are reduced to arguing for the thematic continuity between 1.17 and 1.18 beyond the hook-wording of the ναὶ καὶ οὔ. In reference to the plural referent in 1.18 ("our word"), Thrall (p. 145) argues: "It seems, then, that 'our word' has a dual reference, both to what Paul says about his travel plans [1.17] and also to the message which both he and his associates preach." But, this conclusion is unnecessary; 1.18 marks a new partition heading, signaled by the δέ. This δέ is not simply a "connective in a general sense" (Thrall, p. 144 note 114), but serves to demarcate verses 17 and 18 as treating distinct themes treated in the *probatio*.

Second, in 1.17–24 Paul introduces diverse themes. This fact puzzles interpreters. For example, the train of thought from God's promises, affirmation, sealing and giving of the Holy Spirit in 1.20–22 to Paul's emphatic (ἐγώ) statements justifying his conduct in 1.23 is, to say the least, "some slight contrast with what he has just been saying about the activity of God" (Thrall, p. 159). Furthermore, Paul's justification in 1.23 for not coming ("in order to spare them") is not consistent with 1.24, as Thrall (p. 160) explains: "How would this [idea of sparing] fit the disclaimer at the beginning of v.24? To imply that he forbore to come to exercise his right to punish offenders would, after all, suggest that he does possess a dominating control over his readers' lives." Thrall (pp. 161–63) has no good answer to this lack of logic.

Third, the γάρ at 2.1 does not substantiate 1.24 logically. In fact, strong textual support calls for a δέ instead (Thrall, p. 163 note 246). But, working with the assumption that γάρ is original, Thrall (p. 164) treats 2.1 as substantiating 1.23, *hence skipping 1.24*, which she thus considers a parenthetical remark (so also Furnish, 1984, pp. 151–52).

This puzzlement is unnecessary. Paul's statements in 1.24 do not need to be reduced to parenthetical remarks. Furthermore, the alternation from singular to plural and back, as well as the treatment of different, theologically dense themes, does not need to be an embarrassment for Paul. When one understands 1.17–24 as his discussion of the heads to be treated in his *probatio*, then these problems are no problems at all. Consequently, 2.1 marks the departure from the *partitio* to the beginning of the *probatio*.

8.6   *Probatio*: 2.1–9.15

The *partitio* provides argumentative heads elaborated in the *probatio* (see Table 8.3 above). The rhetorical theorists indicate that the *probatio* should follow the heads in the same order as presented in the *partitio*. These theorists also treat the invention of arguments when discussing disposition (Cic. *Inv.* 1.34–77; Quint. *Inst.* 5.1); but that is the topic of the next chapter.

Belleville (1989, p. 143–44) states that "even many of those who support the unity of the letter think that 2 Corinthians does not evidence much consideration of arrangement or logical sequence." A glance at commentaries reveals various structural depictions and organized schemata (e.g., R. Martin, 1986, pp. vii–viii; and Barnett, 1997, pp. 51–52). The application of historical rhetorical criticism provides one avenue by which to sort through and understand the progression of Paul's argumentation. A detailed discussion of the content and force of the *probatio* would require a commentary. So, what I must do here is to indicate how each movement within the *probatio* is demarcated and what major themes are treated in relation to the whole argument. I hope to show how those portions of 2 Corinthians that have been plagued with doubts on literary grounds (e.g., 2.13/2.14; 6.14–7.1 and chapters 8–9) fit within Paul's broader argumentative strategies.

The structure and thematic coherence of the *probatio*

Paul constructed the *probatio* with five argumentative movements. The beginning and ending movements are separated by intervening distributed narrative material (2.12–13 and 7.2–16). These *bracketing* argument sections (2.1–11 and chapters 8–9) pertain rather specifically to logistical issues with the Corinthians: Second Corinthians 2.1–11 discusses the sending of the letter of tears (1 Corinthians) and chapters 8–9 describe his sending of others in preparation for the collection. It is possible that Paul thought these were his strongest lines of defense. If so, he followed the well-known "Homeric order" for arranging a discourse, with the strongest arguments at the fore and the back (see Quint. *Inst.* 5.12.14). Stephen Usher (1993, p. 17) argues that Demosthenes arranged *On the Crown* according to this principle, since Demosthenes placed his treatment of the laws, where his case was the weakest, in the middle. Before and after his discussion of these laws, Demosthenes elaborated upon his prestigious political career.

However, one may account for the logical sequence of Paul's thought according to *stasis* theory (see Chapter 9.2). I think that Paul's treatment of the primary charge (failing to visit) first is necessary since it is precipitous of other criticisms. For Paul to conclude the *probatio* with his appeal for the Corinthians to complete the collection also is strategic. This final appeal presented the Corinthians with a tangible test of their reconciliation with him. Furthermore, to end the *probatio* with Paul's appeal in the collection before moving to the *refutatio* in 10.1–11.15 is especially fitting, since it appears that these "super apostles" had won the Corinthians' allegiance in the matter of the collection.

Table 8.4 *Thematic coherence in the central arguments of 2 Corinthians*

Theme Verses (RSV)	Rhetoric, God's word, and Paul's proclamation	Commendation	God's purview of Paul's activities	References to Paul's Rivals
2.14–3.1	For we are not, like so many, peddlers of God's word; but as men of sincerity,	Are we beginning to commend ourselves again? Or do we need, as some do, letters of recommendation to you, or from you?	as commissioned by God, in the sight of God we speak in Christ	peddlers of God's word (2.17) needing letters of recommendation (3.1)
4.2	We have renounced disgraceful, underhanded ways; we refuse to practice cunning or to tamper with God's word.	we would commend ourselves to every man's conscience	but by the open statement of the truth . . . in the sight of God	using underhanded ways and tampering with God's word (4.2)
5.11–12	Therefore, knowing the fear of the Lord, we persuade men.	12 We are not commending ourselves to you again.	but what we are is known to God, and I hope it is known also to your conscience	to answer those who pride themselves on a man's position and not on his heart

The *probatio* may be outlined as follows:

A 2.1–11: The Corinthians' disciplinary problems resulted in Paul's decision not to visit them.
Narrative transition in 2.12–13: Paul was looking for Titus; he was concerned for the Corinthians.
B 2.14–3.18: Paul's ministry of proclamation and the glory of the new covenant
C 4.1–5.10: Paul, weakness, and the down deposit of the Spirit
D 5.11–7.1: Paul, persuasion, and the new covenant
Narrative transition in 7.2–16: Titus' report and Paul's own confidence in the Corinthians
E 8.1–9.15: Paul's integrity: the collection and the Corinthians' faith.

Each argument section has a pronounced climactic or summarizing conclusion (2.10–11; 3.18; 5.9–10; 7.1; 9.13–15). Furthermore, *the three central argumentative movements are initiated with related topical concerns*: (1) rhetoric in relation to God's word vis-à-vis Paul's proclamation, (2) the notion of (self-) commendation, and (3) God's purview of Paul's activities (cf. Belleville, 1989, pp. 153–54; and Talbert, 1987, p. 155). We must also observe that Paul explicitly or implicitly mentions his missionary rivals in these sections. See Table 8.4.

These rivals are criticized by Paul in the *refutatio* as the super and false apostles (10.12–11.5, 12–15) (Barnett, 1997, pp. 33–40, 147, 278; cf. Hafemann, 1990, pp. 79, 85–88). So then, the concentration of these critical themes – commendation, rhetorical proclamation, Paul's missionary rivals, and God's purview – in addition to the other transitional devices (the *abrupt* transition from 2.13 to 2.14; διὰ τοῦτο followed by ἔχοντες in 4.1; and οὖν followed by εἰδότες in 5.11) demarcates the three central argument sections.

A key notion is *commendation* (see Hafemann, 1990; Belleville, 1989; cf. Fitzgerald, 1988, pp. 151–53; Barnett, 1997, p. 278). So pronounced is the notion of (self-) commendation in the central three arguments that Fitzgerald (1988, p. 150) argues that chapters 1–7 are "*a letter of commendation, of self-commendation* and the longest example of this type that we possess." Belleville (1989) considers it "a letter of apologetic self-commendation." However, this theme extends to end of the letter (10.12, 18 [2x]; 12.11). Partition theorists have failed to account for the fact that all of 2 Corinthians treats the subject of commendation in view of religion, rivals, and rhetoric. The *peroratio* begins with Paul contesting being *forced to commend* himself (12.11). Paul's self-commendation was defensive. It was required because the Corinthians were commending others (3.1) and wavered in their evaluation of him in view of these other missionary rivals (5.11–12; cf. 10.12, 18; *contra* McCant, 1999).

First argument: 2 Cor. 2.1–11

Quintilian (*Inst.* 5.12.14; 7.1.11) argues that the defense should begin the *probatio* by addressing the strongest argument of the prosecution. Paul begins his line of defense in 2.1–11 by answering directly the initial charge of failing to visit. Since Paul in the *peroratio* repeatedly relates that he is *now* coming to the Corinthians (12.14, 20–21; 13.1–2, 10), one can be certain that Paul's absence was *the primary issue as far as Paul was concerned* (cf. 10.1, 9–11). Paul argues that a letter was needed instead of his visit. If he appeared guilty of anything, this was it (13.7).

One must also recognize that 2.1–11 was a direct response to the criticism that Paul, when absent, writes weighty (βαρεῖαι) letters (cf. 10.1, 9–11). When Paul explained that one person had caused all the grief, he was careful "not to exaggerate it" (ἵνα μὴ ἐπιβαρῶ) (2.5). Notice the Greek root βαρ-. In other words, Paul was careful not to appear *too weighty*. Simultaneously, Paul showed himself to be *not worldly* by indicating his awareness of Satan's intentions or νοήματα (cf. 1.17). This confirms that he is spiritual, since Satan is a spiritual foe threatening himself (cf. 12.7–9) and the congregation (11.3, 13–15; cf. 10.4).

The first argument is concluded with a return to narrative material (2.12–13). This narrative recounts Paul's preaching and search for Titus, who had delivered the tearful letter, i.e. 1 Corinthians. Paul was eager to learn of the Corinthians' response to the letter that was substituted for his visit. Later in the discourse, Paul will recount finding Titus and Titus' report to Paul about the Corinthians' initial change of heart in Paul's favor (7.2–16). The narrative material in 2.12–13 also serves to separate the first argument section from the next.

Second argument: 2 Cor. 2.14–3.18

The second argument in 2.14–3.18 treats interrelated themes. The preaching of Christ by Paul, Silas, and Timothy was *yes*, and this was done to the glory of God (cf. 1.18). Paul argued that he and his associates were announcers of God's word to the Corinthians, i.e. heralds of God's triumph even as God's captives (2.14). The implication is that their travels are subject to God's will; they cannot travel at their will (see 1 Cor. 16.7; Rom. 1.10; 15.32). Moreover, as captives they preached with integrity. The response to such preaching was mixed (2.15–16; 3.13–16).

However, as far as the Corinthians were concerned, the Spirit was given in their hearts (3.3). This argument demonstrates how Paul's, Silas', and Timothy's word is *yes*, since God had confirmed it by the giving of the Spirit. This *divina testimonia* in favor of Paul (cf. Gal. 3.1–5; see Hafemann, 1990, pp. 84–87) was highly esteemed by ancient standards (e.g., Xen. *Apol.* 14; Cic. *Part. Or.* 2.6; Quint. *Inst.* 5.11.42; see Chapter 9.3). In 1 Cor. 2.1–5 Paul had made a similar appeal to "the demonstration of the Spirit" (ἀπόδειξις πνεύματος).

Paul further argues that this preaching, which resulted in the outpouring of the Spirit, reflects the greater glory of the new covenant in Jesus Christ (3.10–11, 18). In order to make this point, Paul engages in *synkrisis* to compare his role with that of Moses. Paul fares better, since he has more boldness to call for repentance. The real difference is that the dispensation of the Spirit is better in that it is permanent (3.12–13). Paul's special relationship to the new covenant reflects well on him.

Interpreters detect a difficulty in the transition from 2.13 to 2.14. Specifically, why did Paul begin his discussion of his preaching ministry here? And, why did he change from singular to plural? The answer to both is simply that Paul changed arguments as indicated in the *partitio* (1.17–24). In 1.17 Paul used the first person singular concerning his explanation for not coming to Corinth. Thus, one finds Paul using the first person singular in 2.1–11. However, for the next partition head in 1.18–20, Paul explicitly switched to the plural, including Silvanus and Timothy as fellow preachers.

A generalizing conclusion (3.18) marks the conclusion of this second argument. Many interpreters view 4.1–6 as concluding the argument in 2 Corinthians 3 (Furnish, 1984, pp. 201–52; R. Martin, 1986, p. 75; Stockhausen, 1989, pp. 16–18, 154–77; Thrall, 1994, pp. 188–90; Barnett, 1997, p. 145). However, Witherington (1995, pp. 385–89; also Bruce, 1971, pp. 194–206) favors taking 4.1–6 with 4.7–5.10. This is preferred, since 3.18 serves as a transition to the next argument by emphasizing the person of the Spirit, the last word of the sentence in apposition to *Lord* ("this comes from the Lord, the Spirit" [καθάπερ ἀπὸ κυρίου πνεύματος]).

Third argument: 2 Cor. 4.1–5.10

The third argument section (4.1–5.10) begins with the transitional expression διὰ τοῦτο, "for this reason," with an adverbial participle (cf. Belleville, 1989, p. 149; 2 Cor. 2.14 and 5.11 also begin with participle clauses). Paul's use of the verb ἐγκακέω ("lose heart") at 4.1 and at

4.16 is significant, because one having experienced as much grief as he had would certainly be a candidate for losing heart (cf. Eph. 3.13). This section aims to show that Paul and his companions are equal *participants along with the Corinthians* (4.13–15) in the gift of the Spirit as a deposit guaranteeing a more glorious future (5.5) despite their present bodily suffering (4.7–12, 16–18; 5.1–4, 6–10). The exact repetition of "the down deposit of the Spirit" (τὸν ἀρραβῶνα τοῦ πνεύματος) from 1.22 in the *partitio* confirms that Paul is following his partition heads. The generalizing conclusion about the future judgment (5.10) ends this section. It also serves as a transition to the next section involving Paul's appeal and exhortation to the Corinthians.

Fourth argument: 2 Cor. 5.11–7.1

With οὖν in 5.11 Paul advances to the next argument section in 5.11–7.1 (Barnett, 1997, pp. 51–52, 277–358). This unit is bracketed by use of *inclusio* concerning the "fear of the Lord/God" in 5.11 (τὸν φόβον τοῦ κυρίου) and 7.1 (ἐν φόβῳ θεοῦ). Paul admitted using rhetorical persuasion (πείθω), but argues that he was motivated by the fear of the Lord and persuades people in God's full sight (5.11). Presumably, Paul's rivals had used rhetorical display and methods to woo the Corinthians away from Paul; at least this is his insinuation. Paul wants the Corinthians to have some reply to them about the nature of his ministry (5.12). He has conducted his ministry so that no one should fault him (6.3–11).

More importantly for the Corinthians and Paul's defense, however, is the appeal that Paul makes to the Corinthians that they be "the righteousness of God" (5.21) in response to God's offer of salvation (6.2), which involves proper behavior and conduct (6.12–7.1). This confirms the uprightness and holiness of Paul's persuasion (cf. Gal. 1.10); he is not promoting immorality among his converts (cf. Rom. 3.8). Rather, he is a minister of the covenant people of God calling them to covenantal faithfulness (6.14–18).

Admittedly, 5.11–7.1 has the least semblance with its partition head in 1.23: "But I call on God as witness against me: it was to spare you that I did not come again to Corinth." In general, commentators neglect 1.23; yet its covenantal language in relation to Paul's *sparing* the Corinthians deserves careful consideration. Furthermore, the *hapax legomena* and *unique theology* in 6.14–7.1 have perplexed interpreters. Although Barnett (1997, pp. 339–40) correctly argues that too much is made of this, Danker (1989, p. 18) comments on the rhetorical effect of the *hapax legomena*. Gordon D. Fee (1976–77; cf. Lane, 1982, pp. 22–23; Barnett, 1997, pp. 337–43) has correctly argued that Paul was confronting the Corinthians' continued idolatry. James M. Scott's (1994, pp. 95–96) contention that 6.14–7.1 is the conclusion to the argument begun in 2.14 is also not without merit, as it is the last of the three central argument sections. What I would add to these interpretations is that 5.11–7.1 is anticipated by the partition head in 1.23, which speaks to covenantal faithfulness.

Covenantal faithfulness establishes the connection of 1.23a to 5.11–7.1 and supports the view that 6.14–7.1 is appropriate to the context of 2 Corinthians. This can be shown in two ways. First, in the *first portion* of 1.23 Paul calls upon God as *witness against his life* (ἐπὶ τὴν ἐμὴν ψυχήν). This is to be distinguished from Rom. 1.9 (μάρτυς γάρ μού ἐστιν ὁ θεός), Phil. 1.8 (μάρτυς γάρ μου ὁ θεός), and 1 Thess. 2.5, 10 (θεὸς μάρτυς), where it is positively stated that "God is a witness" to Paul's conduct. In 1.23 Paul evokes God *potentially* as a witness against himself, indicating that Paul was on trial by the Corinthians as having done something wrong.

To call God as witness (μάρτυς) against one's conduct corresponds to the theme of covenantal faithfulness in view of idolatry and other sins found throughout the Jewish scriptures (see 1 Sam. 12.6; Jer. 29.23; 42.5 [49.5 LXX]; cf. Deut. 31.26; Josh. 22.34; 24.27; 1 Sam. 12.3; 2 Kgs. 17.13; Mal. 2.14; Jdt. 7.28; Wis. 1.6). For example, consider Ps. 50.7 (LXX, my translation): "Hear, My People, and I will speak to you, O Israel; even I will testify against you [διαμαρτύρομαί σοι]. I am God, your God." The psalm gives a listing of sins and ends by reference to the "salvation of God" (τὸ σωτήριον τοῦ θεοῦ – 50.23; cf. 2 Cor. 6.2). Closest grammatically to 2 Cor. 1.23 (with ἐπί) is Mal. 3.5 (NRSV):

> Then I will draw near to you for judgment; I will be a swift witness against [μάρτυς ἐπὶ] the sorcerers, against the adulterers, against those who swear falsely, against those who oppress the hireling in his wages, the widow and the orphan, against those who thrust aside the sojourner, and do not fear me, says the LORD of hosts.

The conjoining of 2 Cor. 1.23, which calls God into court to provide covenantal forensic witness, with 2 Corinthians 6 contributes to the work of William L. Lane (1982). Lane argues that Paul developed themes from the Suffering Servant section in Isaiah (40–55), specifically Isa. 49.1–13 (cf. 2 Cor. 6.2), to express the nature of his mission. What is particularly relevant for the context of idolatry in 2 Cor. 6.14–7.1 is that God is *witness* for his people that there are no other gods within Isa. 40–55. For example, consider the LXX of Isa. 43.10 and 43.12 (LXX, my translation):

"Become my witnesses, and I myself am a witness," says the
Lord God, "and my servant whom I have chosen, in order that
you may know and believe and understand that I am he. Before
me no other god existed, nor after me will there be any."

"I declared and saved. I reproached and there was no foreigner
god among you; *you* are my witnesses and *I* am a witness," says
the LORD.

The motif of God as testifier to covenantal faithfulness is critical, and
includes allegiance to God as the One God. Paul exhorts the Corinthians
to turn from their idolatry back to the living God in 6.14–7.1.

One might think that Paul's defense is lost in this analysis, but it is
not. Reconciliation to God also meant reconciliation to Paul. Lane (1982,
p. 19; cf. 25) argues,

The point that reconciliation to God demanded reconciliation to
his messenger is forcefully made by Paul through the citation of
Isaiah 49:8a in 2 Corinthians 6:2 . . . Paul found in this recital of
the call, disparagement, and vindication of the servant in Isaiah
49 a paradigm for his relationship with the Corinthians.

Thus, for Paul to evoke the covenantal theme of God as witness in 2 Cor.
1.23 anticipated his argument in 5.11–7.1, which describes Paul's urging
the Corinthians to covenantal faithfulness under the dispensation of the
new covenant "in the fear of the Lord."

Thus far I have argued that 1.23a anticipates Paul's fourth argument
section, which culminates in his plea that the Corinthians stop their idolatrous associations (6.14–7.1). The second half of 1.23 also supports this
contention: "it was to spare [φειδόμενος] you that I did not come again to
Corinth." As I shall point out below in my discussion of the *peroratio*,
Paul uses this same verb φείδομαι summarily at 13.1–2 in reference to
5.11–7.1.

Paul's choice of φείδομαι, which is typically overlooked by commentators, carries a significant covenantal notion *associated mainly with the
moral failings of God's people*. In the LXX it is regularly used to render סוח ("to pity") and חמל ("to spare" or "to have compassion") (BDB,
pp. 299, 328). Those who sinned were not to be spared (Deut. 19.11–13,
16–21; 25.11–12), including above all idolaters (Deut. 13.6–8 [LXX,
13.7–9]). The surrounding idolatrous nations were not to be pitied
(Deut. 7.16; cf. Hab. 1.17; Zech. 11.6). The Hebrew prophets often
warned that the Lord would *not spare* his own sinful people (e.g., Jer.
13.14; 14.10; 15.5; 21.7; Lam. 2.2, 17, 21; Ezek. 5.11; 7.6, 8; 8.8; 9.9;

Isa. 58.1), although this did not stop the Israelites from praying that God would (Joel 2.17–18; cf. 4.16 [LXX]).

That Paul would *spare* the Corinthians in view of their rebellious condition is contrary to this picture. However, there was one *foundational instance* in which God had spared his people: *when initiating them as a distinct covenant people after the Exodus*. God had spared them when leading them under the direction of Moses, despite their idolatry as Ezek. 20.13–17 describes (cf. Deut. 33.3; Isa. 63.8–9). Paul's willingness to spare the Corinthians by not visiting them as planned is analogous to God's (and Moses') sparing the Israelites in their idolatry when in the wilderness. Critically, Paul had already invoked this very episode to warn the Corinthians of idolatry in the previous letter (1 Corinthians 10). Of course, Moses was instrumental in sparing them by pleading on their behalf (Exodus 32). Thus, Paul's own comparison with Moses in 2 Corinthians 3 contributes to our understanding of the covenantal exhortation in 2 Cor. 6.14–7.1. He is the Corinthians' Moses and now has acted to spare them a grievous visit by writing them a "heavy and strong" exhortative letter instead, "the letter of tears" or 1 Corinthians. Second Corinthians is his follow-up letter in preparation for his imminent arrival (12.14–13.2).

Lane (1982, pp. 3–6) argues that Paul presented a *rîb* lawsuit against the Corinthians according to the ancient Near Eastern custom of the vassal–suzerain treaty. Paul as God's messenger found the Corinthians guilty of violating treaty terms and was formally presenting a charge against them. Lane argues (p. 10): "The disruptions at Corinth . . . displayed a callous insensitivity to the New Covenant. Paul was mandated by God to express the divine complaint against the rebellious Corinthians and to call them back to the stipulations of the covenant." Although Paul was not following this ancient Near Eastern form of the *rîb*, as Lane himself admits (pp. 15–16; cf. Belleville, 1989, p. 150 note 30), this does not diminish Lane's insight that *Paul here brings an accusation against the Corinthians in covenantal terms*. Lane's understanding (p. 16) of the central argumentative section, if one includes 2.14–17, is quite sound:

> The theological core of Second Corinthians extends from 3:1–7:1, and finds its coherence in the concept of the New Covenant concluded between God and his people. Both the content and the structure of Paul's thought are intelligible from the perspective of covenant lawsuit ideology. Paul's purpose is to call the Corinthians to renew their commitment to the Lord and to complete the obedience they have already begun to manifest in response to

his "letter of tears." By stressing the eschatological superiority of the new ministry with which he has been entrusted by God to the older ministry committed to Moses, Paul was able to throw into bold relief the urgency of his pastoral appeal.

Therefore, far from being an *egressio* (Witherington, 1995, pp. 402–406), 6.14–7.1 is climactic with respect to Paul's purpose in the central argumentative sections (2.14–7.1). As will be explored in Chapter 9, Paul's defensive strategy was *to make a counter-charge against the Corinthians in order to account for his failure to visit.* Because of their gross idolatrous sin, the Corinthians prevented Paul from coming to them *as he had initially planned.* The argument section in 5.11–7.1 comes to an end with the resumption of narrative material in 7.2–16.

The distributed *narratio* in 7.2–16

As promised, I shall offer a few comments on this final narrative section. First, this is not a letter closing (*contra* Belleville, 1989, pp. 149–50). It exhibits the concern to clear Paul from any wrongdoing in the most emphatic terms (7.2) while explaining his favorable view of the Corinthians, despite the fact that he has just given them a weighty exhortation (7.3). It further establishes the extent of Paul's concern for them by relating the nature of his response to Titus' good news about their renewed zeal (ζῆλος) for him (7.7, 11–12), using terms (ἔρις and ζῆλος) typically associated with students' sentiments towards their rhetorical instructors (Winter, 1997, pp. 170–77). Paul had raised this issue in the course of the previous letter in 1 Cor. 3.3 (ἔρις and ζῆλος).

The narrative in 7.2–16 is rhetorically sophisticated, in that it subtly establishes an inconsistency on the part of the Corinthians. They had wavered in their support of Paul, until 1 Corinthians arrived with Titus, the purpose of which was to win their eagerness (σπουδή) for Paul (7.12). For a time they were on Paul's side. However, they turned once again from Paul to his missionary rivals (5.11–12; chaps. 10–11). It thus maintains the spirit of counter-accusation explicit in the previous argument section (cf. 7.3). The test of the Corinthians' allegiance to Paul awaited further clarification in the letter; namely, their complete participation with him in the collection. This narrative section ends the central argument sections and serves as a transition to Paul's final argument by broaching the issue of *mutual boasting* (7.14–16), a theme Paul applies to the matter of the Corinthian portion of the collection (8.24; 9.2–3).

Fifth argument: 2 Cor. 8.1–9.15

The partition head in 1.24 ("I do not mean to imply that we lord it over your faith; rather, we are workers with you for your joy, because you stand firm in the faith") prepares for 2 Corinthians 8–9. These chapters are a unified appeal that illustrates how Paul works with the Corinthians and also encourages them to give to the collection as a response to their faith in God (1.24b; 8.7, 9). Generally speaking, chapter 8 concerns details; chapter 9 provides motivations for the Corinthians to give (Danker, 1989, p. 19; Witherington, 1995, p. 331). Paul does not demand that they give (1.24a); their contribution is not from extortion (9.5). Instead, he has assembled a very respectable entourage of co-workers to assist in this endeavor (8.6, 16–18, 23; 9.3–5; cf. 1.24b). Witherington (1995, p. 413) aptly argues, "By reminding the Corinthians about the collection, Paul gives them an opportunity to be financial coworkers with him." However, Paul does not consider their contribution as a substitute of patronage for himself (*contra* Witherington, 1995, pp. 341–43). The import of the argument is rather that by contributing to the collection the Corinthians can evidence their reconciliation with Paul, their own consistency (since they indicated that they would do so earlier), and their obedience to the glory of God.

However, there is more to the situation. In the previous chapter, it was argued that Paul was accused of πλεονεξία (greed) and that some Corinthians suspected that Paul had ulterior motives for the collection (7.2; 9.5; 12.16–19; cf. 8.5). Additionally, the Corinthians likely aligned themselves with rival missionaries for whom they were prepared to send letters of recommendation with their portion of the collection (see 3.1; cf. 1 Cor. 16.1–4). They had followed Paul's directives (1 Cor. 16.3) and approved and commended these rivals instead of Paul (2 Cor. 5.12; 13.7; cf. 10.12, 18). Thus, on the one hand, 2 Corinthians 8–9 fulfills the need for Paul to defend himself and his intentions about the collection and show himself and his companions approved (see esp. 8.20–22). On the other hand, Paul perceived that the issue of the collection provided an opportunity to test the Corinthians. They will show themselves approved only when they take part in the collection with Paul as planned (8.8; 9.13). Otherwise, they will show themselves to be inconsistent (8.10–15). Rhetorically, the collection was a means to test concretely the Corinthians' stance towards Paul and his gospel. Hughes (1991, p. 259) rightly argues, "If the Corinthians would be reconciled with both Paul and the one whom Paul represents, then their giving would become not merely a financial matter, but a demonstration of their solidarity with Paul's apostolic ministry and mission."

Table 8.5 *Kennedy's basic disposition schema
of 2 Corinthians 8–9*

Speech section	2 Corinthians 8–9
Narratio	8.1–6
Preparation for *propositio*	8.8–9 (8.7 is not mentioned)
Propositio	8.10–11
Enthymematic argument	8.12–14
Support	8.15
Recommendation of Titus	8.16–24
Explanation for writing presently	9.1–5
Epilogue	9.6–15

Table 8.6 *Betz's basic disposition schema
of 2 Corinthians 8 and 9*

Speech section	2 Corinthians 8	2 Corinthians 9
Exordium	8.1–5	9.1–2
Narratio	8.6	9.3–5a
Propositio	8.7–8	9.5bc
Probatio	8.9–15	9.6–14
Commendation of envoys	8.16–22	
Authorization	8.23	
Peroratio	8.24	9.15

I shall end this discussion of chapters 8 and 9 by considering their dispositional structure and relationship to the broader apology Paul is presenting. Kennedy (1984), Betz (1985), and Kieran O'Mahony (2000) present competing understandings of the disposition and setting(s) of the chapters. Kennedy (pp. 91–92) briefly argued that 2 Corinthians 8–9 formed a complete deliberative speech with a discernible disposition. See Table 8.5.

However, although correct about their unity, Kennedy's proposal is imprecise and not well substantiated by specific features in the text. Moreover, he is unable to relate the material content and concerns of 2 Corinthians 8–9 with the rest of the letter, and treats it as one letter among three edited in 2 Corinthians (1–7, 8–9, and 10–13).

Betz proposed in a learned commentary that these chapters are two administrative letters, each evidencing its own rhetorical structure (pp. 38–41, 88–90). See Table 8.6.

Table 8.7 *O'Mahony's basic disposition schema of 2 Corinthians 8–9*

Speech section	2 Corinthians 8–9
Exordium	8.1–6
Propositio	8.7 (8)
Confirmationes	8.9–9.10
1 Why give?	8.12–14
2 Emissaries appointed	8.15
3 Emissaries sent ahead	8.16–24
4 God's reward	9.1–5
Peroratio	9.6–15

Betz presents a most thoroughgoing argument; however, it is not compelling. O'Mahony has thoroughly reviewed and shown the inadequacy of Betz's proposal, concluding (p. 181) that "Betz's rhetorical reading, although rich in detail and background, fails to deal adequately with the data."

More on target is O'Mahony's rhetorical analysis of these chapters, which he argues are unified and display a discernible disposition (p. 165). See Table 8.7.

His careful rhetorical methodology (pp. 35–48) and treatment of figures (summarized on pp. 182–83) serve his analysis well. He concludes that the purpose of Paul's persuasion is to test the Corinthians' resolve to finish their portion of the collection, to reestablish Paul's authority, and to reconnect the Corinthians with the broader fellowship of believers (pp. 161–62).

Problematic, however, is O'Mahony's treatment of 2 Corinthians 8–9 in relative isolation from the rest of 2 Corinthians, and its apologetic aims. He intends to consider the "potential consequences" for the unity of the letter (p. 35), but fails to do so. Particularly, this affects his conclusion that 8.1–6 is to be understood as the *exordium* (with Betz) rather than as a *narratio* (Kennedy, p. 91). However, 8.1–6 contains a historical review, Paul's testimony (μαρτυρῶ), and a careful description of the Macedonians' financial gift to Paul *as distinct from their giving to the collection* (8.5) in defense of Paul's handling of monies. These features suggest rather that 8.1–6 functions as a *narratio* in the broader book context of apology. My dispositional analysis is slightly different also concerning the identification of a *partitio* rather than a *propositio* and in the identification of the *peroratio*. See Table 8.8.

Table 8.8 *The disposition of 2 Corinthians 8–9*

I *Narratio*: 8.1–6 The Macedonians' example in giving
   – initiated with disclosure formula ("We want you to know, brethren")
   – employs Paul as witness (cf. 1.8, 12)
II *Partitio*: 8.7–9
   A 8.7 "Now as you excel in everything – in faith, in speech, in
      knowledge, in utmost eagerness [πάση σπουδῇ], and in our love for
      you – so we want you to excel also in this generous undertaking."
   B 8.8 "I do not say this as a command, but I am testing [δοκιμάζων] the
      genuineness of your love against the earnestness of others [διὰ τῆς
      ἑτέρων σπουδῆς]."
   C 8.9 "For you know the grace [χάρις] of our Lord Jesus Christ, that
      though He was rich [πλούσιος], yet for your sake He became poor, so
      that you through His poverty might become rich [πλουτέω]."
III *Probatio*: 8.10–9.12
   A 8.10–15: The Corinthians' former eagerness
   B1 8.16–24: Titus' and Paul's eagerness [σπουδή]
   B2 9.1–5: The eagerness of the Macedonians and the rest of the Achaians
   C 9.6–12: Theological appeal to give generously since they have been
      enriched [πλουτίζω] by God's grace [χάρις]
IV *Peroratio*: 9.13–15 God's Indescribable Gift

For Paul to include a relatively distinct rhetorical argument within
a larger rhetorical piece is not odd, since he had done so already in 1
Corinthians 8–10, 12, and 15 (see, e.g., Watson, 1989, 1993; Smit, 1993,
1996; Eriksson, 1999a). We also have the example of Andocides' *On
the Mysteries* (discussed in Chapter 5.1), in which, because of the multi-
plicity of issues, Andocides presents several miniature speeches without
destroying the integrity of the whole disposition.

Paul has composed a rather nice deliberative speech within 2 Corinthians urging the Corinthians to give to the collection (note the appeal to
benefit at 8.10 [συμφέρω]; see Betz, 1985, pp. 63–64; O'Mahony, 2000,
pp. 145–46). He has already prepared for this section, not only in the
partitio in 1.24, but also by introducing the general theme of abundance
(περισσεύω) in 1.5 in the *prooemium*. Additionally, Paul's secure hope
(βεβαία ἐλπίς) with respect to the Corinthians (1.7) anticipated Paul's
hope of acquittal that would necessarily involve Corinthian participation
with him in the collection, since βεβαία and περισσεύω are financial terms
(Danker, 1989, pp. 34–35). Although deliberative in import, 2 Corinthians 8–9 affords Paul the opportunity to show himself approved and call
upon the Corinthians to approve of his ministry through the collection.

In other words, as Witherington (1995, p. 412) argues, "The deliberative argument . . . serves Paul's larger forensic purposes."

Furthermore, Paul continues in some sense his counter-accusation, since the Corinthians have not kept their word. Thus, as Betz (1985, pp. 59–60; cf. Witherington, p. 411; O'Mahony, 2000, p. 161) contends, Paul "regarded the collection as a real test for the Corinthians, on the assumption that the continual test of faith is not the sign of a lack of trust but part of the life of faith itself . . . The object of the test was to prove the genuineness (τὸ γνήσιον) of their love, which would only be manifested by the successful completion of the collection."

Concluding remarks on the *probatio*

Paul craftily constructed his apology with a *partitio* that outlined the major argumentative divisions. I argue that the problematic literary features in 2 Corinthians 1–9 may be accounted for on the basis of Paul's dispositional strategies. He bolstered his *ethos* by distributed narratives at 2.12–13 and 7.2–16 in which he recounts his care and concern for the Corinthians as he awaited Titus' report of their reception of the letter of tears (1 Corinthians). Moreover, the distributed narratives isolate the first and last argument sections (2.1–11 and 8.1–9.15) in which critically Paul relates his intentions for and the logistics of his travels and the collection. The transition from 2.13 to 2.14 is thus not problematic, since Paul is taking up his second argument section. He initiates each of the three central argument sections (2.14–3.18; 4.1–5.10; 5.11–7.1) with four interrelated themes: his rhetoric, God's surveillance, (self-) commendation, and his rivals. The troublesome passage 6.14–7.1 is accounted for on the basis of Paul's partition head in 1.23, which evokes the theme of covenantal intervention (Paul *spares* the Corinthians a grievous visit just as Moses spared the Israelites). The covenantal themes of gospel proclamation, glory, and future judgment culminate with Paul's stern call to covenantal faithfulness in 6.14–7.1. Paul's strategy of counter-accusation is evident here and in chapters 8 and 9. These two chapters evidence a high degree of sophistication, both rhetorically and conceptually, since Paul is able to account for his and his co-workers' actions, while simultaneously urging the Corinthians to approve of his ministry by following through on their promise to participate with him in the collection. Ultimately, the approval of their faith was needed.

Finally, my rhetorical analysis illuminates the progression of the *probatio* (2.1–9.15), which may be summarized as follows. Paul did not visit as promised because of moral problems among the Corinthians, which would have been very grievous for Paul to handle given his dire straits. Paul offers forgiveness to the one causing grief, lest Satan gets the best of the situation (2.1–11). The Corinthians themselves had initially accepted the gospel through the proclamation of Paul *et al.* They thus received the Holy Spirit and came under the promises of the new covenant in Christ, which are to be distinguished from the old covenant in the degree of boldness and glory bestowed (2.14–3.18). Paul's gospel is veiled, since not all believe, and his sufferings and disrepute, while seemingly discordant with the new covenant promises, are not in fact discordant. Paul, likening himself to an earthen vessel, received the Spirit just as have the Corinthians, and both await a final court appearance (4.1–5.10). In view of this, Paul as a minister of reconciliation persuades people to accept salvation. The waywardness of the Corinthians jeopardized their relationship with God and Paul, and they risked putting themselves outside the moral parameters and promises of the new covenant (5.11–7.1). There is hope, however, for the Corinthians, who once rallied to Paul and have Paul's and Titus' confidence even yet (7.2–16). By contributing to the collection under the auspices of Paul and his trustworthy companions, the Corinthians will approve of their ministry and give glory to God (8.1–9.15). These arguments are offered as proof of Paul's good intentions in his travel and all other plans, his godly *modus operandi* in matters of conduct and rhetorical speech, and his upright handling of the collection.

8.7   *Refutatio*: 10.1–11.15

As argued in Chapter 5.4, several features can characterize this section. The *refutatio* typically follows the *probatio*, mentions opponents repeatedly and denigrates them, answers criticisms directed against oneself, and contains various refutative techniques, such as not naming opponents directly. In light of my form-critical analysis of extant forensic speeches, 10.1–11.15 is best understood as the *refutatio* in 2 Corinthians, rather than a distinct letter or a speech itself.

First, 10.1–11.15 follows the *probatio* and is not anticipated by the *partitio*. Although working within the general tenor of the charges (Paul has failed to visit and is worldly), the *refutatio* is a distinct, even relished, section in the oration to answer residual issues and to lambaste the opponents (e.g., Dem. 18.124–26). It is clearly demarcated with the emphatic opening statement "I myself Paul" (Αὐτὸς δὲ ἐγὼ Παῦλος) (cf. the introduction to the *refutatio* in Antiph. 1.5, "I am amazed" θαυμάζω δ'ἔγωγε).

A very similar expression, "Behold, I Paul speak" (Ἴδε ἐγὼ Παῦλος λέγω), is found within the *refutatio* of Galatians (see Brinsmead, 1982, pp. 53–54). Frederick F. Bruce (1971, p. 229) correctly states about 10.1 that "the very Paul who is disparaged and misrepresented by his opponents is the one who speaks with the apostolic authority vested in him in Christ."

Second, Paul repeatedly refers to two groups of opponents. In rhetorical studies, the opponents in chapters 10–13 are treated homogeneously (e.g., Betz, 1972, p. 43; Witherington, 1995, pp. 345–51; Peterson, 1998, p. 72). However, Paul's antagonists among the Corinthians (as seen in 10.1–11, 14; 11.4) are distinct from his missionary rivals (as seen in 10.12, 18; 11.4–5, 13–15). Generally speaking Paul addressed the former directly and the latter in the third person (cf. Betz, 1972, p. 43; the one possible exception is the general statement in 10.10). Paul criticized these rivals explicitly (10.12; 11.4, 13–15) and implicitly (10.15–16, 18; 11.3). He feared losing the Corinthians' allegiance through the deception of his missionary rivals (11.3–5, 12–15). Thus, Paul criticized these rivals to free the Corinthians from their spell. Because of them, some of the Corinthians became critical of Paul. Thus, Paul must violently push these missionary rivals aside in the minds of the Corinthians through invective rhetoric to assure positive relations with the Corinthians before he would visit Corinth again (12.20–13.1).

Third, Paul answers various criticisms some of the Corinthians were holding against him, which is expected in a *refutatio*. Betz (1972, p. 43) acknowledges this by arguing that

> Paulus verteidigt sich vor der Gemeinde gegen die von den Gegnern geltend gemachten Bedenken seinem Apostelamt gegenüber. Er äußert sich detailliert zu den einzelnen Anklagepunkten, spricht aber zur Gemeinde, nicht zu den Gegnern, mit denen es wohl auch kein Gespräch geben kann. [Paul defends himself before the community against misgivings effectively prepared by the opponents with respect to his apostolic office. He addresses in detail the individual charges speaking to the community, not to the opponents, with whom there can also probably be no conversation.]

Betz's notion that the rivals are responsible for all the criticism is objectionable. However, what is critical is Betz's observation that Paul replies to *diverse criticisms*. Although a rhetorician would employ the same means of argumentation in both the *probatio* and the *refutatio*, in the latter section the speaker is able to address (*and* introduce!) *various* criticisms himself (Cic. *Inv.* 1.78; specific types of arguments for *refutatio* are discussed in

Table 8.9 *Direct and indirect criticisms addressed in 10.1–11.15*

	Corinthian criticisms of Paul	Addressed by Paul
Paul's speech and authoritative presence	10.1 Humble when present, but bold when absent.	10.2 Paul will dare to speak.
	10.2 Paul lives according to the flesh.	10.3–6 Paul wages unworldly warfare to attain obedience.
	10.7 Paul does not belong to Christ.	10.7 Yes, he does.
	10.8 Paul boasts of his authority.	10.8 This authority is to build up, not tear down.
	10.9–10 Paul is inconsistent: his letters are strong/weighty, and yet his presence is weak and his speech contemptible.	10.11 What Paul says by letter he will do when present.
Paul's variable acceptance of patronage	11.7 Paul preached free of charge.	11.9–10 Paul did not burden anyone.
	11.8 Paul robbed other churches and rejected funds from Corinth.	11.11 Paul loves the Corinthians.

1.79–96; cf. Quint. *Inst.* 5.13). In forensic speeches defendants do not typically recall multifarious charges and reply to them all as Paul does at this point in 2 Corinthians (*contra* Betz).[7] This rather indicates that he has constructed a *refutatio*.

Paul answers criticisms in two sections. In 10.1–11 the criticisms pertain to his speech and authoritative presence. In 11.7–11 the concern is Paul's refusal to accept money while accepting it from others. Table 8.9 lists the direct or inferred criticisms to which Paul gives a response. Many

[7] Betz (1972, p. 44) contends, "Wie in einer Gerichtsrede üblich, zitiert Paulus die Anklagepunkte und nimmt auch sonst fortwährend Bezug auf die gegnerische Anklage, indem er Wendungen, Ausdrücke oder Sachverhalte aus ihr aufnimmt und sie zu seinen Gunsten, das heisst im Sinne der Verteidigung, interpretiert. In diesem zum Teil sehr komplizierten Verfahren besteht die Verteidigung des Paulus." ["As in a court-speech usually, Paul quotes the charges and also typically continuously takes reference from the opposing accusation, in that he takes up phrases, terms, or circumstances from it and interprets them in his favor, that is, in the sense of the defense. Paul's defense consists of this very complicated procedure."]

recent interpreters have aptly analyzed these criticisms (Sumney, 1990, pp. 149–79; Watson, 2002), so only a brief comment on each group is necessary.

Winter (1997, esp. pp. 207–208) and Litfin (1994) have shown how the Corinthians criticized Paul's speech on the basis of sophistic criteria. Paul's letters, not just 1 and 2 Thessalonians but also 1 Corinthians (*contra* Winter, p. 208, esp. note 22), showed rhetorical prowess. They are rhetorically "heavy" (βαρεῖαι), as the evaluation of 10.10 indicates: "For they say [φησίν], 'His letters are weighty and strong, but his bodily presence is weak, and his speech contemptible.'" Concerning 10.10, Betz (1986, p. 41; cf. 1972, pp. 44–45) makes the following keen observation:

> We do not know where this well-composed three-point description comes from. Paul attributes it to one person, but it is unclear whether this person is merely an individual of the church, or a spokesman for a group, or even an investigator appointed by the church to evaluate Paul. The statement looks like a summary from an evaluation report about Paul's performance as an apostle, especially his facilities with the word.

This is true, especially when one understands *Paul's word* to mean his oratorical delivery. As for the origins of the assessment in 10.10, φησίν simply means that this was a circulating evaluation of Paul's speech. This sort of evaluation is best accounted for when we remember the "sophistic mentality" among (some of) the Corinthians (on attacking an opponent's rhetorical ability, see Danker, 1991, p. 276). The critique is not related to Paul's apostleship (*contra* Betz, 1972, p. 45). Winter (1997, p. 203) argues that the critique originated with the missionary rivals who, when attacked implicitly by Paul in 1 Corinthians, returned the fire with a critique of Paul's "inherent deficiencies as a public speaker in order to justify their own ministry in the church." To diffuse this criticism, Paul admitted to being merely an ἰδιώτης τῷ λόγῳ (11.6), which did not necessarily mean that he was untrained in rhetoric, but rather *that he was not a professional rhetorician* (on this meaning of ἰδιώτης, see Winter, pp. 213–15). Winter (p. 220) argues, "The evidence reveals that Paul's *modus operandi* is being judged by sophistic categories (2 Cor. 10.10, 11.6 and 12.14–18). Furthermore, the assault was framed in light of his own critique of the sophistic tradition in 1 Corinthians 1–4." One can perceive that Paul's absence and decision to write rather than visit provided fertile fields for such criticisms to grow into specific charges needing his apology.

The remainder of the *refutatio* consists of two sections in which Paul criticizes his missionary rivals: 10.12–11.6 and 11.12–15. See Table 8.10.

Table 8.10 *Paul's criticism of and difference from his missionary rivals*

Paul's criticism of missionary rivals	How Paul is different [and better]
10.12 Others compare themselves with others and commend themselves; they show no understanding.	10.12 Paul does not dare to compare himself with them.
10.13 [They boast beyond limits.] 10.15–16 [They boast in someone else's work.]	10.13–14 Paul stays within God's assignment. 10.15–16 Paul boasts in his own work. 10.17–18 Paul gives a moral maxim on the matter.
11.3–4 They are likened to the serpent who deceived Eve; they offer another gospel and spirit to the Corinthians.	11.2 Paul is divinely jealous and desires to keep the Corinthians pure in devotion to Christ.
11.5 They are "super apostles" [and deceptive in that they are not really "known"].	11.5–6 Paul is not inferior; if he can't speak, he does impart knowledge so that he is well known.
11.12 They claim equal status with Paul by accepting Corinthian support.	11.12 Paul works free of charge to undermine them.
11.13–15 They are false apostles like Satan himself, disguised as servants of righteousness.	11.16–12.10 This leads to Paul's foolish boast or self-adulation.

Sometimes Paul's criticism of these missionary rivals is implicit, which is indicated by brackets in Table 8.10.

Concerning 10.12–18, Scott Hafemann (1990, pp. 82–83) argues that Paul rejected the authoritative claim of his rivals on the ground that the basis of their claims (self-commendation in comparison with others) was not valid:

> The problem is simply that Paul's opponents are attempting to boast in something for which they have no divine "canon" or attestation of having, namely, a claim of authority over the Corinthians . . . the boast of Paul's opponents is merely an exercise in "*self*-commendation," since they lack the necessary divine accreditation appropriate to the claim in view.

The *divine canon* is the reception of the Spirit through Paul's proclamation. The criticism to which Paul subjected his rivals is scathing, particularly at the end in 11.13–15. They are "false apostles, deceitful workers, disguising themselves as apostles of Christ," deserving a fitting condemnation. In comparison with extant forensic speeches, Paul's caustic remarks are fitting.

Additionally, Paul used methods that are consistent with the refutative tradition. For example, Paul discusses his antagonists using indefinite constructions. DiCicco (1995, p. 177) argues this point well:

> Interestingly enough, as another way of showing his hostility, Paul regularly damns his rivals with anonymity. His usual references to them are: "some" (10:2; 10:12), "themselves" (10:12), "such people" (11:13), "many" (11:18), "anyone" (11:20), and other non-specific references contained in verbs [e.g., 10:10]. Paul's object in this non-naming of his rivals is to reduce them in stature and thus create animosity toward them in the minds of the Corinthians.

This particular feature extends also into the beginning of the next section (τις – 11.16, 20–21). Such anonymity contrasts sharply with the opening of the *Refutatio* in 10.1: "I, Paul, myself entreat you" (Αὐτὸς δὲ ἐγὼ Παῦλος παρακαλῶ ὑμᾶς).

Paul also turned the argument of his opponents against them. We must recall that he was already the victim of this strategy (see Chapter 7.2). For example, he asks those sizing him up in 10.2 (λογίζομαι) to think again in 10.7 (λογίζομαι) (Peterson, 1998, pp. 89–90, who lists others). Additionally, Paul defended his territorial jurisdiction against intrusion (10.13–16); his missionary rivals, one might assume, claimed jurisdiction over the Corinthians, probably because they had received support from the Corinthians (11.7–10). Paul turned the argument against his opponents by implying that they were claiming credit for someone else's work. Paul also identifies them as "false apostles" and "agents of Satan" (11.13–15; cf. 11.3); perhaps the Corinthians described Paul in these terms. Lastly, he responds to the criticism from the Corinthians that his letters are too weighty or βαρείαι (10.10). He receives the charge of clever speech, at least with respect to his letters. However, by implication Paul levers this argument against his opponents by calling himself "inexperienced in speech" (ἰδιώτης τῷ λόγῳ) in 11.5–6 (cf. Dem. 58.61) and by implicitly comparing the rivals to the deceiving serpent (11.3). In contrast to Paul, the rivals must be professional rhetoricians who are not to be trusted, as he had insinuated in the *probatio* (2.17; 4.2).

By using these techniques and by answering and presenting his own critique of his rivals, Paul followed the form of apologetic *refutatio*. One can perceive Paul's rhetorical skill in the construction of individual units

Table 8.11 *Strategic arrangement of material in the* refutatio

Unit A (10.1–11)	Paul answers criticisms of the Corinthians of his authority and speech.
Unit B (10.12–11.6)	Paul critiques the missionary rivals for their boasting/self-commendation (and therefore lack of authority) and their deceptive speech, which likens them to the serpent in the garden.
Unit A′ (11.7–11)	Paul answers criticisms of the Corinthians of his refusal of their support.
Unit B′ (11.12–15)	Paul criticizes the missionary rivals for trying to claim equal status by receiving support and categorizes them with Satan, who is disguised.

within this *refutatio*. See Table 8.11. The arrangement of material consists of an alternation between Paul answering criticisms from (some of) the Corinthians (Units A and A′) and then offering his own criticism of his missionary rivals (Units B and B′). Additionally, when Paul answers criticisms, the criticism is given first; but when he criticizes the missionary rivals, Paul starts with a positive remark about himself before offering the criticism.

There is an inner correspondence for units A and B, and for units A′ and B′ thematically and lexically. Within units A and B Paul addresses matters of authority, deception/inconsistency, and speech. Paul begins responding to criticism in unit A at 10.2 by using the verbs θαρρέω and τολμάω: "I ask that when I am present I need not show boldness [θαρρέω] by daring [τολμάω] to oppose those who think we are acting according to human standards." Likewise in unit B at 10.12, Paul begins his critique by not *daring* (τολμάω) to engage in comparison with his missionary rivals. These rhetorical terms were used in the debate between philosophers and sophists; and Betz (1972, pp. 67–68; cf. Malherbe, 1983, p. 167) is correct to see Paul using these terms accordingly.

Here it is important to see that τολμάω carries the nuance of a prosecutor introducing hybristic charges. Isocrates in *Antidosis* (14; cf. Isocrates' deliberative speech *Archidamus* 33 and Lys. 21.20) makes the audacious statement, "I consider that in all the world there are none so depraved and so deserving of the severest punishment as those who have the audacity to charge others [τολμῶσι κατηγορεῖν] with the offences of which they themselves are guilty." This theme is pronounced in *Antidosis*, particularly at the beginning of the *refutatio* in 196–319 in relation to Isocrates' opponents (2, 23, 139, 209, 212, 217, 221, 228). It was typical to characterize your opponent by saying "they dare to say that . . ." or using similar expressions with τολμάω (Aeschin. *Ctes.* 53; Antiph. 5.57; Dem. 38.6; Din. 1.49; Isae. 1.17, 27; Isae. 8.1, 2, 26, 30; Lys. 14.5; Lys. 19.49, 51; cf. Isae. 3.61; Isae. 10.14). Only the one in a *weaker* position can be so bold as "to assert their righteous claims" (Isae. 9.35).

The second round of criticisms in A′ and B′ concerns Paul's financial independence from the Corinthians. Although Paul rejected patronage from the Corinthians and accepted it from the Macedonians, he still asserted his love for the Corinthians. The missionary rivals accepted support from the Corinthians only to claim equal status with Paul and so disguise themselves as Satan does.

The AB/A′B′ structure would also indicate that the "super apostles" (11.5) and the "false apostles" (11.13) were the same group, since both were associated with the serpent/Satan (Theissen, 1982, p. 48 note 50; *contra*, e.g., Barrett, 1973, pp. 30–32). This association is rhetorically sophisticated, since it communicated to the Corinthians that Paul attributed greater responsibility for wrongdoing to his missionary rivals. These rivals were deceptive, just like the serpent in the garden (11.3) and Satan, who can be disguised as an "angel of light" (11.14). For the Corinthians to resist the deception of the impostors and to recognize their disguise would be very difficult. According to Paul's depiction (11.3–5), the Corinthians found themselves like Eve – potentially deceived. They needed a clear understanding of Paul in relation to themselves (11.6), so that reconciliation could occur. To align themselves with the agents of Satan would be to share the rivals' ultimately grim fate (11.15).

My argument necessitates that interpreters distinguish between the Corinthians' standards of evaluation and the missionary rivals' arguments for authoritative status. As many have noted, the missionary rivals were well received by the Corinthians because they met these standards: They were rhetorically sophisticated (11.5–6), perhaps even displaying an audacious moral strictness (11.20); then they also accepted patronage from the Corinthians (11.12; cf. Hock, 1980, pp. 62–63). In many respects, the rivals embraced this feature of Hellenistic culture. Paul, however, avoided these associations, as 1 Thess. 2.1–10 indicates (Winter, 1993a). However, in 2 Corinthians we are privileged to see Paul constrained *to refute both the grounds of his evaluation by the Corinthians and the claims of his missionary rivals.*

Thus far I have argued how 2 Cor. 10.1–11.15 addresses opponents, answers and offers criticisms, and contains rhetorical strategies consistent with the forensic tradition of *refutatio*. These forensic features account for Paul's invective. Stylistically Paul used irony (εἰρωνεία) rather effectively to defend himself against slanderous remarks entertained by the

Corinthians and the (boastful) practices of his missionary rivals (Forbes, 1986). At the same time, Paul promoted tremendous ill feeling towards his antagonists, both from the Corinthian community and especially his missionary rivals. However, 2 Corinthians 10–13 is more than just a *refutatio*; it contains Paul's self-adulation and the *peroratio* for the whole letter.

8.8   Self-adulation: 11.16–12.10

Paul's extended boast in chapters 11–12 has attracted much scholarly attention. It is my contention that 11.16–12.10 conforms to the apologetic practice of speaking concerning oneself (περὶ ἑαυτοῦ) or self-adulation. Although there has been interest on the ancient topic of self-praise, particularly as enumerated by Plutarch's *On Praising Oneself Inoffensively*, my survey in Chapter 5.5 indicates that in theory and practice self-adulation originated in forensic contexts.

There are several ancient speeches that show considerable analogy to Paul's discourse. For example, Demosthenes in *On the Crown* asserts in the *prooemium* (4),

> To him [Aeschines] the agreeable duty [of accusation] has been assigned; the part that is almost always offensive remains for me. If, as a safeguard against such an offense, I avoid the relation of my own achievements, I shall seem to be unable to refute the charges alleged against me, or to establish my claim to any public distinction. Yet, if I address myself to what I have done, and to the part I have taken in politics, I shall often be obliged to speak about myself [ἀναγκασθήσομαι περὶ ἐμαυτοῦ]. Well, I will endeavor to do so with all possible modesty; and let the man who has initiated this controversy bear the blame of the egoism which the conditions force upon me [τὸ πρᾶγμα αὔτ᾽ ἀναγκάζη].

Just as Demosthenes *was forced* by Aeschines to speak at length concerning himself (cf. περὶ ἐμαυτοῦ at 321), so Paul *was forced* (ὑμεῖς με ἠναγκάσατε at 12.11) to be a fool in commending himself. At 12.11, he self-reflectively refers to his apology in the preceding chapters.

Paul followed the apologetic strategy of self-adulation in 11.16–12.10 by use of appropriate technical terminology. He argues (12.5): "On behalf of such a one [ὑπὲρ τοῦ τοιούτου] I will boast, but on my own behalf [ὑπὲρ ἐμαυτοῦ] I will not boast, except of my weaknesses." Paul's use of the preposition ὑπέρ is calculated in the context of 2 Corinthians

10–12 (Barnett, 1997, p. 33, lists these uses). For example, Paul stresses in 12.7 the surpassing quality (ὑπερβολή) of his revelations and the risk of self-inflation (ἵνα μὴ ὑπεραίρωμαι) because of them. Paul's emphatic statement in 11.23 using ὑπὲρ ἐγώ is choice: "Are they ministers of Christ? I am talking like a madman – I am a better one [ὑπὲρ ἐγώ]." By using technical terminology like ὑπὲρ ἐμαυτοῦ in 12.5 and ὑπὲρ ἐγώ in 11.23 Paul indicates that he is formally engaged in apologetic self-adulation. Such terminology matches a number of apologetic speeches where identical terminology is used after the *refutatio* at the end of the speech.

For example, in Hyperides' *Defense of Lycophron*, after giving the *refutatio* (8–13), the orator makes a clear transition to talk about himself (14): "So Ariston may say whatever he pleases, gentlemen of the jury, and invent lies against me, but surely your verdict upon me must be based, not on the slanders of the prosecutor, but on a review of the whole of my life." After reciting several aspects of his good conduct and honors (16–18), he makes the transition to the *peroratio* with this retrospective statement: "Well, gentleman of the jury, you have heard virtually all that I had to say in my own defense [lit. 'concerning myself']" (ὅσα μὲν οὖν ἐγὼ εἶχον, ὦ ἄνδρες δικασταί, ὑπὲρ ἐμαυτοῦ εἰπεῖν, σχεδὸν ἀκηκόατε). (See also the use of ὑπὲρ ἐμαυτοῦ in Antiph. 2.2.13 immediately after the honorable deeds section in 2.2.12.) Another example can be found in the *dokimasia* trial speech by Lysias, *In Defense of Mantitheus*, in which Mantitheus (20) refers to his recitation of his good deeds as speaking "on behalf of his own actions" (ὑπὲρ τῶν ἐμαυτοῦ πραγμάτων). Other similar examples with ὑπὲρ ἐμαυτοῦ can be provided (e.g., Andoc. 1.148; Antiph. 2.4.11; Din. 1.48; Isae. 10.1). For the similar expression περὶ ἐμαυτοῦ in relation to this section of a forensic speech, see my discussion in Chapter 5.5.

Self-adulation complements the *refutatio*. Where does the *refutatio* end and self-adulation begin? How can we be sure that 11.16–12.10 is the proper delimitation of this section? In 2 Corinthians it is difficult to locate its precise beginning, although 11.16 seems most appropriate, since the number of references to *boasting* increases significantly. Furthermore, there are notably fewer statements directed against Paul's opponents. Victor P. Furnish (1984, p. 484; cf. Barnett, 1997, pp. 18, 528, 534, 577) argues that 11.1 begins the section "A Fool's Speech" from 11.1 to 12.14. However, this is problematic, because Furnish (pp. 511–12) understands 11.16 as a renewal of the appeal to be foolish (accepting 11.17–18 as parenthetical, as does the RSV) and 11.21b–12.10 as "the speech proper." Other interpreters view 12.10 as ending a major section (Witherington, 1995, pp. 442–64, esp. 442; cf. Travis, 1973, p. 531).

Table 8.12 *Boasting and foolishness in 2 Corinthians*

Foolish/foolishness	Within chapters 10–12	Outside these chapters
ἄφρων: foolish	**11.16², 19; 12.6, 11**	
ἀφροσύνη: foolishness	11.1, **17, 21**	
Boast/boasting		
καύχησις: boast	11.10, **17**	1.12; 7.4, 14; 8.24
καυχάομαι: I boast	10.8, 13, 15, 16, 17²; 11.12, **16, 18²**, 30²; **12.1, 5², 6, 9**	5.12; 7.14; 9.2

Tracking the key terms relating to *boasting* and *foolishness* can provide the basis for the view that the self-adulation section begins at 11.16 and extends to 12.10. See Table 8.12.

The idea of boasting, which unites the whole letter, is found in some concentration in chapter 10. However, 10.8 refers only to the possibility of Paul's boasting (a conditional construction), whereas 10.13–17 *and* 11.12 contain his criticism of the inappropriate boasting of his rivals. Furthermore, Paul's boast (καύχησις) in 11.10 is actually given to answer a direct criticism involving his financial independence from the Corinthians. The greater concentration of the occurrences of καυχάομαι is in 11.16–12.9; they all refer exclusively to Paul's boasting, except 11.18. (But even 11.18, which mentions the boasting of the opponents, is Paul's justification for his own boasting.) Paul explicitly indicated that he will boast in 11.16, 18, 30; 12.5, 9 (καυχήσομαι). Paul's self-adulation is concluded by the last reference in 12.9: "So, I will boast all the more gladly of my weaknesses, so that the power of Christ may dwell in me." As far as Paul's foolishness is concerned, permission is asked for *a little foolishness* to be granted him in 11.1. However, Paul answers criticisms (his poor speech; his financial history) and attacks his missionary antagonists (Satan's motley crew) in 11.1–15, so that he is not *truly* foolish until he indulges in a little boasting for himself (11.16–12.10). Paul's statement after his boasting is done in 12.11a ("I have been a fool! You forced me to it") indicates that his boasting is finished and initiates the *peroratio*. Thus, 12.10 is the end of his self-adulation.

How does Paul's boast concerning himself compare with other boasts in forensic speeches? There are at least five similarities. First, Demosthenes was forced (ἀναγκάζω) to speak about himself, as was Paul (see also below). Second, I have already discussed ὑπὲρ ἐγώ in 11.23 and ὑπὲρ ἐμαυτοῦ in 12.5.

Third, Paul affirms his race, heritage, and parentage in 11.22: "Are they Hebrews? So am I. Are they Israelites? So am I. Are they descendants of Abraham? So am I." For Paul to ignore this would, in fact, be shameful and cowardly. This concern has direct correlation to Theon's *Progymnasmata* and forensic speeches. In Theon's discussion of *encomium* in the *Progymnasmata* (9.15–19; cf. Anax. *Rhet. Alex.* 35; Arist. *Rhet.* 1.5.5–6; *Rhet. Her.* 3.6.10; Cic. *Inv.* 2.177; see also Butts, 1986, p. 481 note 7) one's *good breeding* (εὐγένεια ἀγαθή) in terms of race, nationality, and parents is listed first among the "external qualities." In the forensic speeches the deeds of one's father could be evoked to help one's case (Andoc. 1.141–43; Antiph. 5.74–84). Also one's nationality was tied to being a good citizen (Andoc. 1.144; Lys. 7.30–32; Dem. 18.321–22; Hyp. 1.16; Hyp. 4.33, 37; Isoc. 18.58; cf. Hunter, 1990, pp. 314–16).

Fourth, although it is true that Paul in 11.23–33 "employs well known encomiastic conventions" but is *parodying* them (Travis, 1973, pp. 529–30; McCant, 1999), the description of his hardships correlates with Theon's recommendations and the extant speeches. Theon (9.25–33; cf. Anax. *Rhet. Alex.* 35; Arist. *Rhet.* 1.5.9) describes these as "noble actions" (καλαὶ πράξεις):

> Noble actions are both those which are applauded after death (for it is customary to flatter the living) and, conversely, those which are applauded while we are still living . . . Noble actions are also those which we do for the sake of others, and not ourselves; and in behalf of what is noble, rather than on account of what is advantageous or pleasant; and in which the labor is individual, but the benefit is shared; and on account of which most people receive great benefits; and which we do for the sake of benefactors and especially dead ones.

There are many examples in the extant forensic speeches (cf. Antiph. 2.2.12; Dem. 18.321–22; Isoc. 18.62–64; Lys. 7.31–32). One accuser (Isoc. 18.62) argues thus: "Yet surely men who should now be regarded as friends of the people are . . . those who, when the state was suffering misfortune, were willing to brave the first dangers on your behalf . . . and gratitude is due . . . to him who conferred benefits to you." Paul likewise recounts his labors and hardships endured for the church (11.23–29). Also, Paul's "heroic military" exploits of being let down a wall in 11.30–33 (Judge, 1966, p. 45) are not without analogy in forensic speeches. One's military services for the city were especially appropriate in this section of the speech (see, e.g., Isoc. 18.59–61 and Hyp. 1.17).

Fifth, to conclude this section Paul recounts his prodigious religious experiences. He relates the first set of experiences in the third person (12.1–7a), perhaps mimicking the practice of calling upon one's friends and family members as witnesses to testify for the defendant (for examples, see Chapter 5.5). Quintilian (*Inst.* 11.1.22) argues: "Let us therefore leave it to others to praise us. For it beseems us, as Demosthenes says, to blush even when we are praised by others." The second experience – an account of an oracle from Christ the Lord – is given directly to Paul: "My grace is sufficient for you, for power is made perfect in weakness" (12.9a). This also has precedent in the oratorical tradition (e.g., Antiph. 2.2.12; Antiph. 5.81–84; see also Chapter 5.5). Socrates is perhaps the best-known example in antiquity who relates a prodigious oracle from Delphi declaring him to be the most free, upright, or temperate person of his day (Xen. *Apol.* 14; cf. Quint. *Inst.* 5.11.42). But immediately, to lessen the force of this oracle, Socrates recounts an oracle deifying the lawgiver Lycurgus of Lacedaemon. Is Paul mimicking this Socratic tradition by diminishing his own oracle by first relating the visions of another person in 12.1–7a (if these verses are not a reference to himself)? In any case, it is hard to imagine a stronger testimony for Paul's person despite his weakness than the Lord's testimony in 12.9. This statement is climactic for the whole letter by effectively relativizing earthly evaluations of Paul, his ministry, and his weakness by a direct commendatory statement from the risen Christ.

There can be little doubt that Paul followed the apologetic tradition of self-adulation, even though he amply seasoned it with parody by appealing to his weaknesses. He used the technical terms typical of this section; he included themes suitable for self-adulation; and he ended the section climactically with what would have been recognized as the crème de la crème of divine commendation. The purport of Paul's self-adulation met the requirements of ancient apology, but did so *while it undermined the typical social values associated with it.* Paul's apology served both a defensive purpose and a pedagogical one, as he acknowledged at 12.19 within the *peroratio*.

8.9   *Peroratio*: 12.11–13.10

Since I have argued that 10.1–12.10 comprises the complementary sections of *refutatio* and self-adulation, these verses cannot be a part of the "emotional recapitulation of the arguments of the letter" (*contra* Barnett, 1997, p. 18). Rather, the *peroratio* begins at 12.11 and runs until the epistolary closing (13.11–13). Evidence for this conclusion comes from at least six considerations.

First, Paul is most self-reflective about his discourse in 12.11–13.10. I have already treated 12.11 briefly. Paul blames the Corinthians for his need to be foolish: "I have been a fool! You forced me to it [ὑμεῖς με ἠναγκάσατε]. Indeed you should have been the ones commending me." Paul's use of ἀναγκάζω to express why he *must* present an apology is perfectly in line with forensic oratory, as the example from Demosthenes' *On the Crown* quoted above illustrates.

Pleaders often claimed to have been forced into a litigious situation (see Isoc. 15.23; Antiph. 1.2; 3.2.1; 3.3.1; Lys. 12.3, 92, 93, 96; 22.1; Dem. 40.35; Dem. 41.4; Dem. 45.5; Dem 48.1, 2; cf. Dem. 37.43; Dem. 40.2, 11). For example, in Lysias' *In Defense of Mantitheus*, a δοκιμασία speech, the defendant initiated the *peroratio* with the following remarks: "I have had occasion to observe, gentlemen, that some people are annoyed with me merely for attempting at too early an age to speak before the people. But, in the first place, I was compelled [ἠναγκάσθην] to speak in public on behalf of my own honorable deeds [ὑπὲρ τῶν ἐμαυτοῦ πραγμάτων]" (16.20 – my own translation). So also in the *peroratio* of Lysias' *Against Simon* (actually a defensive speech) the defendant argues (48) that he was *forced* to stand trial on account of his interactions with his accuser.

Furthermore, at 12.19 Paul self-reflectively remarks that the Corinthians have perceived 2 Corinthians as a defense "all along" (πάλαι). Self-conscious reference to one's speech as either an accusation or a defense in the *peroratio* is found within forensic speeches (e.g., Aesch. *Leg.* 180.2; Antiph. 5.85.1; Lys. 14.46.1). Peterson (1998) argues on this basis alone that 12.19 marks the beginning of the *peroratio*. He notes (p. 133) that Paul has become self-reflective at this point: "in 12:19 Paul stops to look back over what he has said." However, 12.11 fulfills this equally well and employs a forensic element which expresses why he was compelled to offer his speech ending with self-adulation. That one could begin the *peroratio* self-reflectively without immediately referring to one's speech formally as a defense or an accusation is seen in Antiphon 6.48 and Isocrates 15.320. The precise significance of 12.19 (*defending* and *building up*) is understood only when one comprehends that Paul in 12.11–13.10 is recapitulating all of 2 Corinthians. Specifically, 12.19 recalls Paul's covenantal exhortation and accusation of the Corinthians in 5.11–7.1.

This brings us to a second consideration. When reading 12.11–13.10, it becomes apparent that the Corinthians are expected to render a decision regarding Paul. Paul plays on this in 12.19, but explicitly refers to their decision in 12.13, 18 and 13.3, 6–7 (my translations follow). Thus, in 12.13 Paul pleads, "Forgive me this wrong!" (χαρίσασθέ μοι τὴν ἀδικίαν ταύτην), and in 12.18 he pointedly asks (expecting a positive answer) "Did we not conduct ourselves in the same spirit? Did we not take the same steps?" (οὐ τῷ αὐτῷ πνεύματι περιεπατήσαμεν; οὐ τοῖς αὐτοῖς ἴχνεσιν;) In 13.3 Paul asserts "you seek proof of Christ speaking in me" (δοκιμὴν ζητεῖτε τοῦ ἐν ἐμοὶ λαλοῦντος Χριστοῦ), and in 13.6–7 he anticipates, "I hope you will know that *we* are not unapproved . . . but *we* may seem to be unapproved" (ἐλπίζω δὲ ὅτι γνώσεσθε ὅτι ἡμεῖς οὐκ ἐσμὲν ἀδόκιμοι . . . ἡμεῖς δὲ ὡς ἀδόκιμοι ὦμεν). In 13.1 Paul quotes Deut. 19.15 on what constitutes evidence worthy for a proper verdict to be reached.

That Paul expresses his hope in 13.6 is a common element in forensic cases, as was discussed in connection with the *prooemium* above. Attached to this hope is that the Corinthians "will know [γνώσεσθε] that we [Paul *et al.*] have not failed." *The use of the future tense form here is odd at the end of the discourse.* However, such use of the future tense is an idiom reflecting a future decision to be rendered by a jury. For example, also in the *peroratio* in Isocrates 20.18.2 is the statement by the litigant, "Indeed, concerning the present case you will know rightly [ὀρθῶς γνώσεσθε] and will cause the other citizens to be more orderly and will make your own life more safe" (my translation). Also in Antiphon 5.96 the defendant predicts, "And concerning me you will render a decision [διαγνώσεσθε] in accordance with the established laws" (my translation). These particular examples also parallel 2 Cor. 13.6–7, because both passages encourage the judges to make *the right decision*. See also Antiphon 2.2.12, where γνώσεσθε is used in the honorable deeds section just prior to the *peroratio* in view of the final decision to be rendered (cf. Antiph. 5.85.10; Dem. 48.58.5; Lys. 6.51; Lys.19.11; Lys. 22.17; Lys. 24.27; Lys. 25.7).

In this respect, 13.6 and the expression of hope in 1.13 (followed by the future verb ἐπιγνώσεσθε) in the *narratio* need to be understood together: The evidence provided in the *narratio* will assist the Corinthians in their final decision. (See the use of γνώσεσθε in the forensic speeches cited above in Chapter 8.4.) That this future form of the verb in these settings, which typically introduces evidence (relevant to a proper decision), ought to be seen in conjunction with the final verdict is explicitly portrayed in Demosthenes 22.44: "Then even if it were certain that after this man's conviction no one would pay the tax or be willing to collect it, even so you

must not convict him, as you will see [γνώσεσθε] from this consideration."
After this the pleader produces a short argument using evidence.

A third reason to view 12.11–13.10 as the *peroratio* is that Paul introduces God as the One before whom he speaks in 12.19 and to whom he
prays concerning the Corinthians' choosing to do the right thing (13.7).
Paul is setting before the Corinthians the fact that God is watching over
the verdict that they will render. We should be reminded of Cicero's suggestions (*Inv.* 1.101): "The first topic [under *indignatio*] is derived from
authority when we relate how much care and interest has been devoted to
the subject under discussion by those whose authority ought to have the
greatest weight, namely, the immortal gods." Quintilian likewise argues
(*Inst.* 6.1.34), "Invocation of the gods, again, usually gives the impres-
sion that the speaker is conscious of the justice of his cause." Once again,
the juries in forensic speeches are repeatedly reminded by the pleader
of the gods' interest in the justice of the case (e.g., Aeschin. *Leg.* 102,
180; Andoc. 1.139; Antiph. 1.25, 31; Antiph. 2.1.10; Antiph. 6.3–4; Dem.
18.324; Dem. 26.27; Isae. 2.47; Isae. 6.58; Isoc. 15.281–82, 321; Lycurg.
Leoc. 148; Lys. 4.20; Lys. 6 *et passim*; Lys. 13.95; Lys. 19.34, 54).

Fourth, with respect to the decision to be rendered, Paul gives several
admonitions to the Corinthians: 12.13, "Forgive" (χαρίσασθέ); 12.16,
"Let it be" (ἔστω); 13.5 "Examine yourselves" (Ἑαυτοὺς πειράζετε);
13.5 "Test yourselves" (ἑαυτοὺς δοκιμάζετε). This practice – pleaders
admonishing the jury about their vote – has parallels in the extant forensic
speeches. For example, the pleader in Isocrates 20.21–22 exhorts:

> No, if you will be advised by me, you will not assume that
> position toward your own selves. You will not teach the young
> men to have contempt for the mass of our citizens, nor consider
> that trials of this character are of no concern to you; on the
> contrary, each one of you will cast his ballot as if he were judging
> his own case . . . And so, if you are wise, exhort one another,
> and reveal to Lochites your own wrath, for you know that all
> individuals of this kind despise the established laws, but regard
> as law the decisions rendered here.

Similar examples may be cited (Antiph. 2.1.10; Dem. 26.27; Din. 1.109–
11; Isae. 6.62; and Lys. 4.18–19; 22.20).

Also notable is Paul's urging the Corinthians emphatically in 13.7 to do
the right thing (ἵνα ὑμεῖς τὸ καλὸν ποιῆτε). Καλόν is used in the *peroratio*
in Demosthenes 45.85.10 with reference to a verdict: "For neither would
it be good [καλόν] for you [to allow me to suffer through your verdict in
light of my father's favorable services]" (my translation). Consider also

Demosthenes 49.57.1, where καλόν is used to indicate what would make a pleader's case favorable given a specific hypothetical situation. Also, there is one passage from Demosthenes' *Against Aristocrates* (75; cf. Dem. 25.16) that contains a slight digression on determining whether an action (in this case a murder) was just.

> And yet to every act and to every word one of two epithets is applicable: it is either just or unjust [δικαίου καὶ ἀδίκου]. To no act and to no word can both these epithets be applied at the same time, for how can the same act at the same time be both just and unjust? Every act is brought to the test [δοκιμάζεται] as having one or the other of these qualities; if it be found to have the quality of injustice, it is adjudged to be wicked, if of justice, to be good and honest [χρηστὸν καὶ καλόν].

One wonders whether Paul is drawing on a tradition of evaluating (δοκιμάζω) a defendant's actions to determine whether they are good (καλόν). If so, he inverted the evaluation of himself to the Corinthians: they are the ones who are to act justly. Their evaluation of Paul must start with evaluating themselves (13.5) and then doing the right thing. This strategy would be in keeping with the counter-accusation that is present throughout 2 Corinthians.

Furthermore, the pleader's exhortations to the jury often accentuate the consequences of the decision. For example, in Isocrates 20.18 the litigant says: "And it is the part of intelligent judges, while casting their votes for justice in causes not their own, at the same time to safeguard their own interests also" (cf. Aeschin. *In Ctes.* 156–58; *In Tim.* 192–96; Antiph. 2.2.11; Dem. 22.44–45; Din. 1.66–68, 113; Isae. 2.47; Lys. 13.96; Lys. 19.33; Lys. 22.17–21). Paul plays on this characteristic as well, since he repeatedly refers to his impending visit and clearly portrays the consequences of his visit (12.14, 20–21; 13.1–3, 10). At this point Paul was likely utilizing the topic of comparing one crime with another (under inciting ill-will Cicero includes this as the ninth topic; *Inv.* 1.104; cf. *Rhet. Her.* 2.49). Paul's own crime (cf. 1.17) is that he had failed to visit. However, such a crime was necessitated because of the crimes of the Corinthians, i.e. their immorality, which is bluntly depicted to the Corinthians: God may humble Paul when he does come with the Corinthians' disobedience (12.21). I shall treat this feature of counter-charge within 2 Corinthians more completely in Chapter 9.2.

Fifth, the rhetorical theoreticians advised constructing the *peroratio* by amplification (appeals to emotions) and recapitulation. Amplification is achieved either through evoking ill-will towards one's opponent (*indignatio*) or arousing pity and sympathy for oneself (*conquestio*) (Cic. *Inv.* 1.98; see Quint. *Inst.* 6.1.9–55 and 6.2). Most generally, Cicero argues (*Inv.* 1.106) that one should appeal to one's own weakness as a shared "weakness of the human race." Paul does this in 13.4, 9 (cf. 12.9–10). Furthermore, although he does not make a direct appeal for mercy (ἔλεος), he asks to be forgiven in 12.13. Cicero discusses (*Inv.* 1.109) an appeal for mercy as the fourteenth common topic under *conquestio*. Even if spoken somewhat ironically by Paul or with a slightly offensive tone, the request is nevertheless fitting for the *peroratio* (cf. the sixth common topic for *indignatio*; Cic. *Inv.* 1.102; cf. *Rhet. Her.* 2.49).

Also, within 12.11–13.10 Paul evokes a range of emotions. In 12.14–15 he relates himself lovingly to the Corinthians as a father to a child. To ask the hearers to consider oneself a parent or child is a common topic for *conquestio* according to Cicero (*Inv.* 1.108). In 12.20–21, however, Paul depicts himself as a fearful disciplinarian. Furthermore, in 13.9 he speaks of rejoicing (χαίρω), yet in 13.10 he threatens having to treat the Corinthians severely (ἀποτόμως).

To heighten the intensity and emotion of the *peroratio*, Cicero also recommended the use of weighty terms, the repetition of words, and asyndeton (*Part. Or.* 53–54; cf. Arist. *Rhet.* 3.19.6; *Rhet. Her.* 4.41; Quint. *Inst.* 6.1.2; 9.3.50; for other references see Butts, 1986, p. 397 note 70). Weighty terms in 2 Corinthians 12.11–13.10, some of which are repeated, include, for example, ἀλήθεια (13.8[2]), δοκιμή (13.3), δοκιμάζω (13.5), δόκιμος (13.7), ἀδόκιμος (13.5, 6, 7), οἰκοδομή (12.19; 13.10). Significantly, Paul admits in 13.7 to having the appearance of being unapproved (ἀδόκιμοι): "Now we pray to God that you do no wrong; not that we ourselves may appear approved [ἡμεῖς δόκιμοι φανῶμεν], but that you may do what is right, even though we may appear unapproved [ἀδόκιμοι ὦμεν]" (NASB). To substantiate this feeble admission, Paul argued (13.8) that "we cannot do anything against the truth, but only for the truth."

As for repeated themes, there are the Corinthians' immorality (12.21–13.2, 5, 7) and Paul's impending visit (12.14, 20, 21; 13.1, 10). Finally, this *peroratio* lacks connective conjunctions at some critical transitions, thus displaying asyndeton (12.11, 14, 17, 18, 19; 13.1, 2, 5). This is not to say that 12.11–13.10 does not have its share of coordinating conjunctions or particles: γάρ (12.11[2], 13, 14[2], 20; 13.4, 8, 9); μέν (12.12); καὶ (12.14); δὲ (12.15, 16, 19; 13.6, 7, 9); ἀλλά (12.16).

This leads us, sixthly, to consider how the *peroratio* is a recapitulation of the arguments, inclusive of the *refutatio* and extending back through the *partitio* (but not the *narratio* and *prooemium*) (cf. *Rhet. Her.* 2.47). We must recall the main arguments of 2 Corinthians at this point: his

Table 8.13 *The inverted recapitulation of 2 Corinthians in 12.11–13.10*

Peroratio	Recapitulation in *peroratio*	Sections summarized
12.11–13	Paul's foolishness, commendation in light of false apostles, Paul's genuine apostleship and signs	10.1–12.10
12.14–18	Paul's coming, seeking them, not their money, sending Titus and the brother, not taking advantage of them	7.2–9.15
12.19–13.4	Paul's defense yet upbuilding, they are beloved, strong moral exhortation	5.11–7.1
13.1–4	Paul's coming, witnesses, sin confronted; Paul's speech in Christ, weakness, life, and power	5.11–7.1 and 2.14–5.10
13.5–10	Corinthian self-examination and test, Paul's seemingly acting unapproved, writing presently but coming soon, Paul's moral authority not with severity but for building up	2.1–11

failure to visit (1.17; 2.1–11), his God-derived authority, rhetoric, and moral appeal to the Corinthians (2.14–7.1), the travels of Titus (7.2–16), Paul's collection efforts, involving Titus and the brethren and his own coming (8.1–9.15), and finally his refutation of opponents (10.1–11.15) and self-adulation, culminating in his visions and divine affirmations (11.16–12.10). With only some slight creativity, the ordering of material in 12.11–13.10 indicates that *Paul was here surveying the entire discourse of 2 Corinthians, but in inverted order, retracing the main points of his argumentation.* See Table 8.13. For a more detailed description, see Appendix I.

One can detect similar inverted recapitulations in 1 Corinthians 15 and Galatians, both of which display forensic disposition. First Corinthians 15.50–58 summarizes the discourse in inverted order: 15.50–53 summarizes the *refutatio* (15.35–49) and 15.54–58 recapitulates the *probatio* (15.20–34). The *peroratio* in Gal. 6.11–17, although not as precise, begins by treating Paul's opponents and circumcision (6.12–13), both of which were dealt with in the *refutatio* (4.21–6.10), before moving to recapitulate other significant themes found throughout the letter.

Paul's inverted summary in 2 Corinthians can be detected by tracking key words (and their cognates) and important themes (see especially Appendix I). This conforms to the recommendations of Cicero (*Part. Or.*

59–60) that the enumeration shows diversity and is not a too obvious "embarking on a parade of one's powers of memory." "This danger," Cicero argues, "will be escaped by one who does not repeat all his very small points, but while briefly touching on them one by one brings into focus the actual values of the facts" (*Part. Or.* 60). Paul's summary is not rote. Rather, it accurately reflects his core concerns and values. These are a proper understanding of himself as Christ's apostle and spokesperson, his urgent appeal to the Corinthians for their moral repentance, and Paul's future coming and the nature of his authority, to build them up. The picture before us, then, is that Paul has constructed 12.11–13.10 as a recapitulating *peroratio.* Any full-scale exposition of 2 Corinthians would benefit from a careful study of this feature of the *peroratio.*

8.10 Conclusion

I have argued that 2 Corinthians may be described as an apologetic speech with a discernible disposition. The evidence suggests that Paul composed it according to forensic practice and the rhetorical principles available in his day and age. Many forensic and apologetic features, themes, and strategies have been discovered. For example, the *exordium* in 1.3–7 is well crafted, anticipates major themes in the *probatio,* and concludes with an expression of hope for a favorable outcome in the case. The *narratio* in 1.8–16 recounts facts relevant to the case and prepares for Paul's arguments by disclosing in no uncertain terms his good intentions to come to Corinth. Furthermore, Paul wisely distributed narrative sections throughout the *probatio* (2.12–13 and 7.2–16) which explained his whereabouts and anticipation of hearing from Titus how the letter of tears (1 Corinthians) was received by the Corinthians.

The argument heads in the *divisio/partitio* (1.17–24) outline in order Paul's main argument in the *probatio.* Furthermore, I investigated the architecture of the *probatio,* discovering that the central three arguments in 2.1–7.1 shared important themes (rhetoric, rivals, [re]commendation, and God's purview). Additionally, these sections work within a distinctive new covenantal theology culminating in a call to covenantal faithfulness (6.14–7.1). In this regard, it is significant that Paul begins with a comparison/contrast with Moses' boldness, since Paul's final call to covenantal faithfulness justifies his use of persuasion "in the fear of the Lord" (5.11; 7.1). The two bracketing argument sections (2.1–11; 8.1–9.15) pertain specifically to Paul's relations with the Corinthians on matters concerning his visits and the collection. Specifically, I agree with other interpreters that the argument in 8.1–9.15 evidences its own deliberative disposition, appealing to the Corinthians to participate with Paul in the collection. This critical section contributes to Paul's apology by demonstrating his financial integrity (and that of his associates) while at the same time challenging the Corinthians tangibly to be restored to a proper relationship with him by approving of this ministry, thus participating with him (rather than his rivals) in the collection.

The *refutatio* follows the *probatio*, as would typically be the case. In 10.1–11.15 Paul answers criticisms from some of the Corinthians and directs criticisms to his missionary rivals. The *refutatio* is followed by the complementary self-adulation section of 11.16–12.10 in which Paul must boast about himself, his nationality, his heroic efforts, and his prodigious religious experiences. Although he employs parody here to educate the Corinthians, the inclusion of his foolish boast indicates that he is working firmly within the apologetic tradition.

Finally, in the *peroratio* Paul evidences a concern to recapitulate his letter retracing major themes. It is clear that the Corinthians must make a decision about his conduct. Are he and his associates approved (δόκιμοι) or not? In some respects, Paul admits the appearance of culpability (12.13; 13.7; cf. 7.2b). Associated with this failure to visit, however, Paul criticizes the Corinthians for their moral failings (12.20–21; 13.1–2; cf. 2.9; 5.20; 6.1, 12–16; 13.5). To a large extent, Paul's strategy was to offer a counter-charge. In Chapter 9 I examine this and other aspects of rhetorical invention in 2 Corinthians.

9

THE RHETORICAL INVENTION
OF 2 CORINTHIANS

9.1   Introduction

Turning to rhetorical invention in 2 Corinthians, I am painfully aware that I am working with an ancient text. This text is dynamic, contoured, and cryptic. It is, however, the only *window* we have through which to reconstruct Paul's invention of arguments. Did Paul prepare his apology according to the rhetorical invention process within ancient rhetorical theory and as modeled in forensic practice? My research would indicate that he keenly constructed *a line of defense*. Second Corinthians contains numerous interrelated argumentative strategies and techniques consistent with forensic rhetorical theory and practice.

9.2   Essential issue and *stasis* theory

Can 2 Corinthians be analyzed successfully according to *stasis* theory? If so, would this necessarily indicate that Paul utilized *stasis* theory? The first step to answering these questions is to discover what *stasis* would apply according to the reconstructed situation from Chapter 7. In the second step, I shall apply forensic theory to probe the argumentative landscape of 2 Corinthians.

Qualitative *stasis* in 2 Corinthians

I begin with a preliminary consideration of the nature of the charges and the determination of the overall *stasis* of the case. According to forensic theory we should expect that Paul constructed the main argument in 2.1–9.15 with one primary *stasis* (see Quint. *Inst*. 3.6.9). The evidence suggests that, since he could not deny the charges against him, Paul developed his defense according to the qualitative issue, which was a defendant's most honorable choice (Quint. *Inst*. 3.6.83). In Chapter 7 I argued that Paul was charged with inconsistency on several fronts: using worldly rhetoric, accepting patronage from the Macedonians (possibly stealing from their portion of the collection), and changing his itinerary while failing to visit altogether. By looking at the nature of Paul's defense on these particular points, one can determine which is focal and determinative of the issue.

Concerning the use of rhetoric, Paul could not deny it, since he constructed 1 Corinthians with great rhetorical care. Thus, according to the qualitative *stasis*, it is quite fitting that in 2 Cor. 5.11 Paul admits that he "persuades persons" (ἀνθρώπους πείθομεν) *with the added qualification* that he does so "knowing the fear of the Lord" (εἰδότες τὸν φόβον τοῦ κυρίου).

Concerning his acceptance of patronage, Paul repeatedly distinguished himself from greedy persons (2.17; cf. 4.2), thus *by definition* excluding the possibility that he was stealing monies (cf. Acts 20.33). In 8.1–5 Paul recounted that a portion of the Macedonians' giving went to himself, but that this was "through the will of God" (διὰ θελήματος θεοῦ). Thus, the quality of their gift of patronage is emphasized (8.5). In 11.7–12 Paul entertained the notion that he *robbed* other churches in order to serve the Corinthians, essentially denying this *conjecturally*, but mainly describing the *quality* of his sacrificial actions out of love for the Corinthians. So, to answer this charge of accepting patronage and being greedy, there are features of conjecture, definition, and quality.

Finally, in 2 Corinthians Paul treats failing to visit as primary. Whether this focus is Paul's tactic to manage the situation, the actual main criticism of the Corinthians, or the result of Paul's insight that his absence was the precipitous issue of all others is difficult to determine. Paul forcefully raised the charge of his itinerate inconsistency in 1.17. Thrall (1994, p. 142) argues that it is "an exegetical impasse" how Paul repudiates this charge. Let me venture across.

Since Paul did not come to Corinth but rather wrote a disciplinary letter, his best course of defense involved the *stasis* of quality. Paul's action (writing instead of coming) was admitted, but he argued that it was *the right act* (or *recte factum* in Cic. *Part. Or.* 102). Paul interspersed narrations describing his deep concern for the Corinthians and his good intentions of writing rather than visiting. Paul narrated his travel experiences (1.8–16; 2.12–13) and the beneficial effects of his tearful letter sent in his place (7.2–16). He also accounted for the beneficial travels of his liaisons to the Corinthians, especially Titus (7.6, 13–14; 8.6, 16–18; 12.18). Paul's final words to the Corinthians consisted of repeated references to his impending visit to Corinth in the *peroratio* (12.14, 20–21; 13.1–3, 10).

Cicero (*Part. Or.* 42) describes how the action might be defended in the qualitative issue: "Either . . . the deed was rightly done for the sake of avoiding or avenging pain or in the name of piety or modesty or religious scruple or patriotism, or finally because of necessity or ignorance or accident." These rationales proceed from strongest (avoiding pain) to weakest (accident). Furthermore, Cicero (*Part. Or.* 106) argues that the question is "whether he [the defendant] had the power and the right" to perform the act. An action was performed either by divine or human right (*Part. Or.* 129; cf. *Top.* 90). In either case, by arguing according to the qualitative *stasis* one was enabled to show the *honorable* nature of one's actions. No doubt remains as in a conjectural case; nor is there quibbling over definitions. Rather, the defendant admits to performing the action, but is able to justify it as right, necessary, beneficial, and hence honorable.

I shall present my analysis of the *stasis* of quality along two lines. First, I shall determine the point to be judged (κρινόμενον) within a qualitative case according to Hermagoras' theory as reproduced in Cicero's *De Inventione Rhetorica*. This will contribute to one's understanding of the foundation (*firmamentum*) of Paul's line of defense in the *probatio*; this turns on the issue of his authority (cf. Eriksson, 1998, p. 36). Second, I shall consider the argument strategies and *topoi* particularly recommended in *Rhetorica ad Herennium* and Cicero's *De Inventione Rhetorica* for the presentation of a qualitative case. Here I disagree fundamentally with Anderson's (1996, p. 58) general claim, "Given that the kind of τόποι provided for the στάσεις are related to typical judicial disputes, they are not actually very relevant to Paul's letters." Demonstrably, Paul drew upon *the most fundamental arguments recommended for qualitative forensic cases.*

The Hermagorean line of defense

To begin, it would be helpful if the reader recall from Chapter 4.1 (esp. Figure 4.1) the interchange between the prosecutor and defendant that Hermagoras developed in order to determine one's line of defense. Figure 4.1 concerned Orestes' murder of his mother (Cic. *Inv.* 1.18–19). Cicero presented other cases in a similar format (*Inv.* 2.73, 79, 87; *Top.* 95; *Part. Or.* 103). Such a format, by extrapolating lines of argument from the initial charge and defense, aided the speech's construction. How Paul developed the *probatio* of 2 Corinthians may be investigated heuristically by overlaying the Hermagorean format onto it (P = prosecutor, D = defendant, and J = judge). See Table 9.1.

Table 9.1 *Judicial exchange for determining the line of defense in 2 Corinthians*

P1	*intentio*; κατάφασις	You did not visit us but sent a rhetorical letter in which you deny using rhetoric. Therefore, you are inconsistent and worldly.	indictment
D1	*depulsio*; ἀπόφασις	I did this justly. I am not inconsistent or worldly.	defense
J1	*quaestio*; ζήτημα	Is Paul justified in this?	question
D2	*ratio*; αἴτιον	For you were not prepared morally for my visit. Besides, I was suffering enough as it was; by visiting you I would have suffered more grief. And, I wanted you to have some answer to those boasting in persons.	excuse or reason
P2	*infirmatio rationis*; αἴτιον	You have no authority over us, especially since you yourself work underhandedly and in a worldly manner. You are, in fact, rather embarrassing, because of your appearance and fiascoes. We have others who are credentialed and more physically and rhetorically graceful who are willing to be patronized by us.	rebuttal
J2	*iudicatio*; κρινόμενον	Was it right for Paul not to visit the Corinthians because they were not morally prepared for his visit?	point of judgment
D3	*firmamentum*; σύνεχον	God leads me in triumphant procession as I preach the gospel. My authoritative preaching ministry is a part of God's glory as revealed in Christ in the power of the Spirit under the new covenant, in which both you and we participate, to call all people to salvation, which entails godly living and giving oneself freely and sacrificially to God's work. You Corinthians are still acting immorally and your test of faith is your participation in the collection with me and the rest of the brethren.	foundation or supporting argument

I have attempted to describe the argument flow for 2 Corinthians in an analogous fashion to Cicero's in the qualitative case of Orestes. Admittedly, Paul's argument is more complex, as are the extant speeches. Paul begins his argument by addressing the charge directly in 2 Cor. 2.1–11: the Corinthians needed moral rebuke and so Paul chose not to visit them because he was in enough pain as it was. Then, from chapter 3 onward (at the risk of oversimplification), Paul presents himself and his co-workers as God's authoritatively approved messengers of the greater glory in Christ to the Corinthians (chapter 3). Paul is, despite his sufferings, a co-participant in eschatological realities along with the Corinthians (chapters 4–5). Paul furthermore has the prerogative of exhorting the Corinthians to faithfulness of conduct (chapters 6–7) and charity (chapters 8–9).

The movement from D2 to P2, in order to address the matter of Paul's authority and God's authorization of him, is entirely appropriate for the qualitative *stasis*, particularly of the subtype counter-plea (*comparatio*). In *Rhetorica ad Herennium* 2.21 the author advises, after determining whether or not the action was beneficial, to consider the defendant's right to make a decision that eventually affected the injured party. When applied to Paul, the question would be, "Do you have the right to make this decision in light of our suspicions about you?" Beneath such a question is the more fundamental one: "By what law or authority are you conducting your activity/ministry?" The logic of the *divisio* and *probatio* as described in Table 9.2 answers this question.

From this depiction, one can see that the majority of the *probatio* in 2 Corinthians is given to the *firmamentum* in Paul's line of defense. This is perfectly acceptable (for the case of Orestes see Quint. *Inst.* 3.11.12). Cicero (*Inv.* 1.19; cf. Quint. *Inst.* 3.11.9) states, "The *foundation* is the strongest argument of the defence, and the one most relevant to the point for the judge's decision." Paul's rationale for not coming to the Corinthians (thus sparing them) and the authority of his decision are well argued in 2.1–7.1.

How does 2 Corinthians 8–9 contribute to Paul's defense? First, these chapters are Paul's (continued) appeal for the Corinthians to be reconciled to him. If they complete the work they started (8.10–11; 9.2, 5), then they show that they themselves are consistent and reconciled to him (8.8; cf. 9.12–13). Paul describes their participation as "the harvest of your righteousness" (9.10; cf. 5.21; 9.11–15). Second, these chapters contribute to Paul's defense by indicating that he was not trying to trick the Corinthians. Paul did not coerce the Macedonians to give; nor did he pilfer any portion of their offering to the collection. The Macedonians gave first to

Table 9.2 *The defendant's authority in the judicial exchange of 2 Corinthians*

P1	1.17 Indictment	Paul did not visit but wrote a rhetorical letter in which he denied using rhetoric; therefore, Paul is inconsistent and worldly.
D1	1.17 Paul's defense	"I am not inconsistent or worldly."
D2	2.1–11 Paul's excuse	"I was justified in not coming (2.1) but in writing instead (2.3), because you (or, in actuality, only one of you) were sinning so badly (2.5, 9); this would have been extremely grievous to me (2.1) given my difficult circumstances (2.4), when I needed joy from you (2.2–3)."
P2	Rebuttal	You, Paul, have no authority to make this decision.
D3	2.14–9.15 Foundation	Paul's argument concerning his authority to act
		2.14–3.18 → God confirms Paul's ministry (cf. "God is faithful," 1.18), since by it the Corinthians have the Spirit in their hearts. → This shows forth the greater glory of the new covenant.
		4.1–5.10 → Paul *et al.* are not deceptive, but rather are established alongside the Corinthians in this glory (4.1–15). → Both are sealed by God and receive the deposit of the Spirit (5.5) and await a future judgment (5.10).
		5.11–7.1 → Paul, as one known to God, persuades people to accept God's reconciliation (5.11–21). → Paul's ministry is blameless and presents a covenantal exhortation to the Corinthians (6.1–7.1).
		8.1–9.15 → Paul orchestrates the collection efforts (8.1–5, 16–22; 9.1–5). → Paul encourages the Corinthians to give to the Lord in the collection as a test of their love (8.7–15). → When they do so, they will show that Paul's ministry is approved (8.20–21; 9.13) and reciprocate a mutual boast (8.24).

the Lord and then to Paul "through the will of God" (8.5). Thus, Paul asserts unambiguously that he facilitates the collection "for the Lord's glory" "in the sight of (all) people" and without any fault or grounds for censure (8.20–21). Furthermore, Paul's co-workers (particularly Titus) agreed voluntarily to return to the Corinthians in goodwill (8.16–20).

Paul engaged in no trickery by sending Titus and others back to them (12.16–18).

Suitable *topoi* in a case involving a qualitative issue

The *stasis* of quality had four subtypes according to Hermagoras' theory, which remained uniform in the treatment of invention (*Rhet. Her.* 1.24–25; 2.19–26; Cic. *Inv.* 1.15; 2.71–115; cf. Quint. *Inst.* 7.4.7–17; Hermog. *Stas.* 38.18–39.19). Paul bolstered his argument generally by using argumentative features and *topoi* of three of the four qualitative subtypes. My analysis of the beginning of 2 Corinthians (where one would expect the issue to be raised in conjunction with the *narratio* and *partitio*) indicates that Paul employed counter-plea (ἀντίστασις; *comparatio*), counter-charge (ἀντέγκλημα; *relatio criminis*), and a plea for leniency (συγγνώμη; *concessio*, specifically *purgatio*).[1] To draw upon different sub-stases to construct arguments was encouraged as it would be helpful (e.g., Cic. *Inv.* 2.74, 79, 103).

Many of the *topoi* are present. I have included a table summarizing the *topoi* for each subtype of the qualitative *stasis* in Appendix II. The recognition of these *topoi* is particularly relevant for understanding the argumentative features and themes that I have already observed; for example, Paul's amplification of his sufferings, his exhortation of the Corinthians regarding their moral failures, and Paul's admission to the appearance of failing respecting his visit in the *peroratio*. To confirm the validity of my analysis, I shall first consider the vital *topos* of one's intentions, since all three qualitative subtypes treat it as fundamental. Then I shall discuss the relevance of counter-plea, counter-charge, and plea for leniency for Paul's apology.

Paul's intentions

The defendant's intentions are central in the qualitative issue. The *divisio* of 2 Corinthians (1.17) reveals precisely this *topos*: "Therefore, intending this [βουλόμενος], did I act with fickleness? (Surely not!) Or, those things that I intend [βουλεύομαι], do I intend them [βουλεύομαι] in a worldly fashion, so that the 'Yes, yes . . .' from me is also 'No, no . . .'?

---

[1] On the basis of 1.23, Kennedy (1984, p. 88; cf. Witherington, 1995, p. 361; Peterson, 1998, pp. 37–38) understands that Paul's case turns on the qualitative issue, specifically that of *antistasis*. Kennedy also acknowledges the presence of *metastasis* (counter-charge) in 2.5–11.

(Surely not!)" (my translation).[2] Paul here magnified his intentions. This assertive statement of intention is anticipated by the *narratio*, which was constructed to present Paul's resolutions in the best light. Paul's *ethical digression* (1.12–14) within the *narratio* prepares for 1.15: "And with this confidence, I was intending [ἐβουλόμην] formerly to come to you, in order that you would have a second favor." Paul appears to follow the advice of Quintilian (*Inst.* 3.6.92) to work with the one *stasis* that allows for the greatest force to be made during the statement of the facts. In the *narratio* Paul emphasized his suffering (1.8–11), his mutuality with the Corinthians (1.11–14), and his intentions (1.15–16), each of which contributes to the qualitative *stasis*.

Moreover, Paul's good intentions are amplified throughout the remainder of the letter. He is moved by love (2.4; 5.16; cf. 6.6) and affection, especially for the Corinthians (6.11–13; 7.2–4, 13; 8.7, 16). He is motivated to make God's appeal (5.20) and not to put a stumbling block in anyone's way (6.3); and he is engaged in the service of the saints (8.4, 19), especially in terms of equity and fairness regarding the collection (8.13, 20–21; cf. 9.5).

Topoi *of counter-plea*

Cicero (*Inv.* 2.72) argues that the defensive strategy of counter-plea (*comparatio*) involves "the case where some act which cannot be approved by itself, is defended by reference to the end for which it was done." Should Paul visit the Corinthians, which would result in grief, or should he write instead? Given these two choices Paul argued that he chose the better – writing (2.1–3). Simply to consider whether there was a better course of action is to employ Aristotle's twenty-fifth formal *topos* (*Rhet.* 2.23.26). As Aristotle says, "no one, purposely or knowingly, chooses what is bad."

The defense can employ various *topoi* to bolster its argument. One should amplify the benefit rendered, if possible. Paul did this by arguing that a visit would have been grief-filled. He argued that this possibility *still existed*, since the Corinthians continued in their disobedience (6.12–16; 12.20–21). However, he assured the Corinthians emphatically that

---

[2] There is considerable discussion about the textual history behind the latter portion of 1.17 (ἵνα ᾖ παρ' ἐμοὶ τὸ Ναὶ ναὶ καὶ τὸ Οὒ οὔ) and consequently its precise meaning. For a discussion of both, see Thrall (1994, pp. 140–43). The best interpretation of this result (or purpose?) clause is that Paul is inconsistent in his commitments: He agrees to one thing but does another. Typically, the καί is taken as a coordinating conjunction. My translation takes it as an adverb, "also/even." However one understands the grammar, the doubled ναί and οὔ are regularly thought to be emphatic.

he wrote with abundant love (2.4).³ Finally, Paul amplified the circumstances of his writing – time, place, circumstances, deliberation – in 2.1–9
(cf. 1.8–11). On the suffering associated with the circumstances, see
below under plea for leniency.

One may also infer from Paul's defense which *topoi* he may have
anticipated from the prosecution in a counter-plea case (see Appendix II).
First, the accusation might question, "Why should one action be sacrificed
for another (visiting for writing)?" Paul addressed such a criticism when
he asked the question in 1.17a with χράομαι ("behave") as the main verb
and ἐν ἐλαφρίᾳ ("lightly") expressing the manner of his behavior. This
verb is a rather interesting choice in the context of 2 Corinthians. (It is
found only nine times in the Pauline epistles: 1 Cor. 7.21, 31; 9.12, 15;
2 Cor. 1.17; 3.12; 13.10; 1 Tim. 1.8; 5.23.) In 3.12 Paul argues, "Since,
then, we have such a hope, we act with great boldness" (Ἔχοντες οὖν
τοιαύτην ἐλπίδα πολλῇ παρρησίᾳ χρώμεθα). This statement contrasts
with the accusation of fickleness (ἐλαφρίᾳ) in 1.17. Equally significant
and especially relevant is Paul's expression of divine authorization in
13.10: "So I write these things while I am away from you, so that when I
come, I may not have to be severe in using [χρήσωμαι] the authority that
the Lord has given me for building up and not for tearing down." Paul
argued that he was composing 2 Corinthians to achieve the same goal
(while he was away from them) as in the first letter he had sent. In both
cases, Paul was not acting (χράομαι) lightly, but with divine authorization
to admonish and build up the Corinthians (cf. 12.19). See also below.

Second, already I have discussed that Paul portrayed his intentions
positively, perhaps in answer to or in anticipation of an attack on them.
The prosecution might ask, "Has Paul acted fraudulently? What were his
intentions really?" In 1.17 he insisted that he has not acted in a worldly
fashion (κατὰ σάρκα). He may be echoing the accusation raised by his
opponents, since this same expression is attributed as originating from
them in 10.2. It is possible that the expression κατὰ σάρκα is Paul's reduc-
tion of the opponents' arguments in order to control his own presentation
of the case. (For a similar possibility with 2.17 see Witherington, 1995,
p. 372.) In either case, Paul appears to be subjected to his same criticism
against the Corinthians, who were fleshly (1 Cor. 3.1) (see Chapter 7.2).

Finally, the prosecution could question the authority by which the
defendant chose one action over another. In 13.10 Paul emphatically

---

³ Note the grammatically proleptic and emphatic position of τὴν ἀγάπην before the
purpose clause in 2.4. ἐκ γὰρ πολλῆς θλίψεως καὶ συνοχῆς καρδίας ἔγραψα ὑμῖν διὰ
πολλῶν δακρύων, οὐχ ἵνα λυπηθῆτε ἀλλὰ τὴν ἀγάπην ἵνα γνῶτε ἣν ἔχω περισσοτέρως
εἰς ὑμᾶς.

states on what basis he is writing 2 Corinthians. It is God's authority (ἐξουσία), which was conferred on him for building up the Corinthians (cf. 10.8). The terminology used in 13.10 – writing while absent (ἀπὼν γράφω) in preparation for being present (παρὼν) – is precisely related to the initial situation of writing 1 Corinthians rather than visiting, which resulted in his having to write 2 Corinthians as a defensive letter. Thus, by way of analogy Paul indicates that 2 Corinthians serves essentially the same purpose as did the letter that was originally sent (1 Corinthians) – to strengthen/build up the Corinthians with authorization from God (cf. 10.2, 11; 13.2). Paul's final remark in the letter at 13.10 correlates with my conclusion that the *firmamentum* of his argument (2.14–7.1) is built upon the notion of authority.

Topoi *of counter-charge*

The defensive strategy of counter-charge (*relatio criminis*) attempts to shift the blame onto the offended party. Cicero (*Inv.* 2.78) explains: "A retort of the charge occurs when the defendant admits the act of which he is accused but shows that he was justified in doing it because he was influenced by an offence committed by the other party." Paul can justify writing instead of visiting by issuing a counter-plea: The Corinthians' disobedience was primarily responsible for his failure to visit. Such a defensive strategy would also account for his exhortation of the Corinthians in 5.11–7.1, which is recapitulated in the *peroratio* at 12.19–13.2. In other words, the Corinthians are still disobedient and in need of moral censure. To recall the crimes of someone to use against him or her is number 27 of Aristotle's formal *topoi* (*Rhet.* 2.23.28).

In addition to amplifying one's intentions, Paul magnified the audacity of the crime, not merely on the basis of the pain it caused him, but also because of its painful consequences for all the Corinthians (2.5). Furthermore, the Corinthians themselves were liable for withholding their affections for Paul, and thus for God, and so needed further exhortation (6.11–13; 7.2a; 12.20–21). What is at stake is their participation in salvation as the people of God, those called to be sons and daughters of God (6.1–2; 6.14–7.1).

Additionally, Paul used the *topos* that he acted too leniently. In the *partitio* he stated that he did not come to Corinth in order to spare (φείδομαι) the Corinthians (1.23; cf. 13.2). By writing 1 Corinthians, he inflicted a less severe consequence (recall the "rod" of 1 Cor. 4.18–21; cf. 2 Cor. 2.3–4; 7.2–16). Furthermore, he quickly forgave one particular wrongdoer in 2 Cor. 2.5–10, which showed his benevolent character and leniency, setting a precedent for the Corinthians to imitate with regard to their assessment of Paul.

The defendant may also argue that the crimes would have had detrimental effects on his or her own reputation, had the action under scrutiny *not* been taken. For example, the Corinthians' poor moral state would have reflected poorly on Paul. Thus, Titus' favorable report of the Corinthians' repentance after the (initial) reception of Paul's tearful letter is confirmation that Paul's boast in the Corinthians is secure (7.4, 9–16). If Paul had not written and the Corinthians not shown repentance, then this would have reflected poorly on Paul. Paul furthermore expected repentant behavior regarding the Corinthians' stance on the collection; if they failed to participate, it would be shameful for both him and themselves (9.3–4). He also argued that he would be humbled by the Corinthians' moral failings when he would finally visit them (12.20–21). Paul's fundamental concern for the moral conduct of his Gentile converts is seen elsewhere (see esp. Rom 1.5; 3.7–8; 6.19–22; 15.18; 16.26).

Given the *topoi* available to the prosecution (see Appendix II), Paul may have anticipated particular lines of accusation. First, the prosecution could argue that the crimes of the offended party (the Corinthians) are less serious than those of the defendant (Paul). An apt objection to this is the scale on which Paul views the disobedience of the Corinthians. The moral failings of the one Corinthian provided an opportunity for Satan to outwit Paul and the Corinthians (2.11). Also the Corinthians' sins result in a situation in which they may have "accepted the grace of God in vain" (εἰς κενὸν τὴν χάριν τοῦ θεοῦ δέξασθαι ὑμᾶς) (6.1). Idolatry was no small matter (6.14–16) and could remove the offenders from the status of sons and daughters of God (6.17–18). Furthermore, God will eventually judge their disobedience (5.10).

Second, the prosecution could argue that the defendant did not follow proper judicial procedure, but rather took justice into his own hands. It is intriguing to think that Paul may have been guilty of this by his condemnation of the man in 1 Corinthians 5. Paul's quotation of Deut. 19.15 ("Any charge must be sustained by the evidence of two or three witnesses") in 13.1 may answer (preemptively?) the charge that he had acted alone when pronouncing judgments.

Topoi *of the plea of leniency*

The presence of some admission of culpability (13.7; cf. 12.13) in addition to the amplification of the circumstances of suffering (e.g., 1.8–11) suggests that Paul employed the defensive strategy of confession, called *concessio*, particularly the *purgatio* variety (Cic. *Inv.* 2.94–103). First, he admitted to some failing or the appearance of failing in 13.7, which is characteristic of this subtype. It is rhetorically significant that such an admission does not appear until the *peroratio*, where such an admission is especially fitting. In other words, Paul *succumbs* to the *pathos* appeal one expected in a *peroratio*. It is difficult to evaluate exactly what he is admitting because of the compilation of ἵνα clauses in 13.7. He admits that his and his companions' approved character does not shine forth (φαίνω). Is this because of their sufferings, which appear shameful, or because Paul failed to visit when expected? Given the prominence of this theme of (failed) travel plans, the latter is more likely. Equally significant is his exhortation (13.5) to the Corinthians to examine themselves (ἑαυτοὺς δοκιμάζετε). Although Paul seems to admit some responsibility for not coming and appears to be unapproved, he also wants the Corinthians to admit their own part in contributing to the situation.

Second, in addition to defending one's intentions (see above), the other defensive *topos* is to amplify the horrendous circumstances that eventually resulted in the crime (Cic. *Inv.* 2.102). Paul amplified the circumstances of suffering that necessitated his writing rather than visiting. The *prooemium* immediately demonstrates this through God's offering consolation and mercy to Paul in his sufferings (1.3–4). Also, the *narratio* is primarily concerned about Paul's affliction (1.8) and its terrible effects on him (1.9–11). Barnett's suggestion (1997, p. 83) is not stated strongly enough: "Perhaps his account of the impact on him of this dreadful experience will mollify the Corinthian criticism that he had not come to them directly from Ephesus." These circumstances illuminate Paul's tears expressing grief *over the need* to write the letter (2.4).

Additionally, Paul included extensive *peristasis* catalogues dispersed strategically throughout the letter. Then, Paul ends the speech proper with the climactic *logion* of Christ (12.9a) that God's grace is sufficient for Paul's sufferings (12.9b–10). Paul's sufferings with God's comfort unite 2 Corinthians. Paul attached great theological significance to his sufferings by relating them in the *prooemium* to the sufferings of Christ (1.5).

Just as in the other subtypes, one may speculate that Paul anticipated various topical counter-arguments available to the prosecution with the plea for leniency (see Appendix II). One *topos* appears especially relevant: *It would have been better for the defendant to endure any fate, even death, rather than to yield to necessity if there is any suspicion of baseness.* Paul effectively disarmed such an argument by mentioning his "sentence of death" in Asia (1.8–9). If Paul had left Asia to visit Corinth, this would have been preferable for him. So, the prosecution cannot argue that Paul should have endured any fate (even death), because, in fact, Paul essentially had.

This concludes my analysis of 2 Corinthians in view of *stasis* theory. I have argued that 2 Corinthians shows considerable evidence that Paul composed the *probatio* according to the qualitative *stasis*. The argument moves from the excuse of Paul's decision to write instead of visit (2.1–11) to a set of arguments to establish his authorization to make this decision (chapters 3–9). Moreover, I have argued particularly that Paul used *topoi* from the qualitative subtypes of counter-plea, counter-charge, and a plea for leniency. This best accounts for the focus on Paul's intentions found in the *divisio* in 1.17, since each of these subtypes encourages the common *topos* of the amplifying the defendant's intentions. The analysis of defensive *topoi* also helped to account for Paul's exhortations to the Corinthians (5.11–7.1; 12.19–13.2).

These exhortative sections contribute to Paul's case by reminding the Corinthians of the basis for Paul's choice to write instead of visit (counter-charge); namely, the Corinthians were morally culpable. Also, a substantial benefit was rendered them, since grief was avoided. Thus, Paul preserved the mutuality between Paul and the Corinthians (counter-plea). Had Paul come and confronted the Corinthians' problems, there would have been tremendous grief. Thus, writing instead of visiting was all the more necessary, because of Paul's dire straits (plea of leniency, *purgatio*). The *peristasis* catalogues are probably partially to be accounted for on the basis of the *topoi* associated with the plea of leniency. This conclusion in no way diminishes Paul's paradoxical conviction that the Christian embodies simultaneously the life and death of Christ.

9.3   Inartificial proofs

Inartificial proofs include witnesses and their interrogation, laws, and any other evidence that is not constructed by the orator. Paul used different inartificial proofs in his argumentation. These include witnesses, written evidence, the reception of the Spirit, physical evidence in the form of his own body, the verbal agreement surrounding the collection, and *divina testimonia*. Paul also interrogated the Corinthians with respect to his ministry with them.

An investigation of μάρτυς and its cognates reveals that Paul understood well the significance and proper use of testimony. For example, in the *narratio*, to confirm the integrity of himself, Silas, and Timothy in their dealings with all, especially the Corinthians, Paul called upon the *testimony of his own conscience* (τὸ μαρτύριον τῆς συνειδήσεως) (1.12;

cf. Rom. 2.14–15; 9.1). Quintilian (*Inst.* 5.11.41) preserves an apt apho-
rism: "Conscientia mille testes" ("Conscience is as good as a thousand
witnesses"). In the *partitio* Paul also called God as a witness (μάρτυς)
against himself (1.23). To appeal to the gods was not uncommon (for
references see Windisch, 1924, p. 74). The language of *God as a witness*
evokes images of the covenantal relationship of the people of Israel and
their God (see Chapter 8.6). Thrice Paul calls on God's knowledge of him
to confirm that he conducted his ministry to persuade people (5.11), that
he loved the Corinthians (11.11), and that he was not lying when relating
his narrow escape over the Damascan wall (11.31). In 8.3 Paul testified
(μαρτυρῶ) to the sacrificial giving of the Macedonians, and this within
the *narratio* (8.1–5) of the miniature speech (see Chapter 8.6). Finally, in
the *peroratio* at 13.1 Paul quoted Deut. 19.15 as the proper judicial procedure for establishing charges "by the evidence of two or three witnesses
[μάρτυραι]."

Paul also appealed to physical evidence in *written form*. First, he made
reference to the previous letter that he had written the Corinthians (2.3–
11; 7.6–15; 13.2; cf. 1.13). Indeed, a serious accounting of that letter was
necessary, since some were using Paul's letters as evidence against his
character (10.1, 9–11). Second, he supplied the Corinthians themselves
as his own *letter of recommendation*, "a letter of Christ" (3.2), resulting
from Paul's ministry (3.3). Paul's strategic move makes the Corinthians
powerful divine evidence for all to see (3.2), since the Spirit of the living
God is the medium of writing "on tablets of human hearts" (3.3). Closely
related is the evidence of the "new covenant of the Spirit" (3.6). That
the Corinthians received the Spirit was also evidence of the legitimacy of
Paul's status as an agent of Christ. This has significant parallels in Gal.
3.2–5; 4.6 (see Betz, 1976). Paul's demonstration (ἀπόδειξις) of the Spirit
also played a critical role in his persuasion in 1 Cor. 2.4–5.

Paul presented his own body as evidence. This evidence is critical in
the third argumentative section (4.1–5.10). Paul argued that he and his
companions were involved in a paradoxical situation. They have the new
covenant glory in "jars of clay" (4.7). Paul then related a catalogue of
hardships, which culminates in the affirmation that they bear "the death
of Christ" bodily so that "the life of Christ" might also be revealed in their
bodies (4.10; cf. 1.5; 4.11). The conclusion in 4.12 is "So death works in
us, but life in you." Admittedly, this is a strange point. However, one must
understand the import of this argument section: to show that Paul and his
associates, despite their sufferings, were also recipients of the Spirit *along
with the Corinthians* (cf. 1.21–22). They spoke with "the same spirit of
faith" as expressed in Ps. 116.10 and in the face of affliction (4.13; notice

the context of suffering in Ps. 116.7–10). Paul argued against the criticism that he and his associates did not live up to the life of the Spirit.

Furthermore, Paul is tactical when addressing the matter of the collection, which is another form of evidence (8.4; 9.1, 12, 13). It could be classified as a verbal agreement (see Cic. *De Or.* 2.26.116) between Paul and the Corinthians (8.6–7, 10–11; 9.2, 5, 12–13). Witherington (1995, p. 335 note 27) has made the interesting suggestion that, if we are to accept Betz's proposal that 2 Corinthians 8 and 9 were separate letters sent by Paul at some point to the Corinthians (although see Chapter 8.6), this would not have precluded Paul from *reusing them as "material evidence" in his defense.* Paul encouraged the Corinthians to follow through with their commitment as a means to express their *righteousness* and participation with him (8.7–8, 23–24; 9.1–5, 10–15). In conjunction with this collection, Paul indirectly cited witnesses in his favor: the participation of the Macedonian believers (8.1–5; cf. 8.8; 9.4), Titus (8.6–7, 16–17, 23–24; 9.3, 5; cf. 12.16–18), and unspecified, approved co-workers and representatives (8.18–19, 22–24; 9.3, 5) (see Furnish, 1984, pp. 104–105). Thus, Paul's presentation of these various details respecting the collection contributes to his case by providing direct and indirect evidence that he was *entirely approved* by some and conducted his ministry uprightly and without coercion (8.20–21; cf. 1.24). Furthermore, any suspicions that he had taken any portion of the Macedonians' contribution are shown to be entirely false (8.5).

The most important evidence that Paul mustered in his defense is divine. I have already noted his reliance on the Spirit as evidence of the efficacy of his ministry. Paul had also called God to witness against him in 1.23 in anticipation of the covenantal exhortation in 5.11–7.1. However, Paul argued throughout 2 Corinthians explicitly and implicitly that God approved of him. It may be helpful to recall Quintilian's distinction between supernatural evidence (*divina testimonia*) and divine arguments (*divina argumenta*) (see Quint. *Inst.* 5.11.42). The former is fitting for the present discussion. The latter amounts to a logical argument of authority, one of the *loci argumentorum.* A neat distinction in argumentative practice is perhaps not possible. Nevertheless, I consider references to God's specific actions within narrative sections on Paul's behalf (1.10; 2.12; cf. 7.6) and Paul's religious experiences culminating in an oracle from the Lord (12.1–9; cf. 5.13) to be *divina testimonia.* The numerous other references, many of which are cited below as artificial proofs, would be classified as *divina argumenta.* For example, I have judged 1.21–22, God's establishment of Paul and associates via the Spirit, to be *divina argumenta*, since Paul must argue this point in 4.1–5.10. Contrariwise, that the Corinthians received the Spirit is not in question (3.2–3) and is therefore classified as a *divina testimonia*.

Finally, since the Corinthians themselves are actual evidence for Paul's case, Paul's questioning of them would constitute *interrogation*.

11.7 Did I commit a sin by humbling myself so that you might be exalted, because I proclaimed God's good news to you free of charge?

12.13 How have you been worse off than the other churches, except that I myself did not burden you?

12.17–18 Did I take advantage of you through any of those whom I sent to you? I urged Titus to go, and sent the brother with him. Titus did not take advantage of you, did he? Did we not conduct ourselves with the same spirit? Did we not take the same steps?

13.5 Examine yourselves to see whether you are living in the faith. Test yourselves. Do you not realize that Jesus Christ is in you? – unless, indeed, you fail to meet the test!

These questions are rhetorical ones (cf. 1.17; 3.1; 6.14–16; 11.22–23; 12.15b, 19), but they betray substantial issues to be clarified regarding Paul's ministry with the Corinthians.

9.4   Artificial proofs: *pathos, ethos,* and *logos*

It would be superfluous to describe in detail Paul's *pathos* and *ethos* appeals. In 2 Corinthians *ethos* and *pathos* are overlapping commodities (for both in 1.8–11 and the presence of *pathos* in 4.13–5.10 see Kennedy, 1984, pp. 87, 90). If one is to distinguish them, then the presence of arguments appealing to *pathos* is detected in 1.3–11, 13–16, 23–24; 2.1–11; 3.2–3; 4.1, 7–12; 5.1–8, 12–15; 7.2–16; 8.2, 13–14; 9.1–2, 11–15; 11.23–29; 12.10 and those of *ethos* in 1.12, 17–22; 2.12–13, 17; 3.4–6; 4.2, 5; 5.9, 10, 11, 16, 20; 6.1–7.1; 7.2, 11; 8.20–21; 11.10, 31; 12.1–10; 13.8.

Instances of *pathos* and *ethos*

Paul established favorable *pathos* with the Corinthians by expressing in the *prooemium* the mutuality that existed between him and them (1.6–7). In the *narratio* and *probatio* this mutuality is expressed in terms of comfort and affliction, which means giving assistance and avoiding grief (1.11; 2.1–11; 7.8–16). Quintilian (*Inst.* 4.2.111–15) argues that *pathos* should be found in the statement of the facts, even though the philosophical tradition of rhetoric spurned this. The *narratio* in 1.8–16 and 7.2–16 contains much *pathos*, beginning as it does with Paul's afflictions and sentence of death (on 7.8–16 see Kennedy, 1984, p. 91). Paul opened his heart to the Corinthians and hoped for the same from them (6.11–13; 7.2–4). Furthermore, his repeated references to his sufferings in the *peristasis* catalogues contribute considerably to the *pathos* of 2 Corinthians (see Arist. *Rhet.* 2.8.1–16; cf. *Rhet. Her.* 1.5.8). Paul hoped that his suffering and endurance would engender *pathos* for him in the Corinthians.

These catalogues exhibited Paul's *ethos*. Cicero (*Top.* 76) argues, "The testimony which produces conviction through virtue is of two kinds; one sort gets its efficacy by nature, the other acquires it by hard work." Paul constantly portrayed himself as an ardent apostle, one who has suffered, endured, and testified virtuously to the truth of his case. Simultaneously, his portrayal of these *necessary sufferings* adds credibility to his *testimony* (1.12; 8.3). Cicero (*Top.* 74) explains, "For what men say when they have been worn down by stripes, the rack, and fire, seems to be spoken by truth itself; and what they say under stress of mind – grief, lust, anger or fear – lends authority and conviction, because these emotions seem to have the force of necessity."

There are additionally numerous statements that Paul made about his character and his motivations distributed throughout 2 Corinthians. For example,

1.12b We have behaved in the world with frankness and godly sincerity, not by earthly wisdom but by the grace of God – and all the more towards you.

1.17 Was I vacillating when I wanted to do this? [No!] Do I make my plans according to ordinary human standards, ready to say "Yes, yes" and "No, no" at the same time? [No!]

2.17a For we are not peddlers of God's word like so many; but in Christ we speak as persons of sincerity.

4.2 We have renounced the shameful things that one hides; we refuse to practice cunning or to falsify God's word; but by the open statement of the truth we commend ourselves to the conscience of everyone in the sight of God.

6.3 We are putting no obstacle in anyone's way, so that no fault may be found with our ministry.

8.20–21 We intend that no one should blame us about this generous gift that we are administering, for we intend to do what is right not only in the Lord's sight but also in the sight of others.

These arguments express the intended result of Paul's letter. When the Corinthians have a complete knowledge of him, they will have an opportunity to be proud of him (cf. 5.12) and *vice versa* on the ultimate judgment day (1.14; cf. 5.11).

Another *ethos* appeal is found in Paul's repeated statements concerning his truthfulness.

4.2 By the open statement of the truth [τῇ φανερώσει τῆς ἀληθείας] we commend ourselves to the conscience of everyone in the sight of God

6.4, 7a but as servants of God we have commended ourselves in every way . . . [in] truthful speech [ἐν λόγῳ ἀληθείας] . . .

7.14b but just as everything we said to you was true [ἐν ἀληθείᾳ], so our boasting to Titus has proved true [ἀλήθεια] as well.

11.10 As the truth of Christ is in me [ἔστιν ἀλήθεια Χριστοῦ ἐν ἐμοὶ], this boast of mine will not be silenced in the regions of Achaia.

12.6a I will speak the truth [ἀλήθειαν γὰρ ἐρῶ].

13.8 For we cannot do anything against the truth, but only for the truth [οὐ γὰρ δυνάμεθά τι κατὰ τῆς ἀληθείας ἀλλὰ ὑπὲρ τῆς ἀληθείας].

These emphatic statements are completely in conformity with forensic oratorical practice and serve to bolster Paul's *ethos* appeal in 2 Corinthians (see Chapter 4.3).

The *refutatio* and self-adulation sections also contain numerous appeals to *pathos* and *ethos*, as DiCicco (1995) demonstrates (for *ethos* see pp. 77–112; for *pathos* see pp. 164–87; cf. the discussion of *pathos* in Witherington, 1995, p. 373). Winter (1997, p. 229 note 114) rejects DiCicco's analysis from a general consideration: "If it is correct that Paul rejects these persuasive techniques [artificial proofs] in his evangelism in Corinth (1 Cor. 2.1–5) as has been argued here, it is inexplicable why he would make such full use of them in a later letter to the Corinthians without again calling into question his integrity." I would simply respond by arguing that Paul wrote 1 Corinthians in order to reestablish the Corinthians' *zeal* for him (2 Corinthians 7) in view of criticism that his initial evangelization/speech was not very rhetorically polished. Paul's strategy was turned against him, so that in 2 Corinthians he must defend his rhetoric of persuasion, i.e. his manner of exhortation (see 5.11–7.1). For Paul not to use rhetorical or philosophical argumentation would not be possible; in fact, he used his rivals' rhetorical methods of σύγκρισις against them, as Winter argues (p. 229).

Much of this material in the *refutatio* functions to produce ill-will towards Paul's missionary rivals intruding on his territory (10.12–18;

11.3–6, 13–15, 17–21). But, Paul defends his own *ethos* by (re)claiming his rightful position as founder of the Corinthian community and by recourse to reciting his physical and spiritual lineage in 2 Cor. 11.1–23 (see Arist. *Rhet.* 2.6.11–12). Arguably, the pinnacle of Paul's appeal to *pathos* and *ethos* comes in the form of a divine utterance (also a maxim) in 12.9, which itself is in the form of an *enthymeme*:[4] "My grace is sufficient for you, for power is made perfect in weakness" (see Chapter 8.8).

Arguments from *logos*

Paul's use of *logos* arguments consists of examples, *enthymemes*, maxims, and *epicheiremes*. Probability arguments may be present with the details of Paul's decision not to visit (2.2, 10; cf. 2.5; 4.3; 7.8; 7.12): if he would have come, it would have been a grievous visit.

Use of examples

Second Corinthians is replete with examples. Paul considered the Macedonians (8.1–7) and Christ (8.8–9) as examples of giving for the Corinthians to follow (Betz, 1985, pp. 41–42, 61; Witherington, 1995, pp. 412, 420; Hughes, 1991, pp. 258–59). Christ's suffering and resurrection are instrumental in 4.10–14 and 13.4 for Paul's argument that he, too, has been given the down deposit of the Spirit along with the Corinthians (1.22; 5.5). Paul contrasted the example of Moses' fading glory and its consequences with Paul's new covenant and the Spirit (3.7–15). Paul cites Ps. 116.10 as another example: Paul is like the psalmist who "believes and speaks" in the face of affliction (4.13). In 11.3 Paul used the example of Eve and the serpent as a representation of the Corinthians and the false apostles (see DiCicco, 1995, p. 258). Finally, Paul presents God as an example for the Corinthians to follow respecting his evaluation. God has appointed and affirmed him as apostle (1.1; 10.13), reconciling ambassador (5.18–21), co-worker (6.1), and servant (6.4). God has approved of him and his ministry by providing comfort and attesting to Paul's integrity in multifarious ways (1.3–4, 9–10, 12, 18, 20, 21–22, 23; 2.14–17; 3.4–5; 4.2, 6–7; 5.1, 5, 11; 6.7; 7.6; 8.5; 11.11, 31). Thus, the Corinthians should also approve of Paul.

---

[4] Major premise: God gives power/grace perfectly for humans through their weakness; Minor premise: Paul is weak and seeks God's grace; Conclusion: God's grace is perfectly applied and active in Paul's life.

Maxims in 2 Corinthians

Paul's argumentation contains various maxims, adding ethical authority to his discourse. (Paul used Aristotle's term for maxim, γνώμη, in 8.10 to refer to specific advice given; cf. 1 Cor. 7.25, 40; see Betz, 1985, p. 63.) Some of the maxims are scripture citations either as an argument proof (as in 4.13) or a conclusion (as in 4.6 and 10.17). These scripture citations are all brief and express self-evident truth from the perspective of a Christian community. In 7.10 Paul supports his understanding of repentance with a maxim: "For godly grief produces a repentance that leads to salvation and brings no regret, but worldly grief produces death." Paul also uses a maxim in 9.6 as the initial premise of an argument: "The point is this: the one who sows sparingly will also reap sparingly, and the one who sows bountifully will also reap bountifully." In 10.18 Paul supports his conclusion with a maxim: "For it is not the man who commends himself that is accepted, but the man whom the Lord commends" (see Hafemann, 1990, p. 83). A maxim is used in 11.15: "Their end will match their deeds." Other maxims are found in 8.12; 12.9, 14, and 13.6 (DiCicco, 1995, pp. 256–57; on 8.12 see Betz, 1985, pp. 63, 66).

Enthymemes *and* epicheiremes *in 2 Corinthians*

Paul argues enthymematically and epicheirematically throughout 2 Corinthians. These types of reasoning are sometimes difficult to identify (for Pauline literature see Long, 2002 and 2003; cf. Moores, 1995, p. 35). One clue is the presence of γάρ (Kennedy, 1984, p. 16), but this need not always be present.

For example, the causal participial construction in 2 Cor. 4.1 supports a premise and forms an *enthymeme*: "since it is by God's mercy that we are engaged in this ministry, we do not lose heart." Presented in syllogistic fashion it would be, "IF God has called us to work in this ministry, and IF this calling is by mercy, THEN we can expect mercy in carrying out this ministry, so that we do not lose heart."

Another example is found in 4.13–14, also with a scriptural maxim. These verses contain two participial clauses which provide the reason for the central premise (my translation).

Reason: Since we have [ἔχοντες δὲ] the same spirit of faith according to what has been written, "I believed, therefore I spoke" [a maxim],
Premise: *We* [ἡμεῖς] also believe, therefore [διὸ] we also speak [*in the midst of affliction*; cf. Ps. 116.10],

Reason: since we know [εἰδότες] that the one raising the Lord Jesus will raise also us and will establish us with you.

Moreover, this enthymematic expression is the initial premise of an argument section as follows:

Major premise: 4.13–14 But just as we have the same spirit of faith that is in accordance with scripture – "I believed, and so I spoke" – we also believe, and so we speak, because we know that the one who raised the Lord Jesus will raise us also with Jesus, and will bring us with you into his presence.

Proof: 4.15 Yes [γάρ], everything is for your sake, so that grace, as it extends to more and more people, may increase thanksgiving, to the glory of God.

Conclusion: 4.16a So [διό] we do not lose heart.

This argument can be summarized as follows:

Major premise: We believe and speak (while afflicted).

Proof: All is done for you to spread thanksgiving to many people for the glory of God.

Conclusion: Therefore, we do not lose heart (when we believe and speak while afflicted for you).

Paul's argumentation in the *probatio* and *refutatio* follows the epicheirematic argument patterns as described by Cicero, Quintilian, and the author of *Rhetorica ad Herennium*. I propose the following description of Paul's argumentation cautiously, understanding that research in this area is new (Long, 2002, 2003). See Table 9.3.

The same patterns can be found in parts of the *narratio* and *partitio*. For example, in the *narratio* we have a Premise A (verse 12), Proof A (verse 13a), Premise B (verses 13b–14a), Proof B (verse 14b), and Conclusion (verses 15–16). In the second individual partition head (1.18–20), we have Premise (verse 18), Proof (verses 19–20a), and Conclusion (verse 20b). The presence of γάρ often indicates that Paul is supporting a premise by supplying a proof (2.2, 4, 9, 10b–11a, 17a; 3.9, 11, 14b; 4.5, 11, 15, 17, 18b; 5.2, 4, 7, 10, 13, 14; 6.2, 14b, 16b; 8.12, 13–14, 21; 9.2; 10.3; 10.4–6; 10.8; 10.14; 11.2b; 11.4; 11.9b; 11.13; 11.14; I have included in these references instances in which γάρ introduces the *reason of proof*). Sometimes ὅτι is found (2.15; 8.2, 3–4, 17; 10.10) or some other particle/conjunction (ἀλλά in 3.15; 4.2; 10.12b; δέ in 3.17; 5.11b; ὡς in 5.19; καθώς in 9.9), or nothing at all (e.g., 9.4, 7; 11.8). My analysis also indicates that the arguments are closely linked one to the next. In fact, an argument's logical conclusion is occasionally the premise for the next

Table 9.3 Epicheirematic argumentation patterns in 2 Corinthians

Section	2.14–17	3.1–6	3.7–11	3.12–15	3.16–18	4.1–6	4.7–12	4.13–16a	4.16b–18b
Premise A	14	1	7–8	12	16	1	7	13–14	16b
Proof A	15	2–3	9	13	17a	2	8–10	15	17
Premise B	16b		10	14a		3–4			18a
Proof B	17a		11	14b		5			18b
Conclusion	17b	4–6	[3.12]	15	18	6	12	16a	[5.1]
Embellishment									
Reason of proof					17b		11		

Section	5.1–5	5.6–10	5.11–17	5.18–19	6.1–13	6.14–7.1	8.1–6	8.7–8	8.9–15
Premise A	1	6	11a	18	1	14	1	Partitio	9
Proof A	2	7	11b	19	2	14b–16a	2	A = 7	10–11
Premise B	3	8	11c–12		3			B = 8	12–14
Proof B	4	(10)	13		4–10		4–6		15
Conclusion	5	9	16–17	[6.1]	?11–13	17–7.1	?4–6		
Embellishment			15		?4–10				
Reason of proof			14			16b	3		

Section	8.16–24	9.1–5	9.6–15	10.1–6	10.7–11	10.12–18	11.1–6	11.7–11	11.12–15
Premise A	16	1	6	1–2	7	12a	1–2a	7	12
Proof A	17	2	7	3	8	12b	2b	8	13
Premise B	18–20	3	8		9	13	3	9a	
Proof B	21	4	9		10	14	4	9b	
Conclusion	24	5	10		11	17–18	5–6	10–11	15
Embellishment	22–23		11–15	[4–6]		15–16			
Reason of proof			peroration	4–6					14

argument as in 3.12, 5.1, and 6.1 (each involving οὖν). Two extended examples are given here: 9.1–5 and 3.7–18 (Kennedy, 1984, p. 90, argues that 3.12–4.1 "resembles an epicheireme," but no explanation is given).

Second Corinthians 9.1–5 adheres well to Cicero's *ratiocinatio* (*epicheireme*).

Premise A: 9.1 Now [μὲν γάρ] it is not necessary for me to write you about the ministry to the saints,

Proof A: 9.2 for [γάρ] I know your eagerness, which is the subject of my boasting about you to the people of Macedonia, saying that Achaia has been ready since last year; and your zeal has stirred up most of them.

Premise B: 9.3 But [δέ] I am sending the brothers in order that our boasting about you may not prove to have been empty in this case, so that you may be ready, as I said you would be;

Proof B: 9.4 otherwise [μή πως], if some Macedonians come with me and find that you are not ready, we would be humiliated – to say nothing of you – in this undertaking. [contrary reason]

Conclusion: 9.5 So [οὖν] I thought it necessary to urge the brothers to go on ahead to you, and arrange in advance for this bountiful gift that you have promised, so that it may be ready as a voluntary gift and not as an extortion.

Paul was working from premises (9.1, 3) towards a conclusion (9.5). The argument is that his sending of the brethren to prepare for the collection (minor premise) in no way should impede the Corinthians' eagerness to contribute to the collection (major premise). Paul preserved the dignity of the Corinthians by first affirming the premise that the Corinthians are eager to contribute to the collection. Nevertheless, he sent his co-workers to assist in this. Paul so carefully explained who had been sent, their motivations, and their qualifications, in order to clear himself of any possible appearance of wrongdoing, as is strongly suggested in the *peroratio* in 12.14–18, which recapitulates 2 Cor. 8–9. The argument in 9.1–5 flows to the next argument in 9.6–16, which expounds the rationale for the Corinthians to give "bountifully" (9.6) based upon the abundance of God's grace.

A second example of epicheirematic argumentation is found in 3.7–18. This unit consists of three interdependent movements successively building upon one another. Along with the English text, I have included a brief summary. Also, in anticipation of the discussion of *topoi* below, I have included the argumentative *topoi* that are present. See Table 9.4.

These arguments advance with premises and proofs to the conclusion in 3.18, which brings the material content together in a multi-tiered highly

Table 9.4 Epicheirematic *argumentation of 2 Cor. 3.7–18*

	First movement	
	Biblical text	Summary with *topoi* used
Premise A	3.7–8 Now, if the ministry of death, chiseled in letters on stone tablets, came in glory so that the people of Israel could not gaze at Moses' face because of the glory of his face, a glory now set aside, how much more will the ministry of the Spirit come in glory?	The ministry of the Spirit comes in more glory than the ministry of death. [*topoi* of consequence and more or less]
Proof A	3.9 For [γάρ] if there was glory in the ministry of condemnation, much more does the ministry of justification abound in glory!	For justification is more glorious than condemnation. [*topos* of more or less]
Premise B	3.10 Indeed [καὶ γάρ], what once had glory has lost its glory because of the greater glory;	The old glory is gone compared to the new glory. [*topos* of more or less]
Proof B	3.11 for [γάρ] if what was set aside came through glory, much more has the permanent come in glory!	For the old glory is set aside by the permanent glory. [*topos* of more or less]
	Second movement	
Conclusion AB and Premise C	3.12–13a Since, then [οὖν], we have such a hope, we act with great boldness, not like Moses,	Paul acts boldly (with the Corinthians) compared to Moses . . . [*synkrisis*]
Proof C	3.13b who put a veil over his face to keep the people of Israel from gazing at the end of the glory that was being set aside.	since Moses hid the fading glory with a veil from the Israelites. [*topos* of attributed motive]
Premise D	3.14a But their minds were hardened.	The Israelites were hardened.
Proof D	3.14b–15 Indeed [γάρ], to this very day, when they hear the reading of the old covenant, that same veil is still there, since only in Christ is it set aside. Indeed [ἀλλ'], to this very day whenever Moses is read, a veil lies over their minds;	For even today they are hardened or veiled, since only through Christ is this removed. [*topos* of consequence]

Table 9.4 (*cont.*)

	Third movement	
	Biblical text	Summary with *topoi* used
Premise E	3.16 but when one turns to the Lord, the veil is removed.	The Lord removes the veil. [*topos* of consequence]
Proof E	3.17 Now the Lord is the Spirit and where the Spirit of the Lord is, there is freedom.	For the Lord is the Spirit who brings freedom. [*topoi* of definition and consequence]
Conclusion ABDCE	3.18 And all of us, with unveiled faces, seeing the glory of the Lord as though reflected in a mirror, are being transformed into the same image from one degree of glory to another; for this comes from the Lord, the Spirit.	The Lord unveils us all to see the glory of the Lord and be transformed from glory to glory by the Spirit. [*topos* of consequence]

theological statement. Paul accentuates the Lord's agency, which compels Paul's boldness with the Corinthians for the effect of human moral transformation into the glory of the Lord through the Spirit.

Typically, Paul's argumentation in 3.7–18 has been understood against Jewish modes of exegesis, particularly *midrash* (Windisch, 1924, pp. 117–18; cf. Belleville, 1991, pp. 173–91). Specifically, 3.7–11, which follows the pattern εἰ . . . πολλῷ μᾶλλον, is thought to conform to the Jewish exegetical principle of *kal wa-hōmer* (see R. Martin, 1986, pp. 59–60; Stockhausen, 1989, pp. 28, 109–122). However, Paul's repeated use of this pattern within conditional sentences (3x in 3.7–11) parallels significantly the use of πολλῷ μᾶλλον in conditional sentences in a number of Greek forensic orations. For example, the expression is found in a conditional statement of probability in Demosthenes 22.7.4: "If never punished, then all the more you should be convicted to prevent someone else." Similarly, Demosthenes 24.213.5 (see also Isae. 3.28.7; cf. Dem. 24.171.4) concerns probabilities: "if someone did something wrong, then the jury has more reason to hate and punish that man." But, πολλῷ μᾶλλον need not be used in probabilities (see Antiph. 5.74; Dem. 19.310). In Isaeus 2.26.2 πολλῷ μᾶλλον, which is initiated with a γάρ, is used with a question expecting a positive answer.

These argumentative parallels raise a number of questions as to the origins of the *kal wa-hōmer* exegetical form. What my analysis suggests is that, although interpreters have rightly sought to find the conception of Paul's thought through a consideration of his exegesis of the Hebrew scripture, nevertheless Paul has given *formal expression to such conceptions in ways understandable in the Hellenistic rhetorical milieu.*

What are we to make of Paul's "weighty" argumentation, which includes *enthymemes* and *epicheiremes*? Quintilian (*Inst.* 5.14.27–28) concludes his discussion of these types of arguments with the following remarks:

> [T]hese rules still leave scope for free exercise of judgment. For although I consider that there are occasions where the orator may lawfully employ the syllogism, I am far from desiring him to make his whole speech consist of or even be crowded with a mass of *epicheiremes* and *enthymemes*. For a speech of that character would resemble dialogues and dialectical controversies rather than pleadings of the kind with which we are concerned, and there is an enormous difference between the two. For in the former we are confronted with learned men seeking for truth among men of learning; consequently they subject everything to a minute and scrupulous inquiry with a view to arriving at clear and convincing truths.

According to Quintilian, Paul would be judged more philosophical than rhetorical. In this regard, Betz (1986, p. 40) notices Paul's concern to speak of knowledge "with great emphasis" (2.14; 4.6; 6.6). This suggests to Betz that Paul was criticized for a lack of eloquence joined with knowledge. If this was the case, then the depth and sublimity of Paul's argumentation was not without consequence. In the *refutatio* Paul described his own writing as destroying arguments hindering obedience to God (10.4–6). Indeed, his Corinthian antagonists considered his letters as "weighty and strong" (βαρεῖαι καὶ ἰσχυραί – 10.10). Betz (p. 41) is correct to argue that "these terms . . . refer to a style characteristic of philosophers." Paul acknowledges that he is unskilled in rhetorical performance, "but not in knowledge; certainly in every way and in all things we have made this evident to you" (11.6). In other words, he can argue like a philosopher in his letters. What also contributed to the weightiness of Paul's discourses was the use of *loci argumentorum.*

9.5   Forensic *topoi*

Second Corinthians is primarily forensic in form and function. It concerns Paul's apology for writing a letter (1 Corinthians) instead of visiting, a letter which moreover employed heavy persuasion, thus raising suspicions about his ulterior motives. He was being charged with committing an injustice. In 7.2b, after the central three arguments of the *probatio* (2.14–3.18; 4.1–5.10; 5.11–7.1), Paul emphatically denied any wrongdoing: "we have wronged no one, we have corrupted no one, we have taken advantage of no one" (οὐδένα ἠδικήσαμεν, οὐδένα ἐφθείραμεν, οὐδένα ἐπλεονεκτήσαμεν). The use of asyndeton and anaphora makes the denial of wrongdoing even more emphatic.

After this emphatic denial of wrongdoing in 7.2b, Paul denied that he was condemning the Corinthians (πρὸς κατάκρισιν οὐ λέγω) (7.3). It is no surprise that he immediately redressed the matter of writing his letter instead of visiting and its consequences for the Corinthians (7.6–16; cf. 2.1–11). He also related how joyful he was at the news of their godly repentance, after hearing the report from Titus. Another indication that 2 Corinthians is concerned with justice is found in the *peroratio* at 12.13. Paul demands to be forgiven for not accepting financial support from the Corinthians ("Forgive me this wrong!" [χαρίσασθέ μοι τὴν ἀδικίαν ταύτην]). Clearly, justice was at stake between Paul and the Corinthians. This is the primary concern for forensic rhetoric.

As I continue to consider Paul's use of the various kinds of forensic *topoi*, one should remember the advice of Aristotle and Quintilian. The orator should construct his or her arguments from that which is "peculiar to the subject on which the judgment has to be given" (Quint. *Inst.* 5.8.6; cf. 5.10.125; Arist. *Rhet.* 2.22.1–13). Certainly, this was true for Paul.

I have argued above that Paul used *topoi* related to the qualitative *stasis*. In Chapter 8.9 I enumerated how he used commonplace *topoi* associated with the *peroratio*. These are summarized again here.

1   In the *peroratio* generally one should speak to one's weakness (2 Cor. 13.4, 9).

2   The seventh *topos* under *conquestio* (Cic. *Inv.* 108) is to present the orator as a child/parent (2 Cor. 12.14–15).

3   The fourteenth *topos* under *conquestio* (Cic. *Inv.* 109) is to ask for mercy (2 Cor. 12.13).

4   The first common *topos* under *indignatio* is to indicate that the gods are interested in the case (Cic. *Inv.* 101; *Rhet. Her.* 2.48);

Paul speaks before God and prays to God (2 Cor. 12.19, 21; 13.7).

5   The ninth common *topos* under *indignatio* is to compare one crime with another (Cic. *Inv.* 104; *Rhet. Her.* 2.49): Paul compares his being present via letter (2 Cor. 13.2), his impending visit (13.1, 10), and his apparent failure (13.7) with the Corinthians' immorality (12.20–21; cf. 13.5, 10). This is more a prosecutor's tactic.

What remains to be done is to consider whether Paul constructed his arguments using any of the remaining types of *topoi*: universal *topoi* (*koinoi topoi*), formal argumentative *topoi* (*loci argumentorum*), and *topoi* related to persons and matters (*loci ex personis et rebus*). It would be moot to discuss the latter, since, in fact, 2 Corinthians is replete with details relating to persons, their actions, and motivations, as I have discussed thus far. What is offered below is a brief discussion of the universal and argumentative *topoi* in 2 Corinthians.

Paul employs all four of Aristotle's universal *topoi*. With respect to past and future fact (τὸ γεγονὸν καὶ τὸ μέλλον), I have noted how Paul has carefully related past events pertaining to the Corinthians in the narrative sections and elsewhere (see esp. Chapter 8.4). There are significant future events, however, that he vividly depicted for the Corinthians to consider. First, God will rescue Paul from his affliction (1.10). Moreover, when the Corinthians participate in this by supplication, many people will give thanks (1.11). Second, Paul hoped that by his letter the Corinthians will know him completely (1.13; 13.6). Third, he argued that there will be a day of accounting before God (5.10; cf. 5.3; 9.6) in which Paul hopes that he and the Corinthians will share reciprocal boasting (1.14). As for the *false apostles*, their fate is dreadful, since "their end will match their deeds" (11.15). Fourth, God will supply the Corinthians for their portion of the collection, which will result in thanksgiving and the glory of God (9.10–14). Paul will be coming for their portion (12.14–15). Fifth, Paul will continue not to take money from the Corinthians and will boast about this (11.7–12). He will continue to work in the locale as God has directed him (10.13). Furthermore, Paul "will boast" about himself and his weakness (11.18, 30; 12.1, 5, 6, 9). Lastly, Paul will be visiting them soon and warns them not to be disobedient (13.1–2; cf. 12.14–15).

The other universal *topoi* – possibility and impossibility (δυνατὸν καὶ ἀδύνατον), greater or lesser degree (τὸ μᾶλλον καὶ ἧττον), and amplification and depreciation (τὸ αὔξειν καὶ μειοῦν) – are present as well. Paul often amplified his subject, as is seen in 6.4–10; 8.4–6, 22–23 and

9.11–15; 11.13–15, 20, 22–23, 25–28 (cf. *Rhet. Her.* 4.52 and Quint. *Inst.* 8.4.27; on amplification in 4.8–12, 6.3–7, and 6.8–10 see Kennedy, 1984, p. 91; in 7.2–16 see Witherington, 1995, pp. 407–10). He also depreciated the character of his opponents in their dealings with the Corinthians (10.12, 15, 18; 11.3–5, 13–15, 18–21).

With respect to possibility and impossibility, Paul accentuated his reliance on the power (δύναμις) given him by God (6.7) as displayed in his earthly body (4.7). Even while he is weak (1.8; 12.9–10; 13.9), he is able to destroy arguments (10.4) and to deal firmly with the Corinthians (13.3–4). Moreover, the Macedonians were able (δύναμις) to give within and beyond their ability (8.3) and God will empower the Corinthians with their own giving (9.8). I have already discussed the universal *topos* of more or less in 3.7–11 (see Kennedy, 1984, p. 89).

Throughout 2 Corinthians, one might detect that Paul constructed his arguments using formal argumentative *topoi* (see Long, 1999, appendix V; in 2 Cor. 10–13, see DiCicco, 1995, pp. 241–56). First, by reference to Aristotle's τόποι ἐνθυμημάτων, there are numbers 4 (*more or less*) (e.g., 1.12; 2.7; 3.7–11; 12.18), 7 (*definition*) (e.g., 2.16; 3.1, 7–18; 10.13, 17–18), 9 (*division*) (e.g., 2.15–16; 5.9, 10; 7.12), 11 (*authority*) (e.g., 1.20–21; 2.14; 3.5; 4.1, 6, 7; 5.18–20; 6.1, 16–18; 7.6; 8.5, 15; 9.9), 13 (*simple consequences*) (e.g., 3.7; 13.1–2), 19 (*attributed motive for good or bad as is best for the orator*) (e.g., 2.3–4, 9, 17; 3.13; 5.11; 6.3–10), 20 (*incentives and deterrents for people*) (e.g., 3.7–8; 4.10–14, 15, 16–18; 5.10, 14; 6.1–2; 7.1; 8.2, 7; 9.4, 6–15), 22 (*examining opposites or conflicting actions*) (e.g., 8.10–11; 10.1, 12–15; 11.4, 7–11), 23 (*explaining accusation*) (e.g., 2.15–16; 12.21), and 24 (*cause to effect*) (e.g., 3.14, 16; 6.17; 7.9–10; 8.1–6, 9; 12.20–21). Also possible is Paul's use of the *topos* of *contradictions* (*ex pugnantibus*) as described in Quintilian (*Inst.* 5.10.74) (e.g., 1.12, 13a, 19, 24; 2.5, 17; 3.3, 5, 6; 4.2, 5, 8–10; 5.1–2, 4, 7, 12a, 12b, 13, 15, 17; 6.12, 14–16; 7.7, 9, 12; 8.8, 13–14, 19–20, 21; 9.5, 7, 12; 10.3–5, 8, 12; 11.6, 17; 12.14).

Additionally, Paul employs *synkrisis* (comparison), as many have noted (see esp. Furnish, 1984, pp. 532–33; on *synkrisis* in 3.7–18, see Kennedy, p. 89; on *synkrisis* in 2 Cor. 10–12, see Forbes, 1986, p. 19). Paul explicitly referred to the practice of *synkrisis* among his missionary rivals in 10.12. This is particularly significant because *synkrisis* was an important part of the *progymnasmata* (see Forbes, p. 19).

Moreover, Paul's manner of expressing these *topoi* has analogy to what is found in the orators. First, in 3.7–11 Paul clearly used the argumentative *topos* of greater/lesser. The argument is constructed with a series of conditional clauses followed by πολλῷ μᾶλλον, which follows the precedent set by forensic orators as noted above. Second, Paul's repeated use of the antithetical construction οὐ . . . ἀλλά has many parallels in forensic orations (Aeschin. *Ctes.* 24.13; *Leg.* 27.5, 64.7, 162.7, 167.2; *Tim.* 74.9, 89.6; Antiph. 1.13.5; Din. 1.15.2; Dem. 18.131.3, 234.1; Dem. 19.74.4, 331.2, 336.7; Dem. 20.4.6; Dem. 22.63.3; Dem. 23.72.5, 81.5; Dem. 42.29.7; Dem. 44.55.5; Dem. 51.14.2; Dem. 52.14.4; Din. 3.1.2, 18.2; Isoc. 11.5.3; Isoc. 15.117.4; Isoc. 20.10.4; Lys. 6.13.3; Lys. 7.13.2; Lys. 12.44.4; Lys. 22.3.6, 10.3).

What can one learn from Paul's argumentation according to the analysis above? First, he is a dialectical thinker; his argumentation gravitates towards antitheses to a tremendous degree. He constantly juxtaposes opposing notions in order to draw his readers to a desired conclusion. Second, Paul's argumentation in 2 Corinthians is dependent upon issues of authority, which corresponds with my conclusions about the *stasis* of quality as discussed above. Third, he was persuasive in providing incentives and deterrents for decisions that he wanted the Corinthians and others to make. Paul was keenly aware that cause–effect relations would impact the volition of his audience. Finally, the notions that Paul developed by way of definition – sufficiency, God's glory, commendation, boasting – are critical when 2 Corinthians is recognized as an apology. Why Paul employed such weighty argumentation is perhaps best argued by Winter (1997, p. 230):

> That he failed as a "public" orator when judged by the canons of the first-century sophistic tradition with its emphasis on extempore declamation meant that he was excluded from the circle of virtuoso orators in Corinth who attracted a large public following. This discussion has shown, however, that Paul overcame any oratorical limitations with epistolary argumentation which, with his distinct λογισμοί, could conquer the rhetorical devices of his adversaries.

9.6   Conclusion

Paul consciously employed features of forensic rhetorical invention in 2 Corinthians. This conclusion contributes to my thesis that 2 Corinthians is a unified letter of self-apology deliberately formed according to the theory and practice of forensic rhetoric. Paul has constructed a complex and weighty line of defense that depended upon the establishment of his authority to take a certain course of action: He wrote instead of visited.

While making this defense, he used the qualitative *stasis*. One can detect many of the qualitative *topoi* in 2 Corinthians, such as a discussion of intention and the amplification of benefits rendered and sufferings endured. To achieve persuasion and demonstrate his innocence, Paul employed inartificial proofs, such as witnesses, physical evidence, and oracles, all of which establish goodwill for him, often by displaying his outstanding *ethos*. He appealed to *pathos* throughout and repeatedly asserted his integrity and his allegiance to the truth. Additionally, he used examples, maxims, *enthymemes*, and *epicheiremes* with the assistance of argumentative *topoi*. Admittedly, his argumentation is dialectical and philosophical. Although he would grant that he was *untrained in speech* (ἰδιώτης τῷ λόγῳ) – employing a common rhetorical *topos* – he asserted that he was not untrained in knowledge (11.6). However, he confessed that he persuaded persons in the fear of the Lord to obey his gospel proclamation (5.11).

10

THE RHETORIC OF 2 CORINTHIANS AND
THE NATURE OF PAUL'S THEOLOGY

Second Corinthians is Paul's great apology in which he opens wide his heart and wants the Corinthians to do the same (6.11–13). In it Paul defends his perceived inconsistencies while morally educating the Corinthians in matters of forgiveness, faithfulness, and sacrificial service. Paul argued that since God approved his ministry, so should the Corinthians. Although interpreters dispute the apologetic nature of Galatians and portions of 1 Corinthians, I would maintain that Paul in 2 Corinthians leaves little doubt of his intentions (7.2; 12.19). Paul's apology in 2 Corinthians is masterfully on a par with the epideictic rhetoric of 1 Thessalonians (Jewett, 1986) and the deliberative rhetoric in 1 Corinthians (M. Mitchell, 1991). Paul's repertoire is complete.

By investigating 2 Corinthians through Greco-Roman rhetorical theory and practice I have addressed the question of the unity of 2 Corinthians. I have focused primarily on disposition, invention, and exigency. From a methodological viewpoint I hope that this monograph will contribute to the goal of the "complete analysis of New Testament rhetoric," to use Judge's words (1968, p. 45). I expect that it will initiate further discussion and debate on the nature and character of Pauline rhetoric.

My particular thesis is that Paul deliberately fashioned 2 Corinthians in conformity with forensic practice in the Greco-Roman tradition. Specifically, he was responding to damaging charges about his methods and growing suspicions about his motivations. Therefore, he constructed an official apologetic letter. In order to substantiate this claim, I surveyed several centuries of forensic practice and theory and then investigated the evidence regarding Paul's relationship with the Corinthians, especially in 2 Corinthians itself.

Summary and significance of the forensic rhetoric
of 2 Corinthians

In the opening chapter I briefly reviewed the critical issues surrounding the integrity and chronology of 2 Corinthians. I argued that both the literary and chronological problems should suggest to interpreters that a dynamic exigency existed which likely was met with an equally dynamic rhetorical response. Interpreters must account for this rhetorical dimension in order to appreciate the unity of 2 Corinthians. The appropriate methodology, consequently, is historical-rhetorical criticism.

Only a handful of interpreters have attempted to analyze 2 Corinthians as a unified discourse in its rhetorical milieu. Young and Ford (1987, p. 54) rightly argue: "one critical conclusion does seem particularly important to understanding the text. The purport of the text is enshrined in its 'genre' . . . For this reason we regard it as important to try and establish the unity of 2 Corinthians as an apologetic letter." I have attempted to establish on form-critical grounds what Young and Ford proposed. My conclusion is that 2 Corinthians generically is an *apology*.

In order to establish that 2 Corinthians conforms to ancient apology, I needed to survey a significant portion of the numerous extant examples of forensic rhetoric, which are listed in Chapter 2. From this survey (the results of which are found in Chapters 3–5) I concluded that there are at least twelve distinctive and characteristic features of forensic discourse in the areas of exigence, invention, and disposition. Respectively, I treated these features in Chapters 3–5. Readers should consult the respective chapter summaries for an overview of my most relevant findings.

Then, before considering to what extent 2 Corinthians conforms to forensic rhetoric, I wanted to provide in Chapters 2 and 6 further justification for performing a historical-rhetorical criticism on 2 Corinthians by locating it within its appropriate literary milieu. In Chapter 2.2, I discussed Greco-Roman rhetoric's pervasive influence through the proliferation of speech exemplars and its pliability through theoretical developments. Indeed, forensic rhetoric had an impact on all aspects of the Greco-Roman literary culture, forming the foundation of rhetorical theory and education. Persons then as now (consider American television programs like *The People's Court* and *Judge Judy* and the popularity of the O. J. Simpson trial) were fascinated with forensic discourse. Forensic rhetoric demonstrated tremendous versatility and was applied across both spoken and written media and merged with other major genres, namely, epistolography, drama, and historiography.

Most significantly for my study, ancient apology merged with early epistolary practice. This is the subject of Chapter 6. There I suggested that 2 Corinthians on the basis of its extended setting (1.1 – "to all the saints of the whole of Achaia"), length, extensive argumentation, and lively conversational style is *an official apologetic letter*. Because of its recognizable rhetorical features and its propagandistic appeal, we should liken 2 Corinthians to Plato's *Third Letter* and *Seventh Letter* and Demosthenes' *Second Letter*, each of which is a propagandistic apologetic letter. Furthermore, the manner and method of Paul's argumentation in 2 Corinthians would indicate that he deliberately drew upon broader features of self-apology from the ostentatious traditions of Aeschines' *On the Embassy*, Andocides' *On the Mysteries*, the *apologia* of Socrates, Isocrates' *Antidosis*, and Demosthenes' *On the Crown*.

In the second part of my study I sought to demonstrate that 2 Corinthians conforms to ancient apology in terms of exigence (Chapter 7), disposition (Chapter 8), and invention (Chapter 9). Drawing on recent studies, I aimed in Chapter 7 to show that 2 Corinthians addressed a particular exigency. Paul sent 2 Corinthians to address a flowering seedbed of charges and criticisms. Paul's own criticisms of the Corinthians had been turned against him – he was worldly and unapproved. Specifically, he was charged with inconsistency with respect to his failing to visit when planned, his flagrant use of rhetoric in his letters, and his financial duplicity. At jeopardy was Paul's status in delivering the Corinthians' portion of the collection. The evidence suggests that some missionary rivals had gained the Corinthians' confidence and had secured (promises of) letters of recommendation from the Corinthians (3.1). Paul firmly reminded the Corinthians that they themselves were his letter of recommendation (3.2).

Most intriguingly, 2 Corinthians has similarities with the public scrutiny of officials (*dokimasia*) for public service. Paul was suspected of mishandling and pilfering from the collection (cf. 8.20–21; 12.14–18) and was being scrutinized in this official capacity. Thus, just as he had urged the Corinthians – only *some* of whom he deemed *approved* (1 Cor. 11.19) – to approve of some to accompany him in the presentation of the collection (1 Cor. 16.3), so now he was deemed *unapproved* (2 Cor. 13.7). Because some of the Corinthians likely applied Paul's own particular directives against him, an apologetic letter was necessary. Paul could not simply assert his apostolic status. In order to secure their partnership with him, he presented them with an apt apology.

In Chapter 8 I endeavored to show that 2 Corinthians is structured as an apology. It contains a *prooemium*, a distributed *narratio*, a *divisio* and *partitio*, a *probatio*, a *refutatio*, self-adulation, and a *peroratio*. The function of each section contributes substantially to our understanding of the strategies and aims of Paul's discourse. The dignified *prooemium* (1.1–7) established goodwill by turning the audience's attention to God's mercy in suffering, and the bond that existed between Paul and the audience through mutual identification with Christ's suffering and comfort. At the same time Paul announced his hope *on behalf of* the Corinthians, *as if they were on trial.* The ethical *narratio* related Paul's suffering (1.8–10a) and affirmed his hope in God and hope in mutual prayer from the Corinthians (1.10b–11). Paul based this hope in 1.12–14 upon the testimony of his ethical conduct towards them and their ability to read the present discourse and fully understand him. Particularly, Paul must clarify his intentions regarding his travel failures (1.15–16).

The *narratio* leads directly to the *divisio* and *partitio* in 1.17–24. In these verses Paul directed his attention to the matter of his own inconsistency and itinerate intentions (1.17), his and his companions' divine affirmation as agents of the gospel proclamation (1.18–20 – "*our* word," "preached among you *by* us," "the amen to God for glory is *through* us"), their co-participation with the Corinthians in the down deposit of the Holy Spirit (1.21–22), Paul's sparing of the Corinthians (1.23), and Paul's laboring for the Corinthians' joy in the faith (1.24). The *partitio* outlines the *probatio* using key terms and ideas (see Table 8.3).

Further narrative material at 2.12–13 and 7.2–16 helps to demarcate the initial and final argumentative sections in the *probatio*. The first section (2.1–11) concerns Paul's explanations, intentions, and new directives to forgive the sinful one in light of the letter he had sent in lieu of visiting them. The fifth section (2 Cor. 8–9) is deliberative in import. In it Paul explained the steps he had taken in preparation for the collection, while supplying several reasons why the Corinthians should participate with him in it. Both the first and the fifth sections pertain to logistical matters (travels/letters and envoys/collection efforts respectively) concerning which Paul had been particularly scrutinized (see esp. 1.15–17; 12.14–18; cf. 7.2b).

The three central argument movements in 2.14–3.18, 4.1–5.10, and 5.11–7.1 represent Paul's attempt to clarify the content, character, conduct, and consequences of his gospel proclamation. Each of these units is initiated (2.14–3.1; 4.2; 5.11–12) with four recurring elements: (1) rhetoric in relation to God's word vis-à-vis Paul's proclamation (2.17; 4.2; 5.11; cf. 5.17; 6.7), (2) the notion of self-commendation (Ἀρχόμεθα πάλιν ἑαυτοὺς συνιστάνειν; συνιστάνοντες ἑαυτούς; ἑαυτοὺς συνιστάνομεν), (3) God's purview of Paul's activities (κατέναντι θεοῦ; ἐνώπιον τοῦ θεοῦ; θεῷ δὲ πεφανερώμεθα), and (4) explicit or implicit reference to Paul's missionary rivals. The theological content of these chapters moves from the past events of Paul's initial proclamation resulting in the Corinthians' conversion and their reception of the Spirit (2.14–3.18) to a discussion of Paul's present sufferings (4.8–12) moving towards the future reality of renewed bodies, which is guaranteed by the down deposit of the Holy Spirit, and the universal future judgment (4.13–5.10). Paul's argumentation here is a segue to his urgent rhetorical appeals to the Corinthians "in the fear of the Lord" to be reconciled to God and him and to embrace God's righteousness as God's covenant people (5.11–7.1). The Corinthians' faithful participation with Paul in the collection (2 Cor. 8–9) would reflect their reconciliation with both God and him.

In the *refutatio* (10.1–11.15) Paul redressed the criticisms of his inconsistency on two counts: He has a bold epistolary style in contrast to his weak personal presence (10.1–11) and he received financial support from some when he had refused it from others (11.7–11). However, Paul also critiqued his missionary rivals, who, as he put it, "commend themselves" and encroached on his territory (10.12–18). These *false apostles* were to be compared with the ancient serpent and the servants of Satan because they preached a different Jesus/spirit/gospel (11.1–6) and received financial support in attempts to feign true apostleship (11.12–15).

As would be fitting for a defensive speech, Paul entered into self-adulation (11.16–12.10), although with reluctance and at moments in parody. Paul's relating of his cowardly escape (11.31–33) and third-person heavenly raptures (12.1–5) are prime examples. But, we should not think that Paul did not want the Corinthians to esteem or see something in him that is praiseworthy, something which they should embrace. The list of labors and sufferings (11.23–29) and Paul's statements about what he will boast (11.30; 12.5, 9, 10) cannot be construed merely as parody. There is profound truth in these statements to be imitated, and Paul is implicitly imploring the Corinthians to share mutually in his sufferings, thereby participating in Christ's power (12.8–10). Paul had received a direct affirming statement from the Lord.

This climactic moment in the discourse marks a return to the key theme of the *prooemium* and introduces the *peroratio* in 12.11–13.10. The *peroratio* retraces major argumentative themes in inverted fashion (see Table 8.13 and Appendix I). At the same time Paul made his final appeals to the Corinthians (12.13, 17, 18; 13.5, 7) and repeatedly promised his imminent visit to Corinth (12.14, 20, 21; 13.1, 10). Although he had failed to visit thus far, he would not delay it any longer. All that Paul did while absent he was doing for the Corinthians' edification according to divine authorization (13.10).

During my exposition of these forensic speech sections, I identified specific formulaic forensic *topoi* and idioms. These included, among many others, expressions of hope (1.7, 13–14; 5.11; 13.6), speaking the truth (4.2; 6.7; 7.14; 11.10; 12.6; 13.8), recollecting divine affirmations and an oracle (12.1–10), being forced/compelled to speak on one's behalf (12.11), and a final appeal that the Corinthian jury ought to judge Paul rightly (13.7). In the final analysis, such a convergence of *topoi* and idioms contribute cumulatively to my argument that 2 Corinthians was *conceived* by Paul and *perceived* by the Corinthians as a unified apology.

The significance of my analysis is that those problematic literary characteristics of 2 Corinthians are readily accounted for form-critically when 2 Corinthians is affirmed as an apology. First, the perceived seams at 2.13/14 and 7.4/5 are transitions out of and into well-crafted distributed narrative material (1.8–16; 2.12–13; 7.2b–16). This material relates materially to the case because it clarifies where Paul is, his circumstances, his intentions, his preparations, and his great concern for the Corinthians (despite his failure to visit). In this regard, there is a chronological development across the whole discourse: (1) Paul's dire circumstances and intentions to visit (1.8–16); (2) his decision not to visit but rather write a letter instead and the intentions behind the letter (2.1–11); (3) Paul's search for Titus to learn of the letter's effects (2.12–13); (4) Paul's further clarification of his intentions behind the letter and his rendezvous with Titus, who related to Paul the letter's initial positive results (7.2–16); (5) Paul's preparations for the collection, particularly the sending of Titus and the brethren (chaps. 8–9); and finally, (6) Paul's emphatically promised arrival in Corinth (12.11–13.10).

Second, the disputed material in 6.14–7.1 was shown to belong to the argument unit of 5.11–7.1, which was anticipated by the *partitio* at 1.23. Paul correlated his own experience with the immoral and idolatrous Corinthians with that of Moses and the Israelites in the Exodus event at Mt. Sinai. Just as God through Moses *spared* the Israelites from sure destruction, so too Paul acted to *spare* the Corinthians a painful face-to-face confrontation. Paul was acting as a covenantal representative like Moses, and climactically in 6.14–7.1 he exhorted the Corinthians to a renewed covenantal faithfulness as God's people.

Third, 2 Corinthians 8–9, rather than being two independent letters, is a unified argument displaying its own deliberative disposition with *narratio* (8.1–6), *partitio* (8.7–9), *probatio* (8.10–9.12), and *peroratio* (9.13–15). The import of this *speech within a speech* is to urge the Corinthians to support Paul's efforts in the collection – he and his co-workers have acted with demonstrable integrity for the glory of God. These chapters also contribute to Paul's counter-charge of the Corinthians, because should they refuse to participate in the collection, they will show themselves unable to keep their word (8.10–15, 24; 9.2, 5).

Finally, I argue that 2 Corinthians 10–13 are the final three sections of a defensive speech. The *change of tone* at 10.1 is to be expected, since Paul begins the *refutatio*. At 11.16 he entered into a foolish boast *concerning himself* that extends to 12.10. At 12.11 he self-reflectively reviewed the need for his apology and creatively recapitulated thoroughly its main apologetic points (see Appendix I), while calling the Corinthians to evaluate themselves and him favorably (13.5–7) before his impending visit. Thus, the result of my disposition analysis challenges the standard suspicions about the literary problems in 2 Corinthians in favor of the letter's compositional and thematic unity. Accordingly, I gladly place myself among the growing company of those who acknowledge the compositional unity of 2 Corinthians.

In Chapter 9 I explored the inventive side to Paul's discourse. By nature this chapter is the most speculative, since I attempt to explain the process and strategies Paul followed in the construction of 2 Corinthians. I argue that Paul developed a line of defense according to the qualitative *stasis*. This is the most honorable defense, since the defendant admits *doing the deed*, but *justifies it* on other grounds. Important features of a qualitative defense are the defendant's *intentions* and *authority* to do what he or she had done. *These two elements are central to Paul's rhetorical performance.* He repeatedly explained his intentions to visit the Corinthians in the *narratio* (esp. 1.12–16). Then in the *peroratio*, he repetitiously and emphatically stated his impending visit (12.14, 20–21; 13.1–2, 10). Also he demonstrated his divinely appointed authority with the Corinthians and defended his position throughout the letter, "for building up, not tearing down" (2.1–7; 10.8; 13.1–10). If Paul had visited when planned, this would have resulted in grief (λύπη) (2.1–4, 7), just as the sinful one had grieved (λελύπηκεν) all (2.5). As it turned out, Paul grieved (ἐλύπησα) the Corinthians by his letter (1 Corinthians), which led them to repentance (εἰς μετάνοιαν) (7.8–11). In his conclusion, Paul sternly warned them that he might be divinely grieved (πενθέω) by their *unrepentant immorality* at his imminent coming (12.21). Thus, the situation that he had so carefully tried to avoid (a grievous visit) could yet result.

Moreover, 2 Corinthians exhibits features of each of the four qualitative *stasis* subtypes, most significantly counter-charge (see McCant, 1999). That the Corinthians are on trial can be seen in many ways. First, in the *prooemium* (1.7) Paul has hope not *from* the Corinthians but *on their behalf* (ὑπέρ with the genitive). They awaited a divine trial, as did Paul (5.10), and must examine themselves (13.5) and think rightly about him (13.7). Second, although the Corinthians had charged Paul with failing to visit, he argued that his delay was a *result of their own disobedience* (2.3–11). Third, their immorality persisted to such an extent that Paul must exhort them to righteous living (5.11–7.1). Fourth, Paul urged them to be consistent with their prior commitment to give to the collection

(2 Cor. 8–9). Fifth, Paul *dared to confront* (τολμάω) those who suspected him of acting in a worldly fashion (10.2). Such *daring* was usually associated with those presenting an accusation. Furthermore, he threatened to punish excessively (10.6). Lastly, Paul asked the Corinthians to test themselves to see if they were approved (13.1–7). He also chided them once again for their poor conduct (12.20–21). Thus, a significant component of Paul's self-defense is the common forensic practice of counter-accusation.

In addition to using *topoi* associated with the qualitative *stasis* (see Appendix II), 2 Corinthians reveals other aspects of rhetorical invention. Paul appealed to witnesses (e.g., 1.12, 23; 8.3), laws (e.g., 13.1), and other physical evidences (e.g., his previous letter – 2.3–11; 7.6–15; 13.2). He appealed to *pathos* (*peristasis* catalogues) and *ethos* ("I speak the truth" – 6.7; 7.14; 12.6; cf. 4.2; 11.10; 13.8). Concerning *logos* arguments, Paul used examples (e.g., 8.1–9) and maxims (4.6, 13; 7.10; 8.10, 12; 9.6; 10.17, 18; 11.15; 12.9, 14; 13.6). Furthermore, he constructed 2 Corinthians with *enthymemes* and *epicheirematic* argumentation (premise–proof–conclusion) using various kinds of forensic *topoi*. Paul used common *topoi* and various formal argumentative *topoi* (e.g., authority and opposites). There can be little doubt that he had significant training in rhetorical invention and the construction and presentation of arguments.

Some interpreters will contest my view that 2 Corinthians is primarily forensic in nature as opposed to deliberative or epideictic. I agree that we should not ignore the deliberative/parenetic and epideictic/encomiastic elements and dimensions of 2 Corinthians. However, *even* these elements contribute to Paul's forensic strategy. For example, Paul's exhortation (5.11–7.1) bolstered his case by describing the kind of persuasion he used and by providing further rationale for not coming but writing instead because the Corinthians were so immoral (cf. 12.20–21; 13.1–2). Likewise, Paul's discussion of the collection supplied evidence that he was innocent of wrongdoing (he didn't steal from the Macedonians – 8.5; 11.8; cf. 7.2 and 12.13–18) and that he intended to conduct the collection with manifest integrity (8.20–21). At the same time Paul challenged the Corinthians to act *consistently* with their own promise of participation. In the end, the collection provided an opportunity for the Corinthians to cast a favorable vote for Paul. These two issues, Paul's exhortation and the collection, contributed to a forensic strategy (and *topos*) of counter-charge.

Taking a step back, we must carefully distinguish between *the various needs* Paul's rhetoric met and *the various intentions* of his rhetoric. As far as the Corinthians were concerned, an apology was required. From

Paul's perspective, the Corinthians needed reconciliation, moral reform, and accountability in addition to completing their portion of the collection. However, in 2 Corinthians the emphasis rests upon *the apologetic need*, since Paul must *first* clear himself of any wrongdoing before complete cooperation by the Corinthians could even be conceivable. We must be realistic on this point. Paul could not *simply* argue that God approved of him and that God's court is all that matters, thereby closing the case. Although Paul did argue that God approved of him, he used this as *evidence* in his favor as he proceeded to account for his apparent failures and explain more clearly the nature and character of his ministry. Paul's argument is that, since God approved of him, so should the Corinthians. Additionally, Paul's apology was *absolutely necessary*, since certain rivals had successfully wooed (at least) some of the Corinthians, which resulted in questioning his integrity and authoritative status within the Corinthian community.

While providing a form-critical solution to the compositional problems of 2 Corinthians, this present work also contributes to understanding Paul's relations with the Corinthians. Often interpreters work with the assumption that *the letter of tears* (2.1–5) is simply lost or to be reconfigured from some other portion of 2 Corinthians (sometimes chaps. 10–13). Additionally, interpreters assume that Paul made an *intermediate visit*. However, my rhetorical analysis supports the conclusions of Hyldahl (1973) that 1 Corinthians and the so-called letter of tears are one and the same and that Paul made no intervening visit (none is recorded in Acts). Critical in this discussion is the observation that from the descriptions in 2 Cor. 2.1–11 and 7.2–16 we learn that the material content of the letter of tears corresponds with Paul's *severest, most shameful*, and potentially *most condemning chastisement* of the Corinthians in 1 Corinthians 5–6 after his initial *apologia* in 1 Corinthians 1–4. Also, when Paul describes his *presence* among the Corinthians a *second time while also absent now* (ὡς παρὼν τὸ δεύτερον καὶ ἀπὼν νῦν) (2 Cor. 13.2), he refers to his presence in proxy, which he explicitly evoked in 1 Cor. 5.1–5. We should perceive Paul defending his choice of writing and sending his own presence in that letter in lieu of actually being present. These conclusions should encourage scholars to rethink the time frame and events between 1 and 2 Corinthians (see my tentative reconstruction at the end of Chapter 7.2) and the two letters' interrelated themes of Paul's authoritative presence, Corinthian immorality, boasting, and rhetoric.

Finally, I have endeavored to avoid an exact determination of Paul's opponents in 2 Corinthians. Some of the Corinthians themselves were already criticizing Paul on the basis of sophistic criteria. Those missionary rivals who did arrive – Apollos may have inadvertently started an exodus from Paul on account of his rhetorical polish, Spirit enthusiasm, and baptismal fervor – only exacerbated some of the Corinthians' disesteem for Paul. I suspect that itinerant teachers (or even known rivals) were specifically invited (cf. Acts 18.27) to accept Corinthian patronage of their services during Paul's prolonged absence. It seems certain that they were rhetorically minded teachers and were willing to take Paul's place in the collection, possibly denouncing him themselves. In response, Paul thought himself sufficiently justified to demonize them (11.3, 5, 13–15) because they preached a different gospel and were subverting his authority, his relationship with the Corinthians, and ultimately his special project, the collection.

Understanding Paul and his theology: the unity of 2 Corinthians

It is difficult to speak succinctly and precisely about the relation of Paul's theology and his rhetoric. One could speak of the substructure of his theology and the structure of his rhetoric. However, this may suggest that his theology hardly makes it to the surface. This will not do. A critical starting point for interpreting Paul and constructing a Pauline theology is to recognize and become familiar with the fact that *Paul's theological presentation is rhetorically conditioned*. To what extent can we understand his theology without understanding his historically conditioned rhetoric? The two are inexorably merged.

Certainly something of Paul's message and theology can be caught without such an understanding, for authors use rhetoric to move audiences, and Paul's rhetoric moves us whether we understand how we are moved or not. Consequently, persons can understand him at some level without sophisticated training, *although* maybe not to the extent that he might want them to and not as much as would be completely edifying for them (cf. 2 Pet. 3.14–16). We must reread and rehear Paul again and again. We must remember that 2 Corinthians was addressed to the Corinthians for *their understanding* of Paul and not *our own* (1.12–13). Therefore, something of tremendous value is gained by understanding how the discourse functioned *for them rhetorically*, on terms established, as much as possible, on the basis of ancient rhetorical and forensic theory and practice in its social, historical, and religious milieu. I hope that my analysis contributes to this more complete and edifying understanding of 2 Corinthians.

My analysis of the rhetoric of 2 Corinthians (historically understood) has led me to affirm the letter's unity. David A. DeSilva (1996, pp. 5–6) has some very cogent thoughts pertaining to grasping Paul's theology within the context of questions surrounding the letter's unity:

> Questions of the literary integrity of 2 Corinthians are important, however, not only for matters of historical reconstruction, but for the correct reading of passages within the letters themselves. Every passage taken from a larger letter or narrative must be read and interpreted in light of the whole text of which it is a part – the interpretation of any given passage within 2 Corinthians will change (often only slightly, sometimes more dramatically) according to the interpreter's idea of the "whole" which guides the reading of the "part." Furthermore, an understanding of the literary integrity of the letter leads to a comprehension of the strategies pursued within the text and, finally, of the apostle himself, especially in a letter such as 2 Corinthians, which focuses not on the power and abilities of the man so much as on his weaknesses, even his apparent vacillations and insecurities. Understanding the rhetorical strategy and argumentation of 2 Corinthians thus assists our own struggles with weakness and our encounters with the power of God, which transcends our weakness.

If, indeed, 2 Corinthians was composed as a unified discourse, then to read 2 Corinthians as a composite of letter fragments would result in some violence theologically when attempting to recapture Paul's thought. My hope is that something of his rhetorical method and theological message in 2 Corinthians has been recovered through my analysis so that his focal description of God's work in Christ may be embraced and celebrated.

Personally, I am challenged by the approach that Paul has taken in 2 Corinthians. He speaks to meet the Corinthians *where they are* "while walking in the flesh but not battling according to the flesh" (10.3). Paul's rhetoric fundamentally is *incarnational rhetoric*. It is not a Socratic *true rhetoric* relying on ambiguity, deception, and double-talk (*contra* Given, 2001); nor is it a thoroughly Socratic *parodic rhetoric* (*contra* McCant, 1999). Paul's is a *suffering rhetoric*, and at times a self-deprecating rhetoric, but always a rhetoric *calling the audience to conformity to Christ* and *directing human persons to the purposes and glory of God in Christ*. Paul is himself *incarnated* in and through his speech, even written speech (1 Cor. 5.1–5; cf. 2 Cor. 13.2). More importantly, Christ is *incarnated* through Paul in his speech (13.3; cf. 2.17; 12.19). Paul *is* the aroma of

Christ (2.15). Paul *embodies* simultaneously the sufferings (1.5–6; 4.10) and life (4.10–11) of Christ. Paul *reflects* the new covenant glory (3.12–13) and reminds the Corinthians that all in Christ are being transformed into this glory more and more, whereby they reflect the very face of Christ (3.18). Indeed, the gospel message of Christ is incarnated in Paul's ministry.

This *incarnational rhetoric* enters enduringly into all arenas of human life, with all its ambiguities and contingencies, attempting to communicate successfully to found and fortify *Christ-centered communities*. Paul's speech embodied human speech forms, while also transforming them, in order to battle the values and opinions that are often quite at odds with the truth of the gospel of Christ. Consequently, Paul occasionally employed rhetorical techniques, such as parody, sarcasm, irony, and even name-calling, which are stunning and shocking. They formed one part of Paul's rhetorical arsenal "to take captive every thought for Christ" to bring about complete obedience (10.5–6).

APPENDIX I
HOW THE *PERORATIO* (12.11–13.10)
SUMMARIZES 2 CORINTHIANS

Peroratio	Transitional particle, etc.	Subjects and vocabulary in the *Peroratio*	Corresponding section, subjects, and vocabulary in 2 Corinthians
12.11–13	– no particle – denoted by element of self-reflection – several aspects of previous section summarized	A Fool (ἄφρων) B Corinthians compelled Paul by not commending (συνίστημι) him C Paul not inferior (ὑστερέω) D Super apostles (τῶν ὑπερλίαν ἀποστόλων) E Signs, miracles, wonders of an apostle performed by Paul F Paul did not burden church (καταναρκάω); this is a transitional subject to financial subjects	*Self-adulation:* *11.16–12.10* A Fool (ἄφρων – 11.16, 19; 12.6); foolishness (ἀφροσύνη – 11.1, 17, 21); speaking as fool (παραφρονέω – 11.23) *Refutatio: 10.1–11.15* B Commend (συνίστημι – 10.12, 18) C Paul's inferiority (ὑστερέω – 11.5, 9) D Super apostles (τῶν ὑπερλίαν ἀποστόλων – 11.5) and false apostles (ψευδαπόστολοι – 11.13) E Implied? (or cf. 12.1–10) F Burden (καταναρκάω – 11.9)
12.14–15	– ἰδού – travel plans discussed – change in topic, yet transition	A Paul is coming to the Corinthians B Paul seeks not their possessions (i.e. the collection), but them C Issue of Corinthian love for Paul [This section is closely tied to next]	*Probatio: 9.1–15* A Paul is coming with Macedonians and will collect the gift (9.4) B The Corinthians' possible humiliation is at stake (9.4); Paul is focused on their giving freely (9.13–14)

Peroratio	Transitional particle, etc.	Subjects and vocabulary in the *Peroratio*	Corresponding section, subjects, and vocabulary in 2 Corinthians
			C Corinthians' love for Paul to be proven (8.7–8, 24)
12.16–18	ἔστω δὲ – change in topic	A Paul sent Titus and the brother B Did he or they take advantage (πλεονεκτέω) of the Corinthians? C Reference to right conduct in the Spirit (πνεύμα) [transitional]	*Narratio/probatio: 7.2–8.24* A Titus and brothers (8.6, 16–19, 22) B Paul did not take advantage of them (πλεονεκτέω – 7.2); also, Paul explains Titus' and companions' motivation for coming to Corinth, etc. in detail (7.4–16) C Defilement of Spirit (7.1)
12.19–21	πάλαι – self-reflective from the Corinthians' perspective – change in subject	A Paul not merely defending, but speaking for their upbuilding; B Corinthians are "beloved" (ἀγαπητοί) C Vice List 12.20 (no words matching those found in 5.20–7.3) D Impurity (ἀκαθαρσία) E Deeds practiced (πράσσω) [Transition = "sinned before" (προαμαρτάνω) 12.21 → 13.2]	*Probatio: 5.11–7.1* A Exhortation section; note the concentration of imperatives; see 7.3 B Corinthians are "beloved" (ἀγαπητοί – 7.1) C Purge from all defilement (7.1) D Impure (ἀκάθαρτος – 6.17) E Judged by what is done (πράσσω) in the body – 5.10, which is a transition to the next exhortation section
13.1–4	– no particle – travel plans – different subject	A Paul will not be sparing (φείδομαι) when he comes as he warned before B Two or three witnesses C Proof (δοκιμή) that . . . D Christ speaks (λαλέω) in Paul E Christ's power/God's power (δυνατέω; δύναμις)	*Probatio: 5.11–7.1* A Paul is not sparing (φείδομαι in the *partitio* at 1.23 prepares for 5.11–7.1) B Paul calls God as witness (again, the *partitio* at 1.23 prepares for the covenantal quotations at 6.16–18) *(cont.)*

Peroratio	Transitional particle, etc.	Subjects and vocabulary in the *Peroratio*	Corresponding section, subjects, and vocabulary in 2 Corinthians
		F Despite Christ's weakness/Paul's weakness	*Probatio: 2.14–3.18; 4.1–5.10*
		G Living (ζάω) (in power)	C Paul does not call his argument here a proof (δοκιμή), but it functions that way – God is speaking in Paul
			D Christ speaks (λαλέω) in Paul (2.17; 4.12; cf. 4.2, 5)
			E Power (δύναμις – 4.7; cf. 6.7)
			F Different images and wording = "afflicted" (θλίψομαι – 4.8); "affliction (θλῖψις – 4.17; 6.4); "mortal body" (θνητή σάρξ – 4.11); "death" (θάνατος – 4.11–12); cf. "our earthly home in this tent" (ἡ ἐπίγειος ἡμῶν οἰκία τοῦ σκήνους – 5.1, 4)
			G "Living" (ζάω – 4.11; 5.15; 6.9; cf. "Living God" 3.3; 6.16); "Life" (ζωή – 2.16; 4.10–12; 5.4)
13.5–10	imperatives	A Have the Corinthians passed the test? (δοκιμάζω; ἀδόκιμος)	*Probatio: 2.1–11*
		B It seems as though Paul has failed and has not met the test (13.7)	A Paul checks if they pass the test (δοκιμή – 2.9). This recalls the reason he gives for not having come the first time – the Corinthians' moral failings and his fear of confrontation
		C Paul rejoices (χαίρω) at their strength	B Paul did not visit (2.1, 3).
		D Paul is preparing to be present with them, i.e. to come to them physically, even though writing to them presently	C Paul wanted to rejoice (χαίρω) in the Corinthians (2.3; cf. χαρά – 1.24)
			D Paul was not able to come previously to them, but only by letter (2.3)

APPENDIX II
TOPOI FOR EACH SUBTYPE OF THE QUALITATIVE *STASIS*

This table summarizes the topical theories of the four subtypes of the qualitative *stasis* as described by the *Rhetorica ad Herennium* and Cicero's *De Inventione Rhetorica*. In these works, general suggestions are provided, in addition to specific *topoi* directives for both prosecution and defense. The table distinguishes between *topoi* associated directly with the *stasis* (ST) and the common *topoi* (CT). The specific *topoi* that I argue are present in 2 Corinthians (see analysis in Chapter 9.2) are indicated by italics.

	General topical suggestions
Counter-plea *comparatio*; ἀντίστασις The action taken was the better of the options.	ST = First, which action was the more advantageous, i.e. honorable, practicable, and profitable? Second, was the defendant the one to determine this (what authority)? Third, could this situation have been avoided? (*Rhet. Her.* 2.21)
Counter-charge *relatio criminis*; ἀντέγκλημα The action taken was due to the crime(s) of others.	ST = First, does law permit this? Second, is the counter-charge as serious as the charge against the defendant? Third, should the defendant have waited for a trial before pronouncing judgment? Fourth, should a judgment now be given? (*Rhet. Her.* 2.22)
Plea for leniency *concessio*, particularly *purgatio*; συγγνώμη The action was done by necessity and not with intent.	ST = First, is the defendant responsible for this necessity? Second, what means did he have to lighten its force or what did he do to lighten it? Third, did the defendant try to alleviate the force of necessity? Fourth, was there any premeditation? Fifth, if there was some extreme necessity, was it a sufficient excuse? (*Rhet. Her.* 2.23)

(cont.)

	Topics for the prosecution
Counter-plea *comparatio*; ἀντίστασις The action taken was the better of the options.	ST = *(a) Raise suspicion that the defendant did not intend to act for the better, but acted in fraud of some form (Rhet. Her.* 2.21); (b) Attack the act and show its harm; *(c) One act should not be sacrificed for another* (*Inv.* 2.74–75). CT = *(a) Defendant had no right to choose (Rhet. Her.* 2.22); *(b) Generally, inveigh against the defendant attacking intention* (*Inv.* 2.77).
Counter-charge *relatio criminis*; ἀντέγκλημα The action taken was due to the crime(s) of others.	ST = (a) Defend the one accused by the defense. *(b) Show the crime(s) to be less severe than that of the defendant. (c) Explain proper procedure to conduct a trial, etc., rather than to take justice into one's hands. (d)* Point out laws that the defendant could have appealed to rather than acting on his own authority. And a few others (*Inv.* 79–82) CT = (a) Violence or injustice should not prevail over judicial decisions. (b) What if others did this? (*Rhet. Her.* 2.22; *Inv.* 2.85)
Plea for leniency *concessio*, particularly *purgatio*; συγγνώμη The action was done out of necessity and not with intent.	ST = (a) Prove that the defendant had intent. (b) It should have been avoided. *(c) It is not due to necessity but rather to laziness, carelessness or folly. (d) It is better to endure any fate, even death, than to yield to necessity, especially if there is any suspicion of baseness. (e) Make reference to laws and past precedents similar to this warning against ignoring it* (*Inv.* 2.98–100). CT = (a) Defendant is only prolonging the trial by spewing forth words (*Rhet. Her.* 2.24). (b) Attack plea of confession and avoidance. (c) Question the defendant, taking the focus away from the act committed to its excuse (*Inv.* 2.101).
	Topics for the defense
Counter-plea *comparatio*; ἀντίστασις The action taken was the better of the options.	ST = *(a) Deny this and magnify the action taken as beneficial, etc.* CT = (a) It is not prudent to choose the ruinous over the beneficial. (b) Ask what the prosecutor would have done in the same situation. *(c) Depict the defendant's time, place, circumstances, and deliberations (Rhet. Her.* 2.22). *(d) Intent is what counts. (e) Furthermore, magnify the deed by reference to its advantage, honor, or necessity.* (f) Describe event to convince them that they would have done the same thing (*Inv.* 2.77).

	Topics for the defense
Counter-charge *relatio criminis*; ἀντέγκλημα The action taken was due to the crime(s) of others.	ST = (a) Answer prosecution's charges. *(b) To support the counter-charge the defendant should magnify the audacity of the crime, describing the scene of this crime vividly. (c) Also he should show that the punishment for this crime was too lenient.* (d) Lessen the legal questions of the prosecutor by various techniques, such as pointing out that the crime is universally disgusting (*Inv.* 2.83–85). CT = (a) The crimes were atrocious. *(b) Present and argue that the time, place, circumstances were such that to bring the crimes to trial would have been impossible or inexpedient (Rhet. Her. 2.22; Inv. 2.86). (c) Show that the defendant was well intended. (d) Show that the crime would have damaged the defendant's reputation, etc. had not action been taken (Inv. 2.86).*
Plea for leniency *concessio* particualry *purgatio*; συγγνώμη The action was done out of necessity and not with intent.	ST = *(a) Defend intentions. (b) Magnify "circumstances that thwarted his purpose; saying that it was impossible to do more than he did . . . and that under his name the weakness common to all men may be condemned."* (c) Say that one free of guilt should be free of punishment (*Inv.* 2.101). CT = (a) On the basis of humanity and pity, intention should always be considered and unintentional acts should not be regarded as crimes (*Rhet. Her.* 2.24). *(b) Magnify circumstances which thwarted his purposes; in other words, offer "a lament over his own tribulations and a denunciation of the cruelty of his opponents"* (*Inv.* 2.102).

REFERENCES

Achtemeier, Paul (1990) "*Omne Verbum Sonat*: The New Testament and the Oral Environment of Late Western Antiquity," *JBL* 109, pp. 3–27.

Adeleye, Gabriel (1983) "The Purpose of the *Dokimasia*," *GRBS* 24, pp. 295–306.

Aeschines. *The Speeches: Against Timarchus, On the Embassy, Against Ctesiphon*, trans. C. P. Adams, LCL, Cambridge, MA: Harvard University Press; London: William Heinemann (1919).

Alexander, Michael C. (1990) *Trials in the Late Roman Republic, 149 BC to 50 BC*, Phoenix Tome supplémentaire 26, Toronto: University of Toronto Press.

Alexandre, Manuel Jr. (1999) *Rhetorical Argumentation in Philo of Alexandria*, BJS 322; SPhiloMS 2, Atlanta: Scholars Press.

Anaximenes. *Rhetorica ad Alexandrum*, trans. H. Rackham, in *Aristotle Problems II*, LCL, Cambridge, MA: Harvard University Press; London: William Heinemann (1937).

Anderson, R. Dean Jr. (1996) *Ancient Rhetorical Theory and Paul*, CBET 18, Kampen: Kok Pharos, 1996.

(1999) *Ancient Rhetorical Theory and Paul*, CBET 18, rev. edn., Kampen: Kok Pharos.

Andocides. *Minor Attic Orators*, vol. 1, trans. K. J. Maidment, LCL, Cambridge, MA: Harvard University Press; London: William Heinemann (1941).

Andrews, Scott B. (1995) "The Form and Function of 2 Cor 11.23b–33," *NTS* 41, pp. 263–76.

Antiphon. *Minor Attic Orators*, vol. 1, trans. K. J. Maidment, LCL, Cambridge, MA: Harvard University Press; London: William Heinemann (1941).

Aristophanes. 3 vols., trans. B. B. Rogers, LCL, Cambridge, MA: Harvard University Press; London: William Heinemann (1924).

Aristotle. *The "Art" of Rhetoric*, trans. J. H. Freese, LCL, Cambridge, MA: Harvard University Press; London: William Heinemann (1926).

Aristotle. *Posterior Analytics*, trans. H. Tredennick, LCL, Cambridge, MA: Harvard University Press; London: William Heinemann (1926).

Aristotle. *Topica*, trans. E. S. Forster, LCL, Cambridge, MA: Harvard University Press; London: William Heinemann (1926).

Aune, David E. (1991) "Romans as a Logos Protreptikos in the Context of Ancient Religious and Philosophical Propaganda," in *Paulus und das antike Judentum*, WUNT 58, ed. M. Hengel, Tübingen: J. C. B. Mohr, pp. 91–124.

Bakhtin, M. M. (1986) *Speech Genres and Other Late Essays*, ed. Caryl Emerson and Michael Holquist, trans. V. W. McGee, University of Texas Press Slavic Series 8, Austin: University of Texas.

Barnett, Paul W. (1997) *Second Epistle to the Corinthians*, NICNT, Grand Rapids, MI: W. B. Eerdmans.

Barrett, Charles K. (1973) *The Second Epistle to the Corinthians*, HNTC, New York: Harper & Row, 1973.

Bates, W. H. (1965–69) "The Integrity of II Corinthians," *NTS* 12, pp. 56–69.

Belleville, Linda L. (1989) "A Letter of Apologetic Self-Commendation: 2 Cor. 1:8–7:16," *NovT* 31, pp. 142–63.

(1991) *Reflections of Glory: Paul's Polemical Use of the Moses-Doxa Tradition in 2 Corinthians 3:1–18*, JSNTSup 52, Sheffield: Sheffield Academic Press.

Betz, Hans Dieter (1972) *Der Apostel Paulus und die sokratische Tradition: Eine exegetische Untersuchung zu seiner Apologie 2 Kor 10–13*, BHTh 45, Tübingen: J. C. B. Mohr.

(1976) "In Defense of the Spirit: Paul's Letter to the Galatians as a Document of Early Christian Apologetics," in *Aspects of Religious Propaganda in Judaism and Early Christianity*, ed. E. Schüssler Fiorenza, Notre Dame: University of Notre Dame Press, pp. 99–114.

(1979) *Galatians: A Commentary on Paul's Letter to the Churches in Galatia*, Hermeneia, Philadelphia: Fortress Press.

(1985) *2 Corinthians 8 and 9: A Commentary on Two Administrative Letters of the Apostle Paul*, Hermeneia, Philadelphia: Fortress Press.

(1986) "The Problem of Rhetoric and Theology according to the Apostle Paul," in *L'Apôtre Paul. Personnalité, style et conception du ministère*, ed. A. Vanhoye *et al.*, BETL 73, Leuven: Louvain University Press.

Bieringer, Reimund (1994a) "Plädoyer für die Einheitlichkeit des 2. Korintherbriefes. Literarkritische und inhaltliche Argumente," in *Studies on 2 Corinthians*, ed. Reimund Bieringer and J. Lambrecht, BETL 112, Leuven: Louvain University Press, pp. 131–79.

(1994b) "Teilungshypothesen zum 2. Korintherbrief. Ein Forschungsüberblick," in *Studies on 2 Corinthians*, ed. Reimund Bieringer and J. Lambrecht, BETL 112, Leuven: Louvain University Press, pp. 67–105.

(ed.) (1996) *The Corinthian Correspondence*, BETL 125, Leuven: Louvain University Press.

Bitzer, Lloyd F. (1968) "The Rhetorical Situation," *PhilRhet* 1, pp. 1–14.

Black, C. Clifton II (1989) "Keeping up with Recent Studies: Rhetorical Criticism and Biblical Interpretation," *ExpTim* 100, pp. 252–58.

(1990) "Rhetorical Questions: The New Testament, Classical Rhetoric and Biblical Interpretation," *Dialog* 29, pp. 62–63, 68–71.

Blass, Friedrich (ed.) (1908) *Antiphontis Orationes et Fragmenta: Adiunctis Gorgiae Antisthenis Alcidamantis Declamationibus*, Leipzig: B. G. Teubner.

(ed.) (1962) *Die attische Beredsamkeit*, 3 vols. in 4 vols., 3rd edn., Hildesheim: G. Olms.

Bluck, R. S. (ed.) (1947) *Plato's Seventh and Eighth Letters*, Pitt Press Series, Cambridge: Cambridge University Press.

Bonner, Robert J. (1920) "The Legal Setting of Isocrates's *Antidosis*," *CP* 15, pp. 193–97.

Bonner, Robert J., and Gertrude Smith (1930–38) *The Administration of Justice from Homer to Aristotle*, 2 vols., Chicago: University of Chicago Press.

Bonner, Stanley F. (1969) *Roman Declamation in the Late Republic and Early Empire*, Liverpool: Liverpool University Press.

(1977) *Education in Ancient Rome: From the Elder Cato to the Younger Pliny*, Berkeley and Los Angeles: University of California Press.

Bornkamm, Günther (1965) "The History of the Origin of the So-called Second Letter to the Corinthians," in *The Authorship and Integrity of the New Testament: Some Recent Studies*, ed. K. Aland *et al.*, Theological Collections 4, London: SPCK, pp. 73–81.

Bowers, Paul (1980) "Paul and Religious Propaganda in the First Century," *NovT* 22, 4, pp. 316–23.

Braet, Antione (1987) "The Classical Doctrine of Status and the Rhetorical Theory of Argumentation," *PhilRhet* 20, pp. 79–93.

Brinsmead, Bernard (1982) *Galatians – Dialogical Response to Opponents*, SBLDS 65, Chico, CA: Scholars Press, 1982.

Brown, Francis, Samuel R. Driver, and Charles A. Briggs (1907) *A Hebrew and English Lexicon of the Old Testament*, Oxford: Oxford University Press.

Bruce, Frederick F. (1971) *1 and 2 Corinthians*, NCBC, London: Oliphants.

Bultmann, Rudolf (1985) *The Second Letter to the Corinthians*, trans. from *Der zweite Brief an die Korinther*, trans. R. A. Harrisville, Minneapolis: Augsburg Publishing House.

Butts, James R. (1986) "The 'Progymnasmata' of Theon: A New Text with Translation and Commentary," Ph. D. dissertation, Claremont Graduate School; Ann Arbor, MI: University Microfilms.

Cambell, Karlyn K., and Kathleen H. Jamieson (eds.) (1978) "Form and Genre in Rhetorical Criticism: An Introduction," in *Form and Genre: Shaping Rhetorical Action*, ed. Karlyn K. Cambell and Kathleen H. Jamieson, Falls Church, VA: Speech Communication Association, pp. 9–32.

Carey, Christopher (1994a) "'Artless' Proofs in Aristotle and the Orators," *Bulletin of the Institute of Classical Studies* 39, pp. 95–106.

(1994b) "Rhetorical Means of Persuasion," in *Persuasion: Greek Rhetoric in Action*, ed. I. Worthington, London and New York: Routledge, pp. 26–45.

(1997) *Trials from Classical Athens*, London and New York: Routledge.

Carrino, Elnora M. D. (1959) "Conceptions of *Dispositio* in Ancient Rhetoric," Ph.D. dissertation, University of Michigan, 1959; Ann Arbor, MI: University Microfilms.

Church, David A., and Robert S. Cathcart (1965) "Some Concepts of the Epicheireme in Greek and Roman Rhetoric," *Western Speech* 29, pp. 140–47.

Church, F. Forrester (1978) "Rhetorical Structure and Design in Paul's Letter to Philemon," *HTR* 71, pp. 17–33.

Cicero. *Cicero in Twenty-eight Volumes*, trans. G. L. Hendrickson, H. M. Hubbell, *et al.*, LCL, Cambridge, MA: Harvard University Press; London: William Heinemann (1912–72).

[Cicero.] *Ad C. Herennium De Ratione Dicendi (Rhetorica ad Herennium)*, trans. H. Caplan, LCL, Cambridge, MA: Harvard University Press; London: William Heinemann (1954).

Clark, Donald A. (1957) *Rhetoric in Greco-Roman Education*, Morningside Heights, NY: Columbia University Press.

Clarke, Martin L. (1968) *Rhetoric at Rome: A Historical Survey*, corrected 1st edn., London: Cohen & West, 1968.

Classen, C. Joachim (1992) "St. Paul's Epistles and Ancient Greek and Roman Rhetoric," *Rhetorica* 10, pp. 319–44.

Cole, Thomas (1991) *The Origins of Rhetoric in Ancient Greece*, ASH, Baltimore: Johns Hopkins University Press.

Collins, Raymond F. (1996) "Reflections on 1 Corinthians as a Hellenistic Letter," in Bieringer, 1996, pp. 39–61.

Conley, Thomas M. (1979) "Ancient Rhetoric and Modern Genre Criticism," *CommQ* 27, pp. 47–53.

(1984) "The Enthymeme in Perspective," *QJS* 70, pp. 168–87.

Cope, Edward M. (1867) *An Introduction to Aristotle's Rhetoric*, London: Macmillan.

Costa, C. D. N. (2001) *Greek Fictional Letters: A Selection with Introduction, Translation, and Commentary*, Oxford and New York: Oxford University Press.

Crawford, Jane W. (1994) *M. Tullius Cicero, the Fragmentary Speeches: An Edition with Commentary*, ACS 37, 2nd edn., Atlanta: Scholars.

Crook, John A. (1995) *Legal Advocacy in the Roman World*, London: Duckworth.

Dahl, Nils A. (1977) "Paul and the Church at Corinth According to 1 Corinthians 1:10–4:21," in *Studies in Paul: Theology for the Early Christian Mission*, Minneapolis: Augsburg Publishing House, pp. 40–61.

Danker, Frederick W. (1989) *II Corinthians*, ACNT, Minneapolis: Augsburg Publishing House.

(1991) "Paul's Debt to the 'De Corona' of Demosthenes: A Study of Rhetorical Techniques in Second Corinthians," in Watson, 1991, pp. 262–80.

Demades. *Minor Attic Orators*, vol. 2, trans. J. O. Burtt, LCL, Cambridge, MA: Harvard University Press; London: William Heinemann (1954).

Demetrius. *On Style*, trans. W. R. Roberts, LCL, in *Aristotle* vol. 23, *The Poetics*, Cambridge, MA: Harvard University Press; London: William Heinemann (1927).

Demosthenes. *Demosthenes*, 7 vols., trans. L. H. Vince, C. A. Vince, *et al.*, LCL, Cambridge, MA: Harvard University Press; London: William Heinemann (1930–49).

Derrett, J. Duncan M. (1991) "Judgment and 1 Corinthians 6," *NTS* 37, pp. 22–36.

DeSilva, David A. (1996) "Meeting the Exigency of a Complex Rhetorical Situation: Paul's Strategy in 2 Corinthians 1 Through 7," *AUSS* 34, pp. 5–22.

DiCicco, Mario M. (1995) *Paul's Use of Ethos, Pathos, and Logos in 2 Corinthians 10–13*, MBPS 31, Lewiston, NY: Mellen Biblical Press, 1995.

Dieter, Otto Alvin Loeb (1950) "Stasis," *Speech Monographs* 17, pp. 345–69.

Dilts, Mervin R., and George A. Kennedy (eds.) (1997) *Two Greek Rhetorical Treatises from the Roman Empire: Introduction, Text, and Translation of the Arts of Rhetoric attributed to Anonymous Seguerianus and to Apsines of Gadara*, MBCBSup 168, Leiden: E. J. Brill.

Dinarchus. *Minor Attic Orators*, vol. 2, trans. J. O. Burtt, LCL, Cambridge, MA: Harvard University Press; London: William Heinemann (1954).

Dio Chrysostom. *Dio Chrysostom*, 5 vols., trans. J. W. Cohoon and H. L. Crosby, LCL, Cambridge, MA: Harvard University Press; London: William Heinemann (1932–51).

Dionysius of Halicarnassus. *Critical Essays*, 2 vols., trans. S. Usher, LCL, Cambridge, MA: Harvard University Press; London: William Heinemann (1974–1985).

Dionysius of Halicarnassus. *Roman Antiquities*, 7 vols., trans. E. Cary, LCL, Cambridge: Harvard University Press; London: William Heinemann (1937–1950).

Douglas, Alan E. (1956) "Cicero, Quintilian, and the Canon of the Ten Attic Orators," *MBCB* 9, pp. 30–40.

Duff, Paul Brooks (1993) "The Mind of the Redactor: 2 Cor. 6:14–7:1 in its Secondary Context," *NovT* 35, pp. 160–80.

Edwards, Michael (1995) *Andocides*, Greek Orators 4, Warminster, England: Aris & Phillips.

Edwards, Michael and Stephen Usher (1985) *Antiphon and Lysias*, Greek Orators 1, Chicago: Bolchazy Carducci.

Enderlein, Steven E. (1998) "The Gospel is not Shameful: The Argumentative Structure of Romans in the Light of Classical Rhetoric," Ph.D. dissertation, Marquette University; Ann Arbor, MI: University Microfilms.

Enos, Richard L. (1972) "When Rhetoric was Outlawed in Rome: A Translation and Commentary of Suetonius's Treatise on Early Roman Rhetoricians," *Speech Monographs* 39, pp. 37–45.

(1975) "Cicero's Forensic Oratory: The Manifestation of Power in the Roman Republic," *SSCJ* 40, pp. 377–94.

(1977) "The Effects of Imperial Patronage on the Rhetorical Tradition of the Athenian Second Sophistic," *CommQ* 25, pp. 3–10.

(1980) "How Rhetoric Survived the Decline and Fall of the Roman Empire: A Synoptic View," *WPRC* 2, pp. 1–33.

(1984) "Heuristic Structures of *Dispositio* in Oral and Written Rhetorical Composition: An Addendum to Ochs' Analysis of the Verrine Orations," *CSSJ* 35, pp. 77–83.

(1985) "Ciceronian *Dispositio* as an Architecture for Creativity in Composition: A Note for the Affirmative," *Rhetoric Review* 4, pp. 108–10.

(1993) *Greek Rhetoric before Aristotle*, Prospect Heights, IL: Waveland.

Eriksson, Anders (1998) *Traditions as Rhetorical Proof: Pauline Argumentation in 1 Corinthians*, CB NTS 29, Stockholm: Almqvist & Wiksell International.

(1999a) "Elaboration of Argument in 1 Cor 15:20–34," *SEÅ* 64, pp. 101–14.

(1999b) "Special Topics in 1 Corinthians 8–10," in Porter and Olbricht, 1999, pp. 272–301.

Eriksson, Anders, Thomas H. Olbricht, and Walter Übelacker (eds.) (2002) *Rhetorical Argumentation in Biblical Texts: Essays from the Lund 2000 Conference*, ESEC, Harrisburg, PA: Trinity International.

Fairweather, Janet (1994) "The Epistle to the Galatians and Classical Rhetoric," *TynBul* 45, pp. 1–38, 213–43.

Fee, Gordon D. (1976–77) "II Corinthians vi.14–vii.1 and Food Offered to Idols," *NTS* 23, pp. 140–61.

Fiore, Benjamin (1986) *The Function of Personal Example in the Socratic and Pastoral Epistles*, AnBib 105, Rome: Biblical Institute, 1986.

Fiorenza, Elisabeth Schüssler (1987) "Rhetorical Situation and Historical Reconstruction in 1 Corinthians," *NTS* 33, pp. 386–403.

Fitzgerald, John T. (1988) *Cracks in an Earthen Vessel: An Examination of the Catalogues of Hardships in the Corinthian Correspondence*, SBLDS 99, Atlanta: Scholars Press.

Forbes, Christopher (1986) "Comparison, Self-Praise and Irony: Paul's Boasting and the Conventions of Hellenistic Rhetoric," *NTS* 32, pp. 1–30.

Freeman, Kathleen (1946) *The Pre-Socratic Philosophers: A Companion to Diels, Fragmente der Vorsokratiker*, Oxford: Basil Blackwell.

Freese, John Henry (1926) "Introduction," *Aristotle: The "Art" of Rhetoric*, trans. J. H. Freese, LCL, Cambridge, MA; London: William Heinemann.

Furnish, Victor P. (1984) *II Corinthians*, AB 32A, Garden City, NY: Doubleday.

Gagarin, Michael (ed.) (1994) "Probability and Persuasion: Plato and Early Greek Rhetoric," in *Persuasion: Greek Rhetoric in Action*, ed. I. Worthington, London: Routledge, pp. 46–68.

(1997) *Antiphon: The Speeches*, CGLC, Cambridge: Cambridge University Press.

Gagarin, Michael, and Douglas M. MacDowell (1998) *Antiphon and Andocides*, OCG 1, Austin: University of Texas Press.

Gaines, Robert N. (1985) "Philodemus on the Three Activities of Rhetorical Invention," *Rhetorica* 3, pp. 155–63.

Given, Mark D. (2001) *Paul's True Rhetoric: Ambiguity, Cunning, and Deception in Greece and Rome*, ESEC, Harrisburg, PA: Trinity Press International.

Glad, Clarence E. (1995) *Paul and Philodemus: Adaptability in Epicurean and Early Christian Psychagogy*, NovTSup 81, Leiden: E. J. Brill.

Goebel, George H. (1983) "Early Greek Rhetorical Theory and Practice: Proof and Arrangement in the Speeches of Antiphon and Euripides," Ph.D. dissertation, University of Wisconsin; Ann Arbor, MI: University Microfilms.

Goldstein, Jonathan A. (1968) *The Letters of Demosthenes*, New York and London: Columbia University Press.

Hafemann, Scott (1990) "Self-Commendation and Apostolic Legitimacy in 2 Corinthians," *NTS* 36, pp. 66–88.

Hall, Robert G. (1997) "Ancient Historical Method and the Training of an Orator," in Porter and Olbricht, 1997, pp. 103–18.

Hamberger, Peter (1914) *Die rednerische Disposition in den alten Techne Rhetorike (Corax, Gorgias, Antiphon)*, Rhetorische Studien 2, Paderborn: F. Schöningh.

Hansen, G. Walter (1989) *Abraham in Galatians: Epistolary and Rhetorical Contexts*, JSNTSup 29, Sheffield: Sheffield Academic Press.

Harris, Edward M. (1994) "Law and Oratory," in *Persuasion: Greek Rhetoric in Action*, ed. I. Worthington, London: Routledge, pp. 130–50.

Harris, Gerald (1991) "The Beginning of Church Discipline: 1 Corinthians 5," *NTS* 37, pp. 1–21.

Harrison, A. R. W. (1968–71) *The Law of Athens*, 2 vols., Oxford: Oxford University Press.

Heath, Malcolm (1994) "The Substructure of *Stasis*-Theory from Hermagoras to Hermogenes," *CQ* 44, pp. 114–29.

(1995) *Hermogenes on Issues: Strategies of Argument in Later Greek Rhetoric*, Oxford: Clarendon Press.

(1997) "Invention," in Porter, 1997c, pp. 89–119.

Hellholm, David (1994) "Enthymemic Argumentation in Paul: The Case of Romans 6," in *Paul in his Hellenistic Context*, ed. T. Engberg-Pedersen, Edinburgh: T. & T. Clark, pp. 119–79.

Hester (Amador), J. D. (2000) "Revisiting 2 Corinthians: Rhetoric and the Case for Unity," *NTS* 46, pp. 92–111.
  (2002) "Re-Reading 2 Corinthians: A Rhetorical Approach," in Eriksson *et al.*, 2002, pp. 276–95.

Hinks, D. A. G. (1940) "Tisias and Corax and the Invention of Rhetoric," *CQ* 34, pp. 61–69.

Hock, Ronald F. (1978) "Paul's Tentmaking and the Problem of his Social Class," *JBL* 97, pp. 555–64.
  (1980) *The Social Context of Paul's Ministry: Tentmaking and Apostleship*, Philadelphia: Fortress Press.

Holtsmark, Erling B. (1968) "Quintilian on Status: A Progymnasma," *Hermes* 96, pp. 356–68.

Hughes, Frank W. (1989) *Early Christian Rhetoric and 2 Thessalonians*, JSNTSup 30, Sheffield: JSOT Press.
  (1990) "The Rhetoric of 1 Thessalonians," pp. 94–116 in *The Thessalonian Correspondence*, ed. R. F. Collins, BETL 87, Leuven: Leuven University Press.
  (1991) "The Rhetoric of Reconciliation: 2 Corinthians 1.1–2.13 and 7.5–8.24," in Watson, 1991, pp. 246–61.

Hunter, Virginia (1990) "Gossip and the Politics of Reputation in Classical Athens," *Phoenix* 44, pp. 299–325.

Huseman, Richard C. (1965 [1994]) "Aristotle's System of Topics," *Southern Speech Journal* 30 (1965), pp. 243–52; repr. (1994) *Landmark Essays on Classical Greek Rhetoric*, ed. E. Schiappa, Davis, CA: Hermagoras, pp. 191–99.

Hyldahl, Niels (1973) "Die Frage nach der literarischen Einheit des Zweiten Korintherbrief," *ZNW* 64, pp. 289–306.

Hyperides. *Minor Attic Orators*, vol. 2, trans. J. O. Burtt, LCL, Cambridge, MA: Harvard University Press; London: William Heinemann (1954).

Innes, Doreen and Michael Winterbottom (1988) *Sopatros the Rhetor: Studies in the Text of the Διαίρεσις Ζητημάτων*, Bulletin Supplement 48, London: Institute of Classical Studies.

Isaeus. trans. E. D. Forster, LCL, Cambridge, MA: Harvard University Press; London: William Heinemann (1957).

Isocrates. 3 vols., trans. G. Norlin and L. Van Hook, LCL, Cambridge, MA: Harvard University Press; London: William Heinemann (1928–45).

Jennrich, Walter A. (1948). "Classical Rhetoric in the New Testament," *CJ* 44, pp. 30–32.

Jewett, Robert (1986) *The Thessalonian Correspondence: Pauline Rhetoric and Millenarian Piety*, FF, Philadelphia: Fortress Press.

Jolivet, Ira J. (1999) "The Lukan Account of Paul's Conversion and Hermagorean Stasis Theory," in Porter and Olbricht, 1999, pp. 210–20.

Josephus. 9 vols., trans. S. St. J. Thackeray, R. Marcus, and L. H. Feldman, LCL, Cambridge, MA: Harvard University Press; London: William Heinemann (1956–65).

Judge, Edwin A. (1960) "The Early Christians as a Scholastic Community: Part II," *JRH* 1, pp. 125–37.

(1966) "The Conflict of Educational Aims in New Testament Thought," *JCE* 9, pp. 32–45.

(1968) "Paul's Boasting in Relation to Contemporary Professional Practice," *AusBR* 16, pp. 37–50.

(1980) "The Social Identity of the First Christians: A Question of Method in Religious History," *JRH* 11, pp. 201–17.

(1984) "Cultural Conformity and Innovation in Paul: Some Clues from Contemporary Documents," *TynBul* 35, pp. 3–24.

Kennedy, George A. (1959) "The Earliest Rhetorical Handbooks" *AJP* 80, pp. 169–78.

(1963) *The Art of Persuasion in Greece*, Princeton: Princeton University Press.

(1968) "The Rhetoric of Advocacy in Greece and Rome," *AJP* 89, pp. 419–36.

(1972) *The Art of Rhetoric in the Roman World*, Princeton: Princeton University Press.

(1980) *Classical Rhetoric and its Christian and Secular Tradition from Ancient to Modern Times*, Chapel Hill: University of North Carolina Press.

(1983) *Greek Rhetoric under Christian Emperors*, Princeton: Princeton University Press.

(1984) *New Testament Interpretation through Rhetorical Criticism*, Chapel Hill: University of North Carolina Press.

(ed.) (1989) *The Cambridge History of Literary Criticism. Vol. 1. Classical Criticism*, Cambridge: Cambridge University Press.

(1994) *A New History of Classical Rhetoric*, Princeton: Princeton University Press.

(1997) "The Genres of Rhetoric," in Porter, 1997c, pp. 43–50.

(2003) *Progymnasmata: Greek Textbooks of Prose Composition and Rhetoric*, WGRW, Atlanta: SBL.

Kern, Philip H. (1998) *Rhetoric and Galatians: Assessing an Approach to Paul's Epistles*, SNTSMS 101, Cambridge: Cambridge University Press.

Kinneavy, James L. (1987) *Greek Rhetorical Origins of Christian Faith: An Inquiry*, Oxford: Oxford University Press.

Kirby, John T. (1990) *The Rhetoric of Cicero's Pro Cluentio*, LSCP 23, Amsterdam: J. C. Gieben.

Kraus, Manfred (2002) "Theories and Practice of the Enthymeme in the First Centuries B.C.E and C.E.," in Eriksson *et al.*, 2002, pp. 95–111.

Kroll, Wilhelm (1936) *Das Epicheirema*, Akademie der Wissenschaften in Wien Philosophisch-Historische Klasse, 216, 2, Vienna: Hölder-Pichler-Tempsky.

Kümmel, Werner G. (1975) *Introduction to the New Testament*, rev. edn., Nashville: Abingdon.

Kurz, William S. (1980) "Hellenistic Rhetoric in the Christological Proof of Luke–Acts," *CBQ* 42, pp. 171–95.

(1996) "2 Corinthians: Implied Readers and Canonical Implications," *JSNT* 62, pp. 43–63.

Lambrecht, Jan (1989) "Rhetorical Criticism and the New Testament," *Bijdr* 50, pp. 239–53.

Lane, William L. (1982) "Covenant: The Key to Paul's Conflict with Corinth," *TynBul* 33, pp. 3–29.

Lausberg, Heinrich (1998) *Handbook of Literary Rhetoric*, 2nd edn., Leiden: E. J. Brill.

Lavency, M. (1964) *Aspects de la logographie judiciaire attique*, Recueil de Travaux d'Histoire et de Philologie 32, Louvain: Publications Universitaires de Louvain.

Leff, Michael C. (1983) "The Topics of Argumentative Invention in Latin Rhetorical Theory from Cicero to Boethius," *Rhetorica* 1, pp. 23–44.

Liddell, H. G., and R. Scott. *A Greek–English Lexicon: A New Edition Revised and Augmented throughout*, ed. H. S. Jones and R. McKenzie, 9th edn., Oxford: Clarendon Press (1940).

Litfin, Duane (1994) *St. Paul's Theology of Proclamation: 1 Corinthians 1–4 and Greco-Roman Rhetoric*, SNTSMS 79, Cambridge: Cambridge University Press.

Little, Charles E. (ed.) (1951) *The Institutio Oratoria of Marcus Fabius Quintilianus*, 2 vols., Nashville: George Peabody College.

Livy. 14 vols., trans. B. O. Foster, F. G. Moore, *et al.*, LCL, Cambridge, MA: Harvard University Press; London: William Heinemann (1919–59).

Lloyd, Michael (1992) *The Agon in Euripides*, Oxford and New York: Clarendon Press.

Long, Fredrick J. (1999) "'Have we been defending ourselves to you?' (2 Cor 12:19): Forensic Rhetoric and the Rhetorical Unity of 2 Corinthians," Ph.D. Dissertation, Marquette University, Milwaukee, WI; Ann Arbor, MI: University Microfilms.

(2002) "From Epicheiremes to Exhortation: A Pauline Method for Moral Persuasion in Hellenistic Socio-Rhetorical Context," presented at the conference "Rhetorics, Ethics and Moral Persuasion in Biblical Discourse" at the Moore Haus of Pepperdine University in Heidelberg, Germany, July 22–25, 2002 and found in *Queen: A Journal of Rhetoric and Power: Special Volume 2: Rhetorics, Ethics & Moral Persuasion http://www.arsrhetorica.net/Queen/VolumeSpecialIssue2/Articles/Long.html.*

(2003) "'We Destroy Arguments . . .' (2 Corinthians 10:5): The Apostle Paul's Use of Epicheirematic Argumentation," *Proceedings of the Fifth Meeting of the International Society for the Study of Argumentation*, pp. 697–703.

Longenecker, Richard (1990) *Galatians*, WBC 41, Dallas: Word Books.

Loubser, J. A. (1995) "Orality and Literacy in the Pauline Epistles: Some New Hermeneutical Implications," *Neot* 29, pp. 61–74.

Lycurgus. *Minor Attic Orators*, vol. 2, trans. J. O. Burtt, LCL, Cambridge, MA: Harvard University Press; London: William Heinemann (1954).

Lysias. trans. W. R. M. Lamb, LCL, Cambridge, MA: Harvard University Press; London: William Heinemann (1930).

McAdon, Brad (2001) "Rhetoric as a Counterpart of Dialectic (Ἡ ῥητορική ἐστιν ἀντίστροφος τῇ διαλεκτικῇ)," *PhilRhet* 34, pp. 113–50.

McBurney, James H. (1936 [1994]) "The Place of the Enthymeme in Rhetorical Theory," *Speech Monographs* 3, pp. 49–74; repr. (1994) *Landmark Essays on Classical Greek Rhetoric*, ed. E. Schiappa, Davis, CA: Hermagoras, pp. 169–90.

McCant, Jerry W. (1999) *2 Corinthians*, Readings: A New Biblical Commentary, Sheffield: Sheffield Academic Press.

MacDowell, Douglas M. (1978) *The Law in Classical Athens*, AGRL, Ithaca, NY: Cornell University Press.

(1982) *Encomium of Helen / Gorgias*, Bristol: Bristol Classical.

Mack, Burton L. (1990) *Rhetoric and the New Testament*, GBS, Minneapolis: Fortress Press.

Malherbe, Abraham J. (1983) "Antisthenes and Odysseus, and Paul at War," *HTR* 76, pp. 143–73.

(1988) *Ancient Epistolary Theorists*, SBLSBS 19, Atlanta: Scholars Press.

(1989) *Paul and the Popular Philosophers*, Minneapolis: Fortress Press.

Marshall, Peter (1987) *Enmity in Corinth: Social Conventions in Paul's Relations with the Corinthians*, WUNT 2, 23, Tübingen: J. C. B. Mohr.

Martin, Dale B. (1995) *The Corinthian Body*, New Haven: Yale University Press.

Martin, Josef (1974) *Antike Rhetorik: Technik und Methode*, HAW 2, 3, Munich: Beck.

Martin, Ralph P. (1986) *2 Corinthians*, WBC 40, Waco, TX: Word.

Martin, Troy (1995) "Apostasy to Paganism: The Rhetorical Stasis of the Galatians Controversy," *JBL* 114, pp. 437–61.

May, James M. (1988) *Trials of Character: The Eloquence of Ciceronian Ethos*, Chapel Hill: University of North Caroline Press.

Mitchell, Alan C. (1986) "1 Corinthians 6:1–11: Group Boundaries and the Courts of Corinth," Ph.D. dissertation, Yale University; Ann Arbor, MI: University Microfilms.

Mitchell, Margaret M. (1991) *Paul and the Rhetoric of Reconciliation: An Exegetical Investigation of the Language and Composition of 1 Corinthians*, HUNT 28, Tübingen: J. C. B. Mohr.

Moores, John D. (1995) *Wrestling with Rationality in Paul: Romans 1–8 in a New Perspective*, SNTSMS 82, Cambridge: Cambridge University Press.

Morrow, Glenn R. (1962) *Plato's Epistles*, New York: Harper & Row.

Murphy, Charles T. (1938) "Aristophanes and the Art of Rhetoric," *HSCP* 49, pp. 69–113.

Nadeau, Ray (1959) "Classical Systems of Stases in Greek: Hermagoras to Hermogenes," *GRBS* 2, pp. 52–71.

(1964) "Hermogenes' *On Stases*: A Translation with an Introduction and Notes," *Speech Monographs* 31, pp. 361–424.

Natali, Carlo (1989) "Paradeigma: The Problems of Human Acting and the Use of Examples in Some Greek Authors of the 4th Century B.C.," *RSQ* 19, pp. 141–52.

Nestle, E., and K. Aland (1979) *Novum Testamentum Graece*, 26th edn., Stuttgart: Deutsche Bibelstiftung.

Neumeister, Christoff (1964) *Grundsätze der forensischen Rhetorik, gezeigt an Gerichtsreden Ciceros*, Langue et Parole 3, Munich: M. Hueber.

Ober, Josiah (1989) *Mass and Elite in Democratic Athens: Rhetoric, Ideology, and the Power of the People*, Princeton: Princeton University Press.

Ochs, Donovan J. (1969) "Aristotle's Concept of Formal Topics," *Speech Monographs* 36, pp. 419–25.

(1989) "Cicero and Philosophic *Inventio*," *RSQ* 19, pp. 217–27.

Olson, Stanley N. (1976) "Confidence Expressions in Paul: Epistolary Conventions and the Purpose of 2 Corinthians," Ph.D. dissertation, Yale University; Ann Arbor, MI: University Microfilms.

O'Mahony, Kieran J. (2000) *Pauline Persuasion: A Sounding in 2 Corinthians 8–9*. JSNTSup 199. Sheffield: Sheffield Academic Press.

Palmer, Georgiana P. (1934) "The τόποι of Aristotle's Rhetoric as exemplified in the Orators," Ph.D. dissertation, University of Chicago; Ann Arbor, MI: University Microfilms.

Parks, E. Patrick (1945) *The Roman Rhetorical Schools as a Preparation for the Courts under the Early Empire*, JHUSHPS 63, 2, Baltimore: Johns Hopkins Press.

Perelman, Chaïm, and Lucie Olbrechts-Tyteca (1969) *The New Rhetoric: A Treatise on Argumentation*, trans. J. Wilkinson and P. Wever, Notre Dame and London: University of Notre Dame Press.

Peterson, Brian K. (1998) *Eloquence and the Proclamation of the Gospel in Corinth*, SBLDS 163, Atlanta: Scholars Press.

Plank, Karl A. (1987) *Paul and the Irony of Affliction*, SemeiaSt, Atlanta: Scholars Press.

Plato. 12 vols., trans. H. N. Fowler, W. R. M. Lamb, *et al.*, LCL, Cambridge, MA: Harvard University Press; London: William Heinemann (1914–35).

Plato. *Epistulae*, ed. J. Moore-Blunt. BSGRT. Leipzig: B. G. Teubner (1985).

Pliny. *Letters, and Panegyricus*, 2 vols., trans. B. Radice, LCL, Cambridge, MA: Harvard University Press; London: William Heinemann (1969).

Plutarch's Moralia. 15 vols., trans. F. C. Babbitt, W. Helmbold, *et al.*, LCL, Cambridge, MA: Harvard University Press; London: William Heinemann (1927–69).

Pogoloff, Stephen M. (1992) *Logos and Sophia: The Rhetorical Situation of I Corinthians*, SBLDS 134, Atlanta: Scholars Press.

Porter, Stanley E. (1997a) "Ancient Rhetorical Analysis and Discourse Analysis of the Pauline Corpus," in Porter and Olbricht, 1997, pp. 249–74.

  (1997b) "Paul of Tarsus and his Letters," in Porter, 1997c, pp. 533–85.

  (ed.) (1997c) *Handbook of Classical Rhetoric in the Hellenistic Period: 330 B.C.–A.D. 400*. Leiden; New York: E. J. Brill.

  (1999) "Paul as Epistolographer *and* Rhetorician?," in Porter and Olbricht, 1999, pp. 222–48.

Porter, Stanley E., and Thomas H. Olbricht (eds.) (1993) *Rhetoric and the New Testament: Essays from the 1992 Heidelberg Conference*, JSNTSup 90, Sheffield: JSOT Press.

  (eds.) (1997) *The Rhetorical Analysis of Scripture: Essays from the 1995 London Conference*, JSNTSup 146, Sheffield: Sheffield Academic Press.

  (eds.) (1999) *The Rhetorical Interpretation of Scripture: Essays form the 1996 Malibu Conference*, JSNTSup 180, Sheffield: Sheffield Academic Press.

Poulakos, Takis (1988) "Towards a Cultural Understanding of Classical Epideictic Oratory," *Pre/Text* 9.3–4, pp. 147–66.

  (1989) "Epideictic Rhetoric as Social Hegemony: Isocrates' *Helen*," in *Rhetoric and Ideology: Compositions and Criticisms of Power*, ed. Charles W. Kneupper, Arlington, TX: Rhetoric Society of America.

  (1990) "Interpreting Sophistic Rhetoric: A Response to Schiappa," *PhilRhet* 23, pp. 218–28.

Quintilian. *The Instituto Oratoria of Quintilian*, 4 vols., trans. H. E. Butler, LCL, New York: G. P. Putnam's Sons; London: William Heinemann (1921–22).

Rabe, H. (ed.) (1931) *Prolegomenon Sylloge*, Bibliotheca Scriptorum Graecorum et Romanorum Teubneriana, Rhetores Graeci 14, Leipzig: Teubner.

Rahlfs, A. *Septuaginta*, 8th edn., Stuttgart: Deutsche Bibelgesellschaft, repr. (1979).

Reed, Jeffrey T. (1993) "Using Ancient Rhetorical Categories to Interpret Paul's Letters: A Question of Genre," in Porter and Olbricht, 1993, pp. 292–324.

Robbins, Vernon K. (1996a) *Exploring the Texture of Texts: A Guide to Socio-Rhetorical Interpretation*, Valley Forge, PA: Trinity Press International.

Robbins, Vernon K. (1996b) *The Tapestry of Early Christian Discourse: Rhetoric, Society, Ideology*. New York: Routledge.

Rowe, Galen O. (1997) "Style," in Porter, 1997c, pp. 121–57.

Russell, Donald A. (1983) *Greek Declamation*, Cambridge: Cambridge University Press.

Ryan, Eugene E. (1984) *Aristotle's Theory of Rhetorical Argumentation*, Collection Noêsis, Montreal: Bellarmin.

Sallust. trans. J. C. Rolfe, LCL, Cambridge, MA: Harvard University Press; London: William Heinemann (1921).

Satterthwaite, Philip E. (1993) "Acts against the Background of Classical Rhetoric," in *The Book of Acts in its Ancient Literary Setting*, ed. B. W. Winter and A. D. Clarke, vol. 1, *The Book of Acts in its First Century Setting*, Grand Rapids, MI: W. B. Eerdmans, pp. 337–79.

Savage, Timothy B. (1996) *Power through Weakness: Paul's Understanding of the Christian Ministry in 2 Corinthians*, SNTSMS 86, Cambridge: Cambridge University Press.

Schiappa, Edward (1991) *Protagoras and Logos: A Study in Greek Philosophy and Rhetoric*, Studies in Rhetoric/Communication, Columbia: University of South Carolina Press.

(1999) *The Beginning of Rhetorical Theory in Classical Greece*, London: Yale University Press.

Schmithals, Walter (1973) "Die Korintherbriefe als Briefsammlung," *ZNW* 64, pp. 263–88.

Scott, James M. (1994) "The Use of Scripture in 2 Corinthians 6.16c–18 and Paul's Restoration Theology," *JSNT* 56, pp. 73–99.

Sealey, Raphael (1984) "The *Tetralogies* Ascribed to Antiphon," *TAPA* 114, pp. 71–85.

Semler, Johann S. (1776) *Paraphrasis II: Epistolae ad Corinthos*. Halle: Hemmerde.

Settle, James N. (1962) "The Publication of Cicero's Orations," Ph. D. dissertation, University of North Carolina; Ann Arbor, MI: University Microfilms.

Sinclair, Patrick (1993) "The *Sententia* in *Rhetorica ad Herennium*: A Study in the Sociology of Rhetoric," *AJP* 114, pp. 561–80.

Smeltzer, Mark A. (1996) "Gorgias on Arrangement: A Search for Pragmatism amidst the Art and Epistemology of Gorgias of Leontini," *SCJ* 61, pp. 156–65.

(1997) "Practice and Theory in Gorgianic Speech-Making: A Response to Major and Schiappa," *SCJ* 62, pp. 247–52.

Smit, Joop F. M. (1993) "Argument and Genre of 1 Cor 12–14," in Porter and Olbricht, 1993, pp. 211–30.

(1996) "1 Cor 8,1–8: A Rhetorical *Partitio*: A Contribution to the Coherence of 1 Cor 8,1–11,1," in Bieringer, 1996, pp. 577–91.

Smith, Bromily (1921) "Corax and Probability," *QJSE* 7, pp. 13–42.

Smith, Robert M. (1995) "A New Look at the Canon of the Ten Attic Orators," *Mnemosyne* 48, pp. 66–79.

Smith, Robert W. (1974) *The Art of Rhetoric in Alexandria: Its Theory and Practice in the Ancient World*, The Hague, Netherlands: Nijhoff.

Solmsen, Friedrich (1941) "The Aristotelian Tradition in Ancient Rhetoric," *AJP* 62, pp. 35–50, 169–90.

Soubie, André (1973, 1974) "Les Prévues dans les plaidoyers des orateurs attiques," *Revue internationale des droits de l'antiquité* 20 (1973), pp. 171–253 and 21 (1974), pp. 77–134.

Spencer, Aida Besançon (1998) *Paul's Literary Style: A Stylistic and Historical Comparison of 2 Corinthians 11:16–12:13, Romans 8:9–39, and Philippians 3:2–4:13*, Lanham, MD: University Press of America.

Sprague, Rosamond Kent (ed.) (1972) *The Older Sophists*, Columbia, SA: University of South Carolina Press.

Stamps, Dennis L. (1992) "Rhetorical Criticism and the Rhetoric of New Testament Criticism," *JLT* 6 (1992), pp. 268–79.

(1993) "Rethinking the Rhetorical Situation: The Entextualization of the Situation in New Testament Epistles," in Porter and Olbricht, 1993, pp. 193–210.

(1995) "Rhetorical Criticism of the New Testament," in *Approaches to New Testament Study*, ed. Stanley E. Porter and D. Tombs, JSNTSup 120, Sheffield: JSOT Press (1995), pp. 129–69.

(1999) "The Theological Rhetoric of the Pauline Epistles: Prolegomenon," in Porter and Olbricht, 1999, pp. 249–59.

Stephenson, Alan M. G. (1965) "A Defence of the Integrity of 2 Corinthians," in *The Authorship and Integrity of the New Testament*, Theological Collections 4, London: SPCK, pp. 82–97.

Stirewalt, M. Luther (1993) *Studies in Ancient Greek Epistolography*, SBLRBS 27, Atlanta: Scholars Press.

Stockhausen, Carol K. (1989) *Moses' Veil and the Glory of the New Covenant: The Exegetical Substructure of II Cor. 3,1–4,6*, AnBib 116, Roma: Pontificio Instituto Biblico.

Stowers, Stanley K. (1984) "Social Status, Public Speaking and Private Teaching: The Circumstances of Paul's Preaching Activity," *NovT* 26, pp. 59–82.

(1986) *Letter Writing in Greco-Roman Antiquity*, LEC 5, Philadelphia: Westminster.

Stroh, Wilfried (1975) *Taxis und Taktik: Die advokatische Dispositionskunst in Ciceros Gerichtsreden*, Stuttgart: B. G. Teubner.

Sumney, Jerry L. (1990) *Identifying Paul's Opponents: The Question of Method in 2 Corinthians*, JSNTSup 40, Sheffield: JSOT Press.

Sykutris, J. (1931) "Epistolographie," in PW 5, Stuttgart: Metzler, cols. 185–220.

Tacitus. *The Histories*, 5 vols., trans. C. H. Moore and J. Jackson, LCL, Cambridge, MA: Harvard University Press; London: William Heinemann (1925–37).

Talbert, Charles H. (1987) *Reading Corinthians: A Literary and Theological Commentary on 1 and 2 Corinthians*, New York: Crossroad.

Theissen, Gerd (1982) "Legitimation and Subsistence: An Essay on the Sociology of Early Christian Missionaries," in *The Social Setting of Pauline Christianity: Essays on Corinth*, ed. and trans. J. H. Schutz, Philadelphia: Fortress Press, pp. 27–67.

Thesaurus Linguae Graecae, CD Rom # D, TLG Project, University of California, Irvine (1992).

Thompson, Wayne, N. (1975) *Aristotle's Deduction and Induction: Introductory Analysis and Synthesis*, Amsterdam: Rodopi N. V.

Thrall, Margaret E. (1994) *The Second Epistle to the Corinthians*, vol. 1, ICC, Edinburgh: T. & T. Clark.

Too, Yun Lee (1995) *The Rhetoric of Identity in Isocrates: Text, Power, Pedagogy*, CCS, Cambridge: Cambridge University Press.

Travis, Stephen H. (1973) "Paul's Boasting in 2 Corinthians 10–12," *Studia Evangelica*, no. VI, Berlin: Akademie Verlag, pp. 527–32.

Usher, Stephen (1974) "Introduction," in vol. 1 of *Dionysius of Halicarnassus: Critical Essays*, 2 vols., trans. S. Usher, LCL, Cambridge, MA: Harvard University Press; London: William Heinemann (1974–1985).

(1990) *Isocrates: Panegryicus and To Nicocles*, Greek Orators 3, Warminster, England: Aris & Phillips.

(1993) *Demosthenes: On the Crown*, Greek Orators 5, Warminster, England: Aris & Phillips.

Van Hook, LaRue (1919) "Alcidamas versus Isocrates: The Spoken versus the Written Word," *Classical Weekly* 12, pp. 89–94.

Veltman, Fred (1978) "The Defense Speeches of Paul in Acts," in *Perspectives on Luke–Acts*, ed. C. Talbert, *PRSt*, Edinburgh: T. & T. Clark, pp. 243–56.

Vitanza, Victor J. (1993). "Some Rudiments of Histories of Rhetorics and Rhetorics of Histories," in T. Poulakos (ed.), *Rethinking the History of Rhetoric*, Boulder, CO: Westview.

Volkmann, Richard (1885) *Die Rhetorik der Griechen und Römer in systematischer Übersicht*, Leipzig: B. G. Teubner.

Wallace, Richard, and Wynne Williams (1998) *The Three Worlds of Paul of Tarsus*, New York: Routledge, 1998.

Walz, C. (ed.) (1832–1936) *Rhetores Graeci*, 9 vols., Stuttgart: Cotta.

Watson, Duane F. (1988) *Invention, Arrangement, and Style: Rhetorical Criticism of Jude and 2 Peter*, SBLDS 104, Atlanta: Scholars Press.

(1989) "I Corinthians 10:23–11:1 in the Light of Greco-Roman Rhetoric: The Role of Rhetorical Questions," *JBL* 108, pp. 301–18.

(ed.) (1991) *Persuasive Artistry: Studies in New Testament Rhetoric in Honor of George A. Kennedy*, JSNTSup 50, Sheffield: Sheffield Academic Press.

(1993) "Paul's Rhetorical Strategy in I Corinthians 15," in Porter and Olbricht, 1993, pp. 231–49.

(2002) "Paul's Boasting in 2 Corinthians 10–13 as Defense of his Honor: A Socio-Rhetorical Analysis," in Eriksson *et al.*, 2002, pp. 260–75.

Welborn, Laurence L. (1996) "Like Broken Pieces of a Ring: 2 Cor. 1.1–2.13; 7:5–16 and Ancient Theories of Literary Unity," *NTS* 42, pp. 559–83.

West, William C. III (1973) "The Speeches in Thucydides: A Description and Listing," in *The Speeches in Thucydides: A Collection of Original Studies with a Bibliography*, ed. P. A. Stadter, Chapel Hill: University of North Carolina Press, pp. 3–15.

White, John (1971) "The Structural Analysis of Philemon: A Point of Departure in the Formal Analysis of the Pauline Letter," in *Society of Biblical Literature: 1971 Seminar Papers*, Chico, CA: Scholars Press, pp. 1–47.

(1986) *Light from Ancient Letters*, FF, Philadelphia: Fortress Press.

Wilcox, Stanley (1943) "Corax and the *Prolegomena*," *AJP* 64, pp. 1–23.

Windisch, Hans (1924) *Der zweite Korintherbrief*, KEK 6, Göttingen: Vandenhoeck & Ruprecht.

Winter, Bruce W. (1991a) "Civil Litigation in Secular Corinth and the Church," *NTS* 37, pp. 559–72.

(1991b) "The Importance of the *Captatio Benevolentiae* in the Speeches of Tertullus and Paul in Acts 24:1–24," *JTS* 42, pp. 505–31.

(1993a) "The Entries and Ethics of Orators and Paul (1 Thessalonians 2:1–12)," *TynBul* 44, pp. 55–74.

(1993b) "Official Proceedings and the Forensic Speeches in Acts," in *The Book of Acts in its Ancient Literary Setting*, ed. B. W. Winter and A. D. Clarke, Grand Rapids, MI: W. B. Eerdmans, pp. 305–36.

(1997) *Philo and Paul among the Sophists*, SNTSMS 96, Cambridge: Cambridge University Press.

Winterbottom, Michael (1984) *The Minor Declamations Ascribed to Quintilian*, Texte und Kommentare 13, New York: de Gruyter.

Wisse, Jakob (1989) *Ethos and Pathos from Aristotle to Cicero*, Amsterdam: Hakkert.

Witherington, Ben III (1995) *Conflict and Community in Corinth: A Socio-Rhetorical Commentary on 1 and 2 Corinthians*, Grand Rapids, MI: W. B. Eerdmans.

Wolf, Hans J. (1968) *Demosthenes als Advokat, Funktionen und Methoden des Prozesspraktikers im klassischen Athen*, SJG 30, Berlin: de Gruyter.

Worthington, Ian (1992) *A Historical Commentary on Dinarchus: Rhetoric and Conspiracy in Later Fourth-Century Athens*, Ann Arbor: University of Michigan Press.

(1993) "Once More, The Client/*Logographos* Relationship," *CQ* 43, pp. 67–72.

(1994) "The Canon of the Ten Attic Orators," in *Persuasion: Greek Rhetoric in Action*, ed. Ian Worthington, London: Routledge, pp. 244–63.

Wuellner, Wilhelm H. (1997) "Arrangement," in Porter, 1997c, pp. 51–87.

Xanthakis-Karamanos, G. (1979) "The Influence of Rhetoric on Fourth Century Tragedy," *CQ* 29, pp. 66–76.

Xenophon. 7 vols., trans. C. L. Brownson, O. J. Todd, and E. C. Marchant, New York: G. P. Putnam's Sons; London: W. Heinemann (1918–68).

Young, Frances M., and David F. Ford (1987) *Meaning and Truth in 2 Corinthians*, BFT, Grand Rapids, MI: W. B. Eerdmans.

INDEX OF BIBLICAL REFERENCES

Note: Non-specific references to 2 Corinthians (i.e. general references) are not included.

263

Isaiah
40–55   169
43.10   169
43.12   169
49.1–13   147, 169
49.8a   170
58.1   171
63.8–9   171

Jeremiah
13.14   170
14.10   170
15.5   170
21.7   170
29.23   169
42.5   169
49.5   169

Joel
2.17–18   171
4.16   171

Joshua
22.34   169
24.27   169

Judith
7.28   169

Lamentations
2.2   170
2.17   170
2.21   170

Malachi
2.14   169
3.5   169

Philemon
1.22   150

Philippians
1.8   169
1.12   153
2.19   150
2.23   150
4.15–16   130

Psalms
50.7   169
50.23   169
116.7–10   212
116.10   212, 217, 218

Romans   100
1.5   209
1.9   169
1.10   166
1.11   153
1.13   153
1.16–17   160
2.14–15   212
2.21–23   59
3.7–8   209
3.8   168
6.19–22   209
8.25   150
8.32   59
9.1   212
9.1–2   154
11.25   153
15.18   209
15.24   150
15.32   166
16.26   209

Wisdom
1.6   169

Zechariah
11.6   170

INDEX OF ANCIENT AUTHORS AND SOURCES

Hyperides (*cont.*)
   Defense of Lycophron (Hyp. 1)   21, 93,
     187
     Fr. IV   36
     Fr. IVb. 3.1;   37
     3.4   36
     8–13   90, 93, 187
     9.2   37
     13   90
     14   93, 187
     16   189
     16–18   93, 187
     17   190
     19.1   40
     20   154

Ignatius of Antioch   3
Isaeus   23, 43, 93
   On Behalf of Euphiletus (Isae. 12)   21,
     43
   On the Estate of Apollodorus (Isae. 7)
     21, 43
     32.4   148
     37–41   52
     45.10   152
   On the Estate of Aristarchus (Isae. 10)
     20
     1   52, 93, 187
     7   49
     10   49
     14   185
   On the Estate of Astyphilus (Isae. 9)
     20, 43
     35   185
   On the Estate of Ciron (Isae. 8)   21,
     43
     1   185
     1.4   150
     2   185
     5   148
     10–14   48
     11   49
     13   49
     14.1   56
     15.2   49
     17   49
     20   49
     24   49
     26   185
     27   49
     29   48
     30   185
     34.5   37
     42   49
     43   49

     45   48
     46.5   152
   On the Estate of Cleonymus (Isae. 1)
     21, 43
     6   52
     8   155
     17   185
     27   185
   On the Estate of Dicaeogenes (Isae. 5)
     20, 43
   On the Estate of Hagnias (Isae. 11)   21
     7   155
     9.10   148
     11.2   49
     32.6   40
     36.6   152
   On the Estate of Menecles (Isae. 2)   21
     1   146
     5   49
     16   49
     26.2   223
     34   49
     37   49
     42   52
     47   193, 194
   On the Estate of Nicostratus (Isae. 4)
     20, 43
     18.4   56
     27   52
   On the Estate of Philoctemon (Isae. 6)
     20, 43
     2.7   37
     11.4   56
     48.5   49
     50.5   49
     58   193
     62   193
   On the Estate of Pyrrhus (Isae. 3)   20,
     43
     7   49
     6.7   49
     12   49
     12.4   49
     14   49
     15   49
     24.4   37
     28.7   223
     37   49
     42.4   49
     43   49
     53   49
     56   49
     61   185
     76   49
     80   49

SUBJECT INDEX